Warlords and Coalition Politics in Post-Soviet States

The breakup of the USSR was unexpected and unexpectedly peaceful. Though a third of the new states fell prey to violent civil conflict, anarchy on the post-Soviet periphery, when it occurred, was quickly cauterized. This book argues that this outcome had nothing to do with security guarantees by Russia or the United Nations and everything to do with local innovation by ruthless warlords, who competed and colluded in a high-risk coalition formation game. Drawing on a structured comparison of Georgian and Tajik militia members, the book combines rich comparative data with formal modeling, treating the post-Soviet space as an extraordinary laboratory to observe the limits of great powers' efforts to shape domestic institutions in weak states.

Jesse Driscoll is Assistant Professor of Political Science at the School of International Relations and Pacific Studies, University of California, San Diego. He was an OCV (Order, Conflict, and Violence) Fellow at Yale University and a GAGE (Governing America in a Global Era) Fellow at the University of Virginia, and most recently a member of the Harvard Academy for International and Area Studies from 2009 to 2013. His work has been published in the *Journal of Conflict Resolution*, *Research and Politics*, and the *Journal of Survey Statistics and Methodology*.

Cambridge Studies in Comparative Politics

General Editors

Kathleen Thelen   *Massachusetts Institute of Technology*
Erik Wibbels   *Duke University*

Associate Editors

Robert H. Bates   *Harvard University*
Gary Cox   *Stanford University*
Stephen Hanson   *The College of William and Mary*
Torben Iversen   *Harvard University*
Stathis Kalyvas   *Yale University*
Peter Lange   *Duke University*
Margaret Levi   *Center for the Advanced Study of the Behavioral Sciences, Stanford University*
Helen Milner   *Princeton University*
Frances Rosenbluth   *Yale University*
Susan Stokes   *Yale University*
Sidney Tarrow   *Cornell University*

(continued after the Index)

Warlords and Coalition Politics in Post-Soviet States

JESSE DRISCOLL

University of California, San Diego

CAMBRIDGE
UNIVERSITY PRESS

CAMBRIDGE
UNIVERSITY PRESS

University Printing House, Cambridge CB2 8BS, United Kingdom

One Liberty Plaza, 20th Floor, New York, NY 10006, USA

477 Williamstown Road, Port Melbourne, VIC 3207, Australia

4843/24, 2nd Floor, Ansari Road, Daryaganj, Delhi - 110002, India

79 Anson Road, #06-04/06, Singapore 079906

Cambridge University Press is part of the University of Cambridge.

It furthers the University's mission by disseminating knowledge in the pursuit of education, learning and research at the highest international levels of excellence.

www.cambridge.org
Information on this title: www.cambridge.org/9781107636453

First published 2015
First paperback edition 2017

A catalogue record for this publication is available from the British Library

Library of Congress Cataloging in Publication data
Driscoll, Jesse, 1978–
Warlords and coalition politics in post-Soviet states / Jesse Driscoll.
    pages cm. – (Cambridge studies in comparative politics)
ISBN 978-1-107-06335-8 (hardback)
1. Warlordism–Georgia (Republic) 2. Warlordism–Tajikistan. 3. Coalition
governments–Georgia (Republic) 4. Coalition governments–Tajikistan. 5. Georgia
(Republic)–Politics and government–1991– 6. Tajikistan–Politics and
government–1991– I. Title.
JZ1317.2.D75 2015
320.94758–dc23   2014047366

ISBN 978-1-107-06335-8 Hardback
ISBN 978-1-107-63645-3 Paperback

I get it. I know what you want. I understand. You want to make up a list, on your computer, of all our bad men. 'Terrorists.' You want to cross names off the list when they were killed or jailed. To see that we Tajiks can take care of our own. But we can. We did. You'll see.

Yuri, Dushanbe, 2007

Contents

Acknowledgments

None of this would have been conceivable – or be meaningful to me – without the love and support of my wife Emma; my parents, Mary and Wally; my sister, Amanda; and a number of friends that are increasingly indistinguishable from family. (*"…We're all on one road … and we're only passing through …"*)

This book builds upon an ongoing research program that matured while I pursued graduate studies at Stanford's Department of Political Science. I owe a great deal to the patient guidance of David Laitin, James Fearon, and Jeremy Weinstein, and I owe far more to the friendly assistance of my exceptional graduate student cohort. But the book also exists because of a full decade of itinerant labor. During this time I gratefully accepted institutional and financial support from diverse sources: The Center for Russian and Eastern European Studies at Stanford University; the Russian Language program at Middlebury College; the Caucasus Research Resource Centers (CRRC); the Program on Order, Conflict, and Violence (OCV) at Yale University; the American University of Central Asia in Bishkek; the International Research and Exchanges Board (IREX); the Governing America in a Global Age (GAGE) program at the University of Virginia; and probably a few more that I am forgetting. Jorge Dominguez and the Harvard Academy for International and Area Studies at Harvard University deserve special thanks, both for connecting me with the Cambridge University Press team and giving me time to share my work with a fantastic network of young interdisciplinary scholars. I am grateful to all of these institutions for help getting my career started.

Along the way, many scholars shared critical thoughts on primitive drafts of the manuscript. The argument evolved in response to critiques from Dominique Arel, Robert Bates, Mark Beissinger, Timothy Blauvelt, Keith Darden, Georgi Derluguian, Paula Garb, Hans Gutbrod, Steph Haggard, Stephen Hanson, Miles Kahler, Stathis Kalyvas, Charles King, Bethany Lacina, David Lake, Jay Lyall, Ghia Nodia, Roger Petersen, Robert Powell, Phil Roeder, John

Schoeberlein, Yuhki Tajima, Barbara Walter, and Christoph Zuercher. Special thanks must be extended to James Fearon, who continued to give me advice on how to streamline and simplify the argument long after professional obligations expired. The blunt advice of the anonymous reviewers and series editors at Cambridge University Press is largely responsible for the structure and intellectual coherence of the final book manuscript.

For most of the data in this book I relied on the goodwill and honesty of former combatants in Tajikistan and Georgia. The work must be dedicated, in large part, to Yuri, Vasha, Samojon, Sergei, and others who made introductions, vouched for my character, and shared difficult memories. None of their real names appear in this book for human subjects reasons that should be quickly apparent. Key respondents divulged their stories with the expectation that I would write a fair and accurate history. This book represents my best effort to honor their trust. I reserve a different sort of gratitude for the various families that opened their doors to me along the way – people who were not my human subjects, but whose humanity inspired me to try to write a good book about real people. Memories from the field fade unevenly, but I am always going to wonder what happened to Lira and Jamiliya and Siyl, to Anthony and Nino, to Elizabeth and Katherine, to Bahron and Mahmuba and Ikron and Shodmon. Most of my professional colleagues will recognize that the methods employed in this sort of fieldwork are not well-incentivized by the discipline of political science. As such, I am in an unusual sort of debt to David Laitin, whose scholarship and example convinced me that it really was all right, even in security studies, to lean heavily on the kinds of insights that only emerge through years of patient ethnography. That unusual debt extends to Stanford University's Department of Anthropological Sciences, personified by "Down Town" Melissa Brown and Kylea Liese. And to Azriel, who was one of the first to voice her concerns that this book was a thing of evil. (*Mine!*)

I have an enviable first job. The University of California at San Diego is a wonderful employer. Steph Haggard, Peter Gourevitch, Miles Kahler, and Barbara Walter have all been tremendous professional mentors in different ways. All empowered me, with their scholarship and their gentle advice, to write exactly the book that I did. I have also had the opportunity to teach some of the world's brightest students – some of whom I employed as the book moved toward the final stages of completion. Elaine Denny provided useful feedback on an early draft of the material related to human subjects and issues of anonymity. Karen Simpson and Megan Becker assisted in the preparation of this manuscript with careful copyediting. Daniel Maliniak created original maps, helped with a few of the figures, and continues to keep me honest with the data. John Porten organized the index.

I wouldn't have made it to Stanford at all if I hadn't met Charles King and Michael Brown just exactly when I did as an undergraduate at Georgetown University. If I wind the clock back further, I find that it is important that I use this space to thank Penny Johnston and Mark "Mad Dog" Bowman for different kinds of virtuous labor as underpaid public high school teachers at Mead High School in Spokane, Washington.

But past is past, and I'm working to be here now. My wife Emma was the first person thanked, but she insisted that she be thanked again at the end, as well. It isn't very much fun to live with someone whose work involves writing self-serious paragraphs about the representation of distant people in war zones. Emma, and our wonderful dog Sally, help to remind me that even when I'm most proud of my work, and even when I convince myself that my work is important, the truth is my work isn't my life. It's just work.

I

Revisionist History

As many as 500,000 people lost their lives in the wake of the Soviet experiment. Civil wars were fought in Azerbaijan, Bosnia, Croatia, Georgia, Kosovo, Moldova, the North Caucasus, Romania, and Tajikistan. Though the thought experiment requires a grisly kind of arithmetic, social scientists can assert with confidence that longer civil wars likely would have resulted in many more deaths. How did order consolidate so quickly in the post-Soviet space?

This book presents a host of new data and original game theory to revisit the basic intuition of Thomas Hobbes (1651): anarchy creates strong incentives for people to build states. I demonstrate that political order arose out of violent anarchy because violence entrepreneurs – warlords hereafter – realized that the great powers would pay handsomely for local order. Order facilitates efficient markets (for foreign investors) and local-language intelligence collection (for foreign militaries). Warlords understood that they were in a position to extort certain rents of sovereignty from the international system and wanted to be bought out in the scramble that followed the collapse of the USSR. The ancient truism that "war is bad for business" was quickly grasped by certain individuals who realized that they were in a rare position to extort civilian governments directly – and the international community indirectly – with anarchy. Foot soldiers were recruited from the sub-proletarian underclass through promises of future state spoils. Some warlords initially colluded to provide order, access international wealth, and allocate themselves monopoly rents from the state apparatus that fell under their control. A local puppet president served as a placeholder for opaque coalition politics. Many warlords became violence subcontractors for the regime. Some did not. Complicated bargaining followed. Back-room deals were struck. A great deal of property changed hands. Peace emerged as local criminals developed techniques to hold civilians hostage and rewrite local history to their advantage. In other words, the warlords became the state.

POST-SOVIET SETTLEMENT PATTERNS: SUCCESSFUL THIRD-PARTY INTERVENTIONS?

It is clear that helping people to build states in the wake of civil disorder will be a core foreign policy challenge for the United States and the United Nations for the foreseeable future. The threat of catastrophic terrorism has changed the terms of the debate about national security, increasing the emphasis on threats that can emerge from very weak actors in the international system. Events that transpire in the global periphery can directly threaten the safety of voters living in states shielded by strong professional militaries and oceans.

This book is motivated by a question rarely given voice by Western diplomats or academics: What did the Russians get *right* in their relations with their new periphery? After all, wars that broke out during the Soviet collapse were shorter – and thus far less bloody – than similar civil wars emerging from decolonization. The average length of post-Communist wars is only 3.9 years, compared to an average length of 9.8 years for all civil wars since 1945.[1] Violence in the wake of the Communist collapse was brutal, but drawn-out insurgencies would have produced many more deaths. Appendix A at the end of this volume shows that even with numerous statistical controls, the subset of civil wars resulting from the breakup of the USSR was a group of unusual outliers in terms of overall duration.

Is this unusual regional trend attributable to local politics and path-dependent institutional history? Or is it attributable to the successful actions of a third-party intervention force, with Russia acting as the lead state? Reasonable people disagree.[2] Each cell of Figure 1.1 is meant to represent a different internally consistent narrative of how civil wars remain settled, including different assumptions about the possible role of third-party foreign assistance in shaping peace processes.[3] The horizontal dimension is the assumed

---

[1] Nearly a dozen individual states housed civil wars that each surpassed a half-million deaths – Afghanistan, Angola, Cambodia, China, the Democratic Republic of the Congo, Ethiopia, Greece, Lebanon, Mozambique, Uganda, and Vietnam. These conflicts lasted 16.5 years on average. Lacina (2006) demonstrates that the length of a civil war is a robust predictor of the overall battle deaths.

[2] This disagreement may be no one's fault. Military professionals, diplomats, missionaries, and development assistance professionals often hold different root assumptions about what it takes for a war to stay resolved. Theoretical assumptions inevitably leak into descriptions. By selectively omitting deviant facts, different narratives can be fit to the same observations.

[3] Much of the data produced from humanitarian disaster zones chronicle the critical role being played by the intervention force, confirming the need for ongoing foreign assistance. Heathershaw (2007) argues that in authoritarian regimes recovering from civil conflict, social scientists often become complicit in this interpretative exercise. See also Heathershaw (2008, 2009).

	Decisive Military Victory	Stalemate Between Factions
Possibility of Third-Party Monitoring/ Enforcement	[Postmodern] Imperialism	Liberal Interventionism
No Possibility of Third-Party Monitoring/ Enforcement	Realism	Militia Coalition Politics

FIGURE I.I. Disputed Narratives: What mechanisms keep civil war settled?

military balance between the incumbent and insurgent armies at the time of settlement. The vertical dimension is the assumed ability of foreign powers to monitor and enforce outcomes relevant to the settlement.

In the lower left corner of Figure 1.1 one finds most self-styled "realists." They maintain that the central mechanism that keeps civil wars settled is military hegemony by a sovereign authority within recognized interstate borders. This would have been called "the king's peace" in prior eras. Probably the most famous account of how states emerge from civil war comes from seventeenth century philosopher Thomas Hobbes (1651), who articulates a straightforward case for peace through military conquest by the agents of a sovereign. The social contract, for Hobbes, is imposed. Citizens are made subordinate to the ruler violently, opponents are disarmed, and order emerges.[4] A strong state apparatus is the best inoculation against civil war.[5]

A number of independent research programs – most prominently those of Licklider (1995) and Fearon (2004) – have confirmed that, since 1945, the most stable civil war settlements are those that end with military victory. The military contest often takes a long time – approximately a decade on average.[6] Many "negotiated settlements" are face-saving arrangements that codify the de facto

---

4 This interpretation of Hobbes (1651) draws heavily on the synthesis of the realist canon in Wagner (2007). On pages 126–127, Wagner references the central argument in Fearon and Laitin (1996) to suggest the evolution of the current boundaries of nation-states as "natural" responses to differential comparative advantages in counterinsurgency by different language speakers.

5 For compelling evidence that state weakness is statistically correlated with the outbreak of large-scale civil violence, see Fearon and Laitin (2003).

6 Military victory, when it comes, rarely requires comprehensively and decisively defeating a conventional rebel army on the battlefield. Much more common is selective co-optation of insurgent field commanders during the closing phases of asymmetric irregular war. As such, the coalition of social forces that constitutes "the state" changes from the beginning of the conflict to its end.

military balance.[7] Toft (2010) forcefully argues that deterrence – fear of a technologically enabled security sector – is the mechanism that is most likely to be responsible for post–civil war peace.[8] National veterans are the heroic actors, and the story of their *decisive victory* is passed on from one generation to the next in monuments, museums, and military academies.

Though the collapse of the Soviet Union has been described by economist Douglass North as "perhaps the most striking case of internally induced rapid demise in all of human history," even the most disadvantaged states on the Soviet periphery were "born strong" in important respects, inheriting huge institutional advantages compared to the postcolonial states of Africa that achieved independence in the 1960s and 1970s.[9] Although the Eurasian states that joined the United Nations in the early 1990s lagged behind in terms of per capita gross domestic product (GDP) – difficult to measure in states transitioning to market systems – decades of institutional development translated into huge advantages when it came time for post-Soviet populations to improvise the construction of war machines. There can be no doubt that this is part of the explanation for the quick resolution of the post-Soviet wars. The Soviet experience bequeathed to the first generation of post-independence elites a well-organized party network, borders and administrative units, a centralized media distribution system, a secret police apparatus (with transnational linkages to other republics-turned-states), a national language, an official history (institutionalized with maps, censuses, and museums), as well as an educated and largely literate population that anticipated that these institutions would endure.[10]

Completely different assumptions and mechanisms support a more benign "liberal intervention" narrative of civil war termination, located in the top right quadrant of Figure 1.1. Especially since the end of the Cold War, policymakers have sought solutions to military stalemates that do not rely on grinding military attrition. An empirical research agenda demonstrating the efficacy of

---

[7] King (1997), Fearon and Laitin (2007), and McCormick, Horton, Harrison (2007) propose moderate policies based on this insight. Luttwak (1999) is also consistent with this line of reasoning.

[8] I have located Toft's scholarship in the "realist" camp for the purpose of this chapter because it is clear that she sees herself in opposition to liberal voices (e.g., those in the upper-right quadrant of Figure 1.1). With that said, in my reading Toft is equivocal on the role of foreign governments; she does admit a limited role for foreign governments in promoting "security sector reforms" during the implementation phase of postwar peace processes. She is vexed that U.S. threats to intervene militarily to facilitate decisive victories lack credibility (160–162), so perhaps she would prefer to be identified with the "postmodern imperialists" in the upper-left-hand corner.

[9] North (2006), 4. A broader exposition of his views on the dissolution of the Soviet experiment can be found on pages 146–154 of the same volume.

[10] For a good introductory overview of the nature and sources of Soviet institutional advantages in producing compliant behaviors in the rural periphery, see Roeder (1993); Jones-Luong (2002), chapter 1; and Brown (2007).

third-party interventions to end conflict has coevolved with the expansion of United Nations Peacekeeping Operations (UNPKOs) in the last two decades. Remarkable scientific progress has been made on the question of whether and how outsiders can assist in ending civil wars. They can, and we know quite a bit about how they can. Peacekeepers can provide security guarantees that allow for disarmament (e.g., Walter 1997, 2002), provide neutral monitoring of the terms of agreement (e.g., Fortna 2008), marginalize holdouts (e.g., Stedman 1997), and gradually establish trust between warring parties via multifaceted mediation programs (e.g., Doyle 2006). In the quarter-century since the end of the Cold War, there has been an audience for arguments explaining how a benign international gendarmerie might help establish order. The United Nations – assisted by a plethora of international organizations, social scientists, and private actors – has established many peacekeeping missions. Much of the foreign aid that reaches post–civil war societies is directed towards paying the salaries of, and meeting program goals drawn up by, liberal interventionists. Most of the rotating class of Americans and Western Europeans who staff embassies and the offices of aid organizations housed in the capital cities of the post-Soviet republics imagine themselves to be day-by-day peace builders. Their reports state plainly why they believe their programs are vital to the persistence of peace.

It is common for realists to caricature the arguments of liberal interventionists as utopian.[11] A few contemporary liberal interventionists have met this critique head-on, acknowledging that identities and interests do not need to be fundamentally transformed for a civil war to end. War ends because actors with the capacity to undermine order-providing institutions with violence come to believe that it is not in their best interest to sabotage order. But when locals are stuck in a costly stalemate, neutral foreigners can sometimes save lives by helping the warring sides extract themselves from pointless attrition. An influential deductive approach to civil war settlement over the last decade argues that foreign interveners can shape the postwar institutions by altering players' strategies without altering their underlying preferences. The transformation of conflict identities may be important in the long run, but it is often the work of many generations and is not necessarily relevant to the contours of war termination.

A more urgent task, as Barbara Walter (1997) has argued, is the creation of a secure framework to ensure rebel disarmament. Negotiators attempting to end a civil war grapple with different challenges than diplomats negotiating

---

[11] To the extent that liberals' optimism relies on the gradual transformation of identities or the alleviation of deep grievances, these charges are deserved. Much of the programming of humanitarian relief agencies has a striking resemblance to missionary work. Most of the professional bureaucrats who serve as a rotating middle class, drifting across the world's war zones, are motivated by a desire to assist in transnational and transhistorical processes of social transformation.

an armistice after interstate war. At the end of an interstate war, both armies remain intact and can retreat behind internationally reified boundaries. Ending a civil war, it is argued, requires that one side or the other formally lay down its arms. The winners – who will then control all the guns – have a very difficult time making their commitments to honor the terms of the ceasefire credible.[12] This approach to the problem of civil war suggests that credible third-party security guarantees, and subsequent monitoring, can help sculpt peace accords that would otherwise crumble under the weight of the security dilemma.

But once the possibility of third-party intervention to sculpt war outcomes is considered, it also becomes necessary to consider the upper left corner of Figure 1.1. The threat of transnational mass-casualty terrorism changed the conversation about involvement in other people's civil wars. Certain weak states, once peripheral to American interests, are now treated by great powers as potential security concerns, rather than just troubling manmade humanitarian disasters. The situation is new, and its implications poorly understood, but Western governments grasp that stabilizing weak states is not simply about the humanitarian mission of saving lives – it is also about self-protection. And in this new world, the same constituencies who would balk at their tax dollars ending up in unsavory pockets can be blackmailed into tolerating autocratic corruption. Violence against human dignity is weighed against the risk of ideologically hostile regimes emerging from pockets of anarchy in the Middle East and Central Asia. For certain autocrats, the claim to be "too weak" to control one's territory can, perversely, bring more foreign aid in the service of decisively defeating terrorists. Much of this extortion dynamic depends on variables that are imagined or kinds of intelligence that are intrinsically suspect.[13] *– Jesus, no shit.*

This is neo-con INVADE THE WORLD/INVITE THE WORLD = Problem solved. BS, SECURE BORDERS = problem solved.

[12] This commitment problem complicates the diplomatic resolution of civil wars through many mechanisms. It is thought to render stable postwar power sharing extremely difficult. Fearon and Laitin summarize the core of this asymmetric commitment problem: "Rebel groups aim at regime change because they could not trust the government to implement the policies they desire even if the government formally agreed to do so. After the rebel group disbands, or after the central government regains strength, or because of monitoring problems arising from the nature of the policy aims (for example, redistribution), the central government would renege on policy concessions it made to end a war. Thus rebel groups must often fight for 'all or nothing.'" Fearon and Laitin (2007), 2. For a review of theoretical and formal literature on commitment problems in civil war, see Blattman and Miguel (2009) and Walter (2009).

[13] The word "imagined" is perhaps too provocative, giving the impression that national interests are *completely* constructed. States are constructed as strategic allies partially as a product of their geographic location vis-à-vis perceived enemies, partially based on objective characteristics of a country (e.g., the presence of oil, democratic institutions, nuclear weapons, military bases, diaspora linkages, or density of ideologically radical subpopulations), and partially a figment of political practice. See Gourevitch (1978). During the Cold War, post-revolutionary leaders could install Communist Party Structures (*Single Party Regimes*) and count on some aid from the USSR. Today there is little doubt that democracies in strategically important neighborhoods – Israel, the Philippines, Taiwan, and most recently, Georgia – have been able to attract bilateral aid from the United States by a similar logic.

$$

Direct military interventions into other states' civil wars to shape the contours of settlement, facilitating decisive victory for one faction or another, will be familiar to students of imperial history. The mechanisms tend to emphasize sinister kinds of meddling: sharing signals intelligence and military satellite information, providing sophisticated weapons, liquidating potential spoilers, picking winners, picking losers. The end of the Cold War; the demonstrated ability of weak actors to cause great damage to the interests of strong states; the spread of new technology; and the growing consensus by elites in Russia, China, the United States, France, and Great Britain – the permanent five members of the UN Security Council – that their security interests are tied up in the outcomes of civil wars fought in weak or failed states are combining to facilitate the emergence of a new kind of "Post-modern Imperialism," according to Fearon and Laitin (2004).[14] These behaviors are distinguished from classical imperialism in that the intervener acts on behalf of the entire state system, and does not want to stay in the territory – the intervention force wants to go home as soon as possible, but to do so it must leave a stable partner government in charge of the territory. The kinds of policies that result are not always compatible with the idealized prescriptions championed by the liberal interventionists. But great powers do, if only rarely, find it is in their national interest to guarantee decisive victory for one side or the other in someone else's civil war.

Consider the two maps in Figures 1.2 and 1.3. If one doubts that Russian military power was decisive in shaping the contours of military settlements in the early 1990s, one has only to notice the persistence of breakaway regions in Georgia, in clear contrast to the territorially intact map of Tajikistan. The "frozen conflicts" inside territory claimed by Georgia pit the national government in Tbilisi against Russian-backed secessionist statelets in Abkhazia and South Ossetia. To the question "Why was the map redrawn in the South Caucasus and left intact in Central Asia?" one can do worse than answer with the crude observation that "Political elites in Russia just wanted it that way." As discussed at length in the chapters that follow, Russian peacekeeping – or "peacemaking" as the word *mirotvorchestvo* is more accurately translated – was never meant to facilitate general disarmament. Russian troops – sometimes still in familiar Soviet uniforms, and sometimes wearing black ski masks – and paramilitary units from neighboring republics (the North Caucasus) and states (Uzbekistan) rallied across new interstate borders.[15] In Georgia, borders

[14] The authors identify four general challenges for peacekeeping missions sent after humanitarian disasters break out in badly governed parts of the world: 1) recruitment ("who sends troops?"), 2) coordination ("who acts as the 'lead state,' taking responsibility for critical tasks of coordination?"), 3) accountability ("what happens if peacekeepers are not neutral?"), and 4) exit ("at what point can the intervention terminate?"). As we shall see, these questions had unusually clear answers in the post-Soviet wars: 1) the CIS 2) Russia 3) nothing 4) maybe never. Locals were not tempted to try to "wait out" the Russian military force.

[15] King (2000) and Derluguian (2005), 262–273.

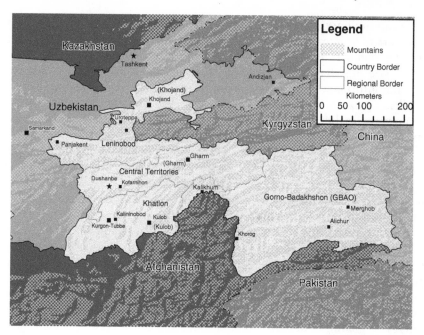

FIGURE 1.2. Tajikistan.

were essentially redrawn by Russia to coerce elites in Tbilisi to join the new Commonwealth of Independent States (CIS). In Tajikistan, after initial lukewarm support for Khojandi secessionists, it was decided in Moscow that Tajikistan would stay intact as a buffer state to shield the rest of inner Asia from chaos in Afghanistan. It was difficult to misinterpret Boris Yeltsin's 1993 statement that the Tajik–Afghan border was "in effect, Russia's."[16]

These mechanisms hint at another partial explanation for the unusually short length of the post-Soviet wars. These wars did not develop into "proxy wars," with different regional powers backing different clients. The violence of the post-Soviet wars occurred in the periphery of the USSR, and against a backdrop of total state failure that was no less revolutionary for being largely nonviolent.[17] Other great powers calibrated their foreign policies to give Russia, a stumbling nuclear superpower, a wide berth. Potential external

[16] On Tajikistan, Fearon and Laitin report: "Russian peacekeepers were able and willing to (in the words of several informants) 'liquidate' spoilers. They were able, as in Tajikistan, to pick a warlord favorable to them and provide him the military support necessary to compel other pretenders into negotiations." Fearon and Laitin (2004), 27. Footnote 56 is informative as well.

[17] Our social science theories are simply not up to the task of task of explaining the contingencies of revolutionary politics, even when the stakes are very high. No one can state with confidence why it was that Boris Yeltsin emerged standing on top of the tank instead of an aggressive military populist.

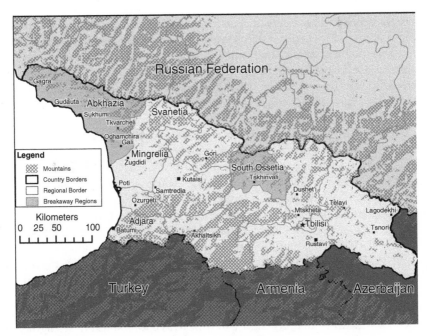

FIGURE I.3. Georgia.

interveners – Iran, Turkey, the United States, or China – might have been able
to find security, economic, or humanitarian justifications to expand their role
in the South Caucasus or Central Asia, setting off a competitive scramble to
affect outcomes. Proxy war dynamics might have ensued. This did not happen,
however, in large part because possible gains were weighed against the risk that
perceived interference into Russia's traditional zone of control would empower
hard-liners in Moscow. Nothing in Georgia, Tajikistan, or Chechnya could be
worth trading Boris Yeltsin for Alexander Lebed. Georgians and Tajiks understood that foreign governments would be second-guessing Moscow's preferences while improvising policy in Russia's traditional sphere of influence.[18]

By the late 1990s, when Russia was more of a "normal country," the
impulse for Western governments to tinker with institutions under the aegis of
democracy promotion and meddle in the security affairs of post-Soviet states

[18] MacFarlane (1999) provides a sympathetic summary of how Russia's geopolitical predicament
was viewed at the time. The message that the United States' central foreign policy priority
vis-à-vis Russia was stable control of nuclear materials by a friendly government in Moscow –
and that every other interest would be subordinated to that goal – was signaled clearly,
early, and often. See Allison and Blackwill (1991), 90–91; Nunn (1991); Kennan (1997);
and Kubicek (1999–2000), 548–549, and the retrospective summary of Cornell (2001), 367.
Despite some pressure from Congress, the only thing that pushed the Clinton Administration
to even entertain discussion of military intervention in Russia's war in Chechnya was the (false)
claim that Dzhokhar Dudayev had acquired a nuclear bomb. See Goldgeier and McFaul (2003),
139–149.

reasserted itself.[19] The results are particularly visible in contemporary Georgia. But one can safely generalize that it was not simply a strong outside intervener tipping the military balance that cauterized the wars that broke out as the USSR collapsed – it was the *absence* of *multiple competing* interveners. So if one is tempted to fall back on the crude realist observation that "Russia just wanted it that way," for completeness one should add "and it matters quite a bit that *just Russia* wanted it that way."

All three of the perspectives sketched earlier – the realist, the liberal interventionist, and the postmodern imperialist perspective – contain important insights into the stable settlement patterns of the post-Soviet wars. A realist approach emphasizes the Soviet institutional legacy – clearly visible in the de facto and de jure borders of the recognized and unrecognized states of the region. New leaders inherited unusually strong coercive machinery, facilitating the rapid creation of sovereign domestic authority structures.[20] A liberal, apologetic for Russia's CIS interventions into its periphery, would emphasize Russia's role in protecting embattled minorities and trying to assist as a third-party peace mediator in a humanitarian capacity. It is a political necessity that any document that passes through the Security Council of the United Nations be calibrated to reflect that narrative.[21] Many harbor conspiracy theories – very difficult to falsify – that Russia's true role was more sinister: strengthening security forces in some places and sabotaging them in others, sharing signals intelligence and military satellite information selectively with clients, and targeting certain individuals for assassination. The provocative phrasing "postmodern imperialism" is meant to emphasize that Russia was not driven by desire for imperial glory, but was executing the will of many foreign actors, all colluding to ensure a decisive outcome in the name of international security.

But my book sustains a different narrative, emphasizing processes in the lower right corner of Figure 1.1. I provide evidence that in Georgia and Tajikistan local militias never disarmed, and that local elites never really followed through on the liberal development script. They instead improvised creative solutions that were self-enforcing. "The state" described here is analogous to a semipermeable membrane for violence entrepreneurs – "warlords" – who weigh their life opportunities as social bandits against their life opportunities as agents of an internationally recognized sovereign. The utility of such an approach would be measured by its ability to generate predictions about when warlords are likely to yoke themselves to the governing coalition and when they are likely to resist consolidation. But if it is the case that incumbent and insurgent militia commanders were potentially interchangeable candidates for

---

[19] I borrow this phrasing from Shleifer (2005).

[20] Roeder (2007) suggests that some aspects of this machinery generate momentum of their own, creating demands for sovereignty that ended the federal experiment of the USSR.

[21] For an outstanding overview to the arguments made by the Russian state to justify its interventions, see O'Prey (1996).

postwar government spoils, then from the point of view of field commanders, civil war settlement was a *coalition formation* process.

This study defines "the state" somewhat pragmatically, as a bundle of formal and informal contracts regulating and incentivizing the behavior of citizens within a particular geographic space (ideally an internationally recognized territory). Shared norms exist that govern enforcement power for contracts, but I believe it is appropriate to consider the point of view of the violence entrepreneurs who compete for the right to selectively enforce those contracts to their benefit.[22] Great power interests and institutional inheritance set the chessboard, but, viewed from the point of view of individual warlords, the nature of the spoils being contested made "robust third-party monitoring" impossible. The micro-contours of post-independence redistribution politics hinged on the particulars of land reform, privatization in opaque and closed-bid environments, complex credit swaps cemented via marriages, money laundering across borders, and asset price-fixing schemes designed to pass debt on to the next generation. Profiting from these kinds of dealings required informal understandings between warlords – and the argument in this book is that those informal understandings, combined with certain inherited state institutions, ultimately provided the orderly structure that foreigners later tried to "shore up" with aid and assistance. Warlords understood perfectly that great powers could not send much money or guarantee regime support until *after* strong local clients had emerged, via a violent process of sorting and attrition on the streets. They bargained among each other and ultimately backed the ascendency of a civilian figurehead. The president rehabilitated warlords and granted them ministry positions in exchange for security. The consolidation process that followed had characteristics of a high-stakes lottery. Unlucky warlords eventually found themselves isolated and liquidated when the winds of political fortune turned. Lucky warlords were allowed to disappear into the police and military bureaucracy, where many still reside.

COALITION FORMATION BY INTERCHANGEABLE PREDATORS

The violent conflicts that emerged out of the collapse of the Soviet Union were often extensions of nonviolent property disputes. These property disputes were often between members of the same ethnic group.[23] All players understood that

---

22 It is plausible to me that the norm of territorial sovereignty – now enshrined in international law and constantly reified in contemporary discourse – evolved as a technology for strong states to efficiently enforce a "division of responsibility that diminishes the number of occasions for violent conflict between or among states." Wagner (2007), 126. See also Chapters 3, 4, and 6 generally. On the closely related question of why the "nation state" (as opposed to simply "the state") has evolved as the primary unit of political order in the modern world system, see Anderson (1991) and Fearon and Laitin (1996). A useful genealogy of the word "sovereignty" is found in Krasner (2001), especially 184–219.

23 See Handelman (1995), Varese (2001), and Reno (2002).

local solutions were necessary. The story of how warlords arrived at these local solutions involved highly contingent local brokering, bargaining, and coalition formation, with a great deal of side-switching and ambiguity of alliances. Russia's geopolitical strength loomed in the background of local strategizing, as a structural constraint to be maneuvered around and the engineer of critical model parameters. But in this account Russia was not a "peace enforcer" in the sense that it did not monitor or enforce the bargains that were necessary to keep peace. This book's account emphasizes the agency of locals, who ultimately selected and maintained order-producing equilibria. It also emphasizes the fundamental interchangeability of warlords as providers of local order.

The nonviolent equilibrium that ultimately emerged in Georgia and Tajikistan did not require disarmament. Indeed, as the far right column in Table 1.1 summarizes, the processes that are described in this book did not require many of the steps that are often presented by liberals as prerequisites to lasting peace. The risk of war decreased even while the postwar states developed in a manner that is thought to exacerbate the long-term risk of renewed violence: autocratic rule centered on a strong president, statelets dependent on external protection, and the normalization of corrupt and patronage-ridden governance. Political order was produced by a process that had little to do with the cognitively appealing script of democratization, legitimacy, or the rule of law. I anticipate that the account of militia politics sketched in the third column will be utterly uncontroversial to Georgian and Tajik citizens who lived through the war and its aftermath.[24] Yet the account will run counter to much of the official history of these two states' civil war settlements. There will be little discussion of party reform or rehabilitation of professional security services. I do not describe attempts to alleviate grievances or heal the rifts between social forces, nor do I chronicle attempts by third-party mediators to facilitate roundtables for patient negotiations between elites. The kinds of things that would count as success stories for most Western conflict resolution professionals are almost completely absent from this book's account.

This book explores the possibility that international mediation and multilateral aid play a critical role in the settlement – but not the role that development professionals believe they are playing. In this book's account, the central mechanism of civil war settlement is bribery. Some warlords collude together to create a state, hoping to secure foreign aid and investment. A clear prediction emerges: as the pool of potential bribes increases, the number of warlords who opt into the state will increase. Warlords keep their armies intact so that they can, in principle, extract rents through the credible threat of a coup. Foreign aid professionals can have a positive effect on war settlement not *despite* but *because* of the fact that these funds can be stolen by violence entrepreneurs. What is important is the liquidity provided by the influx of the donor economy,

---

[24] If there is anything controversial, I anticipate it will be framing the post-Soviet wars in a way that emphasizes actors' material interests at the expense of ethnic identities or ideological beliefs.

TABLE 1.1. *Contested Mechanisms of State-Building after Civil War*

	Proposed Process (State-Building Canon)	Alternative Process (Militia Politics)
PROBLEM #1: "Militia Demobilization" If militias have more guns than the police or army, how does post–civil war disarmament work?	Disarming and disbanding militias through the rehabilitation of security forces; Liquidating "spoilers" with foreign assistance.	Militias consolidate themselves in response to strong incentives to eliminate imitators and control entry into the violence market. Process gets more violent as foreign assistance is imminent, as foot soldiers understand that the stakes are very high.
PROBLEM #2: "Coup-Proofing" How does a civilian president get power away from the armed gangsters who installed him?	Institutionalization and formalization of robust political arrangements – ideally "legitimized" by widespread democratic participation.	"Trust" relationships between presidents and armed groups, based on promises of future aid. Viability of bargains depends on international conditions and ability of president to successfully manage divide-and-rule.
PROBLEM #3 "Positive Sovereignty" How does a weak national government commit to rehabilitate institutions and provide public goods?	Conditional foreign aid; building civil society, standard "Development Economics Toolkit" from international development agencies, technical help with counterinsurgency. *i.e., stealing $ from western working class taxpayers + giving it to the 3rd world.*	A red herring. If bilateral or multilateral aid is sufficient to pay bribes and secure regime without taxing citizenry, there is no reason to expect institutional reform. Politics are about coup-proofing and managing geopolitical narrative to ensure aid flows – not providing public goods.

which is then diverted. The content of third-party aid programs may not be relevant, even though the presence of third-party actors is.

This account emphasizes the ability of domestic actors in a civil war zone to anticipate and frustrate the desires of foreign development professionals to make politics open and transparent. If the main axis of politics hinges on warlords' ability to coordinate and credibly threaten to restart the civil war and the president's use of divide-and-rule tactics to prevent this outcome, it is not obviously in anyone's interest for promises to be codified in writing, or channeled through transparent formal institutions. An autocratic, patronage-based favor economy is central to the provision of domestic order, where wealth is secured through selective enforcement of property rights and certain warlords are permitted to loot the state from within.

Though the paired cases in this study are outliers in certain respects, the kinds of arrangements observed in Georgia and Tajikistan are representative of civil war settlements generally. It is inconvenient for the humanitarian aid complex to openly acknowledge the fact that most states that fought civil wars since 1945 emerged from the violence as dictatorships. Only a quarter of the settled civil war observations in the Doyle and Sambanis (2006) dataset are characterizeable as democratic (combined Polity Score of 6 or higher) five years after civil war.[25] Postwar authoritarian institutions matter – and in Appendix A, statistical evidence will be presented that shows that building parties after civil wars seems to be a relatively popular strategy for keeping the war from breaking back out again.[26] In the post–Cold War era, the modal form of governance after civil war is a "hybrid regime" – a semi-authoritarian regime that holds elections.[27] This book emphasizes that governance reform is partially theatrical: regimes make cosmetic efforts towards democracy and reforms to receive multilateral aid, and then use this aid to pay off criminal factions who keep violence off-camera. AND WHY ARE AMERICANS MADE TO BANKROLL THIS?

An approach that views the state from the bottom up, as an emergent equilibrium of joint warlord strategies, illuminates aspects of war termination that are often obscured. In this book's account, foreign governments can use their financial, diplomatic, and military tools to shape civil war settlements

---

[25] On the standard combined −10 to 10 scale, modal and median polity scores five years after the end of the civil war are −7 and −2, respectively. Given that governments that can insulate themselves from coups are more likely to sustain the transition to nonviolent politics, scholars and practitioners alike will be drawn into the business of assisting with coup-proofing weak states after civil war. Fully functioning democracies are obviously the best long-term inoculation against the threat of a coup – and Wantchekon (2004) provides good reasons for this to be so – but these are relatively rare outcomes in the wake of civil violence.

[26] Girod (2012) provides evidence that elites in the world's weakest and most vulnerable states are fully capable of anticipating the kinds of institutions that foreigners expect to see, and, since the end of the Cold War, can be incentivized by multilateral aid and low-interest international loans to build efficacious political institutions.

[27] For variations on this argument, see Levitsky and Way (2005), Pevehouse (2005), Carothers (2006), and Goldsmith (2008).

indirectly by altering certain parameters – but the strategic choices that create the equilibrium are made by people who will continue to live in the war zone after the foreigners depart. The coalition-formation approach has a number of observable implications that differ from those of traditional two-player bargaining models. Instead of treating the armed strength of a rebel challenger as an exogenous model parameter, this approach seeks to explain variation in the relative size and strength of the incumbent and insurgent coalitions. The central strategic choice in the game presented in this book is whether a warlord will choose to contribute his armed forces to the emerging warlord coalition (the state) or remain outside this coalition (as a rebel).

A coalition-formation approach can shed light on contemporary counterinsurgency practices. Though in principle a large number of rebel "spoilers" may complicate negotiations to end a civil war, in practice much of what militaries actually do in the name of counterinsurgency is obviously aimed at sowing rebel fragmentation so that the state can "pick up the pieces."[28] Embattled governments often create institutions to facilitate side-switching by insurgents as irregular wars grind to a slow finish. Incorporating enemy combatants is a triple-win for the incumbent regime, as it simultaneously reduces the ranks of the enemy, provides an "exit option" for demoralized rebels who do not want to keep fighting, and brings hardened soldiers with local knowledge onto their side. It also mitigates the commitment problem that is so vexing to liberal interventionists, as individual rebels simply do not disarm – they keep their weapons, hedge their bets, and gradually transmogrify into state agents. These processes of defection, desertion, and incorporation are rarely placed at the center of strategic analysis by counterinsurgency professionals. This book is meant as a partial corrective to that trend, emphasizing that extortion and bribery were critical mechanisms in settling the post-Soviet wars.

EMPIRICAL METHODOLOGY

This volume represents my best attempt to synthesize the narratives of many people who experienced the wars of independence in Georgia and Tajikistan

---

[28] On spoilers, see Stedman (1997) and Cunningham (2006). On ruthless counterinsurgency tactics aimed at sowing fragmentation, see Kalyvas (2006) and Davenport (2007). Examples of side-switching between incumbents and insurgents abound. More than 5,000 former rebel fighters from the Moro National Liberation Front in the Philippines were trained, armed, and assigned to active units in the Armed Forces of the Philippines in the late 1990s, according to Felter (2005). The 2006 "Anbar Awakening" in Iraq would have been impossible if former insurgents were not permitted to reinvent themselves and find employment in the Iraqi Security Forces, as Anderson (2007) and Ucko (2009) report. Tarzi (2005), Jalali (2006), Rashid (2008), and Giustozzi (2009), all make it clear that the United States' strategy for post-Taliban Afghanistan involved incorporating prominent warlords, many of whom have found their way into the army, police, private security companies, or into opaque relationships with the Karzai government.

firsthand as party activists, militia members, financiers, or leaders, but also as civilians, refugees, and family support networks. I traveled to Central Asia for the first time in 2005. I spent nearly twenty-five uninterrupted months in Tajikistan and Georgia between 2006 and 2008. I employed ethnographic methods – including living in a remote village on the Tajiki–Afghan border – to gain rapport with interview subjects. I lectured at local universities to cement my bona-fides as a credentialed academic with ties to the Academies of Sciences in Tajikistan, Georgia, Kyrgyzstan, and Abkhazia. I oversaw multiple data collection projects to meet ambitious young students. I gradually forged relationships with academics, journalists, expatriate professionals, current and former government employees, and eventually many former militia members in both countries. I conducted more than 300 interviews, 173 of which were with former combatants. These life histories form the locus of what I believe and understand about the consolidation process.

As social scientists, we want to know, from someone else's perspective, why what they did "made sense at the time." If no counterfactuals can be identified that would have changed their strategies, it is likely that the researcher is asking the wrong questions. If one course-corrects in the field, and tries to find the right questions, then one is theory-building (and no longer hypothesis testing). But the alternative – pressing forward and imposing causal explanations and constraints that are inconsistent with subjects' imagined counterfactuals – squanders the goodwill of busy people. Mathematical modeling is a technology that strives to creates precise, unambiguous statements about the psychological states of these subjects. This is an interpretative task, the result of "guessing at meanings, assessing the guesses, and drawing explanatory conclusions from the better guesses."[29]

As I began to break the process of civil war settlement down into tractable parts, it became possible to refine analogies and construct models that captured strategic dilemmas from the perspective of participants. More importantly, locals helped me discard models and analogies that were inappropriate. I was well positioned to ask follow-up questions, and the answers often led me in directions that would never have occurred to me if I had been building the models from the comfort and safety of my home institution. I often had the opportunity to probe counterfactuals with the relevant local actors: to get them to state plainly what they believed would have happened if things had gone differently. Different individuals often identified the same "critical junctures"

---

[29] Geertz (1977), 20. Rational choice frameworks put the burden on the scientist to be explicit about what "truth" she imagines she has distilled from vapor of cultural nuance. Distillation is inevitable, even for the postpositivist skeptic. More than 99 percent of one's daily ethnographic observations are discarded immediately, inevitably, with or without the filter of theory. The words cannot be transmitted to paper fast enough. But note that if the interpretive process occurs across a linguistic or cultural barrier, then at some point the scientist is required to speak on behalf of "The Other." That simply comes with the territory. Satz and Ferejohn (1994) chart a useful path through the minefield of representational debates.

in the consolidation process – suggesting shared understandings of the choke points through which contingent histories could not pass.

Inevitably I met respondents based on a cascading web of contacts. Given the obvious selection problems implicit in snowball sampling, I was initially reticent to display the quantitative data at all or run regressions. I have since come to the conclusion that the sample is sufficiently representative for the intrasample variation to reveal interesting patterns.[30] Approximately two thirds of the interviews took place in the capital cities of Dushanbe and Tbilisi. The rest took place in regional capitals or rural townships. In both Tajikistan and Georgia the sample is weighted somewhat toward pro-regime militias, which was appropriate for my research question, but which limits the generalizability of valid inferences.

I put time and creative energy into strategies to correct for urban bias and network selection effects. I gradually realized that the same recycled stories were the result of selection effects: I was too often collecting the life histories of the "winners," who had managed to stick around the capital, and missing the perspective of the "losers," who had been forced to retreat to rural areas or migrate. Starting in the fall of 2006 and throughout 2007, I made inroads with failed milita groups to see if this was the case. In Georgia, this meant actively seeking out groups that were purged from the state relatively early (the Zviadists, the National Guard, the White Eagles, etc., instead of just former Mkhedrioni), and groups that operated outside of the capital city (Mkhedrioni branches in Gori, Kvimo-Khartli, etc.).

In Tajikistan, it meant venturing outside of Dushanbe for months at a time. I lived in the village of Kalikhum, on the Tajik–Afghan border, in the winter and spring of 2007. This village was in former opposition-controlled territory, and was one of the primary crossing points for the United Tajik Opposition (UTO) insurgency. I met few combatants during those cold months. I did not penetrate rural social networks in any meaningful way. I kept my eyes open, however, and, through pathways that I could not understand, twenty-nine representatives of

---

30 It is worth emphasizing that these are extremely small countries. Key respondents in both countries were critical in providing multiple introductions in networks that branched out unpredictably in different directions. In Georgia, I had two different retired members of the Ministry of the Interior providing my first set of introductions, as well as a number of random connections that turned into profitable networks (a store clerk with whom I struck up a chance conversation, the bouncer at the nightclub beneath my apartment building, etc.). The Special Analytic Division of the Ministry of the Interior was also an unexpected resource, generous with time and access. In Tajikistan introductions came far slower. A number of embassy and NGO drivers knew my project but did not introduce themselves until I was quite far along in the process, both because of a general cultural aversion to discussing the war and a fear that my project would inevitably attract the wrong kind of attention. Still, my reputation gradually spread, and eventually people came out of the woodwork. As I became confident that I was asking the right questions, I suddenly had more respondents than I could schedule. As word spread that I was a serious person writing a serious book, people wanted to make sure their stories were included.

various Pamiri/Gharmi militias – including two former field commanders – sought me out after I returned to the capital city. Much of my perspective on the civil war can be traced to my long, cold months in those mountains.[31]

All of the militia members I interviewed were men. Because initial introductions were often made in social settings, about a dozen interviews, mostly in Georgia, were conducted with groups of men from the same fighting unit. There is no doubt that this biased these responses somewhat. Particularly when conducting interviews with large groups of Geogians at the same time, there was often a hidden threshold in the interview process beyond which people started contradicting each other, arguing among themselves, and revising each others' statements. The main data that went missing in group interviews – due to strong norms of masculinity that proscribe certain kinds of conversations – is the role of parental pressure, particularly from mothers and mothers-in-law, which emerged only in responses with key interviewees. The model that emerges is therefore biased toward a set of microfoundations that treats the individual (man) as the unit of analysis rather than the family network. I suspect that the shame associated with "letting the family down" motivated many of my respondents to keep fighting, even when things got very bad, but my research design makes it impossible to test this hypothesis.

Many of my respondents used to be employed in the police or the army. At the time of the interview, many were marginally employed.[32] Still, respondents spoke clearly from their social position – often including self-awareness of their own biases. When I asked questions about their behaviors, most could reconstruct plausible explanations. They would try to make me understand that they weren't stupid, crazy, or deserving of pity. They believed they had acted reasonably, even deterministically, under the circumstances. Many held bleak and ironic attitudes, and could angrily recall the jarring transition from being "the law" to being "on the wrong side of the law" in a few arbitrary weeks. The random-seeming nature of coalition formation had a cheapening effect on their views of state legitimacy. The process was reflective. The model anchoring this book reflects shared understandings.[33]

---

[31] Kalikhum was effectively cut off from the capital for nearly nineteen months during the war. This led to a great deal of starvation and many deaths from exposure. But when this period was described spontaneously by schoolteachers, government workers, NGO workers, and medical professionals – the most educated citizens of the village, who would be the ones to know better, if anyone would – the suffering was consistently blamed on "the Russians" who "bombed the roads."

[32] The most productive members of the Tajik male labor force reside in Russia and my data reflect this – more than a quarter of my respondents were only "passing through" the capital city on their way back to construction jobs in Moscow, St. Petersburg, or Siberia.

[33] Respondents were not passive conduits to the past. A few asked me what I was doing so far from home, what incentivized me to chase ghosts or get the names right, what my family thought of my spending nights having conversations about someone else's civil war. I tried to answer honestly, but the changing answers that I gave to these questions were constitutive in ways I did not fully appreciate at the time. I acquired a personal stake in getting the story right.

Respondents tended to be generous with their time and candid with their opinions. Many were flattered that I was so interested in finding the right analogies to capture the essence of their experiences. I gradually learned to ask the right questions and articulate persuasive analogies. How did militia leaders initially emerge during the chaos of the Soviet collapse? What promises did they use to initially recruit foot soldiers? Why did this recruitment spiral out of control in some places and not others? Why did some recruits switch captains or hold steady in the face of vicious street violence while others deserted? How did militias adapt their organizational structures after the war? Why did militia leaders empower a president, if they knew he would eventually be in a position to isolate and liquidate them?[34] For many veterans, the war was a coming-of-age ritual, and they spoke about their militia with the nostalgia that American men from small towns use when they describe the exploits of their high school football team. The initial difficulty of finding respondents in Tajikistan and the nature of the interview process often lent itself to long and relatively unstructured conversations. Georgian veterans tend to enjoy discussing their militia experiences in large groups. Tajiks do not. As any veteran can attest, it is difficult to assess the truth of first-person war stories. I was surely exposed to many tall tales. Data analysis and summary statistics in Chapter 4 are drawn from the subset of questions that were asked universally and for which I believe I received honest responses from most interview subjects.[35]

It is difficult to be specific about how the process changed my orientation toward the research problem, but I did change. As I learned more about how the Soviet gray market functioned to empower certain family networks above others and how familial finance networks could be laid directly atop late Soviet mobilization dynamics, the decision for a certain kind of young male to join a militia began to feel overdetermined. Archived emails show that – for months – the nonmobilizations in Kyrgyzstan, Turkmenistan, and Uzbekistan were the puzzling outcome. For a time I became entranced by factors widely considered to be beyond the ken of rational choice: charismatic leadership, self-reinforcing emotional and crowd dynamics, religious beliefs, and conspiracy theories. Subsequent interpretation is further complicated by the fact that ethnographers do not retain an identity wholly distinct from their subjects. I will probably always think of the Tajik village of Kalikhum as "my" village, though of course it is nothing of the sort. I will probably always carry around a bit of anger on behalf of my subjects. This anger is fully irrational, based on grievances that were never my own. The information transmission process goes both ways. Although few of my respondents will ever read this book, it is likely that as a result of answering my questions and reverse-engineering my reasons for asking them, some of these men understand the wars in the same way that I do.

34 These questions may not be "the right questions" in any objective sense, but they do have the advantage of being questions with locally verifiable answers. The longer you ask these kinds of questions to serious people, in a serious way, the harder it becomes for them to lie as they answer. This is the sort of small-n research design advocated by a colloquium of anthropologists and political scientists in Bowen and Petersen (1999). The accumulated life histories of combatants, elite interviews with commanders, and ethnographic experiences were invaluable in the formation of theory. See Aunger (1995) and Wood (2007).

35 This leaves the social scientist with the difficult problem of what to do with data collected from interview respondents who lied outright. Not everyone trusted me at first. Some respondents

At first, I naively tried to avoid implicating my respondents in descriptions of abjectly criminal activities. It quickly became obvious that this was impossible. I settled for a policy of total anonymity for all respondents.[36] Certain subject matter was carefully filtered by the respondents themselves. It was very rare for anyone to discuss money in specific denominations. I learned a great deal about the banalities of racketeering, price-fixing, money laundering, and other mainstays of the post-Soviet underworld, but specific information about the dispensation of family assets was carefully guarded. Details were not volunteered and I never asked. Resentment toward the current generation of "big men" was tempered by the realities of the embedded favor economy. There are strong norms against taking the side of outsiders against the nation, tribe, or family. I never stopped being an outsider. My field interviews improved substantially when I accepted the limits of my role. I acquired a reputation for being primarily interested in political stories and having no particular local agenda. I also took conscious steps to control the subject matter, intentionally shying away from asking respondents about their own violent activities. The main way I did this was to make it clear that I was studying institutions – militia structures – and not people. I overcame my skepticism of questions like "in your group did you observe..." when I realized that respondents

left the interview not trusting me at all. (Who could blame them?) Strange as it sounds, many of the respondents who assumed I was a spy, or affiliated with the U.S. military, were often *more willing* to engage with me. I can only speculate why this was the case. Perhaps they saw me as being part of the same fraternity of warrior-defenders, or that we shared the experience of making bad youthful decisions and getting in over our heads. But some respondents were certainly sociopathic liars. Some respondents misrepresented basic facts about events, their beliefs, and their roles. There is little to be said here beyond the obvious: I listened hard, asked follow-up questions when I could, and usually stayed until the person wished to stop talking. I can only promise readers what I promised my respondents: that I have tried in this text to represent the spirit of their comments accurately, to never print anything I did not believe to be true, and to present quotes in the spirit in which they were spoken. All subsequent errors in the modeling and interpretation of these soldiers' narratives are my own.

36 I recorded only the subject's first name, or a pseudonym, and interview date to preserve anonymity. In a few cases, the subject insisted that I record his full name. For my own safety, and that of my respondents, I never complied with these requests. The protections that I deemed necessary for myself and my respondents were substantially more serious than anything that anyone in the Human Subjects Committee of my home institution thought to impose. I initially hoped it would be useful to have respondents sketch pictures of the security structures at different periods of time. These exercises quickly devolved into incoherence – pages filled with circles, lines, and scribbled names that I realized would never be coded or systematized. I began to brainstorm strategies to collect individual-level characteristics to predict which militia members joined the state, which factions ended up with which jobs, and which factions were "weeded out." Meandering conversation threads then gave way to more structured discussions about who was getting what, how and when side-switching between militia commanders was considered, etc. Though I eventually became discouraged with the effort to map individual militia trajectories, the exercise provided the impetus for the collaborative efforts with the Small Arms Project to code warlord biographies and the impetus for removing individual identifiers from analyzed data.

could describe their own actions in the third person, with plausible deniability and emotional distance from actions that were regretted in retrospect.[37] But interviews often sprawled, and what I ultimately ended up collecting were life histories. With time, behind the veil of anonymity my methods provided, I received rich anecdotes.

It is reasonable to second-guess the motives of networked strangers who arrive from far away states to ask questions about a war. Having extended conversations about post-Soviet security structures occasionally led to uncomfortable and conspiracy-laden conversations about whether old Russian phone taps had been replaced with American post-9/11 security assistance. Following Derluguian (2005), I took notes but did not record interviews – and am sure that if I had started taping voices I would have received less access and very different kinds of data.[38]

I was living in Kyrgyzstan in 2005 when the Andizjan events unfolded across the border in Uzbekistan.[39] I recall distinctly the feeling of vulnerability when the Internet stopped working correctly. I decided that if I was going to continue

---

37 There is obviously some risk that the leading structure of the interview questions biased respondents toward remembering the worst in their counterparts. This means that the degree of theft and indiscipline may be overstated.

38 In keeping with Whyte (1982) and Emerson, Fretz, and Shaw (1995), sometimes I judged that taking notes would disturb the intimacy of the conversation, though I would, if necessary, pause the respondent to scribble a particularly juicy quote, translated to English in real time. In these cases, field notes were recorded immediately after an interview session. Most interviews were either conducted in respondents' homes or in mutually chosen public spaces. I often compensated respondents for their time with a culturally appropriate token gift (often baked goods or alcohol). In public and social settings, I quickly learned that it was important for me to insist I "host" the interview to maintain control of the environment. This allowed me some control over the timing of the questions, when to stop, and some ability to slow the speed of toasts. On a few occasions, my embarassingly low tolerance for alcohol affected my ability to complete the interview, but in many cases these social settings produced key informants and a range of introductions. My inferences are inevitably "weighted" toward a small number of key informants with whom I established rapport, conducted multiple follow-up interviews, and who supplied introductions with others who corroborated their claims. The majority of interviews were conducted in Russian in Georgia, and in either Tajik or Russian in Tajikistan. Approximately a quarter of the interviews in Georgia and a third of the interviews in Tajikistan were conducted in the presence of a translator (always a young man of university age). Eventually I found that navigating the contours of the language barrier provided many opportunities for follow-up questions, and the intimacy allowed me to guide the interview. My knowledge of the civil wars expanded organically along with my language abilities. The quality of my data also improved as I mastered enough local detail to ask face-saving follow-up questions and signal that I had recognized a half-truth.

39 What is not disputed is that there was an attempted prison break and many, many people died. Then the narratives diverge. Akiner (2005) went to Andizjan two weeks after the uprising to conduct interviews and concludes that the demonstrations were a "carefully prepared" (10) attack on the Uzbek government, organized by armed militants (part of the "Akromiya movement"), who were multinational in composition (30–31, 27–29). Her version of events is contradicted by Bukharbaeva (2005), Daly (2005), the OSCE (2005), Ilkhamov (2006), and Kendzior (2006).

operating in an unfriendly authoritarian environment, I needed to adapt. I quickly educated myself about how Internet servers work, and I stopped assuming my email communications were private. For important topics I began to rely on pen and paper. But these realizations gradually transformed my relationship with "the field." Especially in Tajikistan, it meant proceeding very slowly over months that turned into years. After a few frightening encounters, I was warned by a trusted advisor that my research design was making me look quite a bit like a spy – and that if I ran afoul of the wrong character in the wrong security bureaucracy, it could easily result in my permanent disappearance.[40] After returning to the United States, to limit my own liability, I made a point of destroying all of my field notes that could be used to reconstruct contemporary networks.

As a personal matter, I have opted for a rather distant and antiseptic tone in this volume with respect to acts of violence. After a few uncomfortable conversations, I tried to enforce a general policy of stopping interviews when subjects divulged personal memories of violence or war crimes. This was not always possible. Many interviews had a confessional aspect to them. Some men tried to shock me with graphic descriptions of tactics – inflicted or received – to test, embarrass, or entice me. As an author, I have learned that there is no catharsis to be gained by seeing these descriptions in print. Lurid descriptions of mutilations, written from the safety of the ivory tower, cheapen the horror of the experiences for participants. The deepest scars – posttraumatic stress and survivor guilt – are invisible. Ethnographers working in conflict zones eventually learn what police detectives and competent military professionals have understood for time immemorial: there are serious mental and emotional costs associated with treating sociopaths as subjects.[41]

Sometimes I got scared. The interview subjects always noticed. The interview ended shortly afterwards. That I conducted so many interviews is evidence that, from my perspective, the participants in these wars were not all thugs, gangsters, and sociopaths. I could not have created the necessary intimacy if they were. Obviously there were strategic reasons to present distorted and self-serving versions of certain facts, but most respondents seem to remember

[40] A Tajik doctoral student and personal friend was recently placed under house arrest in Tajikistan, pending a trial for charges of treason and espionage, for qualitative observational research (conducting interviews in Badakhshon) on behalf of a non-Tajik Principal Investigator, who works at a well respected European research institute. He has since been released but it is not clear if he will ever be permitted to return. The risks to my local contact network are just as serious. Though there is technically an amnesty law on the books, many respondents became visibly uncomfortable when the conversation turned to Rakhmonov, contemporary politics, or anything that might pique the interest of eavesdroppers. Journalists are routinely intimidated in Dushanbe. Independent of each other, both of my regular translators in Tajikistan (both aspiring journalists) requested that I omit their names from this volume and all future publications.

[41] I occasionally wonder how my life would be different if I had read E. Valentine Daniel (1996) before going into the field, rather than afterwards.

doing what they thought was appropriate at the time. Respondents were reasonably clear, once I asked the right kinds of questions, about what games they understood themselves to be playing, why they adopted the strategies that they did, and why they succeeded or failed.

I decided early in the research process to build my theory on the perspective of actual people as much as possible. People do not, as a rule, like to be studied. And as Jarvis Cocker observed, "everybody hates a tourist." People do, as a rule, like the idea that their stories will be recorded for posterity. Ethnographers – by their invasive presence – force these decision heuristics into conflict. As the line between researcher and subject blurs, what occasionally emerges is a crucible for creative, cooperative theory-building. People can tell when their words are being received with empathy (i.e., when they are being treated as subjects) and when their words are being clinically recorded for some other purpose (i.e., when they are being treated as objects). I found that once a subject decides that the researcher is actually listening – and taking anonymity promises seriously – the researcher gets much better data.

STRUCTURE OF THE BOOK

My book compares the experiences of two countries that disintegrated violently, but then reconstituted relatively quickly, after the collapse of the Soviet Union. In the cases I selected for this study, the third-party intervention force – a Russian force – was not benign or neutral, and it did not make a convincing attempt to implement liberal policies to facilitate general disarmament. Nonetheless, local actors managed to sculpt self-enforcing arrangements by cannibalizing inherited Soviet institutions. But contemporary order-providing bargains in the two countries are very different from each other. I will argue that the differences are better explained as geopolitical adaptations by local innovators than as structural inheritances from Soviet times.

Because no one anticipated the timing of the Soviet Union's collapse, the disintegration and reconstitution of the successor states provides the closest analogue to a laboratory experiment that students of state failure and recovery are likely to find. A shared institutional and historical legacy guarantees that many unobserved contextual variables were held constant in the aftermath of independence. This book traces the experiences of two Eurasian countries, Georgia and Tajikistan, through the first decade of their independence. Both states collapsed into anarchy as the result of dynamics unleashed in their inaugural elections. The hostile and impassable mountains, the absence of a national army, the easy access to illicit funds from drug corridors, the weighty history of bad governance, ethnic cleavages, opaque clan networks, and foreign-backed insurgencies all combined to make them poor candidates for quick resolution or negotiated peace. At the beginning of 1995, Georgia was in a state of near-total anarchy, with the state apparatus delegitimized and its territorial integrity splintered by multiple successful secessionist movements.

Tajikistan was vying with Chechnya for the dubious distinction of being the most brutal war in the post-Soviet space. To the surprise of everyone – conflict scholars and area specialists alike – stable regimes in both countries consolidated during the next few years. Over the course of the next decade, rulers who were originally installed at gunpoint by paramilitary warlords managed to wrest control of the state apparatus from the armed groups that installed them. Faith in the permanence of the state gradually returned as ceasefires calcified into armistice across Eurasia. Today the settlements appear quite stable.

The divergent experiences of Georgia and Tajikistan provide a rare opportunity to examine "the state" from the ground up: sets of local understandings between armed groups congealed eventually into self-enforcing and predictable strategies. It is possible for social scientists to catch a rare glimpse of the process by which order emerged in the post-Soviet periphery. In both countries, clan-based militias and criminal warlords installed a civilian regime in the capital city that was capable of appealing directly to international donors. The regime started as a cosmetic legitimizing device for violent militias. Armed groups fought each other for the right to extort presidents, who doled out privatization rights and ministry positions to buy loyalty. Over time, post-Soviet leaders learned how to pit their enemies against one another in the coalition formation process. A critical component of this strategy was incorporating former political enemies into the state apparatus, allowing rebels to reinvent themselves as important regime allies. Nongovernmental organizations (NGOs) managed the delivery of humanitarian aid, partial privatization enriched local actors, and warlords became tax collectors. European and American aid for targeted institution building and state reconstruction was captured by local agents, who kept violence mostly out of sight and deep structural reforms off the table. State-building entailed the emergence of unaccountable patronage networks inside regime ministries – the "systematic corruption" decried by intellectuals and NGOs – which gardually harmonized informal wartime institutions with formal state structures.

The post-Soviet wars are often explained as exemplar cases of ethnic war: where historically inherited categories determined, and could thus be used to predict, wartime affiliations.[42] This book takes as its starting point the easily

---

[42] I have in mind Posen (1993) and Van Evera (1994). Kaufmann (1996) argues that once ethnic violence reached a certain threshold, the sides are fixed, the stakes are zero-sum, and negotiated settlements short of secession and population separation are practically impossible. Petersen (2002) emphasizes that deep-seated historical grievances are often articulated by fighters as causal explanations for their behaviors. He argues that, in the aftermath of the Soviet federal experiment, it was clear that the inversion of long-established ethnic hierarchies was inevitable in many of the new states. It was not difficult, in the absence of strong state institutions, to use the powerful emotions that accompanied status reversals to motivate young men to commit acts of symbolic violence against their neighbors. Laitin (1999a) presents a "tipping" model for vigilante violence in a multi-linguistic context, designed to create local status-hegemony

visible counter-trend toward interethnic cooperation – by far the most common outcome between the myriad ethnic groups that did *not* begin killing each other when the Soviet Union collapsed.[43] The idea that the violent homogenization of Abkhazia is somehow more of a "natural" or "inevitable" outcome than the stubbornly enduring peaceful coexistence of ethnic groups in the Ferghana Valley ought to be anathema to modern thinking liberals. When all of the "dogs that did not bark" are taken into account, explanations for violence based on ethnic difference and historical grievance are suspect. Ethnicity was certainly not a very reliable predictor of loyalty in either of the violent state consolidation projects that this book describes.[44]

Much of the data that are presented in this book focus on events in Tbilisi and Dushanbe, the respective capital cities of Georgia and Tajikistan. This is intentional. When Georgian and Tajik soldiers talked about the politics of war termination, the politics that they wanted to talk about was primarily the politics of dividing up the best turf. The capital is where one is most likely to find airports, high-end restaurants and casinos to cater to the wealthy transnational investor class, banks, embassies, physical symbols of state authority (such as the statehouse and parliament building), television transmitters, public utilities' junctions, and centers of cultural production (such as universities and opera houses). Calls for nationalist mobilization that come from the capital city are more likely to be taken seriously by rural youth. Whoever controls the capital city controls the image of that country to the world. A relatively orderly capital city is a keyhole that foreigners are permitted to look through.[45] In this account, the visible signs of well-functioning state institutions – shiny buttons on pressed uniforms, television programming to commemorate national and religious holidays, schools where nationalist myths are standardized as curricula, military parades to display soldiers marching in well-ordered ranks, clerks at desks empowered with stamps, clean parks with well-maintained statues, well-run elections and parliaments – are epiphenomenal of understandings between domestic armed groups. The majority of citizens observe public rituals and are held in awe.

---

for a language group to maximize the life opportunities of the vigilantes' children. For Laitin, violence can be rationalized as facilitating a societal "tip" in the status of one's native tongue, with the benefit being passed on to the next generation in the form of high-paying jobs as government clerks. Fearon (1998) explicitly builds the assumption of zero-sum tradeoffs between the values of different ethnic groups into his model of violent secession.

43 Fearon and Laitin (1996), 716.
44 Though it is beyond the scope of this study, the same is also true in Chechnya. The Russian government enlisted rehabilitated Chechen rebels in the last decade and Lyall (2010) demonstrates that they are unusually effective at the sordid tasks of counterinsurgency. Balta (2007) confirms this account. Enloe (1980) documents military co-optation across ethnic lines around the globe.
45 Bates (1984) demonstrates that whoever controls the capital of an African state can extract wealth from rural poor by leveraging import–export bottlenecks. This is also clearly the case in many post-Soviet republics.

Social scientists often rely on models to understand observations and experiences. Formal models derive their power from their claim of being able to clearly capture the essence of a situation. Models are aesthetically attractive to readers who appreciate clear and explicit presentation of theory. Combining formal modeling with narrative – the "analytic narrative" approach – ensures that the argument is defined precisely.[46] The narrative establishes who the actors are, their preferences, the available set of strategies, and possible outcomes. The formal model specifies how the interplay of strategies worked to create a particular stable outcome (equilibrium). In dynamic settings, the concept of subgame perfection is a powerful explanation for why certain behaviors and ideas "stick" in some conditions and not others. The analytic narrative approach also has advantages for social science presentation because the formal model guarantees that analytical rigor is maintained, but readers are not forced to break the narrative prose for hypothesis testing.[47] Filtering a set of noisy facts about the world through a mathematical prism allows for clear articulation of causal processes and washes out irrelevant details.

In a highly critical essay, Jon Elster (2000) raised a number of programmatic objections to the analytic narrative approach. Eschewing real people in favor of bloodless rational agents has pitfalls, namely, the assumption of rational actors, high levels of aggregation, little concern for intentions and beliefs, and no concern for uncertainty. I am sympathetic to Elster's concern that, as a community, political scientists have become a bit too comfortable taking the logic of the firm and applying it to states, ethnic groups, rebel factions, political parties, and terrorist cells. Everyone knows that none of these organizations really have interests or beliefs: only people do. With that in mind, this book's empirical strategy and presentation are calibrated to be directly responsive to Elster's concerns. The individual human being is the unit of analysis in all of the chapters that follow. I describe a violence market in weak states between warlords and recruits, coalition formation processes between strategizing warlords, and divide-and-rule politics between a weak president and his warlords-turned-ministers. In all of these examples, strategic calculations are made by human beings under conditions of great stress and uncertainty. Neither perfect rationality nor perfect information is taken for granted.

Once analysts abandon institutions as the unit of analysis and replace them with thinking agents, Ferejohn (2004) hints that persuasive accounts of any political phenomenon worth studying – such as the quick resolution of the post-Soviet wars – should include both external and internal explanations.

---

[46] See Bates et al. (2000, 2000).

[47] A reader who dismisses the assembled quotes as an unscientific assemblage of accumulated conspiracy theories, acquired haphazardly from a snowball/convenience sample, can at least have faith that all of the tall tales and street stories congealed into something internally consistent.

External explanations relate to intersubjectively realized constraints that are "out there" in the world. Internal explanations come from within an individual, such as psychological biases, emotional responses, and culturally contingent belief structures, and are much harder to measure.[48] Collecting data on the psychology of civil war actors is difficult and dangerous, and I now appreciate better why studies that provide compelling "internal" accounts of civil war behaviors are so rare.[49] As I investigated the militia structures that formed the fighting units of the post-Soviet wars in Tajikistan and Georgia, I was granted an unusually clear view into the worldviews that informed civil war participants. If social science is judged by its ability to integrate subaltern perspectives into hegemonic discourses – and I see no reason it should not be – then adopting the vantage point of excluded actors, to the extent that these actors let their voices be heard, seems to be a decent place to start. I have reproduced a number of my interview subjects' quotes faithfully, and scattered them through the text.

Chapter 2 presents a theoretical account of civil war settlement in which no one actually disarms. A ruler in the capital city (identified generically as a *figurehead president*) is responsible for acting as the public face of the nation to the international community. The president remains in power by establishing informal patronage networks and distributing wealth to local strongmen (identified generically as *warlords*) who, in turn, use the threat of violence to keep citizens from organizing to challenge the state. Bargains are self-enforcing because warlords who install a president can extort him post-installation with the threat of a coup. As payment for providing order, the president is forced to give the warlords relatively unfettered access to state ministries. Parameters required for an orderly situation to stabilize from the model are clear: shared expectations of foreign wealth and low "reservation" options for warlords who opt to retain criminal empires outside of the regime's

---

[48] Consider the now-classic rationalist account of revolutionary social mobilization presented by Timur Kuran (1991). Costly social mobilization is a coordination problem. Risky protests against the government might be worthwhile if they are likely to induce "tipping" behavior – creating a situation where the regime collapses and there is no authority to retaliate against activists. An individual's choice to participate in a revolution will depend on the tradeoff between an external payoff (i.e., personal rewards and punishments, which will vary depending on whether they are acting alone or in a group) and an internal payoff (i.e., the psychological costs of preference falsification). See Petersen (2001), especially chapter 2, for a discussion of how different community thresholds yield different equilibrium strategies.

[49] Participant observation has been the research design that most consistently yields persuasive "internal explanations" for violence. Seminal ethnographic (and often selfnographic) investigations into the social structures and psychological dispositions that make violence thinkable include Orwell (1952), Capote (1965), Fanon (1968), Herr (1968), Scott (1976), Popkin (1979), Pileggi (1985), Katz (1988), Vigil (1988), Jankowski (1992), Buford (1993), Espiritu (1996), Grossman (1996), Brass (1997), Sacco (2003), and Jackall (2005). For an excellent introduction to the anthropology of violence, see the assembled essays in Scheper-Hughes and Bourgois (2004).

distributive politics framework. These are both parameters that great powers can manipulate without any particular local knowledge.

With the structure of strategic interaction defined and the theoretical framework established, the book unfolds in a roughly chronological manner. Rather than present historical snapshots, each chapter explains a process of equilibrium selection. Each chapter explains how Georgian and Tajik actors understood their choice set at the time, and why they chose particular strategies, intentionally emphasizing processes at the expense of variables.

Chapter 3 defines the primary strategic actors in this study – warlords – and explains how they dragged Georgia and Tajikistan into violent state failure. Central to the story in both cases were escalating fears of radical programs for social redistribution and geopolitical re-alignment. With the authority of old Soviet hierarchies contested, and established favor economies disrupted by emigration and economic collapse, there was deep uncertainty about who would be the terminal enforcer of contracts and provider of order. The paramilitarization of politics fueled cycles of fear, and anarchy washed over the countryside. Russian artillery and air power made certain non-negotiable realities of the post-Soviet international system clear by backing the regime in Tajikistan and backing ethnic minority secessionists in Georgia. But despite military cauterization, Russian soldiers could not credibly commit to policing the particulars of the deals that ended the war.

Chapter 4 describes the process of coalition formation in Georgia and Tajikistan. Certain warlords in both states colluded together to invite a "puppet president" to speak on behalf of the state and shake hands with foreign donors. There were not even superficial attempts at disarmament – militias in the original winning coalition self-consciously *became* the state. Warlords in Georgia and Tajikistan understood that if they could form a coalition, lay claim to the capital city, and act like a unified force – reappropriating symbols and rituals from defunct Soviet institutions long enough to convincingly masquerade as a government – they would gain access to foreign aid and recognition. This would, in turn, allow them to defeat rival factions. Warlords understood themselves to be participating in something analogous to a costly lottery or a game of musical chairs. Some warlords ended the game inside the state and others did not. There was a period of jockeying for position in the postwar government. During this period, militia members – many of whom were recruited based on promises of future state spoils – competed with newcomers in the violence game, emerging from urban slums or refugee camps. The post-war police forces could not cartel the local violence market as militias proliferated. Violence during the "Time of Troubles" was primarily instrumental in this account, allowing militia members to gather information on the strength of various warlords, the resolve of various militia recruits, and, ultimately, the final composition of the ruling coalition. Once it became clear which warlords were winners and which were losers, many foot soldiers abandoned their commanders and returned home.

Chapter 5 examines the process by which the civilian "puppet" presidents ultimately managed to free themselves from the threat of a coup. The story of how divide-and-rule tactics were used to transform this symbolic power into real bargaining leverage is ultimately a story of different militia captains being played against each other. Once merged into the state, armed groups provided contract enforcement and laundered foreign assistance into the local economy, and by keeping the risk of coup constant, ultimately found themselves filling a vital institutional role. Warlords in both states understood the necessity of presenting a united front to extort the president, but faced a severe collective action problem against crafty civilian rulers who took advantage of splits and cycling in shifting warlord coalitions. Detailed case studies trace the particulars of the divide-and-rule strategies used by Shevardnadze in Georgia and Rakhmonov in Tajikistan as their respective super-presidencies consolidated over the 1990s. Divergent outcomes in the first decade of the twenty-first century are briefly sketched. Though Georgia and Tajikistan both gained independence with unconsolidated territory, scrap-heap armies cobbled together from identical weapon systems, and similar values on virtually every structural variable that one would use to predict persistent state weakness, they have embarked on strikingly different geopolitical and institutional trajectories.

Chapter 6 concludes the study with a brief discussion of policy implications, including contemporary observations relevant to the civil war in Ukraine. If the reader concludes that the post-Soviet wars – long considered to be about indivisible issues of identity – were actually resolved through brokering and buy-out, this study has political implications. Normatively, the news is mixed. On one hand, short civil wars save lives. On the other hand, the processes of war termination described in this volume implicate interveners in structural violence, extortion, and bribery.

2

Predator Collusion

A High-Stakes Game

A persuasive account of state recovery must answer two questions. First: How did civilian executives become strong once formal institutions collapsed? The answer, as already forecast in the first chapter, is that they were figurehead placeholders for coalitions of warlords who "ran the streets" out of sight. But because this arrangement ultimately benefitted the president at the expense of the warlords who installed him, it is reasonable to ask a second question: Why did warlords agree to install a president if they knew that a possible result was that he would use divide-and-rule tactics to cut them out of the spoils? The answer is that although some high-profile warlords were jailed or killed in the consolidation lottery, others slid out of view, reinventing themselves as state agents. A few became quite wealthy.

In this simplified account, state-building is a constantly renewing process of contracting and bargaining between violence entrepreneurs. Warlords are locked in competition, and their rivalry can easily turn violent. This violence can end only with military victory or through a process of coalition building. Though they have the option of working together, cooperation is risky. If a group of warlords can assemble a coalition with sufficient military power to seize the capital city and achieve international recognition, it can install a civilian regime. This civilian regime will gain access to foreign aid, military assistance, and low-interest capital investment. The new regime will become the warlords' hostage, and will immediately transfer most of these new rents to them to stay in power. If the gains associated with seizing the capital city and extorting the rents of sovereignty are greater than the expected utility of outright war, all warlords may rationally abjure violence.

This chapter presents an account of civil war settlement under conditions of state failure. Though it is presented in the form of a two-stage, *n*-player coalition game, one does not have to be a student of game theory to understand the argument in this chapter (proofs and formal propositions can be found in Appendix B). In the first stage, warlords choose either to fight or join a coalition and back the ascendency of a president. If no president is installed, the game ends with continued warfare. If a president is installed, a second stage takes place in which the president distributes the wealth of the state – newly increased, as the president is able to get more aid and other benefits from foreign actors – among various warlords. Warlords observe the distribution and choose either to accept the transfer or attempt to remove the president in a coup. All players are assumed to understand this basic game in the same way, second guess each other's strategies, and maneuver strategically. Analysis of the model reveals a few analytically distinct equilibria. One of particular interest is an equilibrium in which all warlords merge into a single coalition – monopolizing the production of violence. Other equilibria describe stalled negotiations or persistent state failure. Order-providing institutions and understandings are sustainable despite the inability of foreigners to monitor or enforce local arrangements. Peace is self-enforcing without the need for an external guarantor.

In the "liberal interventionism" framework referenced in Chapter 1, the central problem of civil war settlement is convincing rebels to disarm. Because warlords' bargaining power is assumed to be inextricable from their capacity as violence entrepreneurs, in this model no one disarms. One might observe certain kinds of cosmetic disarmament – warlords may don suits, affix a party lapel pin, and reinvent themselves as party officials or vote brokers – but they maintain control of men and weapons. Order is contracted through a process of incorporation and buy-out, with payments taking the form of graft: state offices, black-market monopolies, or rigged privatization schemes. "The state," in this account, is a legitimizing device for warlords who have reinvented and redefined themselves.

A GAME

The strategic contest takes place in a small, internationally recognized sovereign state. This state contains lootable resources and government positions, and the conflict is over the right to appropriate these spoils through selective enforcement of property rights. The actors in this contest are warlords – violence entrepreneurs with private armies, locked in a struggle for power. Assume the state contains $n > 2$ warlords indexed by i, $W = \{1, 2 \ldots n\}$. At the beginning of the game, every warlord $i \in W$ simultaneously chooses either to fight or join in a coalition to install a president. Each warlord i has the option to "Fight" to capture the capital city, exclude rivals from power, and expropriate state wealth v for himself.

Fighting imposes costs c on each warlord, as sustaining a militia cannibalizes productive assets and exposes his family to some risk of violence. Civil war is costly and unpredictable from the perspective of a warlord. A charismatic leader's ability to sustain a militia depends on a host of military, social, and psychological variables that cannot be easily predicted (see Chapters 3 and 4). A prominent warlord can be killed by a ricocheting bullet or replaced by a crafty lieutenant (see Chapters 4 and 5). Warlords are forced to choose strategies without full knowledge of how their own relative capabilities will compare to those of their opponents over the course of the war.

A simple way to capture the contingent character of this process is to treat warlords as symmetric and interchangeable. If all n warlords play "Fight," all will receive payoffs of $\frac{v}{n} - c$. This could represent, with an equal probability, either that the territory of the state fragments into proportional warlord fiefdoms, or that one warlord wins and will control all the spoils. Fighting imposes costs either way.

As an alternative to going alone, warlords can work together to "Install" a president. If they succeed, they will form a group with sufficient domestic armed power to provide order in the capital and minimally secure the borders. The coalition will then temporarily abjure violence and back the ascension of a civilian government, headed by a figurehead president P.[1] If enough warlords collude together, a government emerges capable of appealing to international donors directly. The "stability threshold" s represents the number of warlords necessary to control the capital against rival warlords outside the coalition, making it safe for foreign governments to open embassies and diplomatically recognize P's regime. If s or more warlords work together, then a government emerges with sufficient domestic power to acquire foreign aid, claim the country's seat at the United Nations, and secure foreign investment. A second stage of the game begins (which will be discussed a bit later in this chapter). If fewer than s warlords opt to collude together, then the government that is installed will be incapable of controlling the countryside, and warlords revert to fighting. The miscalculating warlords receive a sucker's payoff of $\frac{v}{n} - c - w$ for any warlord i who played "Install" while others played "Fight."[2]

The "stability threshold" s is a fixed parameter. It is a benchmark for how many warlords are necessary to install a president in the first stage of the game. It also represents the minimum number of warlords necessary to keep a president in power in the second stage of the game. In Rousseau's classic stag

---

[1] It would be more realistic to complicate warlords' coalition formation problem, imagining the universe of national intellectuals, statesmen, heads of prominent tribes, or bureaucrats forming a pool of potential presidents $P = \{f_1, f_2, \ldots f_z\}$. In this more complicated, realistic, and dynamic version of the game, when warlords opt into a coalition, they would have to choose not only to "Fight" or "Install," but also to "Install" while declaring loyalty to a potential figurehead. I assume that the process of coordinating on an acceptable figurehead is resolved extra-model.

[2] The size of the parameter w is independent of the number of warlords who played Install, but $w > 0$ by assumption. A failed attempt at coalition formation ought to be costly in some way, if only because resources invested in diplomacy trade off with investments in military strategy. One might imagine that a warlord who incorrectly anticipates a coalition forming suffers a reputation cost in the eyes of potential recruits, having endorsed a vision of an emergent stable coalition that does not emerge (i.e., after miscalculating, warlord i would appear less wise, or less informed, than competitors whose predictions of total war proved correct.).

hunt, all of the hunters have to work together to bring down a stag. But it is not a logical or realistic requirement for all of the warlords to have to work together to install a figurehead president. And unlike many coalition formation games analyzed in institutionalized settings, there is nothing particularly special about the 50 percent threshold for a simple majority. The number of warlords who have to work together to stabilize a state sufficiently in the eyes of the international community varies by context. A low stability threshold means that a government can access foreign aid and investment even if there are large pockets of territory controlled by unaffiliated warlords. A high stability threshold means that a government needs to incorporate most of the warlords before it gets access to these rents of the international system.

Warlords who chose to fight in the first stage rather than support the president will be cut out of these spoils, and they have no realistic chance of displacing the entire coalition of warlords that now claims the capital city. For a warlord i who remains outside of a consolidating state, the next best thing he can do with his private army will yield a payoff of r, with $0 \leq r \leq \frac{v}{n} - c$. The game ends for these warlords.

Based on what I heard during interviews, r can vary a great deal depending on a warlord's economic and social endowments, regional geopolitics, and the ability of the regime to get foreign support to coerce recalcitrant warlords. Some warlords may be able to flee to the mountains or across international borders and keep the fight alive for years. They may be able to start new lives as narcotics traffickers or soldiers of fortune. They may set up "shadow state" institutions in territories beyond the reach of state authorities. They may be allowed to walk away from their armies and simply disappear. Or they may not. They may end up on no-fly lists, tagged and tracked for the rest of their lives by the installed regime. They may be quickly and efficiently executed. They may die slow deaths from starvation and exposure.[3]

The number of warlords who play "Install" in the first round can be called k. Call the subset of k warlords who play "Install" $W^P \subseteq W$, such that $W^P = \{i, j, \ldots q\}$. So long as $k \geq s$, a coalition government forms. Power-sharing follows, and a figurehead president P is installed to shake hands with foreign heads of state. Warlords do not disarm.[4] They keep access to men and weapons through a variety of invisible channels, and are well positioned to extort the

---

3 What individual warlord characteristics might change the reservation value r? The obvious starting point is expectations of great power support to the consolidating regime, but students of counterinsurgency might quickly add to the list, suggesting ethno-linguistic differences, diaspora networks stretching to foreign capitals, transnational criminal linkages, a homeland in impenetrable mountains, access to particularly lucrative drug trafficking routes, ideological or religious predispositions, or managerial genius suitable to managing clandestine networks. Appendix B has an extension showing that heterogeneity in r can yield unique equilibrium predictions.

4 Disarmament of armed rebels has been described as the "fundamental barrier to civil war settlement" in Walter (1997, 2002).

president by threatening a coup. For the president P and the k warlords in W^P, the second stage of the game begins.

The first thing that happens in this second stage is that the influx of foreign aid, foreign civilians, and illicit rent-seeking opportunities increase the lootable wealth in the state from v to v^*. This new wealth v^* comes into existence in a form that is controlled by P, as he is the one who doles out cabinet appointments. If foreign investors want to extract mineral wealth from the country's interior, build an oil pipeline across the territory, or sell liquor or cigarettes in the capital, they will have to broker with the president's agents. The same is true for foreign militaries that want to silence transnational dissidents or liquidate terrorists living in the territory. A president is a focal symbol of order and stability. He is the face of the winning warlord coalition.

Though v^* is nominally controlled by the figurehead president, power still comes from the barrel of a gun. The president does not need all of the k warlords to rule, but will pick $l \geq s$ warlords to form his inner circle. Call the subset of l warlords selected by the president $W^L \subseteq W^P$ such that $W^L = \{i, j, \ldots q\}$. Warlords in W^L merge their memberships with the army and police forces. But the game is not over. The threat of a coup still hangs over all distributional politics that follow. Warlords in W^L are well positioned to replace one civilian president with another if their demands are not met. P must publicly distribute v^* among the l warlords in W^L and himself, with his decision represented by $x = (x_i, x_j, \ldots x_q, x_P)$. Wealth transfers take the form of ministry positions, nonenforcement of tax laws, closed-bid contracts, and rigged privatization schemes, all of which are arrangements designed to be opaque to foreign observers. Each of these warlords observes his transfer and chooses simultaneously whether he wants to "Coup" or "Accept" the president. It is necessary for s or more warlords to choose "Accept" after receiving their share of x, or the president P will be deposed. In this case, P ends the game with a payoff of zero.

Choosing "Coup" invites violence, which imposes costs on the warlord. Call these costs c, invariant from the first stage, for simplicity in notation. He has some positive probability p of successfully deposing the president. If he keeps the president's distribution of x, a warlord would replace P and seize whatever share of the rents the president was planning to appropriate to his office (x_P). But why stop there? Perhaps a warlord could completely exclude rivals after installing himself as head of state, claiming the entirety of v^* for himself.[5] Every

---

5   Embedded in these payoffs is the assumption that the coup winner can maintain the favor of the international community and investors (or extort them with the threat of domestic chaos) so the country will continue to receive v^*. At the risk of jumping ahead, payoffs in a coup should reflect the most optimistic possible post-coup situation from the perspective of a warlord, as after backwards induction, the "ceiling" of a coup payoff will represent the "floor" of a risk-adverse president P's transfer to a warlord. It is plausible that in the event of a poorly executed palace coup, v^* would shrink back down to v. In this case expected coup payoffs are only $pv - c$. If this is were known to be true by the warlords, these losses would ultimately benefit the president P,

warlord is a capable observer of the political environment, so for simplicity let us assume that each warlord i can correctly assess his subjective probability of successfully carrying out a palace coup at a given time.[6] To simplify matters and highlight essentials, let us also assume p is invariant to l, and assume a successful palace coup would net the warlord all of the assets in the state.[7] The coup payoff can be described as $pv^* - c$. At the risk of repetition, if fewer than s warlords play "Accept," then the coalition breaks down and all of the warlords fight among themselves, each hoping to personally ascend to the role of president. In this case, the president receives zero and each warlord in W^L receives his coup payoff $pv^* - c$. If the number of warlords playing "Accept" is equal to or greater than s, P stays in power and all of the warlords in W^L receive their transfer according to x.

What happens if more than one warlord "Coups" at the same time? To maintain the assumption of warlord symmetry, the couping warlords should have equal odds of ending up in power. If there are m warlords attempting a palace coup, they each have an expected payoff of $\frac{p}{m}v^* - c$.[8] But to preview analysis in Appendix B, all that is going to matter is the payoff based on the probability of pulling off a successful coup when no one else is trying to do the same, which has been defined previously as $pv^* - c$. If a warlord i in W^L attempts a coup alone and does not succeed (which will occur with probability $1 - p$), it does not affect other warlords' payoffs so long as s or more support the president.

But what happens to warlords who played "Install" in the first round, but were then not selected to be part of the inner circle? In every case where $k > l$, there will be at least one warlord $i \in W^P \notin W^L$. This unlucky warlord i was not transferred anything as a part of x, and is incapable of challenging the combined force of the l warlords who now back the president. The game ends for this warlord with a payoff of zero. This warlord played the lottery and

who now only has to pay $v^* - l(pv - c)$. One can get approximately the same results by allowing c to be different in the first and second stages of the game (c_1 and c_2), incorporating certain losses in investment as higher costs of fighting c_2 in the second stage.

6 In this stylized setting, incorporated into that probabalistic judgment is not only the simultaneous defection of $k - s$ additional warlords, but also defeating all of them in the scramble that will follow.

7 I have no particular theoretical priors on the question of whether the probability of a successful coup should vary with the number of warlords in W^L. It could be that a large number of warlords in the coalition implies a smaller probability of any one of them successfully seizing power. It seems equally plausible that a larger number of warlords competing behind the throne makes coup prospects for any warlord i *higher* because of collective action problems associated with organizing a counter-coup. General results still hold if we let $p(l)$ be the probability of ending up in power after playing "Coup," as a function of number in W^L, so long as $p(l)$ is decreasing, but not decreasing as fast as $1/l$. The derivative of $l(p(l)v^* - c)$ with respect to l must be positive.

8 At first this probably seems counterintuitive, as it implies that a warlord playing "Coup" alone has a higher payoff than playing p in a group ($\frac{p}{m}v^* - c < pv^* - c$). This confusion is an artifact of the notation – p should change between the two settings. If all k warlords play "Coup," the coup succeeds with certainty ($p = 1$) and $m = k$, so the expected payoff would be $\frac{v^*}{k} - c$.

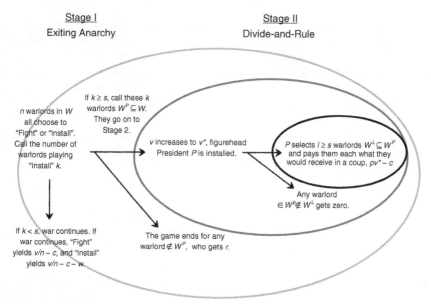

FIGURE 2.1. The Game (off-the-equilibrium-path outcomes not shown).

lost, and will be marginalized by being shut out of state jobs and racketeering rents. His political rehabilitation will be revoked. It will not be taboo to notice his prior criminal behaviors. His army will probably disband itself as soldiers realize their patron cannot pay them.

ANALYZING THE GAME: THREE DIFFERENT STABLE OUTCOMES

Despite the fact that warlords have the first and last move in the game, regardless of parameter values, the figurehead president, once installed, ought to be able to remain in power by buying off a coup. He should be able to appropriate substantial rents for himself from his ability to play warlords against one another. He can build a version of a minimum winning coalition for domestic stability and create a "shadow state," which is exclusively loyal to him and exists in parallel to regular state institutions. A president can – and therefore will – pay s warlords exactly what they would receive in a coup $(pv^* - c)$, pay the rest zero, and keep everything else for himself. Figure 2.1 displays the basic choice sets for warlords who expect that a figurehead president will play the game in this way.[9]

Knowing this, what is a warlord to do in the first stage? It depends on what other warlords are doing. If most are fighting, he should fight as well. But even if enough warlords are working together for a figurehead president to be installed,

---

9   For those readers who are not acquainted with the jargon of game theory, this simplified representation of the game is meant as a schematic of what would happen if every player anticipated that every other player were going to act strategically.

each warlord i must compare his opportunities in W^P to his reservation value r. Because s is static, every warlord i's utility is decreasing in k. Every warlord who plays "Install" worsens the W^L "insider lottery" odds for a warlord in W^P. Because warlords are symmetrical and interchangeable to the president, and the president does not need all of them, in the first stage warlords are gambling when they install a president. Still, if v^* and s are high and the reservation value r is low, a warlord might opt into a high-stakes "liquidation lottery" – a probabalistic game of installing a president with the full knowledge that some installers will be killed as the ruling coalition is trimmed, but others will be in a position to extort the president and get away with it.

In Appendix B, three different classes of subgame perfect Nash equilibria are identified, none of which involve the play of weakly dominated strategies: the *state failure* equilibrum, various *full incorporation* equilibria, and various *partial incorporation* equilibria. These equilibria have different distributional consequences.

- **State Failure: All warlords fight.** The *state failure* equilibrium is inefficient but robust. If all warlords are planning to wage war and seize the capital, an individual warlord i can only make himself worse by not taking part in the scramble.
- **Partial Incorporation: Some install a president, some refuse.** In a *partial incorporation* equilibrium, some warlords form a coalition to install a president and some warlords remain outside the consolidation process. All warlords expect the president will use divide-and-rule tactics to play one against another, assembling the "cheapest" governing coalition of warlords possible, and keeping the rest for himself. Installing the president is a gamble – but a gamble that pays off only for some of the warlords. The odds of being selected as part of the winning coalition W^L diminish as k grows with every additional warlord who opts to enter the state in the first period. For some parameter values, it makes sense for some, but not all, warlords to collude in the extortion game, and warlords in the state coalition prefer that holdouts remain outside state structures.
- **Full Incorporation: All warlords install a president.** In a *full incorporation* equilibrium, all warlords act together to install a president. The president will only distribute the rents of sovereignty v^* among only s warlords, so installing a president is a gamble. Even so, for certain parameters, the potential benefits of being selected to be a member of W^L and extort the president for a share of v^* are sufficiently attractive to outweigh the certain reservation value r one would receive staying outside the state, which induces every warlord to join the state.

What might be observed in a *state failure* equilibrium? Joint strategies by warlords create the Hobbesian nightmare of all against all, as various factions fight each other for survival. Tactical bargains between warlords break down and rampant side-switching and coalition politics make it impossible to identify the "master cleavage" of the conflict.[10] Violent and unpredictable anarchy, chaotic looting, and social disintegration follow. Groups may ravage the countryside with no desire to create order and no political project beyond day-to-day enrichment and survival.

What might be observed in a *partial incorporation* equilibrium? Some warlords have been incorporated into the state apparatus and some have not. Some warlords inside the state do very well, but some warlords who reject state authority do just as well. Civil war may simmer at a low intensity. The sovereignty of the state may be challenged by territorial "shadow states," strong organized criminals who operate in defiance of regime preferences or foreign-backed insurgencies. One might observe stalled peace processes, persistent low-intensity conflict between a loose coalition of urbanized gangsters who control the capital city and rural gangsters who reject the regime's authority, or just a generically "weak state." What all these situations have in common is that some "insurgent" warlords reason that there is more to be gained at the fringes of state control than there is to be gained serving as regime agents.

What might be observed in a *full incorporation* equilibrium? The vast majority of warlords will have been incorporated into the state apparatus and reinvented themselves as regime allies, policemen, or organized criminals with strong ties to the regime. Different organizational and institutional forms comprise the "rules of the game" at this stage, but the underlying arrangements are not considered to be open for modification. Although the threat of a coup hangs over the distribution of spoils, these threats can take the place of actual changes in government. The figurehead president manages a patronage network that allows warlords to reinvent themselves as state agents in the army, ministry of interior, tax police, or local government. Violence entrepreneurs are sated with rents received, and unaccountable patronage networks emerge inside

---

[10] By "master cleavage," I mean the division between the protagonist and the antagonist in the war's "master narrative" – e.g., the incumbents vs. the insurgents, the Islamists vs. the secularists, the red team vs. the blue team, etc. As Kalyvas (2003) forcefully articulated, the reductionist impulse to define a war as being reducible to a two-player game – two "sides" divided by a "master cleavage" – is inherently political, often misleading, and has real implications for how a conflict is rendered in collective memory. One explanation for the systematic bias in favor of narratives that emphasize the "master cleavage," also from Kalyvas (2004), is that journalists and researchers tend to conduct their research in urban areas – where they have access to English-speaking academics, NGO workers, and state representatives – rather than in rural areas, where most of the violence takes place in most civil wars. Another explanation is that civil war actors themselves are often quite sophisticated propagandists, and to attract financial and military from great powers, local allies, or far-flung diaspora groups they misrepresent the content of their motivations or ideology, their unity of command, and any other "off message" detail that might confuse a potential donor with a short attention span. Prominent pleas for disaggregation of the "country-war" as the unit of analysis are Laitin and Brubaker (1998) and Kalyvas (2007).

regime ministries. Relationships with the president and with other warlords – not formal institutions – are the mortar that hold the arrangement together.

Taken sequentially, the three classes of equilibria provide an informal account of how failed states rehabilitate themselves after extended periods of violent anarchy. All warlords recognize that a *state failure* equilibrium is inefficient and to be avoided if possible. Some warlords initially collude to provide order, gain access to international wealth, and gain monopoly rents from the state apparatus that falls under their control. A local "puppet president" is selected as a placeholder for opaque coalition politics. Complicated bargaining follows and backroom deals are struck. As foreign aid and investment increase and the president acquires a reputation for fair dealing, parameter shifts gradually facilitate a switch from a *partial incorporation* equilibrium toward a *full incorporation* equilibrium. In this scenario, peace and order are supported by warlords' ability to extort presidents directly and the international community indirectly. Many warlords transmogrify into violence subcontractors for the regime.

THE STABILITY THRESHOLD AND THE RESERVATION VALUE

To preview the analytic narrative that follows, two parameters critical to the comparison of Georgia and Tajikistan are the stability threshold (s) and the reservation value (r). The story of consolidation in the two decades since independence is the story of declining reservation values. The obvious exception to the general trend of reservation value decline is in the South Caucasus, where certain Abkhaz and South Ossetian warlords remain shielded by Russian military power. The general decline in fortunes for warlords remaining outside the states can be either endogenous to the processes modeled (i.e., as a stable governing coalition emerges, it is increasingly capable of coercing atomized criminal competitors) or exogenous (i.e., outsiders, especially great powers, provide the coercion). Exogenous shifts in the reservation value are of obvious interest for students of international affairs. The obvious exception to the general trend of reservation value decline is in the South Caucasus, where certain Abkhaz and South Ossetian warlords remain shielded by Russian military power. The timing of the 1997 peace accords in Tajikistan conforms with shifts in Russian military policy toward Shah Massoud, the Tajik warlord in Afghanistan, who stopped providing safe havens for warlords across the border. The U.S. invasion of Afghanistan dramatically reduced the expected utility of running a nonstate armed group in Central Asia in a way that Tajik warlords simply could not have anticipated on September 10, 2001. As reservation values fall, the attractiveness of taking part in the v^* lottery – even if it is acknowledged to be a rigged lottery – increases.

The stability threshold s for a particular state is determined by international actors, notably foreign governments and offshore capital markets. It captures how a regime is regarded by important international actors that are in a position to provide recognition, aid, and military assistance. These actors attempt to include in their assessment of local conditions (military technology available to warlords, terrain, distributions of popular support for radicals in the population at large), but their access to information about these conditions is limited. Neighborhood effects matter a great deal. In some settings, foreign powers are desperate to recognize an agent – any agent – to "keep a lid" on revolutionary activism in a state and will send assistance to keep their selected beneficiary in power. If a regime has strong external backers, then the stability threshold s may be $\frac{n}{3}$, $\frac{n}{4}$, or lower. A low stability threshold is more likely when the threat of anarchy from certain out-of-coalition gangsters threatens the collective security of the international community. At the opposite extreme, if foreign powers dislike the political orientation of the de facto government and respond with sanctions or shunning (as often observed in postrevolutionary settings), the stability threshold s, then, may be close to n. A high stability threshold is justifiable when a regime faces strong international pressure and the out-of-coalition alternatives are seen as viable alternatives by the international community.

Analyzing the consolidation game with different stability thresholds is meant to capture differences between post–civil war regimes capable of attracting foreign patrons easily and post–civil war governments that are under constant pressure from outside forces. How does the game play out differently? When s is very high, most of the warlords in a country are necessary to provide order. This increases the "lottery odds" for a single warlord, making him more likely to be in a position to extort the president and get away with it. When s is very low, a small coalition of warlords is sufficient to keep the president in power. Equilibrium predictions are equivocal. If s is low, it is relatively easy to form a government but relatively difficult for the president to credibly commit to distribute wealth widely. This is a situation that has lower "lottery odds" from the perspective of any single warlord, as the president can easily play one out-of-coalition warlord against another and drive expected rents toward zero. By contrast, divide-and-rule is more difficult if s is high, but it is also more difficult to install a president in the first place.

When the stability threshold is extremely high, a *partial incorporation* equilibrium closely resembles a *full incorporation* equilibrium. Nearly all the warlords have to be bought off to achieve a minimum of stability. When the stability threshold is very low, a *partial incorporation* equilibrium has a very different feel – more of a high-stakes standoff between factions. *Full incorporation*, if it emerges at all, does so only when warlords' reservation value r drops precipitously toward zero. Chapter 5 frames Tajikistan and Georgia as exemplar cases of "low stability threshold" and "high stability threshold" consolidation projects.

OBSERVABLE IMPLICATIONS

This chapter was motivated by the question: If warlords were the ones best positioned to profit from the breakdown of social order, and they knew that

I.e., U.S / western Taxpayer = sucker, patsy, chump, milk-cow

they were eventually going to be divided against each other by the president, why would they ever install a president in the first place? The answer is that they anticipate the total amount of wealth in the country to extort (v) will increase once the floodgates of foreign aid (v^*) are opened. The decision to install a puppet president is akin to buying a lottery ticket on inclusion in a winning coalition. Winners get to extort the president for offices, privatization rights, and de facto monopolies. How many opt in to "play the lottery" depends on their outside options, the stability threshold (higher implies better lottery odds), their odds of successful coup once president is installed (more go in if odds are better), and the value of increased revenues from international support (higher is obviously better). Equilibrium selection is fundamentally a matter of local politics, and very difficult to predict in advance. What coalitions emerge is a result of politics, persuasion, personalities, and path-of-play as much as parameters. Informal patronage structures are assumed to run parallel to formal institutions. Warlords opt to civilianize themselves and loot the state from within because they can predict a vast quantity of potential wealth available to the "shadow state" coalition.

Social order after civil war emerges out of collusion by predatory violence entrepreneurs in this account. Instead of treating the armed strength of a rebel challenger as an exogenous model parameter, or giving causal weight to the policies of the third-party intervener, this approach seeks to explain variation in the relative size and strength of the incumbent and insurgent coalitions. The comparative statics of the model are straightforward and intuitive. Conditional on having achieved a *partial incorporation* equilibrium, the likelihood of a *full incorporation* equilibrium should increase with v^*. A higher ratio of v^* to v means more WESTERN wealth for the warlords to steal. The reservation value for staying outside the consolidation process r is also a critical parameter, as discussed earlier. For easy exposition, in Figure 2.2, I assume the most difficult case for consolidation: one in which r never declines. Regardless of how many warlords install a president, in both worlds I hold r identical to the "war economy" payoff, $\frac{v}{n} - c$. This means that by choosing to "Fight" in the first stage, a warlord i can guarantee himself a "war economy" flow payoff. In this simplified setting only positive inducements – higher v^* – can induce a change in strategy. More generally, in this stylization higher costs of war and violence c translate directly into low reservation wage "war economy" payoffs, making it easier for the president to convince recalcitrant warlords to join the state. One might think about of v^* as carrots and c as sticks.

It is clear in the top graph in Figure 2.2, which shows the payoffs in a *partial incorporation* equilibrium, that the payoffs to warlords who remain outside the state are identical to those inside the state. Because warlords are symmetric in power by assumption and indifferent between strategies in equilibrium, the model suggests that it is very difficult for anyone – foreign analysts or the warlords themselves – to predict which warlords will accept the figurehead president and which ones will continue to oppose the state's

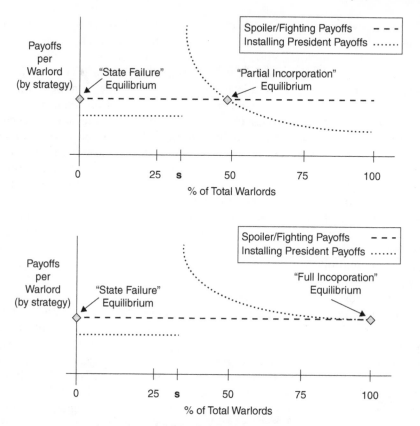

FIGURE 2.2. Comparative Statics: Outsiders assist consolidation by increasing v^*.

consolidation project. Because the president can tailor v^* rewards to field commanders individually, the model implies that in a *partial incorporation* equilibrium no measurable characteristics of a warlord should predict loyalty or defection because they would already be priced into the payoff offer that the president used to buy their loyalty. Homogeneous warlords may, in equilibrium, rationally adopt heterogeneous strategies.

The notion that *partial incorporation* equilibrium can be sustained even with completely identical warlords is a subtle but important departure in this book's treatment of the post-Soviet wars from many other accounts. That certain armed actors attempt to stay out of the consolidation process, calculating that they can do better at the fringes of state control, *may have nothing to do with linguistic or religious difference, regional economic grievances, or anything else.* Many analysts have succumbed to the temptation to label the politicized cleavages that emerged from the post-Soviet wars as "primordial" or "natural." A perspective based on coalition formation, by contrast, is designed

I.E., & TRUMPS IDEOLOGY? ←

to accommodate side-switching political reversals. When v^* gets very high or the reservation value r drops, the model predicts that cultural distance will be paved over, as warlords opt to quietly join the state. Differences can be deconstructed based on cold calculations of interest. The Muslim territory of Adjara can, at the whim of a few people, rejoin the Georgian polity.[11]

These comparative statics are not unqualified. Strategies are determined jointly, and the model explicitly admits the possibility of a violent *state failure* equilibrium regardless of model parameters. This has troubling policy implications for outsiders attempting to shape incentives in failing states. If armed actors have decided to seize the statehouse or extort the president, eleventh-hour wealth transfers may simply increase the value of the prize being contested. Once Georgian and Tajik criminal actors believed that others planned to break from the social contract and attempt to seize the capital with armed force, no amount of aid was likely to halt the slide toward violent anarchy. Put differently, there are two fully sustainable types of "war equilibria" possible in this model, and only one of them, the *partial incorporation* equilibrium, is even in principle susceptible to manipulation by outsiders.

Returning to Figure 1.1 in Chapter 1: the assumption of symmetric warlords anchors this book in the lower half of the table, where foreigners are assumed to be blind to local nuance. Against the anarchic backdrop of state failure, I assume it is too costly for foreigners to shape coalition politics in real time.[12] All of this suggests a relatively blunt set of financial, diplomatic, and military tools.[13] These tools, and their inherent limitations, are clearly familiar to contemporary American practitioners of counterinsurgency, and they were equally well understood by Russian military professionals in the early 1990s. Subsequent chapters will tackle the politics of equilibrium selection, and the movement from one type of equilibrium to another ("state failure," "partial incorporation" or "full incorporation") over time. But the account will emphasize that Russians attempted to shape the contours of war termination indirectly – primarily by inducing warlords to cast their lot with the government (in Tajikistan) or stay outside the consolidating state (in Georgia).

Russia's role in both Georgia and Tajikistan continues to be disputed by local civil war participants and will be the source of debate by future generations of Georgian and Tajik historians. To the extent that there was variation between Russia's policy toward Georgia and its policy toward Tajikistan (as most observers would agree that there was), the model cannot explain it – only assume it. The model cannot account for adaptive changes to postwar social structures in response to foreign aid programs, as v^* is assumed to be divided up in the form of graft. The model cannot explain why some separatists succeeded

11 Marten (2012), 80–84.
12 See, for instance, Filkins and Gall (2010).
13 See Fearon and Laitin (2004), 33, FN 70.

in making good on their demands and others did not.[14] Nor can it explain why violence escalated to war in some parts of the Soviet periphery and not others. ✗ — What exactly does the model do? The model frames the politics of regime consolidation as being primarily about the strategic relationships between warlords as they second guessed each other's strategies. If the president is a placeholder for a warlord coalition, the easy distinction between "formal" (desirable) and "informal" (corrupt) institutions is destroyed. Presidents are installed, or not, because of joint warlord strategies. Once installed, presidential reneging is not constrained by the rule of law, but by the demonstrated ability of warlords to cooperate and collude together – to threaten a coordinated coup if the president breaks his promises, or to demand that some warlords be included in (or excluded from) the inner circle, W^L. Inherited beliefs and social structures constrained the path of play.[15] The model also sheds light on the question of why the period just before and after presidents were installed was so violent. The presidents had not yet selected W^L, and warlords in W^P were jockeying for position in a high-stakes lottery, with a share of v^* as the prize. The model does not attempt to explain the expansion and contraction of militia memberships – it explicitly treats warlords, and the militias they command, as fully interchangeable, identical, and unitary. Viewed from the streets, of course, warlords are not at all interchangeable. Popular and capable warlords could recruit larger armies and demand to be "bought out" by the state. Wartime coalition politics were tremendously uncertain and contingent, and there was great uncertainty about who the warlords were and which ones were strongest. Many foot soldiers came to imagine that their individual contributions of labor to a militia could change the course of the consolidation process. All of this is detailed in Chapter 4.

The model also emphasizes that the president is in an agency relationship with warlords, whose threat of a coup hangs over distributional politics. Incrementally stripping bargaining power away from the men with guns is a local process, with the threat of anarchic violence ever present. The model describes an oligopoly of violence emerging based on structures of personalist rule. These structures are described in Chapter 5.

---

[14] In the language of the model, some warlords have higher reservation wages than others because of historical inheritance, or unusually good luck at attracting foreign assistance. Appendix B has an extension showing that heterogeneity in r can yield unique equilibrium predictions.

[15] Analysis of beliefs generally pushes the scientist toward ephemeral matters: trust, shared values, focal points for identifying when to coordinate for a coup, and other gritty particulars of human political action. These kinds of politics are virtually impossible to analyze in the absence of formal institutions, however, because doing so requires assumptions about what other warlords would do off-the-equilibrium-path. Data on counterfactuals are rarely reliable. Subgame perfection cuts through this knotty problem by assuming that all of the warlords hold the correct beliefs, informed by history and culture, and are at least in part endogenous to the path of play, as described in Ferejohn (1991), 285. See also Bates et al. (2000), 699–700 for a useful discussion of the disadvantages of incorporating models of incomplete information into analytic narratives, and Thelen (1999), generally.

Finally, this account gives tremendous agency to warlords, as the political actors capable of overturning local order. Who were these warlords? How did they come to seize the reins of politics in post-independence Georgia and Tajikistan? Why did violence escalate so quickly? Before we can exit from anarchy, we must first enter it. The narrative journey from independence to state failure begins in the next chapter.

3

Kto Kogo?

The collapse of the USSR was unexpected and unexpectedly peaceful.[1] The ideological superstructure disintegrated, the leviathan ceased to exist, yet across Eastern Europe, Russia, and Central Asia, violence rarely escalated. A few social actors seized security structures and dragged their states into chaos, but this sort of thing was not even attempted in the Baltic states or in most of the new states of Central Asia.[2] In the Kyrgyz city of Osh, in the ethnically mixed Ferghana Valley, there were violent pogroms in 1990 – followed by a court-led investigation by the new Kyrgyz government in 1991, where forty-six of the forty-eight participants in the pogroms charged were found guilty.[3] Georgi Derluguian (2005) recounts the story of the tiny Caucasian republic of Kabardino-Balkaria, where escalation tactics by rowdy warlords were cauterized by local innovation.[4] Are there patterned regularities to the

---

[1] For seminal contributions to social scientists' understanding of the Soviet collapse, see Roeder (1993), Solnick (1998), Bunce (1999), Treisman (1999), McFaul (2001), Beissinger (2002), Brown (2007), Roeder (2007), and Kotkin (2008). For students seeking a shorter summary, see North (2006), 146–154.

[2] Bunce (1999) makes a convincing case that the variation in post-communist violence can be predicted by institutional characteristics, particularly by the composition of the armed forces (102–126).

[3] This event is documented extensively in Tishkov (1995).

[4] Derluguian's tells the tale of the dog that did not bark like this: Kabardino-Balkaria had emerged from an impenetrable mountain backwater to a relatively wealthy ski resort town during the 1980s. The Balkars, 10 percent of the new republic's population, found themselves underrepresented when inaugural elections removed Soviet ethnic quotas. Deadly ethnic war was looming. A local hero, fellow sociologist Yuri Shanibov, stepped in. Transforming himself into the pious Muslim "Musa Shanib," and, backed by a rowdy crew ("athletes – wrestlers, boxers, martial artists – veterans of the Afghan war and simple hooligans [ready] for the fight" 266), he brokered an elite compromise that satisfied the Balkars and staved off a repeat of Chechnya. Or so the story goes. The rarity of English-language accounts like Derluguian's, however, draws attention to an observational bias at work on studies of violence and order:

divergent outcomes – violent or nonviolent, democratic or nondemocratic – in the post-Soviet space? David Laitin (2006), in a playful summary of Derluguian's class-based analysis, speculates the following answer to this important question:

First, there is the *nomenklatura*, the high officials of the Soviet state. … Provincial Soviet life involved families buying state or party appointments, in order to then distribute bribe-friendly posts to relatives. All this was quite comfortable for the *nomenklatura* until the state began to unravel. They then had to make a historic choice: they could steal what they could of state assets and run; they could seek support from the newly reconstituted centre in Moscow to help them regain power; or they could transmogrify into nationalist elites and seek to lead independent states. … Second, there are the national intellectuals, a sub-class of the industrial proletariat. … Universities, Palaces of Culture and local soviets assured positions for this new class of national intellectuals. As Lenin hoped they would, these regional official intelligentsias defused nationalist mobilizations; but since the holders of the positions had no prospects for mobility outside their titular republics – 'their credentials did not travel beyond the republic's borders' – a core of bored intellectuals developed in each republic with close ties both to one another, and to national intellectuals from other republics. … Third, there are the 'sub-proletarians' … [a] 'residual' class [that] includes those who remained outside the state hierarchy, surviving on subsistence agriculture and migration to perform seasonal work, or carry out petty trade. … [T]heir alliances and relationships [determined] … likely outcomes: formal democracy, restored autocracy or chaos. The route to chaos in the Caucasus tended to begin with the retreat of the *nomenklatura*, now facing those they had oppressed and without a Soviet big brother to protect them. They either escaped with the money acquired through the sale of state assets or remained at home and re-identified themselves as national intellectuals. An alliance between national intellectuals and sub-proletarians tended to follow. This alliance, in large part because the national intellectuals could not rein in the rowdy *habitus* of the sub-proletarians, drove all the regions of the Caucasus where it occurred into near chaos, and several over the brink. … The chaos in the Caucasus was but one of three patterns that emerged from the relationship between *nomenklatura*, national intellectuals and sub-proletarians. In the post-Soviet republics as a whole, the most prevalent pattern was the reclamation of power by a powerful rump of the *nomenklatura*, this time capable of controlling the sub-proletarians, with the relatively weak national intellectuals brought into the ruling coalition. These allies feared the rise of sub-proletarians as *mujahedin*, and in the name of secularism and modernity re-imposed authoritarian rule. The Central Asian republics are the key instances of this pattern. In the third pattern, of which the Baltic States are the prime examples, the sub-proletarians were weak. An alliance of the national intellectuals, whose considerable social power derived from their elite positions in pre-revolutionary civil society, and a reformed *nomenklatura*, which re-identified with the national intellectuals – and responded to the lure of membership in the EU – paved the way for a peaceful transition to representative democracy.[5]

> Our community devotes orders of magnitude more energy to writing books about a very rare outcome, the breakdown of order (in, for instance, Chechnya) than we do to writing books about the modal outcome, which is the maintenance of order (in, for instance, Adygeya).

5 Laitin (2006).

Across post-Communist Eurasia, the slide toward violent state breakdown – where it occurred – began when important social actors lost faith in the ability of the new regimes to secure their interests. This loss of faith was not inevitable, even when the weighty structural trends identified by Laitin are taken into account. Though the shock to state capacity that accompanies decolonization often leads to civil war, peaceful decolonization is the modal outcome. Though war occurred in a third of the newly independent states that emerged from the breakup of the Soviet state, in two thirds of the new states violence did not escalate beyond street demonstrations. Roeder (2007) emphasizes that the Soviet legacy bequeathed its federal units (its Soviet Socialist Republics [SSRs]) all of the raw materials for the provision of order: a strong Party system for the distribution of spoils, police and transportation infrastructure, material for a national army, and the institutions necessary to maintain self-renewing self-referential nationalist histories. McFaul (2002) shows that the broad trend across post-Soviet Eurasia was pacts between ex-Communist Party elites to effectively restrict access to the political space and freeze politics in an authoritarian mode. Many of these arrangements can, at some risk of controversy, be said to persist to this day.

What unfolded in Georgia and Tajikistan to make them exceptions to this rule? In these states, elites could not quickly cauterize violence, and the descent into anarchy was horrifyingly rapid. This chapter makes the case that war, as it emerged in Georgia and Tajikistan, can be best understood in the context of a more general scramble for post-Soviet spoils. Though these civil wars are typically discussed in the context of "ethnic conflict," or the preferences of leaders in Moscow, this chapter suggests that the core political failure in both cases was a violent breakdown of *intra*-ethnic bargaining within the post-independence national elite, after certain members of the elite succumbed to the temptation of allying with warlords.

POST-SOVIET PREDATORS: WHO WERE THE WARLORDS?

The breakdown of the Soviet state involved a large-scale defection of the Soviet bureaucracy. The result was a gradual collapse, and in some cases a complete collapse, of the public's faith in the state to provide that most basic public good: security. Three classes of actors began second-guessing each other's strategies.

The first were national elites. There was an obvious symbiosis between the interests of the *nomenklatura* and the various criminal networks that could access state transit networks to move resources within the Soviet Union. Rehabilitating these transit networks, and securing new wealth attained in the post-Soviet fire sale, required forging local alliances with individuals capable of guaranteeing property rights against a backdrop of anarchy.

The *nomenklatura* began crafting a complex set of bargains with a second set of actors, which I have already defined as warlords. These men proved capable of recruiting private armies and "running the streets" when suddenly there was no one to make arrests. Many of these warlords affiliated with new radical parties.

A third set of strategic actors were the street recruits who served at the behest of the warlords. For a number of years, the primary social actors in Georgia and Tajikistan were well-armed militias – with rotating leaderships and flexible memberships – recruited and loosely organized by family, clan, and kinship (*avlod*, in Tajik) ties. Foot soldiers were recruited primarily, but, as we shall see, not exclusively, from the criminal or rural underclass.

As the political order began to fray, many elites in the national republics realized that the end of communism and the transition to independence would bring economic contraction. In the short and medium term, there would be a smaller "pie" to divide, as they anticipated the dual loss of fiscal transfers from Moscow and various efficiencies associated with membership in the Soviet Union. The struggle for control over resources began in the late Soviet period and quickly extended to every facet of social organization. Whether elites were squabbling about how to divide up property rights over natural resources, ownership of factories servicing obsolete industrial production quotas, or even battles over protected institutional niches (e.g., museums, university structures, churches and mosques, sports complexes), similar battles unfolded. Everyone understood that there would be no social safety net to manage the resulting dislocations.[6]

Solnick (1998) chronicles this process analytically, creatively deploying the principal–agent framework. Well-connected party bureaucrats ("agents") strategically timed their "defection" (liquidating state assets, putting the profits into offshore accounts, and moving their families to secure enclaves) against a "principal" (the "Soviet State" or the "median Soviet voter" – both of which were increasingly imaginary). Because this self-serving behavior was possible only if the probability of monitoring and subsequent punishment was small, the dynamics of the resulting state failure took on characteristics of a bank run: once it became obvious that some people were defecting, everyone else wanted to defect as well. Those in power "rushed to claim ... assets before the bureaucratic doors shut for good."[7] Watchful eyes in Moscow could not fix their gaze everywhere at once, and first-movers in peripheral bureaucracies were able to use official letterheads and unofficial influence networks to legalize practices that had been tacitly accepted for decades. Mid-level bureaucrats were well positioned to simply take things they wanted – dachas, town cars, downtown apartment buildings, factories, mineral deposits, commodities futures, and, ultimately, even phones and carpets from the buildings in which they worked.

[6] Olcott (1994), 45.
[7] Solnick (1998), 6–7, 251.

Many accounts of the early 1990s tend to emphasize the continuity of political cadres from the late Soviet period in the Caucasus and Central Asia.[8] Overemphasizing continuity at the top of the power pyramid led many analysts to ignore a parallel trend: traditional elites were inviting new actors into the political arena to secure their holdings. It was a time of unprecedented social opportunity for men who could organize guns. This environment, where money had recently become worthless, rewarded individuals with a talent for activating latent social capital and articulating a political program that could justify using violence against unarmed civilians. As a result, during this period, any journalist or social scientist who went to these collapsing states looking for evidence of "ethnic hatred" or "ingrained patterns of resentment" was sure to find exactly what he or she was looking for. As a general rule, these men who would be warlords had no trouble at all justifying their actions and explaining to anyone who would listen why stakes were indivisible.

The emergent class of power brokers – the warlords – were men who could command respect among a social milieu composed of alcoholics, criminals, day laborers, hooligans, and the serially unemployed. The slow disintegration of order in the late Soviet period provided these sub-proletarians a unique window of opportunity to convert their violent social capital into a better future.[9] Many had settled into pedestrian lives at the time when social order began to collapse. The men who would emerge to lead them were not always from the same social class. The Soviet implosion was a rare second chance for a certain type of person to remake his life. Local drug dealers began to imagine themselves running countrywide smuggling operations. Rural bazaar protection racketeers began to imagine themselves managing urban hotel chains. Dzhaba Ioseliani, the eventual leader of the Mkhedrioni in Georgia, had been a playwright and artist in the USSR. In communist times, "General" Dumbadze worked in a sewing factory, and "Chief" Kobalia managed supplies and inventory at a bakery.[10] Prominent field commanders in Tajikistan included a former construction engineer, a cement factory floor manager, a cotton gin operator, a number of schoolteachers, a visa expediter, a popular singer, a bartender, and a bus driver. The security services, police, and military produced their share of charismatic leaders, and had a comparative advantage in acquiring weapons and recruiting shooters. All of these men had come of age in a system in which familial and kin networks were necessary for everyday life, and they recruited their friends and allies with the understanding that getting a foothold within the new state bureaucracy represented their best chance to increase their life opportunities. The most powerful Tajik and Georgian paramilitary

8 For generalizations based on elite continuity and institutional continuity, see Suny (1995); Jones-Luong (2002); Collins (2006); and McFaul (2002).
9 I gratefully borrow the phrase "sub-proletarian" from Georgi Derluguian, who borrowed it from Pierre Bourdieu's observations of social structures in Algeria.
10 Darchiashvili (1997a).

commanders – Tengiz Kitovani and Sangak Safarov – had both served time in the Soviet prison system.

Not everyone was equally talented at this sort of social organization. It required not only day-to-day charisma and a gift for improvisational management, but also the rarer ability (much prized in CEOs) to project and impose a strategic vision. It also rewarded natural talent for oratory – or at least for a particular kind of calibrated hate speech. Amidst the collapse of Soviet social order, many learned for the first time that they had a gift for "power language" and guiding the mob, and could deploy symbols and phrases to generate authority out of thin air.[11] With a certain natural leadership, aided by a few resources such as weapons, ammunition, and some guarantee of immunity from prosecution, certain men found themselves transforming their prison gangs, martial arts dojos, or even (in the case of Dzhaba Ioseliani) their theater clubs into potent political and economic actors. One could rise from obscurity to local celebrity by demonstrating a willingness to make good on violent threats.

Many warlords reappropriated religious symbols and iconography. It is not fully inaccurate to say that the Mkhedrioni ("The Knights of Georgia") were a paramilitary wing of the Georgian Orthodox Church. Many recruiters and enforcers displayed ornate crosses. Many opposition leaders in Tajikistan were holy men, and in the euphoric aftermath of the USSR some of them competed with each other to articulate the most extreme possible positions. It is easy to exaggerate the importance of religious ideological content by simply taking these extremists at their word. But as the quotes in this chapter make clear, most of these ecclesiastical arguments were weaponized primarily in interaction with locally relevant gendered claims. The ancient, emotionally salient claim that the war's winners would lay claim to the bodies of the losers' females was made early and often. MAN'S BASIC NATURE DOES NOT CHANGE, BIOLOGY IS

There were three analytically distinguishable pathways to wealth for these warlords. The first was to encourage their followers to go out, take things, hurt people, and then to sell protection against the anarchy that they could unleash. HARD WIRED

The second, requiring more subtlety, was to serve as a broker, contract enforcer, and "silent partner" for political or economic elites. At least for a time, neither the Soviet state nor the post-independence governments could serve these functions. Some warlords took advantage of new economic opportunities and became businessmen themselves. Once an import–export bottleneck was controlled by the warlord, there was a temptation to cut politically connected civilians out of the loop.

11 A classic observational study of crowd dynamics used the following phrasing: "When studying the imagination of crowds we saw that it is particularly open to the impressions produced by images. These images do not always lie ready to hand, but it is possible to evoke them by the judicious employment of words and formulas. ... Reason and arguments are incapable of combatting certain words and formulas." LeBon (1895), 96–97.

The third was aggrandized extortion, such as threatening the president with a coup and the entire state with a return to general civil war. As the following chapters show, in the 1990s, Georgian and Tajik warlords realized they had the ability to replace presidents, trigger investor pullouts, and drag their countries into anarchy. This extortion dynamic is easy to miss in two-player bargaining models, or in approaches that define "warlords" as criminal actors distinct from the state.[12] Warlords had only to make these threats credible to be bought off – not to actually make good on them.

The kinds of informal arrangements that emerged in parallel to state institutions are well understood. The most important relationship for any would-be criminal businessman was with "a roof" – a patron with ties to the shadowy political superstructure, capable of structuring the formal "rules of the game" to the advantage of insiders. This arrangement is described by North, Wallis, and Weingast (2009) as "The Natural State" or a "Closed Access Society":

The natural state reduces the problem of endemic violence through the formation of a dominant coalition whose members possess special privileges. The logic of the natural state follows from how it solves the problem of violence. Elites – members of the dominant coalition – agree to respect each other's privileges, including property rights and access to resources and activities. By limiting access to these privileges to members of the dominant coalition, elites create credible incentives to cooperate rather than fight among themselves. Because elites know that violence will reduce their own rents, they have incentives not to fight.[13]

Warlords were ideally suited to serve as pivot players in this relationship.[14] Some members of the emerging political class began to use militias as a source of political insurance against being cut out of the spoils of privatization. For warlords, these arrangements offered a rare opportunity to improve their lives. Their challenge was to convert their ability to organize armed social capital into wealth, power, and possibly even job security and respect over the long term. What followed was essentially the high-stakes coalition formation process modeled in the previous chapter: Winners would receive a position in

---

[12] Kimberly Marten (2012) defines warlords as always and already distinct from the state in her theoretical framework: "[T]he principal actor (the state) relies on an agent (the warlord) to fulfill assigned tasks. ... A warlord bargain is logically akin to the problem faced by states that employ private security contractors as a cost-saving measure, and risk having their overall strategic plans undermined by undisciplined tactical behavior that they cannot control." 30.

[13] North, Wallis, and Weingast (2009), 18.

[14] For extensive details of the kinds of bargains that emerged in Georgia and Tajikistan, see Aves (1996), Jones (1997), Akhmedov (1998), Nourzhanov (2005), Pirseyedi (2000), ICG (2004), de Waal (2005), Rubin (1998), Torjensen (2005), and Slade (2007). In Georgia the most profitable smuggling industries were either drugs, black market currencies, or citrus fruits from Abkhazia, which could be resold on the Siberian black markets at a huge markup. Cotton mono-cropping dominates the Tajik economy, as documented in Van Atta (2008).

a government security ministry, gain control over a populated fiefdom (often a privileged position in a wealthy *kolkhoz*, or de facto mayoral rights over a small town or city), receive monopoly taxation rights for a bazaar or a lucrative gray-market bottleneck, or obtain the ability to dictate property rights over cash crops and mineral deposits. Losers faced exile or worse.

Violent social mobilization was an outgrowth of predatory politics that were ubiquitous during the breakup of the Soviet Union. The details of how these processes spiraled out of control to total state failure require more local flavor, which will be added presently. For a time, predatory criminal militias were in the best position to take advantage of this uncertainty. Subsequent chapters of this book will provide evidence that the nationalist warlords understood that they were temporarily vital but functionally interchangeable with each other as local order-providers, and thus ultimately disposable when the political winds changed. But certain lucky warlords managed to play the violent high-stakes consolidation game successfully, emerging from the lottery as very rich men.

WHY DID THE FOLLOWERS FOLLOW?

What leads someone to join a violent militia? There are three broad answers to this question. The first suggests that "the costs of collective action" are simply exaggerated. To the extent that post-Soviet militia formations conflated the rhetorical power of nationalist politics with the intoxicating allure of criminal fraternities, members may have simply calculated that they could have a pretty good time as violent extortionists when there was suddenly no one to arrest them.[15] For certain young men ritualized kinds of violence are a great deal of fun.[16] So long as this violence was committed by agents of local majorities against unprotected minority targets, these actions did not come with a risk of retaliation or escalation.[17] At the extremes of this line of argument one can notice that the breakdown of social order allowed certain sociopaths to do what they wanted to do anyway: rape and kill their neighbors and afterwards seize their neighbors' apartments. Certain men found that they

[15] See Keen (1998), Kaldor (1999), King (2001*a*), and Zuercher (2005). A hauntingly memorable expression of this argument as applied to Bosnia's war can be found in Sacco (2003).

[16] See Buford (1993), Mueller (2000), and especially Petersen (2002). Various musings on human nature consistent with this insight are scattered throughout Keegan (1994).

[17] When mobilization was not perceived as being risky, violence against helpless minorities was sometimes just a pick-up game; (see Mueller (2000), Fearon and Laitin (2000), and King (2004*a*) on this point). But there is increasing consensus that practically nothing that happens in a civil war zone can be described adequately without some account of how armed groups organize themselves, and how they relate to the civilians who give them moral and economic encouragement. Prominent scholarly contributions have documented how social belief structures sustain militia solidarity in the face of disciplined state resistance (e.g., Petersen [2001], Wood [2003]); emphasized social stigma against violating taboos (e.g., Brass [1997], Ellis [1999]); or shown how the structural constraints that shaped militia recruitment shaped subsequent tactics and strategy (e.g., Fairbanks [2002], Weinstein [2006]).

enjoyed the psychotic rush of breaking taboos against violence and the power
that came from the reversal of long-held status hierarchies. As one of my Tajik
respondents admitted:

"If they hit one us they knew the rest of us ... we would send more people after them,
after their women, their children. And they knew that we would remember. We would
keep coming and coming and never stop, never! Not until they are dead or they run –
run to Moscow or Tashkent, to drive a cab and live like a slave with no visa. If they
wanted to live here [in Dushanbe], they knew they would need to deal with us. ... If you
have a gun, and I just have this [bottle], but I'm willing to use it on you, and you're
afraid, I will win. That's what war is!"[18]

Sociologists specializing in gang behavior tend to take umbrage at this
caricature of the criminal mind. Most police officers and military professionals
would take umbrage as well. Not every soldier, gang member, or criminal
who commits violence suffers from psychopathology. Many participants in
the post-Soviet wars were clear-headed and relatively well-educated products
of the Soviet lower middle class. This suggests a second set of answers, one
emphasizing the sociology of institutions. The psychological, moral, and social
character of militia solidarity groups anchors identities for disaffected young
men while inculcating members in a culture of violence.[19] Militia organizers in
weak states free ride on masculine norms of honor, potent religious and national
scripts, and other engines of social solidarity.

Students of economics and management science can be counted on to
invoke a third class of answers: Militia recruits clearly responded to material
incentives. From the perspective of a rural Georgian or Tajik, or a high school
dropout in the capital city, part of the appeal of participation in these popular
movements was that they lowered the barriers for entry into a respectable
life. They knew that, if lucky, in return for their sacrifices they would be
allowed to don uniforms and join the ranks of the state security services. Social
rewards would be passed on to families of the winners at the expense of the
losers. Treating militia formations as organizational structures allows them to
be modeled as if they were aberrant firms: consuming resources, organizing
labor, and ultimately producing violence.[20]

None of these three approaches is obviously wrong. Coding each of my
173 interviews by rhetorical content reveals systematic patterns in respondents'

---

[18] Interview conducted May 21, 2006 in Dushanbe.
[19] Useful contributions informed by this tradition include Albini, Rogers, and Shabalin (1997);
      Goldstone (1994); Blasi, Kroumova, and Kruse (1997); Darchiashvili (1997b); Tishkov (1997);
      Derluguian (2005); Whitlock (2005).
[20] Useful contributions informed by this tradition include Popkin (1979); Mason and Krane
      (1989); Gambetta (1996); Dixit (2004), and more recently, Weinstein (2006), Berman (2009),
      and Shapiro (2013). Post-Soviet case data consistent with this school of thought can be found
      in Volkov (1999, 2002) and Varese (2001).

TABLE 3.1. *Cheap Talk: Some of the Same Scripts Were Well Rehearsed*

Variables	All (%)	Georgia (%)	Tajikistan (%)
Agreed that "You Can Only Trust Your Family"	82	81	83
Stayed Because Life Was Better Inside Group	94	94	94
Militia Sometimes Engaged in Theft or Rackteering	90	84	96
Stayed Because Friends Were in the Militia Too	74	78	70
Joined to "Help Win the Civil War"	76	68	84
Most Militia Members Talked about Politics	36	30	42
Joined to Protect Their Families	83	83	84
Joined to Influence Politics in the Capital City	83	90	77
Stayed for Promise of a Job	71	68	73
Observations	173	84	89

accounts of the sustaining mechanisms for militia membership.[21] Note in Table 3.1 that certain reasons for joining a militia were common. Local concerns dominated recruitment narratives. The awareness that these militias were players in a larger game for political dominance in the capital cities of the newly independent states penetrated deep into the ranks of the militias. Most joined with friends.[22] Most could articulate the cause for which they fought. Most were emphatic that they joined to protect their families, but this was easily reconciled psychologically with heading to the capital city when the time came as it was obviously where the high-stakes political questions would be resolved and where the crowds would demonstrate. Groups were organized with an eye toward potential personal gains from war: securing their family property first,

---

[21] I borrow the distinction between "triggering mechanisms" and "sustaining mechanisms" from Petersen (2001), 13. The influence of Elster (1989) on Petersen's argument is clearest on pages 82–88 and 113–123.

[22] Militia members in both states often used the plural ("we") when discussing decisions to join a militia, switch commanders, or return home during the violent purges of the "Time of Troubles". When militia members had to lobby together to demand payment from a political or warlord patron, these ties proved quite important. I speculate that the psychological mechanisms that kept soldiers working together through difficult times – honor and shame – were channeled primarily through these initial solidarity networks, as these men knew they would eventually return to the same families, village, and neighborhood networks where there were few secrets and no privacy. It is also notable that dense social networks connecting militia members to each other did not always stretch upward to the commander, though this was more likely to have been the case in Tajikistan. Slightly more than half of the Tajik respondents reported having a family member in the same militia, as opposed to only seven Georgians. This sheds light on the higher likelihood of Georgian militia members to switch commanders during the course of the fighting than their Tajik counterparts, constrained by *avlod* obligation ties.

but also taking things from their neighbors and anointing new political patrons who would turn a blind eye to their theft.

Most militias were not sites for ideological indoctrination. Only 40 percent of Tajik respondents and 30 percent of Georgian respondents characterized their armed groups as being social environments where they remember most people being motivated by politics. Banditry, roadblocks, racketeering, and other predatory behaviors were commonly reported in both states. Many of the men who were best positioned to take advantage of the breakdown of the economic, political, and social order were those with little to lose: criminals, manual laborers, sub-proletarian petty entrepreneurs, and the serially unemployed. Others were simply young enough to have no real responsibilities. Excitement, social recognition, and the opportunity to shoot guns with friends were all mentioned as motivations in the early phases of independence.

Social mobilization was dangerous in the late Soviet period because it meant challenging ruthless and well-tested Soviet security structures, but these structures vanished in 1991. Most participants invoked "arming for community defense" dynamics, suggesting instability was stoked by the kinds of local security dilemmas envisioned by Posen (1993).[23] After the easy answer was coded, however, follow-up questions often revealed exactly what Kalyvas (2006) would have predicted: A complex local milieu of local jealousies, very old family and neighborhood feuds, and no shortage of class- and clan-based resentment. Many recruits were being mobilized to go take things ("take things back") from rival groups. Many reported encouragement by girlfriends or female family members in doing this. Because recruits expected to keep what they looted, up to and including homes and property, many began to think of themselves as soldiers of fortune, serving as armed representatives of family interests.[24] There was consistent agreement that the family was the relevant unit of practical politics, and the "selective incentives" offered were often framed as side payments to mothers, mothers-in-law, or extended family.

But when pressed, more than two thirds of interview respondents admitted that they stuck around because they wanted a job. A general focus on social solidarity and criminal entrepreneurship in militia groups should not obscure

---

[23] Posen (1993) argues that the offense–defense indistinguishability problem in irregular war can be a self-fueling engine of conflict. Self-defense militias can easily go on the offense, and it is impossible to misunderstand or ignore this fact. He also suggests an incentive to strike first in this setting, as whoever holds the territory being fought over at the time the international observers arrive to begin peacekeeping and mediation efforts tends to hold it indefinitely. See Petersen (2011) for an extensive treatment on the implications of this second hypothesis.

[24] For consistent interpretations, see Rubin (1993), Goldenberg (1994), Fairbanks (1995), Aves (1996), Bornet (1998), Brenninkmeijer (1998), Zviagelskaya (1998), Anchabadze (1999), Fairbanks (2002), Darchiashvili (2005), de Waal (2005), Torjensen (2005), and Zuercher (2005).

the main currency that was used to recruit militia members during this period: an emerging "futures market" in political favoritism, contracted by warlords at the time of recruitment. In the post-Soviet wars, the decision to join a militia amounted to risking one's life in exchange for some short-term mix of security and loot, and the long-term promise of better life opportunities if a recruit aligned himself with a worthy patron. In interview after interview, I learned that militia recruits were often explicitly offered the opportunity to rise along with their field commanders, who (by this point) had convinced their men that they were going to be architects in the new national future. In practical terms, this meant the potential for the marginally employed leftovers of the Soviet system to reimagine themselves in jobs with pensions, and even some possibility of social respect and family prestige.

A problem with this recruitment technique was that it was all based on what economists call "cheap talk." No one knew which warlords would emerge as real political players over the long haul. National currencies had not been established and the ruble was in a free-fall, making spot payments for labor impossible. When militia members began to use violence to kill and maim each other, joining up was tantamount to placing a bet on their patron emerging in the faction that controlled ministries within the capital city after the sorting was through. In other words, joining was analogous to playing a costly lottery. To make the matter even worse, there was a problem of intertemporal commitment. There was no way to write a contract that would be enforced at a later time. Should a warlord beat the odds and successfully ascend to prominence, he would no longer *need* any individual who had risked his life to contribute to the warlord's rise. He might be tempted to keep the spoils solely for his family network. So although it was true that aligning oneself with the correct militia captain might secure a recruit access to the wealth associated with control of the state in theory, in practice this wealth would be realized only if the warlord who recruited him both emerged as a powerful member of the new governing apparatus *and* was willing to dole out patronage to loyal subordinates when the time came.

How was this constraint overcome? Many respondents emphasized that the transactions in the militia labor market were not about money. They described organizational patterns more often associated with faith-based enterprises or a religious revival. Warlord success in sustaining recruitment was often reducible to the intangibles of charismatic authority: Who had the power to make young men *believe* that their contribution and sacrifice could tip the odds in their militia's favor? Many men described enduring terrible costs because they had strong convictions that their commander's understanding of conflict dynamics warranted sacrifice. One of the hallmarks of a successful paramilitary commander was an ability to predict politics and rationalize wartime events. The key to keeping morale high was constructing reasonably coherent narratives about why they would win – or why they could not lose. Certain symbolic events (e.g., displays of Russian air power, elections, foiled

TABLE 3.2. *Beyond Cheap Talk: Evidence of Complex Recruit Motivations*

Variables	All (%)	Georgia (%)	Tajikistan (%)
Joined a Militia in an Urban Area	67	92	43
Most Militia Operations "Close to Home"	22	18	27
Had Family Members in the Same Militia	31	9	52
Really Trusted His Commander	47	30	62
Joined or Stayed in a Militia for "Good Times"	29	46	13
Observations	173	84	89

assassination attempts) had dramatic effects on militia memberships, shattering the credibility of certain commanders (whose predictions had been falsified) and increasing the cache of others (whose predictions had been verified).[25]

In anticipation of the case studies that follow, Table 3.2 displays a summary of the differences in recruitment patterns between Tajik and Georgian militias. Most Georgians reported that they joined a militia in an urban setting, recalling their initiation conversations at bars and cafes, at rallies, or in underground political clubs. Most Tajiks in the sample report being recruited in their rural homesteads. This should not be interpreted as evidence that Georgian paramilitaries were a uniquely urban phenomenon. A few of my respondents hailed from rural areas, and I am certain that if I had spent more time in rural areas of Georgia, I could have discovered many more. But they described a pilgrimage of friends borrowing a car and heading to Tbilisi or a nearby town to be "introduced" to a local boss. By contrast, even the modest 43 percent of Tajiks who claim to have been recruited in cities is probably a bit of a misleading figure because rural regional capitals, such as Kurgon-Tubbe and Kulob, would probably not be considered "real cities" by most Georgians in the sample.

Another striking difference, revisited in the text that follows, is that Georgians were far less likely than Tajiks to report really trusting their commander throughout the war. This is likely both a cause and an effect of the common practice of militia members defecting from one militia captain and joining another. This practice, which is discussed at length in Chapter 4, was pervasive in Georgia and comparatively rare in Tajikistan. About 40 percent of the Georgians and 30 percent of the Tajiks who took part in the urban warfare in my sample were "opportunistic joiners," which is to say they were men who

---

[25] A theory based on what recruits *believed* to be true at the time is difficult to test. Convincing recruits to risk their lives in war is difficult, as most of the important benefits of a victory will be realized independent of individual participation and the risk of dying usually outweighs any individual benefit. See Olson (1965), Tullock (1971), Popkin (1979), Lichbach (1995), and Grossman (1999). There was no effort made to systematically interview non-joiners or gather information that could be used to test theories of recruitment in a rigorous fashion.

joined their militia only after the end of major fighting (coded by the scourging of the lowlands in Tajikistan, or the end of the Abkhaz campaign in Georgia). Georgians were more likely to switch factional alliances during this period than Tajiks. Only 13 percent of the members of the Popular Front reported switching commanders, which is approximately the same fraction of Georgians in my sample who did *not* switch factions.

Finally, more than three times as many Georgians as Tajiks admitted that one of their primary motivations for joining or staying with a militia was "fun," "excitement," "a good alternative to boredom," or related concepts. Social mobilization in Georgia escalated over many years, amidst the euphoria of a nationalist movement that saw itself as the harbinger of a brighter future. In Tajikistan, mobilization took place primarily after the unexpected dissolution of the USSR in 1991, and in an environment of fear that descended, rapidly, into terrible violence.

ESCALATION PROCESSES IN TWO POST-SOVIET STATES

At least since the Brezhnev era, in peripheral republics like Georgia and Tajikistan, true power lay in a coalition composed of the Party, which policed entry into the political arena and managed relations with Moscow, and the "shadow economic elite," which provided luxury goods and allowed access to real wealth. There was often a visible class structure in the late Soviet periphery. For example, one set of families would occupy the state house and manage external relations, while another set would run the streets and tax the bazaars.[26] In the final throes of the Soviet experiment, it was extremely demoralizing to be a member of the first group, voicing the slogans of scientific socialism, while watching criminal capitalist entrepreneurs secure offshore holdings. Georgia's preeminent political scientist, Ghia Nodia, summarizes the social understanding of the *nomenklatura* on the eve of independence in the following way:

The delegitimization of the public sphere implies that decent people should avoid politics, or enter them only grudgingly, on the grounds that 'someone has to do the dirty work.' And since entering politics means demeaning yourself, perhaps you should reward yourself by being dishonest for your own personal benefit. The term 'public good' does not exist and is hard to translate.[27]

---

[26] For an primer on social and economic relations in the Soviet periphery see Derluguian (2005), especially chapters 3 and 4. See also Simis (1982), especially 65–95, 126–143, 157–179, and Remnick (1994), 180–215.

[27] Nodia (1996). This resonates with the more general summary of North, Wallis, and Weingast (2009) in their discussion of the "natural state": "Personal relationships, who one is and who one knows, form the basis for social organization and constitute the arena for individual interaction, particularly personal relationships among powerful individuals. Natural states limit the ability of individuals to form organizations. ... Identity ... is inherently political." 18.

Against this backdrop, the rise of politically connected militias in the post-independence capitals of Tbilisi and Dushanbe raised the stakes of politics quickly. When new political parties were flanked by young men with Kalashnikov rifles, it was reasonable for civilians to panic. As these new political parties began to flirt with extreme arguments, such as advocating radical redistribution of wealth and geopolitical realignment, counterrevolutionary militias formed. Although it is beyond the scope of this book to address the question of why the problem of post-independence resource redistribution led to violence in these two states and not others, the scholarly literature suggests three kinds of salient factors.

First, groups that anticipated becoming relative losers in the consolidation process were able to resurrect their chances by enlisting help from beached Russian military units. It is very difficult to account for the mobilization strategy of the Abkhaz secessionists or the Popular Front for Tajikistan (PFT), or either of their rapid escalations to violent tactics, while omitting expected Russian military assistance as a causal variable. Lukewarm support from the Kremlin for the fledgling Nabiev and Gamsakhurdia governments was interpreted in the periphery as a signal that players in Moscow preferred regime change. One of the main determinants of which countries fell victim to serious civil violence was a belief by latent insurgent groups that if they raised the specter of violence and disorder, they could draw Russian military and political aid to their cause, in a humanitarian capacity, adding men and material to aid in their struggle. In Abkhazia, Adjara, South Ossetia, Tajikistan, Transdenestria, and Karabakh, expectations of Russian acquiescence or support were instrumental in crisis decision making.[28]

Second, constructing ethnic and regional difference as a zero-sum game was unusually easy in Georgia and Tajikistan for reasons that are presented at length in the text that follows.[29] The various warring groups could draw on Soviet institutional resources, which were mapped onto ethno-federal hierarchies, to recruit armies quickly and to infuse certain questions of solidarity

---

[28]   For a fuller explication of this argument, see Laitin (2001).
[29]   I tend to be skeptical of these kinds of arguments on their merits. Although it is certainly the case that different ethnic and regional groups in Georgia and Tajikistan saw themselves as distinct, cultural distance is a poor predictor of violent conflict. Cultural frictions over appropriate gender relations, abstract fear of "The Other," and profound aesthetic disagreements are likely inevitable. Laitin (1977), 139–161, presents a set of arguments suggesting that differences in worldviews caused by language differences may be a permanent fixture of the human condition. Nonetheless, as long as representatives of different groups can calculate costs and benefits, there are almost always bargains or arrangements that can resolve these differences nonviolently. Even in the absence of deterrence – such as when the Soviet state apparatus simply disappeared – it is empirically possible for people who do not much care for each other to coexist in amicable silence. Politics between ethnic groups only become zero-sum as a result of political construction. De Figueiredo and Weingast (1999) present a formal model of how violence can construct ethnic identity. For a review of this literature's findings and testable hypotheses, see Fearon and Laitin (2000).

or distributional politics with a "natural" sense of identity.[30] Preexisting autonomous republic boundaries and *kolkhoz*-level hierarchical authority structures were a huge asset in mobilizing the masses. People knew where they fit on the map. Area specialists were not surprised to see Georgia break down along ethnic lines and Tajiks mobilize based on *kolkhoz* and *avlod* structures.

Third, and perhaps most importantly, these states achieved independence with no national military. The Transcaucasus Military District remained under Russian control. The 201st Motorized Division in Tajikistan continued to take orders from Moscow. Local police forces could keep order for a time, but in a situation with no leviathan of last resort, local gangsters were tempted to escalate tactics and dare retaliations that they knew would probably not come.[31]

In Georgia, as nationalist militia groups and extremists rose to political prominence in Tbilisi, minority ethnic enclaves began to fear for their safety in the new Georgian state. Some communities organized militias to defend themselves. Many more accommodated themselves to the new politics, waiting for the violent nationalism to blow over. A few others explored the possibility of Russian military protection, and improvised efforts by rump Soviet security forces to protect Ossetian minorities were decried in Tbilisi as Russian meddling in Georgian sovereign affairs. Georgian nationalists in the capital began to fight among themselves over how to interpret the new state of affairs. Some factions tried to deescalate the tensions and serve as moderate peace brokers, but they could not restrain aggressive warlords. What emerged was political gridlock and an angry echo chamber among the new elites in Tbilisi, with ethnic minorities listening fearfully across a language barrier.[32] As the Soviet Union unraveled, these escalations eventually led to full-blown wars of secession in South Ossetia and Abkhazia, and the general disintegration of state authority.

A similar drama played out in Tajikistan. Islamic activists entered into tactical political alliances with democratic nationalists. Agendas for radical redistribution were discussed for the first time in generations. Elites from the wealthiest and most politically connected regions – who had monopolized state positions and reported directly to Moscow for decades – feared the entry of new groups into the power structure. As Tajikistan was an impoverished cotton colony with some of the worst inequality in the former Soviet Union, stakes were tremendously high. Most of the Russian middle class fled, leaving a civil society void. Proposals for redrawing the internal boundaries of the republic, essentially proposals to replace old gerrymandering with new gerrymandering, threatened established regionally based patronage networks that kept rural

---

30   See Toft (2005) and Roeder (2007). For a carefully reasoned response to Roeder, see Lacina (2014).

31   For an analogous argument tested in the context of Indonesia's transition to democracy in the mid-1990s, see Tajima (2014).

32   This is a distillation of many complex events summarized in Darchiashvili (1997a), Cornell (2001, 2002), Darchiashvili and Nodia (2003), and Wheatley (2005).

populations dependent on urban elites in Dushanbe and Khojand.[33] Once these proposals were on the table, they could not be easily removed. These embattled elites joined forces with rural criminal networks and local strongmen, who cannibalized local military garrisons to create voluntary village defense units.[34] The result was political fragmentation and brutal war.

GEORGIA: 1989–1994

In its first three years of independence, the Georgian state confronted four different ethno-territorial secessionist challenges, a military coup, economic collapse, and rural warlordism. Cumulatively, the wars had a relatively modest human toll compared to wars in Tajikistan or Chechnya. They culminated in full-scale ethnic cleansing and the displacement of as many as 200,000 ethnic Georgians, but probably no more than 20,000 total deaths. The legacy of this violence is substantial, however, casting a long shadow over the current Georgian political landscape.

As Tbilisi evolved in the Russian cultural imagination as an island outpost of civilized luxury on the unruly mountain frontier, wealth and social opportunity accrued to the urban ruling class in Georgia over many generations.[35] Georgians who attended the right schools and managed their careers carefully could access all that Moscow had to offer, fully enjoying the social, cultural, and economic benefits afforded to the Communist Party elite. Some have suggested that in Georgia the Communist Party had more in common with an aristocratic social stratum than an actual political party.[36]

Outside of Tbilisi, the situation was very complex. Soviet ethno-federal structures that protected minorities were particularly important to social order in Georgia, given the well-understood political advantage that the majority group held in the union. A "separate-but-equal" system had allowed dozens of demographically small – but linguistically distinct – groups to live peacefully as neighbors in the South Caucasus for a half-century.[37] The dominance of

---

33   See Dudoignon (1998), Rubin (1998), Roy (2000), Whitlock (2005), and Collins (2006). For some, references to political Islam cloud what would otherwise be a relatively straightforward story of postcolonial distributive politics. For others, it is naive to separate the issue of political Islam from neighborhood geopolitics given the close geographic proximity to Afghanistan and linguistic proximity to Iran.

34   These groups began to carry out offensive operations outside their home territories almost immediately. Bushkov and Mikulskii (1995), Kuzmin (1997), and Markowitz (2012), 60–65.

35   In the Soviet ethnic status hierarchy urban Georgians enjoyed most of the important social protections associated with "favored lords", in the typology presented by Laitin (1998), 59–82.

36   Aves (1993), 230. The perceived social status advantages that Party affiliation conferred on Georgians is reflected in their party membership. With 8.5 percent of the Georgian population registered as official members of the Communist Party, Georgians had one of the highest party membership rates in the twilight of the USSR, besting Russians (7.9 percent) and Azeris (5.4%).

37   See Martin (2001). Blauvelt (2013) reports that Georgian is the most widely spoken of four languages in the Karvelian group of South Caucasian languages (the other being Mingrelian,

ethnic Georgians increased in the republic over the seventy years of Soviet rule, but Georgia remained ethnically diverse. According to the 1989 census, Georgians made up 70 percent of the population, followed by the Armenians (12.7 percent), Russians (6.3 percent) and Azerbaijanis (5.7 percent). Georgia had a number of enclaves where Georgian was barely spoken, and a politically estranged class of elites who mediated between their Abkhaz, Adjar, Armenian, Azeri, Laz, Mingrelian, Ossetian, or Svan-speaking constituencies and the powers-that-be in Moscow and Tbilisi.[38]

Georgia's descent into civil war is difficult to disentangle from the delegitimization of communist ideology, which left a gaping political vacuum. Independence meant that Moscow would no longer be the site of future elite pilgrimages, or the guarantor of minority rights.[39] This meant that ethno-federal preferences, job quotas, and protected slots for minority-language primary education were all suddenly negotiable. As the inaugural election empowered a generation of self-assured Georgian elites, the threat of permanent second-class citizenship began to crystallize in the minds of ethnic minorities. Under the best of circumstances, it would have been difficult to convince Abkhaz, Adjars, Armenians, Azeris, and Ossets that they would fare as well as minority groups within a rapidly nationalizing Georgian republic as they had fared under the "affirmative action empire" of the Soviet Union.[40]

Laz and Svan). Though Russian historically played an important role in administration and in inter-ethnic communication, Georgian was made the official language during Georgia's brief period of independence in 1918–1921, and following the Soviet military conquest, the Georgian SSR was one of the few union republics that successfully implemented paperwork in the titular language under the Soviet "indigenization" policy. Publishing in Georgian and Georgian-language educational institutions, libraries, and cultural and literary organizations were supported during the Soviet period, and local Georgian leadership made fluency in Georgian a criterion for cadre advancement within the Republic. Russian was still necessary for educational and professional advancement opportunities on the all-Union level and access to literature and popular culture, and served as the language of inter-ethnic mobility for ethnic minorities in Georgia. Instruction in Russian was mandatory, though primary and secondary education was also available in "official minority languages": Abkhaz, Armenian, and Azerbaijani.

38 At this point, some readers will be tempted to ask why the population did not all "just become Georgian" or "just learn Georgian." The short answer is that Georgian is difficult to learn, they resented the forced choice, and they calculated that their children would "never be Georgian enough" to ascend to a position of power in Tbilisi. For experimental evidence that they were correct in their estimation, see Driscoll and Blauvelt (2012). Moreover, deeply ingrained legacies of ethnically defined identity were at the heart of the Soviet experiment. For those who wished to become bilinguals, Laitin (1998) provides myriad rationales for the language of social mobility to be Russian, not Georgian. Laitin (1994) notes that multilingual settings often empower a small set of linguistically gifted elites, who can become trilingual with lower-than-average investment and "charge for translation services." 622.

39 By "educational and administrative pilgrimages" (142), see Anderson (1991), 142. See also 137–143 generally.

40 For expansions on this point, see Martin (2001) and Laitin (1998), chapters 3, 4, and 12. For similar arguments applied to South Ossetia and Abkhazia in particular, see Derluguian (2005)

From the perspective of ethnic minorities, what made things worse was
that the emergent elites were often relatively well-known criminals. Criminal
entrepreneurship in crass collusion with security services was nothing new in
the South Caucasus. Organized crime had flourished for decades with a wink
from Tbilisi, and since the 1970s, these networks had gained notoriety as *vori v
zkone* ("Thieves in Law").[41] Individuals with ties to wineries, citrus orchards,
hazelnut farms, and other luxury goods could profit by exploiting the shortages
and bottlenecks inevitable in a command economy. As latent tensions between
Russians and Georgians grew heated via electoral rhetoric, it was increasingly
"impossible to separate political violence from struggle for economic power"
among this elite.[42] By the late 1980s, as a natural transit point to the Black
Sea, Turkey, and the European markets beyond, Georgia had an off-the-books
"shadow economy" that was estimated to be one of the largest anywhere in the
Union.

The slow collapse of authority sent uneven ripples through the Soviet
military and security hierarchy. In the South Caucasus, lucrative rents
associated with guaranteeing road, border, and bazaar security passed to
actors with the ambition and entrepreneurial spirit to monetize transnational
security networks. As the de facto sources of order inside the boundaries of
a new state, military field commanders found themselves guaranteeing vital
transit lines. These men evolved somewhat naturally into brokers – first for
bullets and ammunition to militias, and later for gasoline, drugs, cigarettes,
alcohol, consumer staples, and everything else. Alliances began to form between
uniformed state agents and criminals, as one respondent recalled:

"It was May of 1989 ... I remember because I was just home from prison ... An old
school friend, who was then in the police, was the first to talk to me about real politics.
I remember he said 'This can't end except with blood. Everyone is watching Berlin,
watching the Baltics, watching Budapest. There are not enough eyes and ears to pay
attention to us down here. If things go the way they are going, this will all fall in our
laps.' At first I thought he was trying to trick me, to get me to say something that would
send me back to jail ... but all the plans were his. He had friends in The [Communist]
party that could get us guns, ammunition ... my job was to talk to people I knew who
could shoot [straight] and be trusted."[43]

Independence came to Georgia on the wave of nationalist challenges on the
Baltic model. Mass protests against Soviet power were held, culminating
in demonstrations with many thousands of participants in the capital.[44]

233–237, Laitin (1999a) 48–56. In particular, residents of Abkhazia, where the Abkhaz had
    slowly become a demographic minority in their own Soviet autonomous republic, believed
    they were on the brink of being stripped of their linguistic, social, and economic autonomy.
    See Cornell (2002).
41 See Mars and Altman (1983).
42 Slider (1997), 168.
43 Interview conducted November 1, 2006 in Tbilisi.
44 Slider (1997), 159–162.

Communist authorities were utterly discredited by their decision to violently disperse a demonstration on April 9, 1989, leaving nineteen dead and hundreds injured. The martyrs empowered radical voices at the expense of moderates, creating a set of self-sustaining anarchist attitudes that spread from educated youth throughout the intelligentsia. This political culture festered during the long window of political paralyzation between 1989 and 1991 – a period in which all state institutions began to be seen as illegitimate.[45] Koba, one of my first key informants, presented the following account of his decision to join the Mkhedrioni ("The Knights of Georgia"):

"I had never considered breaking the law ... My mother always told me to be good, to stay out of trouble, and that I should try to keep my grades good so I could join The Party like my older brother Levan ... But then when the Russians killed the women on April 9 [1989], everything changed for me. ... They murdered women for demonstrating peacefully against their fascist state. They used gas, and they cut up their bodies with shovels. How could we stand by while they did this to us? Our sisters? Our mothers? What kind of men would we be? My father and I discussed this many nights ... [A] friend from school said he could introduce me to Dzhaba [Ioseliani], so I went to a meeting. After hearing him speak, I knew that he was the man who would save us. ... He was our Martin Luther King."[46]

There are elements of this story that were common across Georgian recruitment narratives. The first is the reference to the April 9, 1989 massacre of female activists as a focal event evoking an emotional response.[47] It delegitimized the authority of the Soviet police apparatus, and served as a gendered rallying cry for young Georgian males to redeem themselves with reciprocal violence. Second, the presence of family dynamics and the subtle importance of parental approval surrounding the decision to join a violent militia group emerged during many of my extended life interviews with key informants.[48]

---

45 Nodia (2002), 424 and Areshidze (2007), 19.
46 Interview conducted February 28, 2006 in Tbilisi.
47 Stereotypes of Georgians as an "emotional" people were regularly invoked in descriptive accounts of the rise of the militias. This sort of facile cultural stereotyping cannot explain why violent mobilization succeeded in Georgia and not in other republics. (A primary stereotypes of Tajiks is of a quiet and subservient people). Yet cultural memory is real. The visceral emotional response to the April 9 events still resonated in the imaginations of my respondents more than fifteen years after the fact – manifesting in raised voices, angry gestures, and (in one case) the suspension of an interview, when the respondent flew into a rage when I seemed unsuitably unmoved. — SOUNDS LIKE THE "STEREOTYPE" IS PRETTY ACCURATE
48 Although family dynamics are impossible to code and not the focus of this research design, it would not be inconsistent with my data to hypothesize that joining a militia was a life path that would be discouraged for married sons with obligations or who were seen as obvious social risers, and subtly encouraged for sons who had not demonstrated an aptitude for school or a strong work ethic. There are a number of anecdotes from my data of families intervening when a "promising" son allowed himself to be drawn into the violent milieu of militia politics. One particularly prominent case – a former Minister for Culture and Sport for the Saakashvili government – served with his Mkhedrioni unit in Abkhazia before his parents bought him

Third, the transcendent, charismatic authority of the personage of Dzhaba Ioseliani featured in many accounts of Mkhedrioni recruits. Informal networks that connected recruits to groups of university art students or other activist communities with anarchist ties were reflected in stories. Fourth and finally, my interview data reveal a ubiquitous willingness on the part of Georgian nationalists to blame "the Russians" for everything that went wrong during this period.

Anti-communist, anti-political, anti-state, and anti-Russian rhetoric began to blur together. It is difficult to overstate the visceral anti-Russian character of Georgian nationalism. Xenophobic rhetoric migrated into the mainstream of political speech acts. It became commonplace to label political opponents and ethnic minorities as nefarious foreign agents. The blunt stick of language laws escalated the stakes of politics sharply, as the Georgian leadership gave official status to the Georgian language. This curtailed job opportunities and social mobility for minorities, and made it clear that the wave of nationalism would not simply "blow over."[49] Many Russian-speaking ethnic minorities felt they were being asked to choose between cultural assimilation, ghettoization, or permanent resettlement outside of Georgia. Much of the Russian population left Georgia and did not return.[50] *YEAH, SO? ARE WE SUPPOSED TODAY?*

Many former Mkhedrioni members described its founder and spiritual leader, Dzhaba Ioseliani, as an anarchist at heart – someone more interested in tearing down the old order than in presiding over new institutions. As a teacher of theater, he also had superb instincts for what kinds of symbolic actions would allow youth to feel that they were taking part in a communal ritual. One respondent recalled how he joined the Mkhedrioni by literally being swept up in a crowd on its way to picket and protest the "occupation" at a Soviet military base.[51] Two other Tbilisi youth reported joining after attending public demonstrations outside the Ministry of the Interior, protesting the "humiliations and abuses" that the Abkhaz and South Ossetians were inflicting on "defenseless Georgian minorities," and demanding action.[52]

In this anarchic millieu, democratic reforms accelerated in the late Soviet period, leading to modern Georgia's first authentically multiparty elections on October 28, 1990. Zviad Gamsakhurdia's "Round Table – Free Georgia"

WELL IF There's one thing we need more of in the U.S., it's violent foreigners
a one-way ticket to Atlanta, Georgia and enrolled him in dentistry school. See Derluguian (2005), 32 for a related set of insights from the North Caucasus.

[49] See Derluguian (2005), 202. Svante Cornell chronicles the historical reasons that the Abkhaz feared cultural assimilation in Cornell (2001), 155–170, with particular attention to this period.

[50] Census data show that the Russian-speaking percentage of the population declined from 6.3 percent in 1989 to 1.5 percent in 2002.

[51] Interview conducted November 21, 2006 in Mingrelia.

[52] Interviews conducted October 24, 2006 and November 16, 2006 in Tbilisi. The second respondent, Data, enlisted in the National Guard, rather than the Mkhedrioni, and left to South Ossetia to fight for his brethren in December 1990.

coalition won convincingly over the Georgian Communists (64 percent to 30 percent). In November 1990 Gamsakhurdia was elected overwhelmingly as Chairman of the Supreme Council of the Soviet Republic of Georgia. Gamsakhurdia quickly cut funding to the security and intelligence services (believing them to be organs of Moscow), discouraged Georgians from taking part in conscription drives for the Red Army, and explicitly endorsed the creation of a new locally recruited paramilitary National Guard. He came to realize that the power of the Mkhedrioni to control the streets was a serious threat to his legitimacy, and made an attempt to put them down with the help of the new National Guard, which had been organized by an old friend, Tengiz Kitovani. (Kitovani had served time in the Soviet prison system, and is discussed at length in the text that follows.) Gamsakhurdia was assisted with security detachments from Moscow, which included forty tanks. Ioseliani was taken into custody and held in a KGB prison until December 1990, but many of the guards were sympathetic to his cause and his messages filtered out to his commanders.

Locally recruited militias rushed to fill the void in public order. Elites in the capital city had no ability to control the violent forces that had been unleashed. David Darchiashvili recalls that in these early stages the Mkhedrioni and other groups were quite savvy about the political climate and presented themselves as a patriotic, order-providing alternative to the corrupt Soviet police forces: "The theft and murder all came later, of course, but in the early days the Mkhedrioni checkpoints wouldn't harass you for your money ... they made people feel safer."[53] It became fashionable for emerging political parties to support parallel youth movements, which often had paramilitary characteristics. During this period, rural respondents described migrating to Tbilisi en masse, preparing for a showdown with the Russian-backed police if necessary. When I asked a militia member named Vasiil what he thought would happen in the capital, he answered "I didn't know ... no one told us. We were just told that it was a good time to be in the capital. That the police and the Russians were scared ... and that it was our time."[54]

In May 1991, after the Georgian parliament had declared its independence from the Soviet Union, Gamsakhurdia was elected President with more than 85 percent of the vote. His popularity began to fade almost immediately. Dictatorial, willful, paranoid, and self-aggrandizing aspects of his personality surfaced. Gamsakhurdia's erratic decision making included a refusal to sign any defense or economic agreements with the USSR, the haphazard restriction of free speech by closing of opposition newspapers (lamely citing paper shortages), imprisoning underworld figures and parliamentary representatives by seemingly random logic, stochastically reshuffling his cabinet, and repeatedly

---

53 Interview conducted November 19, 2006 in Tbilisi.
54 Interview conducted November 20, 2006 in Tbilisi.

declaring martial law to cover his political tracks. The original members of his "Round Table" coalition began to abandon him. He turned to the streets.

By this point, the fragmentation of Georgia's security infrastructure had produced more than seven fully separate militias.[55] To some degree, all were involved in extortion, smuggling, and racketeering. Some of them were led by individuals with no police background. Tengiz Kitovani, a criminal associate of Gamsakhurdia, had used the anarchic collapse of the state to reinvent himself as a soldier of fortune. He achieved fame agitating for Georgian rights in the ethnic minority enclave of South Ossetia. He transformed his group into a mercenary armed wing of the Union of Georgian Traditionalists, then shifted his support to Gamsakhurdia and his "Round Table – Free Georgia" coalition. As he rose in prominence and multiplied his political connections, Kitovani emerged as an immensely powerful patron to middle-tier police officers who were looking to distance themselves from the shame of state affiliation in the pre-1989 period. One former combatant put his conversion in religious terms, "I had been a part of an evil machine, and I was not proud ... accepting Kitovani's friendship was like being forgiven for my sins."[56] Gia Karkarashvili, a relatively obscure captain in the Soviet army, acquired instant local fame when he and a number of other disgruntled members of his unit deserted and founded the "White Eagle" militia group. This group affiliated itself at various points with the Mkhedrioni, Kitovani's National Guard, and would eventually form the nucleus of Georgia's state army under Shevardnadze.[57]

During the 1991 August coup in Moscow, Gamsakhurdia used the crisis as a cover to dismiss Tengiz Kitovani and subordinate the National Guard under the auspices of the Ministry of the Interior. Gamsakhurdia also sacked the popular Prime Minister, Tengiz Segua, and radically centralized power by personally assuming direct control of the KGB, the Ministry of the Interior, and the Ministry of Justice.[58] Kitovani refused to obey the order and simply left Tbilisi, moving to a nearby armed encampment with the bulk of his troops.[59]

---

[55] Interview conducted December 6, 2006 in Tbilisi.
[56] Interview conducted February 7, 2006 in Tbilisi.
[57] Karkarashvili inspired tremendous loyalty on the part of his men, and when he was dismissed in the late 1990s many members of the unit defected to launch irregular raids across the unrecognized border with Abkhazia. Interviews conducted October 29, 2006 in Kvimo Khartli, and November 16, 2006 in Tbilisi.
[58] O'Ballance (1997), 104. Amidst the euphoria of epochal social change and the first authentic election in living memory, Gamsakhurdia's speeches included a number of unfortunately phrased comments, in Georgian, directed at non-Georgian minorities. Gamsakhurdia later denied having actually mouthed slogans such as "Georgia for Georgians." Parsing speeches for double-entrendres and hidden meanings to determine if he was, in fact, speaking in code to fringe nationalist elements of his own coalition, requires a linguistic fluency that I do not possess. I will simply add that neither did most citizens of listening nervously from Abkhazia, Kvemo Kartli, or Samtse-Javakheti. Nor did most citizens of Moscow, where most politically relevant television and radio broadcasts still originated.
[59] Wheatley (2005), 55.

These recruits formed the core of the militia army that would invade Abkhazia one year later.

In the interim, Kitovani deployed a few trusted subordinates with orders to visit Abkhazia "with no guns – just clipboards and notebooks" to map the locations of waterfront properties and farms with profitable citrus orchards.[60] By this point commanders were fairly brazen economic brokers, not even bothering to hide their ties to organized criminal groups with transnational ties across the former Soviet Union (the *vori v zkone* in particular). A fair number of respondents voluntarily admitted to becoming involved with the National Guard or the Mkhedrioni in this period because they hoped that it would serve as a conduit into a glamorous life of international crime. A representative quote: "There are not so many ways out of my village, if you are not in the right family. For me, I saw a chance to … get rich, like Pacino in Scarface."[61]

A massive hostile demonstration on September 2, 1991 ended with the police firing into the crowd to disperse it, a chilling parallel to the April 9 martyrdom of Georgian activists. As a direct result of these events, the regime lost the support of both the elites and the masses. Tbilisi descended into months of chaos and anarchy, with open gang warfare between different militias with vague and rotating political attachments. In rural areas, many non-Georgian ethnic enclaves had organized militias of their own, or sought protection from beached Russian military units. These actions were seized on by Georgian nationalists as proof of disloyalty.

Gamsakhurdia will primarily be remembered as an erratic politician who needlessly antagonized Georgia's superpower neighbor and escalated tensions with ethnic minorities. As a partial corrective, it is important to recall that as the creeping escalation of violence between fringe Georgian nationalists and Ossetians threatened to draw Russia into Georgian affairs, Gamsakhurdia kept dialogues open with the nationalists in Abkhazia and succeeded in striking a power-sharing agreement to assure Sukhumi its sovereignty. These hard-won agreements were made irrelevant when a coup removed him from office.[62] After weeks of hiding in a Soviet nuclear fallout shelter, Gamsakhurdia fled the capital city on January 6, 1992, leaving Tbilisi in the hands of Dzhaba Ioseliani, Tengiz Kitovani, and Tengiz Segura, who reinstated himself as prime minister.

---

60 Interview conducted February 7, 2006 in Tbilisi.

61 Interview conducted October 19, 2006 in Chinvali. Viewed through this (admittedly cynical) lens, Gamsakhurdia's unforgivable sin may have been shutting down economic relations with Russia without providing an alternative outlet for either the entitled entrepreneurial class or for the rural proto-criminal underclass who saw a better labor market in Moscow and St. Petersburg than Tbilisi. I am grateful to Timothy Blauvelt for this speculation.

62 See Jones (1996) and Zuercher (2005). Gamsakhurdia's final miscalculation was his attempt to centralize control over the militias that kept him in power. This backfired. Obviously the coup-plotters and their intellectual supporters had a more charitable interpretation of their actions. For an unusually thoughtful reflection on this period, see Areshidze (2007), 29–32.

In the immediate wake of the paramilitary coup, the new republic was bankrupt, with no credit to purchase food or fuel. The Abkhaz, South Ossetians, Adjars, and Armenians of Akhalkalaki were de facto independent. Gamsakhurdia – who for all his faults *was* the country's elected leader – had successfully rallied an insurgent army of "Zviadists" and crossed the border into Chechnya to launch an insurgency. Tengiz Segura, now prime minister, went hat in hand to Moscow, then to the Commonwealth of Independent State (CIS) summit in Minsk, and then to the United States and other Western capitals, but was time and again rebuffed in his pleas for aid. The coup leaders had no idea how to resurrect the carcass of the state, no hope of international recognition, and no money to pay police salaries or retain military soldiers. Georgia was a failed state, with no obvious path to recovery. GEE, That's Too BAD. BUT, YA KNOW, I JUST DON'T SEE HOW THAT'S THE FAULT OR THE PROBLEM OF THE U.S. TAXPAYER.

TAJIKISTAN: 1990–1992

Tajikistan's state failure produced, with the possible exception of Chechnya, the most brutal of the post-Soviet wars, with per capita violence on a scale unmatched anywhere in the region. For a country containing fewer than 2 percent of the citizens of the Soviet Union, it produced 37 percent of the casualties of the post-Socialist wars.[63] At least a sixth of the population was displaced by the fighting, including the permanent exodus of virtually every member of the Russian and East German professional class. The World Bank and International Monetary Fund (IMF) estimate that today the per capita gross domestic product (GDP) in Tajikistan is approximately one-tenth what it was before the slide into violence.[64]

---

[63] The 37 percent figure was calculated using the conservative 41,300 figure cited in the Lacina (2006) replication data for all the wars that broke out on the territory of the former Soviet Union between 1991 and 1993, including in the denominator the estimations of deaths in wars in Chechnya, South Ossetia, Abkhazia, and Ngorno-Karabakh. Because so many of the civilian deaths were due to disease and exposure in the frozen mountains of Afghanistan, we will probably never know the true number of deaths in the Tajik civil war. The 50,000 number is regularly cited; estimates by specialists range from fewer than 10,000 (cited by Christoph Zuercher in a 2011 Stockholm International Peace Research Institute (SIPRI) workshop) to estimates as high as 100,000 (cited by Sergei Gretsky, who can credibly claim to have lived through the Tajik civil war as a close observer). Thanks to the United Nations and the International Committee for the Red Cross/Crescent (ICRC), there is much more reliable data on population displacement. In the opening phases of the war approximately 300,000 ethnic Russians and Russian speakers from other republics – the core of the Soviet-educated professional class in Tajikistan – emigrated, never to return. More than half a million additional Tajiks and Uzbeks fled their homes (600,000 is the estimate that the United Nations relief missions used in their internal correspondences in 1995). This does not include the tens of thousands of "predatory migrants," who seized homes in Dushanbe abandoned by fleeing Russian speakers, or rural *kolkhoz* property abandoned by the losers of the civil war.

[64] Nakaya (2009), 1–2.

The social mobilization that led to the Tajik Civil War took place in the poorest, most rural, and most mountainous corner of the Soviet Union.[65] Unlike Georgia, Tajikistan did not achieve independence after years of social mobilization for independence. It was "pushed out" of the USSR by Yeltsin's government after the failed coup and the secession of Belarus and Ukraine.[66] In the years preceding the transition to independence, long latent tensions over scarce resources had begun to emerge. Rural parts of this cotton-monocropping republic were functionally self-governing. The collective farm (*kolkhoz*) was the relevant unit of social organization for many citizens. Formal authority structures wobbled atop local informal networks, and rural Party *nomenklatura* were difficult to distinguish from the shadow economy elite. A lucky individual who emerged with the influence to serve as a Party intermediary could profit by navigating the space between official Communist Party production quotas and local productive capacity. But wealth-generation opportunities were rare, and largely concentrated in labor-intensive agriculture (cotton), light industry (military-industrial production), and mining (gems, gold, and aluminum). Not incidentally, it was also on the military front-line of a decade-long war, sharing a border with Afghanistan. Tajikistan was the only Persian-speaking SSR in the Union.

One of the peripheral Tajik adaptations to Soviet totalitarianism was the tendency to avoid committing very much to writing. Relations between neighboring communities in rural parts of the country were governed by oral agreements and informal understandings when possible. Legislative acts and formal appointments to the hierarchy – the visible state, assigning jobs by quota to minority groups, so relevant to politics in Georgia – had little to do with the structures that shaped relevant life choices for most Tajiks.[67] Instead,

---

[65] Gretsky (1995), 1. The Panj River runs through the rugged and treacherous Pamiri mountain range, forming the political border with Afghanistan. In my interviews with combatants, it was clear that many drew inspiration from their grandfathers who fought in the Basmachi revolts of the 1920s and 1930s, in the same terrain with the same hit-and-run guerrilla tactics. I have heard it said that if one places a map over the territories that the Red Army never quite subdued when they declared victory in the late 1930s, it bears an eerie resemblance to the parts of Tajikistan that were the last hold-outs on the 1997 Peace Process.

[66] Derluguian (2005), 168. Olivier Roy provides a nuanced alternative reading of the historical data, suggesting that the Central Asian republics, like the republics in the Caucasus, were bound to shed ties with "a Soviet model that had become exclusively Slavic." See Roy (2000), 128. Either way, when the Soviet Union broke apart, Tajikistan was dependent on Moscow for 46 percent of its 1991 budget. This figure was actually quite representative of other Central Asian states, as well – Uzbekistan, with all its urban wealth and relative industrialization, received 43 percent of its 1991 budget from Moscow. It is with these facts in mind that Georgi Derluguian writes the following: "To the credit of the *Far Eastern Economic Review*, when the Western media were still celebrating the springtime of nations, this journal in 1992 ran the cover story under blunt title 'Dumping Central Asia.'" 357 FN 4.

[67] See Rashidov (1993), 296.

kolkhoz heads and state farm (*sovkhoz*) directors – particularly the "cotton barons" of Khatlon, Kulob, and Leninobod – were the dominant social actors.[68] Most of the literature identifies the roots of the Tajik civil war in a half-century of divide-and-rule policies that split elites among various regions and "clans" during the Soviet period.[69] Since Stalin's death, Moscow and Tashkent had consistently allowed a few families, based primarily in the region of Khojand, to police entry into the state apparatus.[70] These elites zealously guarded the rents that came from their privileged positions. On the eve of independence, elites from different geographic regions were divided by deep personal mistrust. Regionalism (*mahalgaro'y*) had evolved over generations. Gretsky (1995) describes the resulting social stratification and inequality:

[W]hen the Khujandis ascended to top party and government positions in Tajikistan in the 1940s they endorsed localism as the corner stone of their policy, and kept regional rivalries boiling, while reserving for themselves the role of arbiter. Under the Khujandis, localism assumed such proportions that it began to somewhat resemble the Indian caste pyramid with its division of labor. In Tajikistan, the popular wisdom put it in the following way: 'Leninobod governs, Gharm does business, Kulob guards, Pamir dances, Qurghonteppa ploughs.'[71]

Political and economic impoverishment went hand-in-hand. *Glasnost* and *perestroika* brought forth latent competitive pressures from elites in Tajikistan's

---

[68] Rumer (1989). The notion of "family" in Tajikistan is the subject of a dense anthropological literature that I have not mastered. I inadvertently stumbled into a language problem through my effort to ask the same questions of Tajik and Georgian militia members. Of the eighty-nine former combatants who fought in the Tajik civil war, more than *half* of them claimed to have at least one family member serving in the same militia group. This was the result of a translation problem on my questionnaire because "family" in Tajikistan includes a broad network of extended patronymic affiliations, based on blood ties and strategic marriages. The "*avlod*" (family) is hierarchically organized, with elders (who can be male or female) at the top and junior members obligated to them. Each *avlod* is identified by its location of origin, and there are also social rankings of these *avolds* by prominence, creating what Matveeva (2009) has described as a "caste system" (7). Unlike the Georgian clan networks, these ties did not represent viable pathways for social mobility or economic opportunity outside of the republic, except for a few family networks that stretched across the border to the ancient Tajik cities of Bukhara and Samarkand (now part of the territory of Uzbekistan). For a general discussion of Soviet failure to penetrate the clan structures in Tajikistan, see Rakowska-Harmstone (1970).

[69] For outstanding overviews of the use and misuse of "clan politics" as an explanation for the war in Tajikistan, see Roy (2000), 14, 92–100, Rubin (1998), 147–152, and Akiner (2001), 26–27, 65.

[70] Kathleen Collins (2006) argues that Tajikistan was unique among the Central Asian republics in that it was the only republic where interclan "pacts" were never forged in the 1980s. In my reading of her argument, she gives causal weight to Moscow's desire to keep a state free of any groups that might have ties to revolutionaries in Iran or Afghanistan, which was reverse-engineered by the Khojandi elite in the Uzbek-dominated northern region of Leninobod. 102–117 and 130–140.

[71] Gretsky (1995).

impoverished areas around Gharm, who believed they had been forced into second-class positions outside of communist networks. Not surprisingly, these rural citizens tended to have more pious religious worldviews than their urban counterparts.[72] Though it is oversimplistic to think of Tajikistan's civil war as a clash between different regionally-based family networks, birthplace provides a good rule-of-thumb for determining which faction a particular person supported in the war that emerged after independence. Conservative "neo-communist" forces recruited from regional groups that had benefitted disproportionately in the late Soviet period – Khojandis, Kulobis, Hissoris, and Uzbek minority groups. Their opponents recruited heavily from rural Islamic activist networks that had deep support structures in Gharm and the rural lowlands, and ethnic Pamiris, who had been overrepresented in the police and Soviet security structures since the start of the Afghan war.[73]

A number of populist Islamic parties mobilized in 1990 and 1991, led by eloquent spokespersons among the urban intelligentsia. Both factions claimed – in Tajik and Russian – to represent moderation and democracy. They stood in opposition to the inherited Communist party apparatus and recruited primarily from populations traditionally excluded from power. As Akiner (2001) foreshadows, "[Islamic Renaissance Party] representatives insisted that they were 'against forcing people to accept our path,' but even at this stage their bodyguards were toting Kalashnikovs." [74] In February 1990, when Tajikistan was still a part of the USSR, hundreds of citizens poured onto the streets of the capital to challenge the police in response to a rumor that scarce housing in downtown Dushanbe would be set aside for resettled Armenians. Later accounts suggest that the violence, which produced as many as 25 deaths and 800 injuries, was organized by criminals – an omen of what was to come.[75]

After First Party Secretary and President Kakhar Makhkamov supported the Moscow putschists in August 1991, he was forced to resign in the face of mass

---

72 The best account of opposition ideology is probably Dudoignon (1998). A good companion piece is Whitlock (2005), who describes the allure of "underground Islam" in late Soviet Tajikistan.

73 Though Pamiri cadres were purged from the upper echelons of power in the Tajik state in 1937, the unusually strong cultural value placed on education led Pamiris to be overrepresented in professional classes that were dominated by Russians and East Germans: doctors, academics, and civil servants. As the Soviet war in Afghanistan escalated through the 1980s, Soviet security services heavily recruited from this population, which was often linguistically proficient in Persian and Dari, yet less prone to being cultural sympathetic with the Sunni Tajiks in Afghanistan. As a result, Pamiris were relatively overrepresented in the state security forces at the time of independence.

74 Akiner (2001), 34. See Tadjbakhsh (1993) for a first-person account of the party organization during this period.

75 See Auten (1996) and Nourzhanov (2005), 115.

protests.[76] Tajikistan gained independence on September 9, 1991. Rakhmon Nabiev, a former party secretary representing the traditional ruling families of the northern region of Khojand, assumed the republic's presidency. He dissolved the Communist Party and attempted to legitimize his ascendency in an October presidential election, where he ran against Davlat Khudonazarov, a Pamiri intellectual who was the former head of the Soviet Union of Cinematographers. The election was remarkably open, fair, and rigorously contested by regional standards. Nabiev defeated his opponent with the support of a convincing majority, with 85 percent of Tajiks casting their votes.[77] The ascendence of Nabiev was taken as a signal of political continuity.[78]

Opposition forces from regions traditionally locked out of power, particularly Gharm and the eastern Gorno-Badakhshon Autonomous Oblast (GBAO), feared that their window was closing. Some members of the opposition tried to declare the election fraudulent. At some point there was a decision to test the rhetorical promise that the new state had made regarding freedom of assembly by using street power to get their way.[79] In December 1991, the Speaker of the Supreme Soviet, Safarali Kenjayev, declared martial law and a state of emergency. The head of the Ministry of the Interior, Mamadaez, Naujavanov, a Pamiri from GBAO, refused to implement his orders. In retaliation, Naujavanov was relieved of his position. At the time of independence, the Pamiris of GBAO were overrepresented in the Ministry of the Interior.[80] Naujavanov's dismissal stoked fears among Pamiris that they were being purged from the state apparatus. To many ethnic Tajiks, his dismissal was surely warranted, and a long overdue correction for Russian affirmative action favoring Pamiris.

---

[76] Even after Makhkamov stepped down from office, the Ministry of the Interior refused orders to impose a state of emergency, and allowed more than 10,000 demonstrators to continue paralyzing the capital city of Dushanbe for weeks.

[77] According to Grotz (2001), 466. Nourzhanov and Bleur (2013) reports that 58 percent casting votes for Rahmon Nabiev, 34 percent for Davlat Khudonazarov, 5 percent for Saifiddin Turayev, and marginal support for three other candidates (290). Muriel Atkin (2002) corroborates the 58 percent figure for Nabiev but reports that Khudonazarov achieved only 30 percent of the vote (100). Gleason (1997) claims 58 percent and 29 percent. Grotz (2001) reports 56.9 percent and 30.1 percent (466). Khudonazarov was endorsed by the Democratic Party of Tajikistan, the Islamic Renaissance Party of Tajikistan, La'li Badakhshon, and Rastokhez. Nabiev was supported by the Communist Party of Tajikistan. The details of when these various parties were founded, registered, and suspended are well documented in Babak, Vaisman and Wasserman (2004), 269–321.

[78] Collins (2006), 102–117 and 130–140.

[79] For a more sympathetic view of the opposition demands their political platform, see Akbarzadeh (1996), 1108–1112.

[80] There were also many Pamiris who had received special military training as a result of the Soviet military engagement in Afghanistan. Ever fearful that militant ideas would spread north like a contagion, transmitted perhaps by the charismatic personality of Shah Massoud, Moscow wanted to make sure that there was a non-Uzbek, non-Tajik force of military specialists in Tajikistan's security structures. Roy (2000), 139–140.

As the snows melted the following spring, demonstrators from traditionally disenfranchised regions of the country gathered in Dushanbe and staged a mass protest in Shahidon ("Martyr's") Square, calling for Nabiev's resignation. Fearing that the government would give in to the demands of these agitators, a counter-demonstration formed in nearby Ozodi ("Liberty") Square, featuring mobs of Nabiev supporters – men from Kulob, Khojand, Tursunzade, and the Dushanbe sprawl.[81] The President was unable to deploy the security ministries to disperse these demonstrations because the security ministries were themselves gridlocked between supporters of the opposition and supporters of the new regime.

In the midst of this gridlock, Nabiev – who had already announced his intention to demobilize and disband the Tajik army because he could not pay them – ordered that approximately 2,000 machine guns be distributed to conservative "activists" in Ozodi Square. This was one of the final tipping points to the fragmentation and disintegration of the post-Soviet security infrastructure.[82] The government also released thousands of violent criminals from prison to swell the ranks of its supporters in Ozodi. Kenjayev resigned. On May 5, the Kulobi and Khojandi mobs left Dushanbe in protest. Rather than disband, they organized in their regional strongholds for insurgency, proclaiming their intent to recapture the state by armed force. With the withdrawal of the Leninobodis and their Kulobi allies, the new government was dominated by its loudest and most radical voices. This included a large number of men who were identified – fairly or unfairly – as Islamic fundamentalists, flush with confidence from their successful street protests. Armed militias proliferated in the capital city claiming opaque ties to political parties with radical platforms. Though Nabiev technically remained the President, in practice executive power passed to a small cadre of Pamiri and Gharmi intellectuals headed by Akbarshah Iskanderov, the Deputy President and Prime Minister. Prominent Kulobi and Khojandi elites refused to recognize the legitimacy of the new elite. War followed.

There was substantial unrest and fear in rural areas, as different rural farms organized their young men for war. With no reliable news service, it was difficult for anyone in a rural area to know what was actually happening outside

[81] The question of why agricultural Kulobis saw themselves as natural allies of the old guard Khojandis of Leninobod is addressed explicitly by Lena Jonson and Akiner (1998). In the 1970s and 1980s, Kulob extorted the regime with the threat of subtly escalating violence and forcing the attention of Moscow. Members of the "shadow elite" simply started killing police officers, knowing that if the Khojandis were to call Moscow or Tashkent for help, it might invite cadre reshuffling on the grounds that they could not manage their own republic. As a result, the informal arrangements brought the Kulobis into the Khojandi power structure as "junior partners" – essentially criminal enforcers for wealthy families that owned factories in Leninobod. For a description of how Khojandi cadres played divide-and-rule games to monopolize power for generations, there is no better introduction than Collins (2006).

[82] See Akiner (2001), 37.

of a very small locality. By the beginning of summer 1992, it became clear to
elites in the capital that the governing bargains that had upheld order in the
Tajik state were disintegrating. But news traveled unevenly through *kolkhoz*
networks to outlying rural areas. Village defense militias began to form across
the countryside unevenly. From the perspective of most citizens – including
most militia recruits – there was no way to determine what information was
reliable. It was clear that longstanding political bargains were unraveling
against a backdrop of extreme uncertainty and fear.

By midsummer 1992 the war was fully underway in rural areas. The
basic strategy of both sides was essentially identical – to violently liquidate
the rural population bases from which their opponents recruited.[83] Local
strongmen cannibalized local military garrisons to create voluntary village
defense units. These militias quickly became the primary actors in the civil war.
In the words of one European observer, "Neither side distinguished itself by
humanitarian conduct in the war; ultimately, the side that won committed more
atrocities."[84] Gharmi militias attempted to blockade the region of Kulob, which
was identified as being the main military stronghold of pro-Nabiev groups.
The blockade failed. Kulobi militias emerged as the dominant fighting force
in this period, and displayed a willingness to employ unspeakably gruesome
anti-civilian tactics.

A recurring theme that emerged through extended interviews was an
awareness that the real threat was that the wrong group would end up
in control of the capital city. Even in isolated rural areas, militia recruits
remembered registering awareness that there were profoundly threatening
changes afoot in Dushanbe that had the potential to affect everyone's lives in
the long term, regardless of how the war was resolved. Many of my respondents
had never traveled more than a few dozen kilometers from their place of birth,
let alone to the capital city, before the war. When they described the recruitment
dynamics, it was not surprising that they drew on proximate frames of reference
to describe their mobilization. Their decisions were governed by local insecurity
and local power dynamics constituting what Olivier Roy describes as the "war
of the *kolkhoz*."[85] But local politics in Tajikistan were always in the shadow of

---

[83] The worst atrocities against civilians took place the densely populated rural south where clan
groups were interspersed due to Soviet resettlement policies in the 1940s and 1950s. Use of
population displacement as a strategy to "lock in" a particular demographic group's power
before a peace settlement is a relatively common and well-documented phenomenon. See, for
example, Posen (1993) and Naimark (2002). For an analysis of war crimes in the Tajik civil
war, see Rubin (1993), Bornet (1998), Brown (1998), Gorvin (1998), and Whitlock (2005).
[84] Denber, Rubin, and Laber (1993), xviii.
[85] When Olivier Roy describes the Tajik civil war as a "War of the *Kolkhoz*" he is referring to the
fact that these extremely localized solidarity networks determined social mobilization patterns,
and pitted different village farming communities against one another as they organized militias
and frantically sought allies. In rural areas where state penetration was weak, local feuds
had long been diffused through cross-cutting horizontal networks of elders and influentials
(*gaps* and *gashtaks*). Now these same social networks were used to mobilize young men

Dushanbe, where the real decisions were made, decisions that determined who would get rich and whose children would stay poor. Abdulrahim, an ethnic Uzbek, recalls a speech by "Baba Sangak" Safarov in November 1992, as he rallied troops to march on the capital:

"Baba Sangak [Safarov] called us together … he knew that most of us didn't want to leave our families … we were brave fighters, but we just wanted to defend our homes … but we all decided to go. He said 'They won't come here to block the roads next time, you know – they'll just get the Russians to do it next time, and we won't be able to beat them. If we don't take this chance, Kulob is finished, and everything we just fought for is for nothing. Your daughters will be forced to wear the veil and be thrown from school. Your sons will work in the cotton fields and die poor. And your grandchildren – if they are lucky – will have Pamiri or Russian last names.' That is why we went. To protect what is ours."[86]

These sorts of arguments became commonplace among the literate class. The weeks of public demonstrations in Dushanbe between April and May of 1992 provided a perfect incubator for this sort of radical propaganda to fester on both sides. When the crowds were dismissed, they carried these honed polemics back to their communities. The sense that *"everything* was at stake" became a common theme in important public spaces, such as mosques, *gap* meetings, *kolkhoz* association roundtables, and *chaihonnas* (tea houses), and in private spaces, like around dinner tables, in the hours spent with close friends and co-workers. If a mullah or local police chief could quietly convince the matriarch or patriarch of an influential *avlod* that it was necessary and appropriate to contribute young men to a larger cause, most of the work was already done.[87] Strong hierarchical family ties, reinforced by gendered obligations to "protect the family," probably removed much of the agency from the militia recruit. One of the striking differences between the responses of former Tajik militia members from their Georgian counterparts was that the Tajiks tended to convey a general discomfort with the idea that "joining" a militia was actually choice at all.[88] The instinctive tendency to deny one's

for war. The central question – and one that varied within districts and even within *rayons* (precincts) – was whether these informal networks had sufficient social standing to persuade local law enforcement to defect from their loyalty to the regime and lend their arms to the militias. The general pattern seems to have been that a charismatic field commander, who often emerged from within local security services or the criminal underworld, recruited a core of enthusiastic supporters, and then was legitimized by a local authority figures such as the civil administrators, Islamic mullahs, or *kolkhoz* heads.

86 Interview conducted July 27, 2005 in Kalininobod.
87 Nourzhanov (2005) describes these linkage mechanisms in villages highlands of Kofarnihon, Jirghatal, and Komsomolobod, where "revolts" by "opposition militias" were actually just local police and military garrisons switching sides. Markowitz (2011, 2013) interprets cross-regional data in a way that is consistent with this account.
88 It was regularly described as a forced choice, or a situation where "everyone had to join." Further questioning led to admissions that not everyone joined – that, in fact, many of their

own agency and put the recruitment decision outside of one's own hands was prevalent throughout Tajikistan.[89]

The war activated long-buried community resentments, both within and between *kolkhoz* structures. One common cleavage in the cotton-producing lowlands was between traditional family networks (that could trace their lineage back many generations) and the "Gharmis" (highlanders that were forcibly resettled in the 1940s, 1950s, and 1960s as part of a Soviet population management effort). These groups had long seen themselves as competitors for scarce land and water resources. This trend was particularly acute for recruits who hailed from the rural lowlands of Khatlon, where combatants described intense pressure from family members and community elders to enlist in a self-defense militia and protect their community. "Every [family] had to send a son to go with Baba Sangak [Safarov]," said Oqil, a Kulobi soldier whose family lived in Qabadian about an hour outside of Kurgon-Tubbe. "They ["Gharmis"] had blocked the roads, and we were under siege. They even sabotaged the [irrigation canals], so by the late summer we would have no water. We had to break the blockade."[90] Ghulomjon, a "Gharmi" from the nearby village of Shahri Tuz, presented the mirror-image of the same fears: "Our Rais [district head] came to our home one night and asked for us to donate our rugs and gold, to go to Afghanistan to buy guns. He said that he had heard that the [old government] had opened the prisons and given the criminals guns, and that the local police garrison was disbanding. ... I anyway knew their commander could not be trusted since he was from Kurgon-Tubbe, and would eventually go to be with his family."[91] As Table 3.1 shows, the vast majority of respondents emphasized these sorts of self-defense and family-defense narratives, which often segued into emotional accounts of violent tactics inflicted on family members.

In the highlands of Gharm and Gorno-Badakhshon, militia mobilization was also stoked by local resentments and cleavages against "outsiders," who, in this case, were representatives of urban social networks that had been installed atop the local *avlod* by political decisions made in Leninobod or Dushanbe and backed by Moscow. While walking past the remnants of a now-abandoned *kolkhoz* meeting house, burned during the war, a former combatant from a neighboring town volunteered the observation: "It isn't like it was their farm ... the Russians gave them that farm, for doing someone some favor fifty

---

friends had opted not to join – but it was a patterned contrast with Georgian recruitment narratives.

[89] See Whitlock (2005), 165–168, for additional narratives in this vein.

[90] Interview conducted February 25, 2007 in Dushanbe. There is clearly coercion at work, though less explicit than kidnapping or forced conscription. Respected family elders would be "asked" to "volunteer" one son to join a self-defense militia, with the implicit risk that if this patriotic service were not fulfilled, the family would be branded as disloyal and lose the protection of its local warlord.

[91] Interview conducted February 13, 2007 in Dushanbe.

years ago no one can remember."[92] A striking point of agreement among militia members is that *their* group – whichever group it was – had been unfairly subjected to property expropriation by "the Russians" at some point in the past. It was common to hear that "the best land" and "the best jobs" that had been taken from them and gifted to someone else. The same *gap* and *avlod* structures that were so effective at spreading information and diffusing local tensions also served as powerful receptacles for memories of collective grievance.

Moreover, people intuitively understood that political independence from Russia would provide the opportunity to renegotiate local power and property rights structures. Given the role of cotton in Tajikistan's economic structure, it was not a wise idea to watch this process unfold from the sidelines.[93] A former commander made this point forcefully, when asked about whether he ever used religious appeals to recruit people:

"Islam? Sure, we're all Muslims – but that wasn't why people followed me ... They followed me because I told the truth about the future. Everyone was saying it was a new day, that the future would be bright. But I knew the truth. The future was already spoiled by the cotton. Do you know what cotton does to your hands? Your face? Over a lifetime? No one wants that for their children, their nieces. ... All the while the radio, the politicians – there is an election in the capital, all Soviet lies – they are talking about peace and freedom, like we were idiots, like we could not see with our own eyes. The truth was clear: Some people were going to end up picking cotton, and some other people would lend them money. Call it 'the will of Allah.' Once you say it like this, it is not difficult to recruit friends. Then all that is left to purchase weapons ... and with the [Afghan] border so close and military garrisons everywhere, it was not difficult to do what I did ... once you talked about cotton."[94]

At first, the Russian government, acting through the 201st Motorized Division, tried to assist in the creation of a government of national unity. Though Russian troops remained inside the garrison, it was well understood that Russia's role as kingmaker would be necessary to legitimize any coalition that formed. But recognition was not forthcoming. Perhaps without realizing how it would be interpreted by analysts in Langley and Moscow, Tajikistan's state television network scaled back Russian-language programming and began broadcasting Persian-language programming from the Islamic Republic of Iran.[95] These naive geopolitical missteps, along with general fears that the government could not be a reliable partner, led Russian elites to reject calls to aid the interim government in putting down the rebellions.

---

92 Interview conducted July 30, 2007 in Kalininobod.
93 Cotton mono-cropping dominates the Tajik economy to this day. The most lucrative wealth creation opportunities come from brokering deals with rural *kolkhoz* in the unconvertible local currency, then reselling the final products on the world market and banking the profits in an offshore foreign account. For a detailed discussion of this system, the general contours of which were well understood in the late Soviet period, see Van Atta (2008).
94 Interview conducted May 21, 2007 in Bishkek.
95 Roy (2000), 140.

As the Tajik state disintegrated, the scramble for power was abetted by the intervention of regional governments and nonstate actors. In August 1992, General Abdul Rashid Dostum, a prominent Afghan warlord and an ethnic Uzbek, sent men and material to aid Sangak Safarov and the Popular Front. Ahmed Shah Massoud, a rival Afghan warlord and ethnic Tajik, sent roughly equal numbers of men to support the embattled regime.[96] The government in Uzbekistan was explicitly willing to choose sides and back the well-established Khojandi families, hoping that Tajikistan would emerge as a docile client-state to shield the region from the threat that the chaos of Afghanistan would spread northward.[97] The new Uzbek regime trained, equipped, and provided air support to the Popular Front throughout the spring and summer, and allegedly even sent Ministry of the Interior personnel to assault Dushanbe directly in December 1992.[98]

Russia's official policy was far more circumspect. Russian armed forces stayed neutral, backing both sides indirectly by guarding critical infrastructure in Dushanbe (e.g., bread factories) to ensure that the violence did not spread north to the factories in the Khojandi rust belt.[99] As it became clear that Tajikistan was at serious risk for becoming a theater in the Afghan civil war, the Kremlin finally made the decision to throw its weight behind the Popular Front.[100] In September, Moscow formally declined Iskanerov's plea to send troops or weapons to pacify Kurgon-Tubbe.[101] Dushanbe would fall to the militias of the Popular Front just weeks later. Opposition forces would regroup in Afghanistan and launch an insurgency based in the country's mountainous eastern regions. This warlord counter-coalition, politically reborn as the "United Tajik Opposition," kept the insurgency smoldering for approximately five years.

After seizing the capital, the Popular Front soldiers were encouraged to partake in "punitive reprisals" against supporters of the previous regime – particularly the Pamiri minority group. It is estimated that at least 4,000 families were driven from their homes during the five-week period between January and March of 1993.[102] In January and February of 1993 – the first few

---

[96] Nourzhanov (2005).

[97] Olcott (1997), 123–138.

[98] Denber, Rubin, and Laber (1993), xix.

[99] Gretsky (1995, 1997).

[100] Tajikistan is regularly described as a "center seeking" civil war and Georgia a secessionist conflict. The narrative in this chapter muddles this clean distinction. The growing influence of "center-seeking" Georgian paramilitaries in the politics of the capital city *induced* regional minority groups to bid for secession. This pattern was replicated in Tajikistan after the Popular Front seized the capital. The difference is that the bids for "shadow state" independence in Khojand, Kurgon-Tubbe, and Gorno-Badakhshon failed for lack of a foreign patron, so these secessionist dynamics tended to go unrecorded.

[101] Neumann and Solodovnik (1996).

[102] There are high estimates of tens of thousands of Gharmis and Pamiris being driven from Dushanbe and the surrounding urban and suburban slums during this period.

months after Rakhmonov was installed – collective farms in the south that had not supported the Popular Front were targeted for elimination. Violence was ghastly. Systematic population displacement tactics included the widespread use of public torture, mass shootings, and gang rape. Approximately 90,000 civilians are estimated to have been forced to flee south, fording the icy Amu Darya River to seek refuge in northern Afghanistan. Property and land were transferred to the family members of Popular Front commanders.[103] Many of the men who orchestrated and participated in this campaign of mass killing were immediately granted roles in state security services, locking in the new property rights regime.

THE POST-SOVIET FRONTIER: RUSSIA AFTER EMPIRE

Fighting in both Tajikistan and Georgia was sporadic and disorganized, with criminal hooliganism and violence against civilians far more common than pitched battles.[104] The impromptu armies that fought in these wars often used stolen buses and tractor-trailers as troop transports. Military tactics and basic skills – sighting, shooting, and weapon maintenance – were learned by trial and error by many participants. Given the haphazard organization of these impromptu armies and the low quality of the recruits, it is not surprising that Russian military units intervened to settle almost every single decisive military battle fought on the former territory of the USSR.[105] It was only with military assistance from Russia that South Ossetian and Adjaran militias held back Georgian paramilitaries. Tacit aid from nearby Russian bases eventually became explicit when Abkhaz secessionists were aided by Russian airpower and paramilitary fighters from the North Caucasus in their rout of Georgian army and paramilitary units in September 1993.[106] Artillery from the Russian Black Sea Fleet played a crucial role in the defeat of the Zviadist insurgency, deterring armed resistance in Mingrelia in November 1993.

Having gone to such trouble to define terms formally in Chapter 2, it is a noticeable step backwards to make sweeping claims about what "Russia wanted" or how "Russia acted." Observers continue to disagree on the

103 Olivier Roy (2000) and Charles Fairbanks (2002) have described the neo-feudal arrangements that emerged in rural Tajikistan as the traditional *kolkhoz* and *sovkhoz* structures were doled out to the extended families of victorious warlords. Gorvin (1998) and Whitlock (2005) hint that some of the broad patterns of property rights distribution that were conferred violently in the war persist to this day.
104 The style of fighting in Georgia's wars are well described in Zuercher (2005), especially 115–152, and Popkov (1998). Credible descriptions of the violence in Tajikistan are rarer, but accounts in Rubin (1993), Nassim Jawad and Tadjbakhsh (1995), Leeuw (1999), ICG (2004), and Torjensen (2005) ring true.
105 See de Waal (2003), 200–216 on Russian military influence in Ngorno-Karabakh, which was fought with grisly attrition tactics by Armenian and Azeri military formations. Images were broadcast for consumption to Russian-speaking ex-republics.
106 Derluguian (2005), 236–239.

question of how much this Russian military intervention was the result of deliberate policy in Moscow and how much was the result of improvisational maneuvering on the ground. Though it is difficult to weave a narrative of this period without reverting to realist shorthand, it should be emphasized that Russia was managing its own kind of revolutionary state failure at the time.[107] O'Prey (1996) describes Russian military policy toward civil wars along its borders as "schizophrenic" (415) during this period, suggesting that confused policy – even within a single country – probably reflects a breakdown of command and control.

Was Russia guiding the coalition formation process from behind the scenes? I shared this conspiratorial hypothesis in early interviews in Georgia and was generally rebuffed with tongue clicks and disappointed head shakes. Gia, a former member of the National Guard, said of the Russian role in Georgia's internal wars:

"You need to know what color the pieces are before you can play chess, you know? After Gamsakhurdia, we didn't even have a board! They knew that they couldn't just occupy our country. It's not like Chechnya – we are our own country ... so they knew they needed Georgian friends they could trust, who would not be crazy like Zviad [Gamsakhurdia], and that had the real support of the people. ... but what was the support of the people without an army?"[108]

Russia's 201st Motorized Rifle Division remained in Tajikistan throughout the civil war and served as a kind of weapons depot, allowing Tajik conscripts to desert and fight for their home militia, so long as they left the heavy artillery, helicopters, and combat airplanes behind. Most of my Tajik respondendents reportedly believe that Russian strategic planners were tacit partners in war crimes, allowing mass killings to assess the relative strength of the various warlord factions. A few went further, suggesting that Russian snipers and poisoners had acted directly to trim the opposition of its more radical voices – presumably deterring others from putting voice to dangerous ideas. These conspirational theories are admittedly difficult to falsify. Shirin Akiner's blunt appraisal that "had the Russians wished, they could have decisively altered the course of the war at any time" (46) was confirmed in author interviews with current and former government military personnel. A former lieutenant field commander articulated the general consensus on why they did not: "They

---

[107] There were three different kinds of violent processes playing out simultaneously in Russia. There was revolutionary change – largely peaceful, but punctuated by a military coup – at the top of the power hierarchy in Moscow (see Roeder [1993], Remnick [1994], 431–490; Solnick [1998], and Kotkin [2008]). There was an unreported spike in the Moscow and St. Petersburg murder rates, as criminal organizations competed to fill the void left by the retreating Soviet state; (see Handelman (1995), Volkov (1999, 2002), Varese (2001), and Reno (2002)). And there was violence in the North Caucasus, as Chechnya attempted to secede from Russia.

[108] Interview conducted October 19, 2006 in Chinvali.

wanted us to kill each other, so that we would all see which of us was the strongest ally. Then they step in and smile and talk about peace."[109]

With many carrots and many sticks, it is easy to blame every contour of the outcomes on the Russians. But which units, exactly, were in a position to stop the Kulobis from using scorched-earth tactics to displace populations in the Tajik lowlands? Who could have arrested the bloodletting in Tbilisi in the wake of the Gamsakhurdia coup? Responsible treatment of counterfactuals must acknowledge the possibility that military victory by alternative coalitions in Tajikistan would have led to mass killing in the lowlands of Khatlon with the proper nouns reversed. Perhaps Gharmis would have been the ones revisiting old humiliations on Kulobi *avlod* networks. It is easy to imagine scenarios in which ethnic Georgians in Sukhumi were the ones seizing the best real-estate and – with assistance from Kitovani and armed patrons in the capital – pushing former Abkhaz neighbors north across the frozen mountains into Russia. Russian military professionals could not have been blind to these scenarios. Casual Slavic racism toward peripheral non-Russian peoples is well-understood; the ethnic status hierarchies that defined the Soviet Union were – are – as real as any other sociological construct. Russians, in my experience, still do not afford the victims or perpetrators of violence in their peripheral wars equal intellectual, cultural, moral, or political status. Tofik, who had served in the 201st Motorized Division in Dushanbe, analyzed the Russian dilemma:

"The thing that you have to understand is that the [Slavic] commanders ... they didn't want to stay here. Their families were scared. The Germans and the Russians ... everyone who could leave was leaving! They wanted only to leave the house in order, to stop the Afghan war from coming north. Things would never have gotten so bad if Nabiev had been able to keep a strong hand, like Karimov [in Uzbekistan] ... the Leninobodis, the Kulobis – they were so clever! They knew that the Russians, the Americans, the Uzbeks – no one wanted this country run by clerics like in Iran ... [B]ut why would we [the army] take sides when things are so uncertain? Our commanders had orders to stay out – they said, 'if you want to go to your families and take your guns, you go – but the machines stay, and you can't come back. That would put us all at risk' ... After the Popular Front had already won, then they knew which side they had to be on."[110]

Russia – the former imperial power and future third-party intervener – would be forced to broker with whatever local coalition emerged from the violent crucible. Consider the blunt characterization of a Russian soldier, Sergei, speaking on Russia's role in settling the Tajik civil war:

"After Afghanistan nobody in Moscow had time for another complicated war. [The Tajiks] are so friendly and passive, so I think most people were surprised at how quickly things fell apart here. And once everyone had guns, how could you tell who was who?

109   Interview conducted August 9, 2007 in Dushanbe.
110   Interview conducted February 23, 2007 in Tbilisi.

We got a briefing from a KGB officer in Bishkek before we came down here – he told us that we shouldn't even bother trying to figure this place, with its inbred family politics ... It was really a no-win for Russia – if we left, things would have gotten very bad, and we would have just had to come back ... The Tajik government – if you know them, you know they are peasants and thieves. But what could [Russian Foreign Minister Yevgeny] Primakov do? He said 'Let them have their broken little state, with their cotton and their stupid hats.' After all, war makes its winners ... We care only for the border."[111]

Sergei's quote captures the basic dilemma of Russian military intervention amidst state failure in Central Asia and the South Caucasus. Even when a strong state has clear interests at stake in the outcome of a conflict, no difficulty projecting power, and tremendous access to local intelligence, the unpredictability associated with state failure makes it very difficult to track or shape outcomes. Unlike in Chechnya, where the Russians were willing to fight dirty to keep the population in the Federation, there were no serious plans to occupy and repress the Georgian or Tajik populations directly. Russia's dilemma in both theaters was that although their military units could decisively defeat local armed actors whenever they amassed troops to fight, and thereby secure territory for shadow-state secessionists, it was difficult to sustain the claim that anything achieved would be of lasting strategic value from a Russian point of view. What was needed was for a coalition of Tajik and Georgian violence specialists to emerge capable of managing their own pockets of lower class radicals. The strategic dynamics that emerge once this insight is embraced are modeled in the previous chapter. The details of what this process actually looked like as it unfolded are outlined in the next chapter.

111   Interview conducted April 16, 2007 in Kalikhum.

4

Warlord Coalitions and Militia Politics

For many, the answer to the puzzle of short wars along the post-Soviet periphery is overdetermined: Russia intervened, *only* Russia intervened, and the totalitarian legacy of scientific socialism bequeathed institutions hard-wired for centralization. Large, slow-moving structural variables – inculcated beliefs and geopolitical realities – made for quick and stable war outcomes. But this chapter provides evidence that the great powers did not send money or guarantee regime support until *after* strong clients emerged, through local agreements among armed groups. In the language of the model: Russia was essential to establishing the stability threshold s; outsiders dangled v^*, and locals adjusted. Aid produced new rents, which incentivized warlords to cartel the production of street violence, establish local order in the capital, secure international borders, and keep violence out of sight. Understandings between militia captains had to emerge on the ground before foreigners could help to shore up the fledgling regime with aid and assistance.

This chapter begins by describing the process by which heads of state were selected and installed. The presidents who were selected to head the warlord coalitions in Georgia and Tajikistan were nationalist technocrats with established reputations for honesty and fair-dealing. The people doing the selection were warlords – and in a few cases war criminals with notorious reputations. The figurehead presidents then managed shifting, overlapping coalitions of these criminal interests.

The remainder of the chapter explains how warlords came to understand which of them were "winners" and which were "losers" in the consolidation process. Ceding power to a civilian figurehead carried risks for warlords. Almost everyone had a criminal background and knew that his political immunity could be revoked if the political winds changed. In the interim period after installation but before the "coup-proofing" process was complete, political uncertainty translated into street violence. The number of armed actors expanded during this period. To the extent that there was any disarmament, it was by the losers of the consolidation process who were abandoned by their soldiers once it was clear that their patrons would never be in a position to give them jobs. A model that treats all warlords as essentially interchangeable in this process – subordinating the causal weight of social networks, warlord ideology and charisma, and clandestine foreign interventions – is sure to be a messy fit to either the Tajik or Georgian reality. Whether it is a worse fit than rival two-player "incumbent vs. insurgent" models is for the reader to judge.

EQUILIBRIUM SELECTION: PUPPET PRESIDENTS

In this book, order emerges when some warlords recognize that there are rents to be gained (v^*) from creating a territorial cartel of violence. The central observable implication of the theory is that the postwar government ought to be composed of a large number of warlords and a figurehead president. This president is forced to do the bidding of the warlords who install him because these warlords continue to control the guns, and the president understands that if he does not, he will be replaced by some other public intellectual or representative of the *nomenklatura*. How does this account square with the historical record?

Consider Table 4.1, which displays the coalitions that emerged out of anarchy in Georgia and Tajikistan. In this table a "warlord" is a socially recognized actor who commanded at least thirty armed men at a time.[1] In the inaugural cabinets there was cosmetic attention to creating a sense of political continuity for civilians, with familiar Soviet ministry titles doled out and familiar faces appointed to positions of power. But many of these appointed figures were notoriously characters from the criminal underworld. In Tajikistan, Sangak Safarov, the head of the army, had served twenty-three years in jail for murder. Deputy Prime Minister Rustam Mirzoev had been previously convicted of gang rape – not once, but twice. Yakub Salimov, the face of the Dushanbe mafia, was selected to be the Minister of the Interior. Rauf Saliev, a well-known Dushanbe racketeer and established drug kingpin, was selected to head the new Secret Police. Even the spokesperson for the political opposition – Prime Minister Abdumalik Abdullojonov – had a reputation for being friendly with Khojandi organized crime networks. This was a coalition of conservatives, assembled with an eye to foreign audiences in the emergent Commonwealth Independent State (CIS) security framework. They hoped to signal the emergence of a stable polity that could reassume its place in the old Soviet ethnic hierarchy, subordinated to the suzerainty of Uzbekistan and remaining under the watchful eye of the KGB.

---

[1] The "criminal" moniker is applied conservatively only to individuals who are regularly referenced as criminals in the secondary literature.

TABLE 4.1. *Who Was in Charge after the Post-Soviet Wars?*

Name	Warlord?	Criminal?	Position in Government
The Presidium State Council of Georgia			
Tengiz Kitovani	Yes	Yes	Head of National Guard
Dzhaba Ioseliani	Yes	Yes	Head of the Mkhedrioni
Eduard Shevardnadze	No	No	"Head of State"
Tengiz Sigua	No	?	Prime Minister
First Cabinet of Emomalii Rakhmonov			
Emomalii Rakhmonov	No	No	Head of State/President
Abdumalik Abdullojonov	No	?	Prime Minister
Rustam Mirzoev	No	Yes	Deputy Prime Minister
Yakub Salimov	Yes	Yes	Minister of the Interior
Ghaffor Mirzoyev[a]	Yes	Yes	Deputy Minister of Interior
Sangak Safarov[a]	Yes	Yes	Head of Armed Forces
Alexander Shishlyannikov	No[b]	No	Minister of Defense
Saidamir Zukhurov	No[c]	No	Chairman of National Security Council (NSC)
Rauf Saliev	Yes	Yes	Head of Traffic Police (GAI)
Shurob Kasimov	Yes	Yes	Head of Special Forces
Mahmadnazar Salikhov	No	?	General Prosecutor

? = Reasonable people disagree.
[a] Unofficial cabinet members (attended meetings in "advisory" capacity).
[b] Ethnic Russian, Armed Service Representative of Uzbekistan.
[c] Representative of KGB.

The same basic story plays out in Georgia, but without the Russian influence and with power much more centralized in a celebrity head of state, Soviet Foreign Minister Eduard Shevardnadze. In Georgia, Dzhaba Ioseliani, the head of the Mkhedrioni, was responsible for hatching the plan to invite Shevardnadze back to his homeland to serve on their military council as the head of "his" newly independent state.[2] The conversation between Kitovani and Ioseliani, which debated the wisdom of bringing Shevardnadze back, has spawned many urban legends, but it is clear that the main actors involved in the conversation were anxious about the possibility of being marginalized in a future coalition. Recalling the tactics Shevardnadze used to ascend to the post of the First Secretary of Georgia's Communist Party, Kitovani predicted that they

[2] Wheatley (2005), 69–70. Jonathan Wheatley had the opportunity to personally interview Ioseliani. Ioseliani claims that he was the one who personally telephoned Shevardnadze, and that Kitovani wanted to bring Shevardnadze back as foreign minister only (98, FN7).

would be "dogs on a leash or jailed" within five years.[3] Ioseliani carried the day, arguing that Shevardnadze had spent a lifetime cultivating a reputation for honesty, chaste loyalty to the ideals of the Communist Party, and taking care of his friends. Despite their initial reluctance, both Tengiz Segura (another architect of the military coup against Gamsakhurdia, but with no particularly strong social base) and Kitovani were swayed by the logic that they were more likely to stay afloat financially with Shevardnadze at the helm than with some unknown alternative. There was agreement, however, that Shevardnadze was a potential danger: Ioseliani recalled an understanding between himself and Kitovani that the old man's "hands must be held."[4]

When Shevardnadze returned to Georgia in the spring of 1993, these men were immediately promoted within the power structure and merged their militias into the state armed forces and security services. At this time Zviad Gamsakhurdia was technically still the president of Georgia – it was not until the constitutional referendum of 1995 that Shevardnadze could claim that title for his own. He was initially just one member of an ad hoc military council, a consensus body composed of Ioseliani, Kitovani, and Gamsakhurdia's former Prime Minister Tengiz Sigua.[5] Shevardnadze made symbolic gifts to the warlords, distributing uniforms and titles. Kitovani became the Minister of Defense. Ioseliani held many formal titles including Head of the Emergency Reaction Corps (an autonomous subdivision of the armed forces). One of Ioseliani's hand-picked lieutenants, Temur Khachishvili, became the Minister of the Interior. Kitovani was permitted to parade with sophisticated military hardware procured from high-placed Russian military connections, such as a computerized T-72 tanks. Ioseliani sat beside Shevardnadze in the State Council. Shevardnadze also expressed his friendship with Ioseliani and Kitovani in regular public statements, suggesting that he was personally insulted when people referred to those men as criminals. One of the first things Shevardnadze did was politically rehabilitate the coup-plotters in the most public manner possible, stating in an interview with the *Moscow News*:

Discussing the criminal records of certain people who are my partners now is offensive to me. One should not be reminded of sins committed in youth. On the contrary, I admire the people who had enough strength, will power, and courage to overcome all and make a new start in life. I categorically disagree with those who keep reminding them of their past. Now they are great statesmen. ... Before returning to Georgia I resolved to forget old grudges and abstain from witch hunts.[6]

---

3 This particular quote is almost surely apocryphal, but I reproduce the quotation marks because
   it has the ring of truth. Interview conducted December 14, 2006 in Tbilisi.
4 Wheatley (2005), 70.
5 Wheatley (2005), 69.
6 Quoted in Goldenberg (1994), 93.

The Presidium State Council was run as a consensus body: Every member had a veto over every decision. Every member also had proposal power. This was an unwieldy way to get much of anything done in terms of domestic policy. Not surprisingly, it did not last long. What was most clear from this arrangement was the experiment being embarked: Shevardnadze was allowed to take responsibility for forging an autonomous foreign policy for Georgia, delegating to a small number of warlords the task of keeping the capital city from rioting. This provided a window of time to see what Shevardnadze could do. Five months later, on a hot day in August, Kitovani's militias – now acting in their capacity as the Georgian national army – would invade Abkhazia under the pretense of taking the war to Zviad Gamsakhurdia and his "Zviadists."

In Tajikistan, there was no analogous celebrity figurehead to serve as a focal point for coordination. Safarali Kenjayev, a Hissori who was the former Speaker of the Supreme Soviet, was the founder of The Popular Front of Tajikistan (PFT), a loose coalition of paramilitary groups united by a desire to defend the interests of the groups that had gained the most during the late Soviet period. His faction of the Popular Front was actually the first to capture Dushanbe in October 1992. For a window of about eighteen hours, his men occupied the relevant buildings in the capital city. But other warlords did not coordinate on his ascendency. His soldiers were driven from the capital when it became clear that neither the Russian garrison in Dushanbe nor PFT troops from the south were rallying under his flag.

In mid-November 1992, after three different national rulers had been forced to flee the capital city, the 16th Session of the Supreme Soviet convened in the unusual location of *Arbob Kholkhoz*, a collective farm on the outskirts of Leninobod. This city was the political stronghold of the traditional Khojandi families who had encouraged the formation of the Popular Front. PFT field commanders were visibly in attendance. "Baba Sangak" Safarov himself guaranteed security for the event, and was present at every major meeting. Many of the Gharmi and Pamiri representatives refused to make the journey owing to security concerns and were thus not present for voting.[7] It was decided at this meeting that Nabiev would resign as president and that the office of the presidency would be temporarily abolished. Parliamentarians in attendance voted Emomalii Rakhmonov, a completely unknown figure, into the dual offices of Head of State and Head of Government.

There was no doubt in the minds of any of the assembled representatives that Rakhmonov was Safarov's candidate. They were both Kulobis, both from the same region of Kulob, Dangara, and even from the same subregion of Dangara. In fact, Rakhmonov had been elevated to the post of Sovkhoz Chairman of the Kulob Soviet only a few weeks before this meeting, after the previous Sovkhoz head had been murdered by Safarov on the 28th of October.[8] A

---

7 Whitlock (2005), 177 and Nourzhanov (2005), 118.
8 See Nourzhanov (2005), 117.

government representative recalls a conversation with Rakhmonov the night before he was installed as Head of State in the following way: "He made it clear that the country needed peace, and that peace would require difficult choices. But those choices were not going to come any more at the expense of Kulob. He wanted to build a strong state ... based on the values he had learned in Kulob, and to give charity to the people who had helped him climb."[9] In the prophetic words of Barnett Rubin, the installation of Rakhmonov represented the first signs of "a shift from 'those who held the factories and party personnel committees' to 'those who held the guns.'"[10] Approximately one month later, on December 10, demoralized Pamiri militias finally capitulated and Popular Front forces entered Dushanbe. The capital would not change hands again.

NO DISARMAMENT AND NO EXTERNAL "SECURITY GUARANTEES"

The model in Chapter 2 assumes that after installing a president, warlords will maintain effective control of men and weapons. Power is still about controlling violence, and militias provide leverage to extort the civilian president for ministry jobs. Warlords are permitted to reinvent themselves as reformed political figures, but they keep soldiers on call, ready to mobilize at a moment's notice.

This account closely matches the empirical reality of these post-Soviet settlements. Voluntary warlord disarmament was not an option. In both the hinterlands and secessionist "shadow states," combatants dug in. In the capitals, as civilians watched police forces become saturated with militia members, there were perverse incentives for young men to try to reinvent themselves as warlords and shoot their way into the ruling coalition. Friction between the police and militias was often emblematic of friction between individuals on different sides of the semipermeable state membrane. Weapons proliferated. Many joined the state security services expecting that they would get access to better guns and newer equipment, making it easier to return to the mountains.[11] Abdullo, a Tajik field commander, reflecting on why his United Tajik Opposition (UTO) unit allowed itself to be integrated earlier than those of some of his rivals, recalls that when he had his men take a vote, one of the arguments that carried the day was "wanting to try the new American AK-47s."[12] It was widely understood that field commanders expected to keep some sort of face-saving fallback position if promises were broken down the road. The pervasive culture of street violence and the demonstrated inability of the regime to keep its promises meant that retreating to the mountains

[9]   Interview conducted March 13, 2007 in Dushanbe.
[10] Rubin (1998), 129.
[11] In model parameters: lowering the cost of fighting c and/or raising the reservation value r.
[12] Interview conducted August 11, 2007 in Dushanbe.

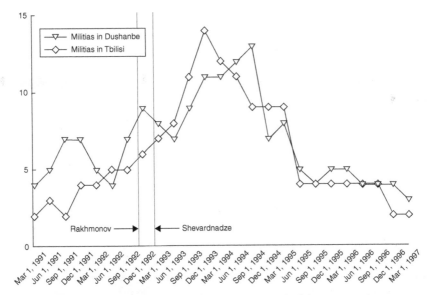

FIGURE 4.1. Nonstate Militias in Dushanbe and Tbilisi, 1991–1996.

was never far from anyone's mind in this period. As Koba, one of my key Georgian informants put it, "the Gamsakhurdia coup sent a clear message: If you can shell the statehouse ... you probably won't be the one starving in the mountains."[13]

Rather than disarmament, what can be easily observed in Figure 4.1 is a proliferation of active militias in the immediate aftermath of Rakhmonov and Shevardnadze's ascensions to power. This was a period of unprecedented militia expansion and fragmentation.[14] The locus of bargaining had shifted to the capital city, and the rush for spoils created perverse incentives for militia expansion.

---

13 Interview conducted December 3, 2006 in Tbilisi. This is not the same "Koba" referenced earlier in the text.

14 The data on the number of militias in the capital over time were coded using newspapers, public records, and trusted third-party reports from the period. Interviews with former combatants were used to clarify the identification of marginal cases where the autonomy of a particular field commander was contested. For a militia to qualify as an independent observation, it had to have at least thirty members, a name, a socially recognized leader who spoke on behalf of a group, and a presence inside the capital city. I constructed a timeline at three-month intervals for both countries; they are superimposed on the same graph for comparison. Coding decisions related to the month-by-month timing of fractionalization of the "umbrella" groups and subordination within ministries were somewhat arbitrary; the broad temporal patterns were uncontroversial when I displayed them to key Georgian and Tajik respondents. The specific names of factional commanders are omitted for reasons discussed in Appendix C.

State weakness is often presented as a permissive condition for the proliferation of violence entrepreneurs – and in one sense it was in these cases. After
all, there was no one to make arrests. But note that, in this account, it was
actually the expectations of a *strengthening* state that led to the expansion
and fragmentation of militias. The promise of future bilateral aid from foreign
donors increased the value of the prize being fought over. Violence between
factions was replaced by violence that was essentially within the winning
faction. Sustained and intense intraethnic violence followed.

Militias did eventually disappear, not because they were disarmed, but
because their memberships disintegrated or switched commanders as warlords
were forced out of the violence game. This happened rapidly. Though none
surrendered their weapons, many groups "dissolved" – whatever social capital
that sustained them broke apart, and recruits went their separate ways. Viewed
through this lens, the violence during this period is best understood as a product
of a high-stakes tournament between paramilitary militia groups, competing to
be part of the winning coalition selected by the installed president. Aided by
young men recruited with promises of plunder and patronage, some militia
captains became valuable assets for the regime, while others were driven from
the capital city at gunpoint.

It is difficult to sustain the case that any of this was the result of plans
hatched in Moscow. As a Tbilisi diplomat put it: "Independence for these
republics meant that the angry people with the long last names just weren't
Moscow's problem anymore."[15] Eduard Shevardnadze was an agent of the discredited Communist Party and the even-more-discredited Gorbachev regime.[16]
Rakhmonov was a complete unknown – a political wildcard compared to
the fully vetted prime minister, Abdumalik Abdullojonov. This is not to say
that Russian preferences for foreign aid, military assistance, and diplomatic
recognition were absent from the minds of Georgian and Tajik warlords. It is
just that local actors were more than capable of anticipating Russian demands
and providing foreigners with much of what they expected to see before anyone
in Moscow thought to publicly ask for it. A common strategy employed by both
Rakhmonov and Shevardnadze was the practical move of installing a Russian
general as the Minister of Defense (or an ethnically Russian Uzbek general in the
Tajik case), which pre-positioned them to leak information back to Moscow.
I interpret this move as evidence that the new governments had a potential
agency problem with Moscow that they were anxious to solve.

---

[15] Interview conducted April 28, 2006 in Tbilisi.
[16] Eduard Shevardnadze tried to go "over the heads" of local militia actors and secessionist
warlords alike and deal directly with players in Moscow to reincorporate Abkhazia and South
Ossetia. He was rebuffed, partially for refusing to join the CIS and partially because of personal
disputes with elites in Moscow who wanted to see him fail. Later, forces in Moscow would be
implicated in multiple assassination attempts against him.

Chapter 2 provides an account of "full incorporation" after insurgents' reservation values drop and they scramble to cut the best deal that they can. The basic logic of the mechanism suggested by the model – declining reservation values – can occur with or without third-party security guarantees to a postwar regime. This part of the account also fits the post-Soviet empirical record quite closely. Russian elites did not even bother articulating an interest in serving as honest brokers, and were overall neither capable of, nor interested in, punishing regimes in newly sovereign states for reneging on local promises to insurgent warlords. Moscow's consistent rhetorical promise, to the extent that it was coherent, was to aid the Tajik government as it pressed hold-outs and to defend secessionist minority enclaves against the threat of the Georgian paramilitaries.

In Tajikistan, reasonable people have confused the actions of prominent Russian field commanders or members of the Soviet 201st Motorized Rifle Division, who would give or sell weapons to both sides, with official Russian policy. In my view, Russian policy was calibrated toward cauterizing violence and stopping the chaos from spreading beyond Tajikistan's borders. Russia's nightmare was that Afghan warlords and American-funded Mujahideen would ally with the UTO and infect the entire region with radical ideology.[17] Russia was also interested in a great many other things. Russia needed to manage the relationship with the newly sovereign state of Uzbekistan, which wanted to continue supporting traditional Khojandi client networks with strong Uzbek ties. Russian diplomats prioritized establishing legal precedents for CIS intervention into the near abroad. As will be discissed in detail later, diplomatic efforts by Moscow to facilitate peace talks (often jointly with Iran and the United Nations) occurred alongside direct military support for counterinsurgency. Keeping the Tajik state intact as a buffer zone, and hoping that radical Islamists would self-select into that mountain theater to be killed, passed as strategy in the early 1990s. The Yeltsin government otherwise had its hands full trying to establish its own domestic authority at home.

What possible "security guarantees" could the Russians have credibly offered to Tajik civil war participants under these conditions? There was no indication that anyone in Moscow thought it was even worth learning the names of the main actors in the Tajik civil war until sometime midway through the 1997 Peace Process. As a former high-ranking UN member and observer of the inter-Tajik peace talks stated, "The main misunderstanding of

---

[17] Akiner (2001) reproduces rumors of more than thirty military training camps, mostly on the territory of Afghanistan, run by Mujahideen and Arab instructors (FN 16, p. 43). Ahmed Rashid (2002) suggests that by the end of the Tajik civil war, the UTO began to act like a real army, mostly because of the training and support from the Uzbek warlord Abdul Rashid Dostum, who was operating in northern Afghanistan. Most former Russian military and civil war participants interviewed tended to be skeptical of Rashid's position, emphasizing that different field commanders remained essentially self-financing and autonomous by colluding with state militias to transport narcotics.

the United Tajik Opposition was that they were 'united.' The second major misunderstanding, at least by the end, was that their 'opposition' was political in any way. The war gave these men cover, but their motives never matched well with their rhetoric. … These were gangsters, pure and simple."[18] There was little political coherence binding together the opposition militias of the UTO. Many warlords used *noms de guerre* or sent cousins or nephews to negotiate in their stead. From the perspective of civilians living in contested regions, this was a time of unchecked banditry, looting, and terror.

The situation in the South Caucasus, where the conflict broke down over territorial lines, was different. Russian policy in Georgia raised the reservation value for Abkhaz and South Ossetian warlords so high that no offer from Shevardnadze could make them better off than they already were behind the shield of Russian guns and UN flags. This *did* had the effect of providing security guarantees to certain non-Georgian ethnic insurgents who had seized administrative structures in Abkhazia, South Ossetia, and Adjara.[19] But the direct result of this support was the ethnic cleansing of Georgians by Abkhaz and South Ossetian militias. The next two decades of cold tension make it clear that Russian policy did not provide an efficacious framework for general disarmament or conflict deescalation. Just as Russian backing for ethnic minority militias had served as a recruiting tool for the Mkhedrioni and National Guard units (who could then claim to be acting to protect, or avenge, their brethren), ongoing Russian support for the territories reinforced the necessity of a strong Georgian army to stand up to Russia, undo military humiliation, and recapture lost territory.

URBAN WARFARE: THE TIME OF TROUBLES

By January 1, 1993, war reporters would describe both the Tajik and Georgian capitals as controlled by a militarily dominant coalition of paramilitaries. The Popular Front had driven their opponents across the Tajik border into Afghanistan or into the impassable Pamiri mountains of Badakhshon to freeze to death. The forces of the Mkhedrioni and the National Guard – which would soon prove incapable of imposing their will on the Russian-backed secessionist enclaves of Abkhazia, Adjara, or South Ossetia – were in control of Tbilisi.

While war had raged in rural areas the state apparatus had continued to provide many public goods for most civilians in the capital. Buses continued to run. Schools continued to operate. Citizens kept their heads down and went about their routines. Bread factories kept pushing out *non* (bread) in Tajikistan, and the metro subway system kept hauling young men and women

---

[18] Interview conducted December 4, 2005.

[19] Darchiashvili (1997a), 2-7. It practically goes without saying that certain Georgian nationalists tend to see Russian fingerprints everywhere. This approach whitewashes the nihilistic anarchism that took root among the Georgian political elite, the ethnically exclusivist radical populism that seized the streets, or the criminal behaviors of the new military caste.

to dates across Tbilisi. Most of the militia members believed that they were owed something by the civilians back in the capital who were the beneficiaries of their protection and sacrifice. A key respondent voiced a common complaint heard by many veterans of Abkhazia:

"Back in Tbilisi life went on pretty much as before. There were parties, wine, weddings, graduations … People bought cars and planned for their future. But we'd been fighting for their behalf! For their kids! I watched friends get shot! For them! And then it was over and we came home they were like 'Oh, that war was such a tragedy.' They didn't help, and didn't know a thing about it! So yeah, we were mad."[20]

Militia members confronted an unpaid Soviet-era police structure that was cut off from political and material patronage in Moscow. Urban citizens recall two distinct waves of urban violence after Dushanbe and Tbilisi fell into the hands of ruling paramilitary factions. The first was a chaotic reign of terror when militia members were encouraged by commanders to claim their share of the spoils of victory in the form of looting.[21] Bahron, who was a pastoralist in Kulob and never had visited Dushanbe before the war, remembers a sense of betrayal and resentment that he felt toward the civilians in the capital:

"We came into this city and realized that they had everything, these Pamiris and Leninobodis. We finally saw with our own eyes that [their commander] Hussein had been telling the truth – the Russians had been sending money to Tajikistan for years, but these men in the capital had stolen it! All their homes had glass windows and gas. We knew … that we had been fools to spend so many winters in the cold."[22]

This relatively short period of unchecked looting, lasting only weeks, was replaced by a very long, very tense stand-off between the armed groups. The second wave of urban violence came only many months after the carnival of violence had subsided after the end of major combat operations. With both capitals awash with cheap weaponry and angry young men, militia captains became power brokers, managing the resentments and expectations of their soldiers. Insecurity gripped the urban centers of Dushanbe and Tbilisi for months. As warlords began to merge their forces with the security services of the captured regime apparatus, appropriating for themselves positions in the Ministry of Defense, Interior, State Security, and other power ministries, it became impossible for civilians to tell police from criminals. Residents of Tbilisi and Dushanbe recall this period as "The Time of Troubles."

And then the violence stopped. Lifetime residents of these capital cities agree substantially on the month – sometimes down to the week or the day – that order was restored in their neighborhood. Violence broke out in these states slowly, as a result of accumulating processes of escalation through the late

---

[20] Interview conducted December 4, 2006 in Tbilisi.
[21] This resonates with more general accounts of "carnival" and "revenge" following military victory by criminalized armies in Yugoslavia and elsewhere. See Mueller (2000), 54–56.
[22] Interview conducted August 14, 2007 in Dushanbe.

Soviet period. Peace, by contrast, broke out virtually overnight.[23] Figure 4.1 suggests that by the end of 1995, most militias had retreated or dissolved. Dushanbe and Tbilisi were patrolled by uniformed police officers, some of whom did not feel the need to carry weapons. To the delight of the international aid community and foreign diplomatic corps, prominent militia commanders were arrested. Anarchy on the streets subsided.

Driving militias from the capital city was considered a tremendous victory for state-building. But where did these police forces come from? What processes were sustaining urban violence during the "Time of Troubles," and why did those processes come to an end? And if it was possible for the forces of order to triumph so quickly and completely, why did it take so long for the "tip" toward order and security to occur?

The "Time of Troubles" occurred in the relatively brief period after Dushanbe and Tbilisi had changed hands, but before the emergence of a secure regime, when militia members had the opportunity to convert their short-term social capital into long-term life opportunities. It was a window of time characterized by deep uncertainty about the final shape of the postwar coalition. It was also a period when the foot soldiers felt the window closing on their ability to make heroic demonstrations of their worth to their commanders. Competition became violent, as the wartime coalition splintered apart and different militia groups cannibalized each other's memberships. Political actors supported large militias as insurance against being trimmed from the spoils of victory. As described in the previous chapter, many militia members were lured into service by non-collateralized promises of future employment by their patron. Once external events clarified membership in the ruling coalition, large militias became obsolete. The promises of many would-be patrons were suddenly worthless. It took only days for militia recruits to switch commanders or quit the streets.

Scholars' failure to account for the sudden disappearance of urban militias reflects a more general failure to properly account for the motivations of combatants in the post-Soviet wars.[24] That the bargains between warlords

---

[23] The autumn of 1994 for Tajikistan and the summer of 1995 for Georgia are typically cited. In Dushanbe, stability and order did not emerge seamlessly; there was territory just outside the city limits where government forces could not safely traverse until the late 1990s. But there was a second-tier drop-off in urban violence in late 1994 when the departure of the militias removed the feeling of an urban war zone, making the city center safe for foreign embassies, intergovernmental organizations, and NGOs to open their doors.

[24] There are two main reasons that the spectacle of urban violence has received relatively short shrift. The main reason is that the patterns of urban violence cut cleanly across the "master cleavage" of the civil war: Georgians were murdering other Georgians, and Tajiks from the same region were killing each other in the streets of the capital. The urban violence simply did not fit the story that most people were telling. As such this period of *intrafactional* violence tends to be treated as an afterthought in otherwise excellent case studies. It is typically described as a period of general state failure, criminalized "bandit patriotism," or (most commonly of all) "anarchy." Even the best descriptive accounts of the period tend to describe it in vague

and their subordinates could disappear overnight undermines the idea that
the sustained presence of militias can be explained by theories that rely on
slow-moving structural factors such as state weakness, easily accessible cultural
repertoires of violence, deep primordial solidarities, or psychopathy.[25] Up
until the moment that they departed the streets of the capital, *the departing
militia members explicitly considered themselves part of the state*, and believed
themselves to be well positioned to contest their share of the rents of
statehood. Rather than imagining these groups through the various analogies of
"ethnic armies," "mafia businessmen," or "criminal thugs" during this period
these groups can be productively thought of as participants in a high-stakes
tournament. Warlords struggled with the problem of recruiting and retaining
volunteers in an environment where money had lost value. Militia members
were trying to help their paramilitary captain secure a good position in the
consolidating regime among a complex and uncertain environment.

How were the stakes of this violent tournament understood? Having lived
through the rampant corruption of the late Soviet period, the emergent
violence entrepreneurs understood that the best opportunities for a better
life required affiliation with the government. Interviews with militia members
from rural areas revealed shared understandings with their urban counterparts
on this point: life was better inside the state. Foot soldiers watched as
warlords and their lieutenants secured virtual empires inside the new ministries,
inheriting centralized proto-industrial economies, with numerous bottlenecks
in the provision of public goods, each an opportunity for rent-seeking. The
ability to issue passports or transit permits, or operate buses or trucking
businesses without fear of being stopped at checkpoints, blurred the line
between smuggling and trade. Consumer goods of all kinds traveled by road to
the post-Soviet capitals. Liquor, gasoline, drugs, and cigarettes were the most
profitable trade goods, but food was imported as well. Entrepreneurs with

---

terms (e.g., "militias ruled the streets"), then provide a description of a changed situation
with no reference to what mechanisms produced or sustained the change (e.g., "order was
restored"). For Georgia, see Aves (1996) 5, 54–55; Darchiashvili (1997b), 3; O'Ballance (1997)
112, 133, 152–160; Leeuw (1999) 182–183; Demetriou (2002), 26; Devdariani (2005), 167;
and Zuercher (2005) 137, 148; There is virtually no scholarship on the urban aspect of the
war in Tajikistan. The narrative of state failure and anarchy emerged as a constant theme in
conversations with current and former European embassy employees and local academics – see
Akiner (2001), 37–44; Whitlock (2005); and Lezhnev (2006), 51–72. A secondary reason is
that most of the men who were the targets and perpetrators of violent tactics were disposable
and anonymous. The bilingual elites of the Soviet academy were (understandably) unwilling
descend into the streets and survey the opinions of the angry, violent, unpredictable young men
from rural areas who had taken over the streets.

25 For explanations that rely on state weakness, see Gambetta (2002), Volkov (2002),
and Lezhnev (2006). For explanations that rely on cultural repertoires of violence, see
Mardin (1978) and Shabad and Liera (1994). For explanations that rely on psychological
predispositions, see Fanon (1968), Stinchcombe (1968) and especially Mueller (2000) and
Petersen (2002).

money, property, or connections could buy police divisions wholesale with a few well-placed appointments. Private armies could mediate contract and wage labor disputes. Criminal kingpins and warlords were the pivot players, as they managed the armed forces that could bring the whole system down. As the security services formed and re-formed, commanders used their armies like lobbyists to jockey for power, influence, and privileged jobs.

The fighters, who had often made great personal sacrifices in an attempt to transform their society, wanted these jobs. The wars terminated in a way that settled none of the underlying grievances that motivated young men to fight. If they could not achieve their deepest desires, they could at least be realistic about compensation for their sacrifices and labor. Not all jobs were equal. The most coveted positions were in subsections of the Ministry of the Interior and the Border Guards, as it was well understood that these jobs could be immediately converted into tax farming and smuggling rents. Because the politics of privatization were being worked out at the same time as the civil wars were being settled, being in the police was a path to nearly instant racketeering wealth. The liquidity of property rights made mutually beneficial transactions between criminals and residual *nomenklatura* transparent. In both countries, the traffic police was a regulated system of roadblocks, controlled stops, and bribes. The worst jobs tended to be in the army, as it often left soldiers stationed outside the capital or tasked with conducting grinding, thankless counterinsurgency operations in the mountains. Particularly in Tajikistan, the army came to be seen as a dumping ground for the least politically connected militias. But at least it was a job.

The evidence that follows suggests that there was a powerfully simple logic to the violence in this period. Militia members were recruited into militias by either the lure of short-term benefits (e.g., excitement, racketeering rents) or the hope of long-term jobs in the consolidated regime. These benefits were weighed against the probability of injury or death that came with entering the violence game under the leadership of a particular militia captain. Promises of jobs were always conditional on the militia captain being incorporated into the regime. Because it was impossible to predict what the final membership in the ruling coalition would be, it was very difficult for warlords to make promises of spoils credible to their memberships.

One of the main strategic behaviors that militia recruits engaged in when faced with this uncertainty, was switching militias. As Table 4.2 makes clear, side-switching during and after the civil war was relatively common, particularly after major combat operations were concluded. It was common for small groups of men recruited in the same neighborhood or village to "move together," as this would give them protection and bargaining power within the new militia structure after switching commanders.[26] Side-switching

---

26 As Table 3.1 from Chapter 3 reports, identical percentages of Tajiks and Georgians (about 80 percent in both subsamples) expressed that one should never really trust anyone "not in

TABLE 4.2. *Evidence of a Street Violence Market: Militia Members Switched Patrons*

Variables	All (%)	Georgian (%)	Tajik (%)
Switched Commanders at Least Once during Civil War	35	45	25
Switched Commanders at Least Once after Civil War	31	47	17
Quit His Militia When He Felt His Life Was at Stake	38	52	24
Observations	173	84	89

was more prevalent in Georgia than in Tajikistan. In Georgia, these close trust networks could be reinserted as a full-module into a different commander's network (allowing "horizontal" movement between militias). In Tajikistan the *avlod* obligation networks that connected recruits and commanders (a "vertical" relationship, sustained by the shared shame of disappointing an invisible audience of second cousins and distant matrons) yielded systematically different behaviors: Tajiks in my sample were unlikely to desert from a militia even when their lives were at stake, and members tended to remain in the service of the commander who recruited them. The obvious impetus for side-switching was when a commander was killed. In Georgia, by contrast, almost half of the respondents in my sample switched commanders at least once during the war, and nearly four-fifths switched at least once.[27]

As discussed in the previous chapter, all of this manifested as an emerging futures market in political favoritism. Violence during this period was an indirect byproduct of high-stakes bargaining between paramilitaries competing over the spoils of victory. Some militia captains – with the assistance of young men recruited with promises of plunder and patronage – became valuable assets for the regime and earned shares of black market goods and services. Others were driven from the capital city at gunpoint. Understanding how militias were recruited can provide insight into changes in the meaning of the violence as the war progressed. The price of social order, at least in the minds of many soldiers, was making sure that the distribution of wealth and influence squared with leaders' demonstrated ability to organize violence. If it could not, there were strong incentives for newcomers to try and break into the system, hoping to be bought out.

your family," which speaks to similar cultural scripts on this matter across both of the study populations.

[27] Tajik respondents were also more than twice as likely to report that they trusted their immediate commander. My data make it impossible to discern whether this was a cause or effect of the pervasive Georgian militia-switching.

Kinda like the
U.S. military

A POLITICAL ECONOMY OF MILITIAS: EXPANSION AND
CONTRACTION IN FOUR PHASES

In the post-Soviet wars, the decision to join a militia amounted to risking one's life in exchange for a short-term mix of security and loot, and the long-term promise of better life opportunities if a recruit aligned himself with a worthy patron. The participants in this violent scramble understood that some warlords would be in the coalition assembled by the president and others would be marginalized. The men who were the most likely to join these militias tended to be either serially unemployed or temporary true believers. There was an overabundance of young men willing to forego safer life opportunities for the excitement of holding a gun. Separating the wheat from the chaff required a sort of tournament among militia captains: a sorting process to determine which individuals had the most talent for convincing others to fight on their behalf.

One of the central characteristics of the post-Soviet wars is that they were fought with voluntary labor in states with few meaningful institutions. There was no trusted national currency, no banking system, and no courts to enforce contracts. The nature of the spoils being fought over required political capital – but the political center had already been shown to be vulnerable to rapid disintegration. The leaders ("warlords") and followers ("recruits") had come of age in a social system where kin networks were necessary for everyday life. Friends and allies drew on dense networks of social capital, and joined militias on the intuition that getting a foothold inside the new state bureaucracy represented their best chance to increase their life opportunities. In one sense, there were a few analytically distinguishable kinds of uncertainty: uncertainty by a recruit over the character of the warlord (whether a patronage relationship was incentive compatible), uncertainty by a recruit over which warlords would emerge inside the "shadow state" at the end of the coalition-formation process (whether the warlord would ever actually be in a position to dispense patronage), and uncertainty by the patron warlord about the quality of a recruit.

The brutal tournament cut through these layers of complexity to address the central question: When the chips were down, which warlords could organize violence most efficiently? This question could be answered only in real time, and with deeds, not words. The brutal urban warfare that emerged during the "Time of Troubles" resolved the three kinds of uncertainty in the emerging market for militia labor. It reduced uncertainty for militia members about which warlords were able to recruit large groups of capable fighters, driving charlatans and incompetents away. It reduced uncertainty for militia captains about the loyalty, fighting capability, and overall resolve of their men. And, in the end, it reduced everyone's uncertainty about which warlords were likely to end up in the winning coalition and be able to deliver on their promises of patronage. The gang war in the streets accomplished what the war itself had not – it screened the unfit members from the mob, let everyone gauge their relative strength accurately, and finally allowed them to select a minimum winning coalition.

Most civilians' primary memory of this period is being caught between different spheres of authority. The practical effect was often competitive racketeering: double and triple taxation for those unlucky stragglers who could not, or did not, hide their wealth. Consider this story from a Dushanbe-based musician:

"I had a friend who loved rock music. After independence... he could make good business on the street just selling copies of his Led Zeppelin tapes. The problem was that guys who worked for the government ... they never paid. They'd come and pick over his merchandise, take what they wanted. Then the tax police would come and do the same thing. Then guys from the army. Then some guys came who claimed they were with the mayor? Then the same local police came by again – guys from [his neighborhood]. He tried to complain. They said there was nothing they could do – that everyone had to chip in and be patriotic. So after a while, he just stopped. He figured somebody would steal from him no matter what, but he didn't count on lots of different people stealing.[28]

ANARCHY? SAME AS HOBBES STATE OF nature?

With no functioning state authority capable of centralizing control of the militias and paying wages, there was not an obvious solution to the problem of public order. Disputes over who exactly was permitted to profit from informal tax structures led to infighting between warlords. Directors of profitable national industries began to be killed with regularity. Informal taxation schemes were improvised to divide up territory and spoils between warlords. There was no recognized authority to split tax rents. As the various warlords ascended to ministry positions, new lieutenants had to step up and prove themselves.

Various militia captains – the de facto providers of urban order – were suddenly thrust into the midst of everyday governance dilemmas that could not be delegated or deferred. How would food be distributed to families who could not afford to pay? Where would the influx of refugees from rural areas be housed? What sorts of punishments should be meted out against people accused of crimes? Who gets to carry a gun? What should be done with aspiring journalists who are bearing witness and naming names?[29]

---

28 Interview conducted February 21, 2007 in Dushanbe.
29 It was especially unsafe time to be an aspiring journalist or photographer. Armed actors, especially in Tajikistan, had an interest in keeping certain details from being recorded. A partial list of murdered Tajik journalists from this period, assembled in Panfilov (2003): Murodulla Sheralizoda (May 5, 1992), Olim Zarobek (May 6, 1992), Shirindzhon Amridzhon (May 26, 1992), Emilia Podobed (June 1992), Turadzhoni Kobil (October 1, 1992), Olimdzhon Iorasen (October 1992), Tabakkal Faizullo (October 1992), Ahror Sharif (December 9, 1992), Saidmurod Iorien (January 1993), Abdulhakim Shukurzoda (April 21, 1993), Pirimkul Sattori (May 28, 1993), Hushvaht Haidarsho (May 19, 1994), Hamidzhon Hakimov (November 18, 1994), Muhiddin Olimpur (December 12, 1995), Zuhuruddin Suiiari (April 26, 1996), Viktor Nikulin (March 28, 1996).

The solutions to many of these problems required cooperative arrangements between different neighborhoods. This meant either cooperation between militia captains or expansion of one militia at the expense of another. So long as the residual fears about the potential for a reignited wider conflict justified their existence, there was substantial social support for popular captains to keep their armies intact and throw their weight around the capital. But some inevitably began to gaze nervously up the hierarchy, trying to determine who had actually secured a "roof" and who had not.[30] Competitive pressures led militia captains to expand their recruit pool and to target each other.

There were two different sorts of newcomers to the violence game: new foot soldiers (essentially "new cheap labor," seeking to prove themselves as muscle) and new organizers (essentially "new violent social capital," seeking to establish themselves as political entities and potential patrons). Because all of these groups lacked formal uniforms and many commanders relied on pseudonyms and *noms de guerre*, it was relatively easy to put on a black leather jacket and take to the streets. Some of these men came from various corners of the capital, and some came from rural areas or other towns. Once a few promising up-and-comers had been incorporated into the police force, there was no obvious way to limit entry into the violence market. The general tactic was to promise permanent jobs (with pensions) in exchange for service. This futures market in political favoritism depended on a recruit's belief that his patron would eventually be in a position to make good on this promise.

It is important to note that there are two separate audiences for the theater of militia arms-racing. First, the different militia commanders were competing with each other for limited space at the political trough. Political parties were brokering with armed groups and choosing which militia factions could make good on offers of security. Weak commanders were potential targets for dismemberment by established captains or by new organizers trying to break into the violence game by making a name for themselves. Second, commanders had a similar incentive to signal to potential militia recruits that they were capable patrons. Recruitment was based on promises – "cheap talk" – mediated by potential members' expectations that the warlord would be capable of paying them down the road. This was a probabilistic assessment. Was a captain's star rising or falling? A militia captain who could not convince recruits to join up or recruit allies would be identified as weak and vulnerable. The sense

---

30 The language of the "roof" is inherited from Soviet times. As Fairbanks (1996) notes, strong informal rules from Soviet times prohibited the betrayal of patrons. Advantage was gained by loyalty to the party apparatus and deference to a small number of "administrative gatekeepers" (369–372). The well-studied tendency for "cadres" to move vertically and horizontally through the Soviet party structure is a phenomenon that has analogies in most armies, political parties, and bureaucracies. This is perfectly compatible with prominent models of clientelism or patronage politics developed in other parts of the globe: ideally, someone two or more tiers higher in a hierarchy will ensure that a lower-ranked individual's interests are represented.

that "winners win," and that success was the best predictor of future success, drove many militia captains in Tajikistan and Georgia to escalate neighborhood violence. Captains took serious risks to provoke responses from other militia captains so that they could establish a reputation for courage and staying power. It was better to be an agent of a strong, politically ascendant warlord than a weak one.

The processes unfolded in five analytically distinguishable phases. ✳

? HE only CLEARLY IDENTIFIES 3

Phase 1: Warre

The breakdown of social order that accompanied the first months of independence provided an opportunity for unemployed youth to shoot guns, escape the boredom of their daily lives, experience the thrill of taking part in demonstrations, and commit petty criminal acts. As noted earlier, all of the armed groups that fought in the post-Soviet wars developed criminal characteristics and recruited from the urban and rural underclass. Yet to treat these groups as nothing more than roving bands of criminal alcoholic youths intentionally misunderstands the nature of the social bonds that kept these groups in the field.[31] A Tajik field commander, explaining why he recruited primarily from his karate dojo, stated: "I needed men who were serious. I knew things would get bad, and I wanted men who I trusted to watch my back."[32] A former Mkhedrioni member echoed this – "Of course there were kids and drunks around. But that's not what [the bosses] needed. They needed reliable people. We were building an army, not a gang. We were reclaiming the nation from the Russians."[33] Interview respondents in both countries often freely admitted that other men in their unit were alcoholics, drug addicts, and troublemakers who liked violence for its own sake – but they were also usually quick to note that those men tended to be bad soldiers who could not see the big picture or keep their peers' respect.[34] No one wants to risk his life for a drug addict or sadist.

---

[31] My attempt to describe these groups is found in Chapter 3. For an eloquent presentation of a simpler alternative perspective, see Mueller (2000).

[32] Interview conducted July 26, 2007 in Dushanbe. Later in the interview, he added: "Not everyone likes to hit."

[33] Interview with Nicholas Rurua, currently serving in the Georgian parliament. Interview conducted December 03, 2006 in Tbilisi.

[34] This is broadly consistent with a number of sociological works on the organization and composition of gangs. Peripheral members are often relatively violent and difficult to control, but the members of this disorganized milieu tend to be trying to impress the core of competent and disciplined organizers who manage economic and political relationships. See Jankowski (1992) and Venkatesh (2007, 2008). Almost none of my respondents identified themselves as free-riders, of course. It is possible that this reflects a systematic bias in my interview pool, but I believe it is more likely that interview respondents presented idealized versions of their own motivations and actions and attributed less favorable characteristics to others.

The "master cleavage" of the war dominated targeting decisions and pogrom behaviors in this period. In Dushanbe, Gharmi, Karategini, and Pamiri neighborhoods were essentially cleansed through targeted campaigns of murder and rape. The property deeds of the victims' homes – sold at a tremendous loss – were transferred to real estate speculators with political connections to the Popular Front or the new regime.[35] In Georgia, though there was a similar deluge of anarchy in which ethnic minorities faced harassment and humiliation on the streets, neighborhoods were not purged in the same way. Families could largely stay indoors and wait out the chaos. In response to this wave of urban violence, many citizens closed their businesses, stayed indoors, or fled the capital. Many people kept their distance from the militias in the 1991–1993 period. The collapse of public order and economic life meant that the spoils of victory were uncertain, and joining one of these groups required participating in a culture of violence that was repulsive to civilized people.

Phase 2: Opportunistic Joiners in the Aftermath

Recruiting dynamics changed once the capital city was under the control of a strong militia coalition. Potential recruits realized that there was a real possibility that victorious militia commanders would actually be able to make good on their promises. But the final ruling coalition was still in flux. Everyone knew that political fortunes were uncertain. On one hand, it was very difficult for anyone to determine which commanders were lying (to themselves, as much as to potential recruits) about their future political fortunes, or to determine which commanders were simple opportunists. On the other hand, capturing the capital city or acquiring a position of status was no longer hypothetical – political power was suddenly fluid and tangible. Ministry portfolios were actually being doled out, often to well-known criminals, as political acknowledgment of certain individuals' armed strength. The stakes of victory in the consolidation game were clarified as foreign aid began to trickle into state coffers.

Without any functioning state bodies to arrest them, and without any real risk of dying in war to deter them, many young men were attracted to the seductive glamour of life with a nationalist militia.[36] A tertiary milieu of young

---

35 The character of the ruling coalition that supported Rakhmonov was never clearer than in the treatment of "enemy" ethnic groups after the state was seized. Militia members in Tajikistan were encouraged to "drive [the Pamiris] back to their mountains" by their captains, leading to a highly organized campaign of civilian displacement and property expropriation by the new Kulobi rulers. Interview conducted August 4, 2007 in Kulob. This had the effect of raising the political stakes of politics significantly in Tajikistan, making control of the state apparatus an all-or-nothing game. It was a tactic that was quite useful in uniting the various factions of the Popular Front for a time.

36 Interviews with participants and "opportunistic joiners" revealed three broad sets of explanations for missing the war. First, many were simply deterred by the threat of dying in the

men – the sort who already knew that they were not likely to grow up to be middle-class professionals – were always available, anxious to ascend through violent rituals to manhood. In the chaotic environment sketched previously, it was relatively easy for a newcomer to "pass" as a member of almost any group, if a few others would vouch for him.[37]

At the same time that the supply of youth on the streets was expanding, field commanders, militia captains, paramilitary lieutenants, and other wartime coalition members who controlled the capital were increasing their demand for new recruits. With the spoils of victory being divided in real time, everyone – militia captains, paramilitary lieutenants, and foot soldier recruits alike – came to understand that the process of moving from a "winning wartime coalition" to a "minimum winning coalition" would be competitive. There would be relative winners and relative losers. Some of the warlords would be pushed out of the ruling coalition and others would reappropriate their hard-earned wealth. The short civil wars meant that the militia coalitions had seized the capitals without developing any institutions to redistribute spoils equitably.

Though the concern of being written out of the coalition was more acute in Tajikistan than in Georgia, militia members in both countries who had fought since the beginning recall this period of uncertainty largely the same way: They went from not being sure if their group could win the war to not being sure if they could keep what they had won. In a few short weeks, the inherent tensions relating to the divisibility of state spoils started to splinter the unity of the umbrella militia coalitions. Identifying oneself as "Mkhedrioni" or "Popular Front" was increasingly meaningless and redundant – what mattered was one's particular factional commander, and groups began to identify themselves to each other by referencing their patronage relationship. Fears of being manipulated and discarded were rampant.

Urban militias were, at this point, a crude but well-understood kind of political insurance. Their primary purpose was to remind other social actors that there would be serious consequences if the warlord, or the group he claimed to speak for, was cut out of the distribution of pork. But the outlines of a stable core coalition were beginning to take shape, and individual militia members could take concrete actions – such as recruiting friends or switching commanders – to improve their lot.

---

fighting. Second, respondents who had families had to see to their safety during the war, which often meant fleeing with their children or parents to rural safe zones or to live with urban relatives. A third explanation was simply that their offers of service were rejected by whoever was recruiting in particular area, usually because they had clan or ethnic criteria for group membership. A Georgian respondent reported with great seriousness that he was "too fat" to join the Mkhedrioni in his neighborhood in 1992, though this did not stop him from eventually signing up a year later after the war in Abkhazia was settled. Interview conducted November 11, 2006 in Kutaisi.

37 Certain tattoos helped distinguish long-time members of the *vori v zkone* ("Thieves in Law") in Georgia; there was not an analogous signaling mechanism in the Tajik prison system.

Phase 3: Attrition and Selection in the Time of Troubles

Urban violence escalated. In Tajikistan, once it became obvious that armed groups from the region of Kulob had begun to consolidate their position inside ministries at the direct expense of other allies in the Popular Front, a steady stream of Hissori, Khojandi, and Lakai foot soldiers began to drift into Dushanbe. As a former combatant from the region of Khojand recalled this period, "We knew we needed more men, so that Kulov [the captain] could speak with a louder voice. ...[S]o we brought friends."[38] Georgians could also draw on clan and family networks that stretched to rural areas. Oleg's anecdote is representative: "My brother told me that he was sure to get a job in the Special Reaction Emergency Unit if his group was strong enough to get noticed by Dzhaba [Ioseliani, the head of the Mkhedrioni]. ... He said that it would be good for the whole family, so I sold one [of the family horses], took my hunting rifle, and went to get a car in Rust'avi [to come to Tbilisi]." Oleg was a self-described family man who had fled with his family, staying neutral during the worst phases of the civil war violence, but his family pressured him to help his brother get a good job during the scramble for post-Soviet spoils.[39] "The state" may have been just a handful of half-empty buildings in the capital city, but in the words of a former Popular Front member in Tajikistan, "Everyone got it ... whoever controlled the police ... controlled the bazaars and the streets. And whoever controlled the streets could whisper in the ear of the big man [Rakhmonov], who would stand like a statue."[40]

As it became more and more obvious that the symbols of the old state, symbols of the Georgian church, and political slogans were providing cover for open banditry, militia commanders' moral authority declined. This opened the door for a third group of militia recruits: local self-defense militias that formed as a response to the disorder and chaos that the "first wave" of militias unleashed. These men, many of whom were career police officers, self-consciously described themselves as cut from a different cloth than those in the militias that emerged from anarchy. Rather than being motivated by abstract fears (e.g., Russian influence), they often described their fears as local and tractable. They often reported disgust at the criminal elements within the mass movements. These urban formations described themselves as protectors of innocents from arbitrary violence, providers of local public goods (most notably security), and generally fair providers of order – similar to how the Mkhedrioni presented themselves in the pre-independence period. Their challenge to the Mkhedrioni and National Guard formations was met with predictable violence. Various "neighborhood defense committees" formed out of youth gangs emerging from the slums of Tbilisi and the outskirts of Dushanbe, and the members began to operate in unpaid parallel positions to the

---

38 Interview conducted May 14, 2007 in Bishkek.
39 Interview conducted November 2, 2006 in Tbilisi.
40 Interview conducted July 17, 2007 in Dushanbe.

lowest levels of the power ministries in both capitals. The basic arrangements described were strikingly similar: a leader was given permission to collect taxes on behalf of a particular militia commander in exchange for local autonomy and free access to the electricity and water grid, with the vague promise that their positions would become salaried at some point in the future.

It did not take long for newcomers to realize they might be able to shoot their way to more power. A common strategy was building up a competent group of violence specialists, taking territory, and eventually merging forces with a captain who would share his veteran nationalist credentials. Levan, a neighborhood organizer who was later incorporated with his men into the local police, understood that holding firm would eventually allow him to be "bought out" and described the bargaining matter-of-factly:

"The Mkhedrioni were serious at first ... but then some of the best of them died in the war, I think. Anyway, after a while, their men asked for too much ... there were beatings and then shooting at night and then a rape, and it got to be too much to bear. So we organized ourselves ... and eventually their bosses came to ask me if I wanted to work in the Ministry [of the Interior]. I said no ... [but then] they offered again, and I accepted."[41]

Militia members who were active in Dushanbe and Tbilisi tend to recount the interfactional violence of the 1993–1994 period through one of two self-serving narratives. The first story was the hardened, virtuous "true believer" militia members fighting against upstarts, criminals, and opportunistic newcomers. A member of the Georgian National Guard put it like this:

"Kids from the city ... they watched movies, they thought they wanted to be war heroes like Rambo. But they had missed the war. They knew nothing. We needed another war to scare out the kids [who] never went to war. So we needed to bring the war here."[42]

The alternative version was that it was the "real" soldiers who were the goons and cowards, less equipped for this new period of violence than new recruits coming up from the streets, who had ties to the solidarity communities emerging in various urban slums and squatter camps. To hear them tell it, these newcomers were just as ruthless and organized in their application of violence as the first wave of fighters but possessed better discipline, better intelligence thanks to ties to the community, and perhaps simply a greater willingness to stand and fight to hold their turf. What both groups agree on is that this period was far more dangerous than participating in the rural phase of the civil war. As one veteran-turned-nightclub-bouncer put it: "There were frontlines in

---

41 Interview conducted November 17, 2007 in Tbilisi. Readers might note the casual reference to the Ministry of the Interior as "The Ministry" – clearly its own center of institutional gravity.
42 Interview conducted November 3, 2006 in Tbilisi. Abdullo, a Dushanbe police captain, stated: "No one would back down without a fight. So, we fought." Interview conducted February 2, 2007, in Dushanbe.

Abkhazia, and if you weren't brave you could hang back. But here [in Tbilisi], there were no frontlines. Everyone is just a drive away."[43]

The first few months of violence took their toll on many of the prominent warlords and militia armies. Militias organized around charismatic authority were vulnerable to decapitation. In Georgia, Deputy Minister of Internal Affairs Gregori Gulua and Deputy Minister of Defense Nika Kekelidze were brutally assassinated within weeks of each other in the spring of 1994. Assassination of prominent militia leaders induced rapid and unpredictable shifts in the political fortunes of subordinates. In March of 1993, two of the most prominent Tajik warlords – Sangak Safarov and Faizali Saidov – were both killed in a shootout.[44] Until that time, Rakhmonov had been seen as the hand-picked representative of Safarov, the most prominent commander of the Popular Front.[45] Suddenly the seat behind the throne was vacant.

This kind of violence had two effects. The first effect was attrition because it raised the costs of organizing based on raw opportunism. Men who joined these groups with a "live only for today" attitude were poorly suited for this new crucible. Even more important than weeding out the unfit soldiers was weeding out unfit warlords. If a leader could not sustain optimism about his ability to make it into the state, or maintain a reputation for generously distributing spoils to his men, his men were likely to switch to a different commander (in Georgia), replace him with a better commander (in Tajikistan), or simply quit. A secondary effect was the creation of common knowledge in the violence marketplace regarding the relative strength of different warlords. Both Tajikistan and Georgia are honor-based societies. Blood-feuds are enforced. Public actions that could risk spirals of violence were costly signals of willingness to endure extended retaliatory violence. The strong

---

43 Interview conducted October 28, 2006 in Tbilisi.
44 Experts still disagree on the precise details of Safarov's death. Olivier Roy (2000) and a few others believe that the argument between Safarov and Saidov escalated over accusations that Saidov was "too soft" on returning Gharmi refugees coming down from the mountains of Afghanistan (49). Safarov, Roy claims, feared that with the Gharmis driven from the region, the ethnic balance would shift in favor of the Uzbeks in areas around Kurgan-Tupe; Saidov's mother was Lakai Uzbek, and he rejected any right of return for the Gharmis. Gretsky (1995) plausibly claims that this was a dispute about control of the new national army. Nourzhanov (2005) articulates the consensus belief on the deaths of Safarov and Saidov: "the whole accident was planned in Dushanbe … Kulyobi commanders were liquidated by the very same people whom they had put in power" (118).
45 President Rakhmonov deftly handled the political situation in the wake of this unexpected event to demonstrate that he enjoyed the support of a plurality of remaining Kulobi militia commanders, heading off the first serious intra-Kulobi power struggle. As the various militia captains chose sides, or hedged their bets by pushing for increased regional autonomy outside of the capital city (the strategy of Ibodullo Boimatov and Mahmud Khudoiberdiev, two extremely influential non-Kulobi warlords), the Tajik army "became nothing more than an arms depot for the new political party." Interview with UN representative, conducted August 16, 2005 in Dushanbe.

were sorted from the imitators, the confident from the brash. After a year of this, there were no imitators.

The most common flashpoints for symbolic violence were the checkpoints and roadblocks that various militia members established inside the urban areas. Checkpoints at major street intersections made it possible to control which vehicles moved in and out of particularly wealthy neighborhoods, black- and gray-market bazaars, or areas with large amounts of foot traffic. These areas provided a key source of income for self-financing urban militias and were signs of prestige and strength for the captains who controlled them. A murder taking place in a protected bazaar would drive off merchants, lowering the tax base for the warlord offering protection. A shooting or public beating at a roadblock would test the mettle of the soldiers who remained. Different paramilitary factions would intentionally march their troops through parts of town controlled by other militias, openly risking provocation and escalation. In Georgia, one Mkhedrioni described his clash with another sub-group of "new" Mkhedrioni:

"They came at us at night, when we were walking home. ... They surprised us, and [aimed – gesture] guns on us. Then they took turns beating us with boards. ... One of them broke my finger kicking me while I tried to [protect – gesture] my head. When they were done, one of them said that they didn't want to have to come back, but that it was payback, and that if we came back next time they would use the guns. ... [W]e wanted to take the fight to them, but Davit [our boss] calmed us down. They both went and talked to Dzhaba, and he sorted it out. They didn't come to our street anymore, and we never saw each other again."[46]

Militia membership based on vague associations had gone from being a relatively fun and even lucrative lifestyle choice to being an extremely dangerous vocation. As noted previously, the point of these acts of violence was not just the control of the checkpoint or the taxes from the bazaar – the point was to see which groups were actually capable of convincing their men to stick around and endure punishing losses and which groups were trying to fake their way through the consolidation process. A Kulobi foot soldier said of this period, "We stayed in the streets because we needed to show Rustam [our

---

46 Interview conducted November 14, 2006 in Tbilisi. This account highlights the important role of informal institutions in conflict resolution – in particular the charismatic authority of Dzhaba, the head of the Mkhedrioni. The form that the resolution took (division of territory) also reflects a political bargain between commanders to collude to share the rents (in the literal sense of apartment rents) in different parts of the capital city. It is also clear from this anecdote that Dzhaba had no ability to control the day-to-day operations of the lower-ranks of "his" hierarchy. Wheatley (2005) observed that, whatever its origin myth, by 1994: "[S]maller criminal gangs (often referred to as 'Mkhedrioni' but quite clearly beyond the control of Jaba Ioseliani and other leaders of the 'official' Mkhedrioni) dominated at local level, typically offering protection to local communities against other marauding gangs. Very often the leaders of these gangs would assume nominal state positions, such as that of mayor or district administrator (*gamgebeli*)." 80.

boss] that we were capable of staying in the streets. We were told 'no one has use for cowards.'"[47]

Clashes gradually became more and more dangerous. Competition for urban territory was often settled with guns or pipes, and bodies were often left on display to show the cost of being affiliated with a weak faction. Armed shootouts with high-powered weapons – and, in more than one case, even the shelling of urban neighborhoods with mortars – were the end result of these escalating displays of paramilitary strength. Sasha, a member of a Hissori faction of the Popular Front, described the summer of 1994 as the most dangerous period of the war:

"It was the worst time … it was so hot during the days, and there was no gas, no water. And every week, we would stand at our post in the heat. And in the night, there was always gunfire … One night our wall [checkpoint] was attacked by men with grenades and explosives, who sprayed bullets all down the street to drive us away – but we took shelter and returned fire into the darkness … Those men that ran away weren't welcomed back … It was very dangerous, and no one was making money on the job … But we couldn't leave … not without just all going home [leaving Dushanbe and going to Hissor]. There were three other factions [of the Ministry of the Interior] that were waiting for an opportunity to take our taxes, to show that [our commander] was weak, to take his job and send us all into the army. We did not fight a war to be unpaid infantry for Kulobi generals."[48]

Or consider this quote from Georgia:

"Everyone knew which was our restaurant; it was Levan's space – Mkhedrioni space … we even had a picture of Dzhaba on the wall … we would all meet up there after work [at the Ministry] to relax. But everything changed when Levan got pulled up to work [in the Ministry of Justice] with [Tedo] Ninidze … Then he was big time … there was one night … it was February 1995 … we realized that the room was thinning out … people were all going back to the toilets but not returning. Men in ski masks had come in through the back, and were were waiting for us there, one at a time. They put our faces in the toilets and … knocked out my teeth on the porcelain. … They said that we should tell Levan what happened. … when we did, and he told us that we should think about joining the Army, that we could get hot meals and better work there … and that we wouldn't be able to stay at the Ministry.[49]

Some recruits, expecting good jobs in the state bureaucracy, could convince themselves to endure these kinds of risks.[50] Dense social networks and ties

---

47 Interview conducted August 15, 2007 in Dushanbe.
48 Interview conducted February 7, 2007 in Dushanbe. Note the explicit ranking of jobs in terms of perceived enrichment opportunities: The Ministry of the Interior, where one could expect relative autonomy and many opportunities to interface with merchants and extort civilians, is the prize. Valued much lower is a uniformed job in the military hierarchy.
49 Interview conducted October 25, 2006 in Tbilisi.
50 Generalizations in this section are drawn from a statistical analysis of only the sub-sample of respondents who reported being present in the capital city for the "Time of Troubles," excluding fighters who fought only in the rural parts of either conflict.

TABLE 4.3. *Which Militia Members Quit When Their Lives Were at Stake?*

Variables	(1) Full	(2) Favored	(3) Only Georgian	(4) Only Tajik
Georgian	0.853# (0.695)	0.957* (0.495)		
Joined after Fighting	2.311*** (0.600)	2.390*** (0.502)	2.237*** (0.639)	2.777** (0.931)
Joined to Protect Family	−1.465* (0.727)	−1.470* (0.716)	−1.703* (0.832)	−0.608 (1.710)
Operated Close to Home	1.465* (0.609)	1.558** (0.599)	1.321# (0.765)	1.996* (1.021)
Switched Units during War	0.141 (0.516)			
Switched Units after War	0.273 (0.657)			
Trusted Commander	−0.707# (0.496)	−0.658# (0.474)	−0.522 (0.603)	−0.710 (0.851)
Stayed for a Better Job	0.043 (0.611)			
Stayed for Fun	−0.837# (0.545)	−0.863# (0.531)	−0.397 (0.624)	−1.949# (1.243)
Wanted Influence in Capital	−0.568 (0.661)			
Constant	0.169 (1.111)	−0.254 (0.848)	0.751 (0.875)	−1.139 (1.884)
Observations	115	120	69	51
Pseudo-r^2	0.281	0.286	0.229	0.351

Logit regression results with *Quit When Things Got Violent* as dependent variable. Standard errors in parentheses. *** $p < 0.001$; ** $p < 0.01$; * $p < 0.05$; # $p < 0.25$.

of reciprocal obligation convinced many militia recruits to endure with their commanders through this violent tournament. But which of the two self-serving narratives sketched at the beginning of this section was more accurate? What kinds of militia members had the comparative advantage during the consolidation phase?

Table 4.3 is an attempt to address these questions systematically. In my sample 43 percent of respondents – half of the Georgians and about a third of the Tajiks – reported that they retired from militia activity because they feared for their lives. Because this variable is dichotomous, a logit estimator can be employed to see what individual characteristics made a militia member relatively likely to quit in the face of violence compared to his opponents who stayed in the fight. The independent variables included in the regression are also coded as binary variables for ease of interpretation. Models 1 and Model 2 present the cumulative and favored models. In my sample, "opportunistic joiners" – new entrants into the violence game who joined the civil war after the bulk of the violence was completed – were more likely to quit the streets when violence intensified. Social ties between commander and recruit predicted staying power. Men who fought through the civil war had established close ties to their patrons and had a higher expectation of a good job (conditional on their militia being a part of the solidified winning coalition, of course). In addition to the simple "opportunism" dummy, two additional indicators of dense social ties emerged as statistically significant, though only marginally so in some specifications. The first was a dummy variable for Georgian paramilitaries – which, as discussed earlier, were substantially more prone to defection and side-switching – and the second, a dummy variable for the question of whether a militia member reported "really trusting" their commander. Plainly, Georgians in my sample were more likely to quit when faced with violence. Recruits reporting that they trusted their commanders also reported that they were willing to take risks for them.

Members of a militia that formed out of self defense – who reported "joining primarily to defend their family" – were relatively willing to endure violence.[51] This variable can be interpreted as sorting "opportunistic" joiners from "late" joiners. Urban self-defense militias that formed during the postwar chaos were well-incentivized to stick around. Urban hangers-on who joined after the fighting, but were not actually acting in defense of the neighborhood, were likely to quit in the face of determined terrorism. The minority of respondents in both states who reported carrying out militia operations close to home were more likely to retire from militia life when faced with serious violence, which can be explained by a closer examination of these thirty-nine cases. In twenty-eight of them, the "home region" that the respondent described was a particular neighborhood of the capital city, meaning this was an additional proxy variable for (largely late-coming) Tbilisi- and Dushanbe-based gangs. My interpretation of this trend is that militia recruits whose homes were in urban areas were more likely to have friends and family that could help get them visas out of the country or resettle them in a stable job. Many urban militia recruits had better "exit" options. Rural migrants were, as a rule, more desperate, and, as a result, more willing to endure violence to avoid returning home.

A disturbing and unexpected pattern appears in the data: militia members who reported "fun," "excitement," or "enjoyment of the experience" as

---

[51] I attribute this trend to a higher level of psychological satisfaction and cognitive consistency associated with being "on the defensive" in an anarchic social environment.

a motivation for joining a militia or sustaining militia membership were, statistically speaking, more likely to sustain ties with a militia when confronted with violence. Given that it was the opportunistic Georgians ("Mkhedrioni Youth") who, for the most part, were reporting having joined for fun, my prior expectation was that multicollinearity would wash out statistical significance, or that the coefficient would be signed in the opposite direction. To make sense of these trends, Models 3 and 4 subdivided the data further into Tajik and Georgian militia members. A few new patterns emerge. The "opportunist" and "close to home" variables provide powerful, if indirect, evidence that the militia members who were most willing to risk their lives were those who joined early and were contributing their social capital to a warlord's political project on behalf of their civilian social network. Those networks were stronger when they originated in rural, rather than in urban, areas. In Tajikistan, *avlod* ties bind tight. Georgian responses to the questions about "protecting one's family" and "really trusting the commander" drove the general results in Models 1 and 2. In Georgia, only recruits who were successful at finding militia commanders whom they trusted enough to persevere through the "Time of Troubles" stuck around. There was insufficient variation in the Tajik responses to these questions to generate meaningful statistical significance in the face of controls.[52] And the puzzle of the "good times" variable is resolved: the effect was driven by the small number (11) of Tajiks who responded in the affirmative, rather than the large number of Georgians (33) in the various subsamples. Returning to the interview transcripts, I realized that this trend was driven by a mix of hardened veterans of the Soviet campaigns in Afghanistan and a few very scary characters who reported "enjoying" their time in the militias because they enjoyed the power that came to them from the sudden reversal of long-established hierarchies.

Militia members considered their life opportunities inside a politically aspiring militia in contrast to the relevant counterfactuals. These calculations took place in a complex social environment where there was never enough information to confidently assess whether one was placing the right bet. Men were weighing the costs and benefits of sustained membership, taking calculated risks, and implementing their best strategies on a day-to-day basis. This is not to imply that these men engaged in hyperrational behavior on a day-to-day basis, nor is it to dismiss the emotional and psychological complexity that surely surrounded every individual decision to enlist in a militia, participate in violent actions, take beatings, watch friends be shot at close range, or eventually attempt to return to civilian life. Patterns in the data simply suggest that they understood themselves to be embedded in a high-stakes

---

[52] An alternative explanation is that the same sorts of psychological and emotional mechanisms in the laundry list above (e.g., the tyranny of sunk costs, shame, etc.) may have made it difficult for the respondent to admit that he had never really trusted his commander in the first place – but only in Tajikistan.

bargaining game and weighed the consequences of their actions. Players at the bottom of the hierarchy were watching the political consolidation process at the top with a great deal of attention and focus. Foot soldiers were keenly aware of the week-to-week and even day-to-day shifts in the fortunes of prominent militia commanders as they navigated the thicket of *nomenklatura* politics, and were constantly reevaluating their own safety and prospects at the bottom of the power structure based on their expectations of what was happening to their patron. In general, the relative power of different leaders came to be measured by their official title in the regime. Moreover, there was a rough consensus that the best jobs would go to the men who demonstrated an ability to absorb punishment and stand firm, and if a leader acquired a reputation for weakness, his men would surely seek a different patron. In dozens of interviews, respondents said that the violence gave them a chance to see whether their commanders were "real men."

Denouement and Deterrence in the "Time of Troubles"

After a few months of urban attrition, militia competition normalized. As the supply of recruits dried up, some of the youth gangs disbanded completely. Yet, as large militias continued to fragment, it became clear that there was, in fact, a limit to the number of potential contenders who could compete in this tournament. Only those warlords with access to deep reservoirs of social capital and powerful friends could survive for long. Groups became smaller, better organized, and their leaders began to view each other differently. This new period featured smaller numbers of determined and committed men, all acutely conscious of the fact that they might, at any time, be forced to prove that they were worthy of inclusion in the ruling coalition. Cosmetic displays of force became less necessary, but trust between warlords did not emerge automatically. And no one really disarmed.

In this new environment, fierce, well-armed, and unpredictable militias on every street corner were gradually replaced by "connected men" who traded on their reputation for friendship with other respected and prominent militia heads. Positions inside the government became an acceptable metric for keeping score of political favors, as tactical bargains calcified into strategic alliances. Many "deposed" or "excluded" warlords during this period were still making decent sums of money managing drug transit lines, sitting on import–export bottlenecks, or managing bazaars – high reservation values r, in the language of the model from Chapter 2. The loss of an esteemed position in a ministry, however, indicated a decline in a warlord's long-term bargaining power vis-à-vis other warlords, as it indicated that he had lost his protection from the president and his time in the winning circle would eventually draw to a close. It was a sign of true strength to openly flaunt the authority of the president, normally only undertaken by warlords who had a firm territorial base and foreign guarantees of their security, such as Aslan Abashidze in

Georgia or Mahmud Khudoiberdiyev in Tajikistan. These early moves toward a formalization of expectations, transparent assessment of risks, and stable political relationships between a fixed number of militias began to congeal into something recognizably state-like. A Mkhedrioni member in Rustavi summed this transition from violence to connections well: "At first none of us knew who was who ... [but] after a few months, it was really clear who the big men were. Then it just becomes about who you know, and if you have respect."[53]

As it became obvious that the umbrella organizations had outlived their usefulness as mechanisms of patronage, and affiliation with a large number of undisciplined street hooligans began to be seen as a liability, militia formations began to restrict their membership to the core of original friends and allies. The threat of violence was still ever-present, but as reputation began to take the place of brute force, it became possible for militia members to cease carrying weapons, which reduced the frequency and intensity of armed brush-ups on the streets.[54] This made it easier for the captains to make credible promises to their subordinates. As family networks reasserted themselves and unaffiliated opportunists fell away, another mechanism raised the costs of violence: blood feud deterrence. Once all the players knew each other, individualized attribution for murders was relatively easy. And since, at this point, no one took seriously arguments about "revolutionary times" or "anarchy," the escalation of blood feuds was reported to be a plausible deterrent for respondents in both countries. Efforts were made to keep civilians in their neighborhoods where they could be easily controlled and taxed. To this day, most adult residents of Dushanbe can recall the name of the warlord who controlled their neighborhood bazaar through this period.

It also became clear during this time that allegiances between militias, and across different ministries of the new government structures, provided a better source of funding and resources than the unaffiliated racketeering projects. Friends in high places could make sure that their subordinates got access to government supplies of ammunition and intelligence and allowed them easier coordination with police and army forces to arrest, intimidate, or disappear opponents. Control of state ministries also lowered the transaction costs associated with smuggling gasoline, narcotics, tobacco, and weapons. In fact, practically all of the economic activities that had allowed militias to be self-financing during the initial period of state failure were fairly natural

---

53 Interview conducted November 22, 2006 in Rustavi.
54 When asked about this, most Georgian militia members insisted that this was because of leadership effects at the highest levels. Both Kitovani and Ioseliani were already dreaming of a future where they would rehabilitate themselves and transmogrify into "legitimate players" in Moscow's emergent class of businessmen, playing down their criminal ties. They impressed the need for restraint and a culture of moral virtue for their men. There is a famous (though possibly apocryphal) story that Kitovani ordered one of his junior lieutenants to be publicly tortured and killed for raping (or perhaps simply sexually harassing) a young woman whose uncle was a Georgian Orthodox priest.

candidates for economies of scale, best achieved through a state monopoly inside the Ministry of the Interior.[55]

One of the major prizes during this transition period was downtown real estate. A number of neighborhoods adjoining the main downtown thoroughfare (Rudaki in Dushanbe, Rustaveli in Tbilisi) contained apartment buildings that had been granted by the Soviet state to members of the local intelligentsia, academics, artists, and local party notables. In Dushanbe, many of these individuals had used their connections to simply flee the country with whatever they could carry, leaving their apartments in the hands of friends and relatives. In Tbilisi, by contrast, deeds, titles, and property rights tended to pass without much incident to their previous Soviet owners, though keeping one's family apartment ultimately required friends in high places. By midway through 1994, a number of innovative militia captains in the Ministry of the Interior (notably Kakha "Black Panther" Tamunindze, who also had connections in the Office of the Prosecutor General) began to force families near Rustaveli and in the Old City to pay protection money, gradually raising informal taxes until they finally acquired title transfers. The only protection against this sort of expropriation was for a family member to acquire political protection from someone in the political hierarchy even higher than the militia captain. Often this was Shevardnadze himself, who took special care to cultivate favors among the intellectuals. In Tajikistan, the intimidation of civilians who happened to be sitting atop valuable real estate was often more crude and cruel.[56] In both capital cities, many of the refurnished houses that are today rented to Western Embassy personnel, aid workers, and diplomats were acquired at gunpoint during this period.

Coalitions of strong militia captains colluded to protect common interests. Together they were capable of acting collectively against opponents or new entrants into the violence game. In time, trust and reputation became resources that were just as important as men or weapons, and political relationships gradually replaced visible demonstrations of group strength. A more orderly sort of bargaining was possible, with smaller numbers of disciplined individuals as enforcers. The situation in the capital city moved from something that could be described as "anarchy" to something that looked far more organized. Essentially, it was a stand-off between competing armed factions, each with powerful patrons within the government. This process favored the militias that

---

55 Akiner (2001) and Zuercher (2005). Shevardnadze brought warlords with interests in the black markets for oil futures, scrap metal export, drug trafficking, and currency speculation – all businesses that thrived in periods of stability – into the Ministerstvo Vnutrennikh Del (MVD), the old Soviet Ministry of the Interior. The highest level of the Ministry of the Interior was composed of a mix of old friends from Shevardnadze's time in the ministry and co-opted Mkhedrioni organizers.

56 In Tajikistan, brazen quasi-legal land grabs by politically protected individuals persist to this day. The 2006 bulldozing of one of Central Asia's oldest Jewish synagogues for the construction of a third presidential palace is an exemplar of this trend.

could play politics, and it was the crafty leaders, those who were able to foster close ties with other militias, build tactical and strategic alliances with other states' intelligence services, and secure access to financiers and commercial front companies to launder money and distribute illicit goods, who came to be recognized as the dominant players. Violent political competition had reached an equilibrium. Thus, the ruling coalition was born in the streets.

UNCERTAINTY AND UPDATING

For Georgian or Tajik citizens living through this period of transitory anarchy, the view from 1994 was bleak. Neither civil war seemed to be on the path to resolution. Enemies had been driven into the mountains, but with foreign support they could easily return. As a veteran noted: "At first, we thought that Gamsakhurdia and his army would return ... After the debacle in Sukhumi, my friends and I returned to the capital city to see what [the Russians] would do next to undermine us. Would they stir trouble in Adjara? Javakheti? Akhalkalaki? Or try again in the city [Tbilisi]? No matter what, we had to be vigilant and ready."[57] In Tajikistan, the UTO had regrouped in the mountains of Afghanistan and were attempting to reinsert themselves into Tajik politics. The important questions for the victorious militias revolved around distributive politics, and how the new state would be organized. Everyone knew that Rakhmonov and the Kulobi coalition that installed him would claim the state apparatus for themselves at the direct expense of the Leninobodi families that had run the state continuously since the 1950s. But the situation was still fluid, and most predicted that Kulobi rule would be a passing phase, with politically connected Leninobidis returning to their traditional positions at the upper tier of the state. If the Kulobis of Leninobod made a serious bid for power with backing from Uzbekistan and Moscow, the war could easily have restarted.

The drawdown in militia membership was precipitated by a consensus among militia members on the streets that the window for being "bought out" by the state had closed. In both states, this new expectation was driven by a focal event that shored up uncertainty on the same two questions. It became public knowledge that certain militia captains would be excluded from the future state coalition, which rendered a large number of promises from the upper ranks worthless. Many hopeful street-level organizers and runners were suddenly operating without "a roof"; they no longer had political protection from other factions, de facto immunity from the fumbling legal system, or a patron to advance them through the ranks. At the same time,

---

57 Interview conducted December 3, 2006 in Tbilisi. This particular respondent also captured the mood at the time, which was that the humiliating defeat in Abkhazia needed to be revenged. "We needed a new military, a strong military! We needed to build ourselves strong, to return to Abkhazia! Otherwise, the Russians would just come again and again. [Russians] needed to be shown."

it also became public knowledge that "insider" militias were sufficiently well organized to jail members of fringe militia groups (and if it came to some last-ditch confrontation were probably capable of annihilating them). In other words, a minimum winning coalition had emerged, and the oversupply of militia members burdened this coalition. Given this transparent collapse of "demand" for militia groups, the pool of ambiguously affiliated gunmen dried up overnight.

What was necessary for the general decline of militia politics was an exogenous shock – something completely unexpected that would force everyone to update their beliefs. This event had the effect of clarifying which warlord commanders were going to be "in" and "out" of the warlord coalition, which allowed their soldiers to cut their losses and quietly flee the scene. Just as important, the response of the "inside" militias had to be sufficiently coherent and convincing to demonstrate that they were actually capable of winning against any viable coalition of enemies. This sort of certainty would have been impossible before the "violence market" had opened up and provided different warlords with the ability to demonstrate that they could recruit and maintain a militia at a relatively low cost. It is beyond the scope of any general theory to predict something that locals could not predict themselves.

In Georgia, the event that shored up certainty about coalition membership was a failed assassination attempt on the president, Eduard Shevardnadze, on August 29, 1995. Most agree Dzhaba Ioseliani and the Russian-affiliated Minister of Defense, Igor Giorgadze, orchestrated the attempt. Shevardnadze survived the car bomb by pure luck. When the president made it a public fight between himself and the coup-plotters – standing minutes after the car bomb before a hastily assembled parliament session – everyone wanted to be on his side. His survival changed everyone's calculations about the future. It became clear that his regime would persevere in the near term and the public outcry associated with the assassination attempt provided a buoyant month of popular legitimacy. Ioseliani was finished. Mkhedrioni members who had integrated themselves into the Ministry of the Interior turned on Dzhaba immediately, practically falling over one another to arrest him. Street-level Mkhedrioni enforcers and Giorgadze's loyalists in various subsections of the Defense Ministry immediately left Tbilisi. Giorgi, a former member of the National Guard who now works as an embassy driver, spoke for many: "We were running the streets … we were kings of this city. And then, overnight, we all just ended up in jail."[58]

The assassination attempt also put to rest the idea that Shevardnadze's survival was dependent on networks in Moscow. At least some Russian actors – likely well-placed political players given Giorgadze's conspicuous decision to flee to Moscow in a Russian military aircraft – had the means and wherewithal to attempt to install a different puppet president. There was a strong sense

[58] Interview conducted October 24, 2006 in Rustavi.

that Georgia was under siege, but also a sense that, if Georgians rallied behind Shevardnadze, he might be able to purge the state of the Russian vipers.[59] The contingency of everything described in the next chapter must be reemphasized, however. If Shevardnadze had died, Ioseliani might still be running large parts of Tbilisi. In the words of Alexander Rondeli: "If those had been East Germans who designed the bomb and timer instead of Georgians, we'd be just like Armenia now."[60]

In Tajikistan, Rakhmonov organized the 1994 election to shore up his claim to power. A defining feature of Tajikistan's politics in the mid-1990s was the uncertainty over the degree of foreign support that the government would receive from Russia and Uzbekistan. To return briefly to the language of the model, one might say that players were uncertain of the stability threshold s. No one knew whether Rakhmonov and his Kulobi backers would really be allowed to rule without sharing meaningful power with Uzbekistan's traditional clients, or if some sort of tacit Russian (or Uzbek) "security guarantee" would kick in. The election broke down along predictable regional lines.[61] Everyone anticipated that Rakhmonov would have an advantage in the capital city and its environs, as well as his traditional power base in the south. Seventy-nine percent of the population of Khojand (31 percent of the population) and 96 percent of voting Badakhshonis (3 percent of the population) chose Abdumalik Abdullojonov, the Prime Minister from a well-known Khojandi family. But these opposition votes were swallowed under the demographic weight of the newly created superdistrict of "Khatlon," which was created by merging three oblasts in the southern region – Hissor (5 percent of the population), Kulob (12 percent of the population), and Kurgon-Tubbe (21 percent of the population). The entirety of this newly created district of Khatlon was delivered to Rakhmonov, with 99.5 percent of the votes counted for the sitting president.[62]

---

59 Recall from the model: A very high stability threshold s increases the probability of any single warlord being pivotal, making presidential promises to pay off warlords more credible than they would be otherwise.

60 Interview conducted at the Georgian Foundation for Strategic and International Studies (GFSIS) in Tbilisi, November 2, 2006.

61 Whatever one thinks of the validity of these numbers, the ability to conduct an election under conditions of abject state failure is an impressive display of the administrative capacity that the Soviet legacy bequeathed. Voter turnout was reported at 88.33 percent; the percentage of the total voting age population who participated was 77.28 percent. Though Gorno-Badakhshon was functionally independent at the time, it is important for the dynamics that followed to to note that they did vote in this election. The election was also a referendum on the new constitution, and 90 percent of voters chose to adopt it. See Grotz (2001), 20, Atkin (2002), 104, and IDEA (2011).

62 See the Current Digest of the Post-Soviet Press: 1994–1995, vol. 46, no. 45, pp. 20. Population numbers are from the 1989 census, reported in Nourzhanov and Bleur (2013), 285. It should be emphasized that the Khatlon region of Tajikistan was the site of horrible anti-civilian tactics aimed at terrorizing civilian populations out of their homes, and many of the people

After the stunning results, Rakhmonov announced he would be reshuffling his cabinet, elevating his core Kulobi supporters at the direct expense of the Hissoris, Khojandis, and other traditional Uzbek clients within the Popular Font. From the perspective of domestic power consolidation, it was a risky and brilliantly brazen move, presenting the Russian government with a clear take-it-or-leave-it offer. They could either explicitly endorse the presidency of Rakhkmonov or declare the elections invalid and return the country to war. Moscow opted for stability on Rakhmonov's terms. Fifteen billion rubles were sent to the Dushanbe regime, which paid government salaries for the first time since independence. Tajikistan's presidential election was hailed as proof of "progress towards democracy."[63] All of this outraged the government of Uzbekistan, and it was certainly not the end of challenges to Rakhmonov's rule, as we shall see in Chapter 5. But, in general, militia captains who wished to remain in the capital city were forced to acknowledge that Rakhmonov was there to stay, not a temporary placeholder before the Khojandis reclaimed the presidency. Factional fighting shifted substantially to clashes outside of the city limits of Dushanbe from this point forward.

Both regimes also laid the groundwork for the peaceful withdrawal of militia forces by lowering the stakes of politics for losing militia captains and even providing different safety nets for the paramilitary foot soldiers who were shut out of the consolidation process. Both states passed blanket amnesty laws for acts of wartime violence, absolving militia members of responsibility for crimes during the transition period. Ongoing insurgencies in rural areas of both states meant that militia groups could withdraw from the capital and carry the fight to "the enemy" – integrating with the state army or border guards – without anyone losing too much face. Ongoing border friction in Abkhazia and the insurgency in the highlands of Tajikistan provided convenient places to send unruly militias for both post-Soviet presidents throughout the 1990s. The opportunities for war profiteering and narcotics smuggling made these sorts of internal exile options relatively profitable for the militia captains. Emigration from the state was another common safety valve, especially in Tajikistan, for violent paramilitary fighters who wanted to start new lives. Relatively stable employment opportunities emerged for these men as bodyguards or private security for the new urban businessmen; emerging transnational smuggling organizations that were operating with tacit regime approval provided another exit strategy. Both regimes were careful to cultivate a reputation for allowing former militia commanders to retreat from the political arena with dignity and keep their wealth without the risk of future retaliation, so long as they kept out of politics. It took time and demonstrations for warlords to believe that they could simply walk away from the violence game, and sometimes these promises

conducting the election were the beneficiaries of these land-grabs. The election effectively ended all conversation about postwar land redistribution in Tajikistan.

63 Atkin (1997*b*), 303.

were revoked capriciously. But many doors were left open for unlucky warlords to exit.

Merging militia forces into the rump bureaucracy was a violent, uncertain, and competitive process. Militia commanders convinced their memberships – all of whom wanted to be compensated for their sacrifices – that they had a shared interest in eliminating imitators and claiming the lion's share of state spoils for themselves. New contenders could not be deterred, however, as there was an overabundance of foot soldiers who saw militia membership as their best way out of the subproletarian underclass. "War of attrition" dynamics helped to create common knowledge about the balance of power between warlords. The upsurge in violence was the result of calculated, violent competition. Warlords were trying to gauge each other's actual strength before agreeing on how to divide state spoils, and militia recruits were trying to gauge warlords' access to state spoils before committing to militia membership. None of this had anything to do with "anarchy" or security dilemmas, except as a permissive cause. It was the fact that all actors could see the *end* of transitional chaos on the horizon that made urban violence between militias necessary.

These militas became increasingly indistinguishable from patronage-based political parties or lobbying groups. Wage competition between various militia groups gradually sorted the violence market. The memberships of these militia groups expanded, and then contracted, based on a few parameters: the overall urban risk for potential new militia recruits, the attractiveness of "exit options" from militia life, and expectations about whether a captain would stay a part of the ruling coalition. Militia members watched anxiously as power consolidated, knowing that they were bit players in the drama of consolidation politics. Focal events made it clear that in the halls above the streets, a stable coalition had emerged. But nothing in this account implies that "the state" suddenly became strong enough to take on militias and restore order. Rather, in Tajikistan and Georgia "the state" was itself formed from a subset of militias and warlords who had their armed checkpoints, bazaars, shadow-economy enclaves, and local tax collection legalized by the decrees of a government they installed. Many of the ministers, deputies, and uniformed members of the Georgian and Tajik security services were affiliated with militias at the time when the streets went quiet.

Thus far, the narrative has treated civilian elites – including the president – as interchangeable and disposable. Multiple presidents had already been removed in coups. The initial bargain that brought warlords into the state was predicated on the promise that the president cede warlords positions in the government. Though formal institutions were vital to serve as a go-between for aid, legitimacy, and policy concessions, violence entrepreneurs could always threaten to smash these institutions if they were not given their fair due. As they began their tenures as heads of state, neither Rakhmonov nor Shevardnadze had any real control over the patchwork of paramilitaries that had penetrated the state apparatus. At some points, both rulers were literally prisoners in the presidential palace. Regional experts bluntly characterized civil–military relations as "feudal."[64] The same bonds of trust that were used to survive the war and the "Time of Troubles" could be used to organize a coup against the president, and this fact was well understood by all parties behind the throne. Even in the late 1990s the presidents were sometimes described by militia members as "marionettes."[65] How these "puppet presidents" cut their strings is the puzzle that motivates the next chapter.

[64] Jones (1996), 46, Fairbanks (2002), 136–150.

[65] I heard this term used to describe Shevardnadze in my very first life history interview with a former Mkhedrioni member, conducted February 27, 2006 in Tbilisi. In one of my last interviews in Tajikistan (conducted August 16, 2007 in Dushanbe), a Kulobi member of the Popular Front dismissed Rakhmonov in the early 1990s as a *"kukla"* (puppet).

5

Coup-Proofing

Georgia and Tajikistan were essentially ruled by criminalized military juntas in the early 1990s. Presidents were installed to act as figureheads. The same insivible bonds of trust that were used to recruit soldiers and coordinate military actions during the war could be – and had been – used to organize coups in both states. Because this fact was well understood by the president and the warlords behind the throne, the president implemented policies to satisfy this critical constituency. Ministry appointments were handed out to cronies, closed-bid privatization schemes were implemented to benefit mafia captains, and arrest warrants targeted businessmen who could not acquire sufficient political protection. At first, the presidents were puppets, with powerful armed groups and underworld financiers holding the strings. A long-time associate of Eduard Shevardnadze, who served in the government during this period, recalled the daily ritual of humiliation and extortion in the following terms:

"Dzhaba [Ioseliani] or one of his lieutenants walked in every day with a bunch of papers for him to sign – usually documents of ownership or deeds and titles to houses and apartment flats. ... There were arrest warrants [for political enemies] as well. They didn't walk in with guns, but ... there were guns in the building. He had to sign them. He had to sign them all."[1]

Yet by the late-1990s, both presidents had successfully placed themselves securely in the center of the web of relationships holding their respective states together, and it was difficult for anyone to imagine either state functioning

---

[1] Interview conducted in Tbilisi November 29, 2006. For excellent descriptive accounts of this period, see Gretsky (1995); Aves (1996); Brown (1998); O'Ballance (1997); Demetriou (2002).

without these men at the helm.[2] The focus of this chapter is on how Eduard Shevardnadze and Emomalii Rakhmanov managed to ascend to the top of their respective political hierarchies.

The analytic narrative presented in this chapter describes how the two presidents, in their weakly institutionalized postwar settings, contended with multiple potential challengers simultaneously. If the logic of the n-player model is correct, there should be evidence of the warlord coalition changing over time to accommodate shifting domestic and international pressures. The figurehead does not change: In postwar settings, individual leaders become focal points, bottlenecks in the "two-level games" that are so critical to international diplomacy.[3] In the context of the politics described in the previous chapter, this meant managing one public persona for the benefit of foreign powers, important transnational donors, and trilingual elites to assure v^*, and a separate persona for the shadow-elite who can make good on private, overlapping, and sometimes contradictory promises while the pie is divided.

The domestic institutions that might in times of peace be used as commitment devices to hold coalition memberships steady were captured by militias and divided as conflict spoils. There was no one to punish presidents who reneged on promises. Proposal power in the coalition formation process created an oligopoly centered on the president, who controlled the timing of cabinet reshuffling and could thus choose a moment when a warlord was politically alienated or ascendant to declare it was time to reshuffle a ministry. This chapter emphasizes that what "divide-and-rule" actually looked like is long periods of presidential inaction: waiting for warlords to alienate or embarrass themselves, then selectively paring them from the coalition. The equilibria that emerged in Georgia and Tajikistan were quite different, and most of the chapter is devoted to describing them. Two parameters – the reservation value (r) available to nonconsolidated warlords and total available amount of wealth that the president has to distribute (v^*) – explain the shift from a situation where the president was the puppet of warlord interests to one where he held the strings.

Though most of the chapter focuses on the leadership styles and strategies of the two presidents, it concludes by returning to the warlord perspective: Were warlords *actually* interchangeable as coalition members or armed agents of the state? Qualitative data from Georgia and an analysis of warlord biographical data from Tajikistan suggest that, broadly speaking, they were. This chapter also presents the summary results of systematic statistical analysis to reveal which observable characteristics of Tajik warlords – home region, which side they fought on, how many soldiers were under their command – predicted

---

[2]   See O'Ballance (1997) and King (2001*b*). Similarly, by 1999 Emomalii Rakhmonov started to relentlessly centralize as much power as possible, finally turning on his own inner circle starting in about 2002. See ICG (2004).

[3]   Putnam (1988).

political fortune in the consolidation phase. In my interpretation, these data reinforce the appropriateness of the lottery metaphor that anchors Chapter 2. At the time of decision, warlords could not predict who would be politically rehabilitated as a nationalist war hero, who would fade quietly, and who would be violently liquidated. Evidence of warlord miscalculation – warlords joining the president's coalition and later regretting their choice – is consistent with this book's theory. Who would win and who would lose as consolidation unfolded was simply not predictable.

THE MODEL REDUX: HOW DID "PUPPET PRESIDENTS" CUT THEIR STRINGS?

If there were difference in coup-proofing strategies between the two states, the difference cannot be the result of inherited Soviet institutions. Both Georgia and Tajikistan states shared a Soviet institutional legacy. Kotkin (2002) cynically observes that it is "clear from today's Russian-speaking populations in most of the newly independent states, as well as the self-declared additional Trashcanistans within them: the various post-Soviet nations emerged deeply Soviet." Twenty years after independence, institutions and behavioral patterns in post-Soviet states share important similarities. One similarity is very strong executives. As summarized in the first chapter of this book, post-Soviet leaders inherited populations with restricted choice sets and all the national symbols of state authority, including a time-tested party system to manage the aspirations of talented elites, uniforms and statue-lined streets for parades, museums and archives, a school system for the education of children, a national television network, and much more.[4] Across most of post-Soviet Eurasia, self-reinforcing

---

4   A centralized radio and television network, broadcasting a single narrative from the titular capitals, is often underappreciated in the laundry list of compliance-generating technologies. Anderson (1991) argues that technologies that disseminate information at low cost – such as radio, newspapers, and television – allow modern states to manipulate the social sense of time. The mechanism is sociocognitive. A mass reception of the same narratives in the same language at the same time – watching the same television serials as they air, hearing the president speaking on the radio, or downloading the same "Internet memes" – is a modern national ritual: An "extraordinary mass ceremony" in which "each communicant is well aware that the ceremony he performs is being replicated simultaneously by thousands (or millions) of others" (35). In social science jargon, one could say that public and synchronized mass communication technologies lower the cost for political leaders to create "common knowledge" (images and narratives that every citizen knows that every other citizen knows, as summarized in Chwe [1998]). In previous epochs, this task had been the sole domain of religious authority. Warren (2015) and Herman and Chomsky (1987) provide theory and empirics on how these technologies produce docility among state populations. I recall being in the rural village of Kalikhum when the lights were turned on for the first time in months, in concordance with the springtime *Navruz* holiday. The national television channel played songs of peace, and Rakhmonov's face was plastered on the screen. I knew that if it were not for that man, the lights would still be off, and I knew that my host family understood this in the same way.

processes of single-party hegemonic stability were unleashed once the chaos of the transition subsided and the electricity was turned back on. Rural votes could be traded for access to scarce public goods. Once foreign relations were secured and neighbors stopped backing coup-plotters, all that was left was to neutralize the risk of insurgency from the internal hinterlands. This task was accomplished with ritual elections, occasional violence, and constant surveillance. Potemkin institution-building in the capitals was paired with a return to Soviet vote-farming in rural areas. Strong presidents, in this account, emerged via a path-dependent logic to take the place of Party Secretaries.

Emphasizing the constraints of inherited culture and path dependence comes at the expense of human agency. The model that anchors this book, by contrast, has no functioning institutions at all. Institutions are assumed to be captured by violence specialists. Mishandled distributional politics can escalate to the violent overthrow of the regime in power, as Georgian and Tajik history show. Inherited institutions did not prevent the removal of Gamsakhurdia or Iskanderov. The "coup-proofing" strategies of Shevardnadze and Rakhmonov were necessary to avoid a similar fate.

As a starting point for comparing these strategies, the previous chapter revealed an important similarity: both men paid off warlords in order to stay in power. To capture the vulnerability of presidents in this period, violence entrepreneurs are given the last move of the game in the model presented in Chapter 2. In essence, warlords are given a collective veto over distributional politics. If the president fails to democratize, provide public goods, punish corruption, or allow for a flourishing civil society, the cost to him is losing potential support from civil society or donors.[5] If, on the other hand, the president fails to pay off enough warlords, there will be a violent coup and he will be replaced. The militia-permeated institutions described in Chapter 4 are evidence of how these payoffs manifested.

Part of the explanation for variation in coup-proofing strategies is the different geopolitical situations that the two states faced. I argue that international system-level constraints set the structural parameters of the game, and in particular the stability threshold s, which changed the way the game was played in Georgia and Tajikistan. Russian policy toward the newly independent states was haphazard and sometimes improvised, to be sure. But, in broad brushstrokes, Russia pursued different strategies in response to state disintegration in the South Caucasus and Central Asia. In Georgia, Russian foreign policy had dual justifications: keeping leverage over the new state by threatening to support local ethnocracies and protecting innocent civilians from ethnic cleansing.[6] Thus, indigenous Georgian state-building efforts were

---

[5] This could be parameterized as a lower v^*.

[6] The well-known secessionist regions of Abkhazia, South Ossetia, and Adjara fit into neat spaces on preexisting Soviet maps, and the lesser known Armenian and Azeri enclaves of Akhalkalaki, Dmanisi, Ninochminda, Marneuli, and Bolnisi all managed to trade votes for

undermined. In the language of the model: the stability threshold was higher in Georgia, where a regime was consolidating in explicit opposition to, and in defiance of, Russian interests.

However, in Tajikistan, where a strong bulwark was needed against the radicalism in Afghanistan, state-building efforts were simply not allowed to fail. The potential for irregular infantry units and dangerous ideas to filter north across the Panj River to infect the other states of Central Asia was terrifying. Russia's foreign policy was chaotic and disorganized in the early 1990s, but Boris Yeltsin's 1993 statement that the Tajik–Afghan border is "in effect, Russia's" left no doubt that Russian leaders identified a vital interest in containing the consequences of Tajikistan's state failure. If Iranian or Afghan-backed guerrillas had been able to use the impenetrable Pamiri Mountains as a base to spread war into Kyrgyzstan and Uzbekistan, the Uzbek government would likely have redrawn the map of Central Asia by incorporating the Tajik region of Khojand – or perhaps all of the Ferghana Valley – as a buffer state. The expansion of Uzbekistan would have had unpredictable effects on Turkmenistan and Kazakhstan, with their abundant oil and gas reserves. These were all terrible outcomes that would have come at the expense of the regional security arrangements Russia was frantically sculpting.[7] To return to the language of the model: the stability threshold was lower in Tajikistan, where a regime was consolidating in explicit support of Russian interests.

Differences in the consolidation projects of Shevardnadze and Rakhmonov are consistent with what the model would predict if one country had a high stability threshold and the other had a low threshold (see Figure 5.1). Revolutionary nationalism in post-independence Georgia had a distinctly militant and anti-Russian flavor. Shevardnadze's foot dragging on joining the Commonwealth of Independent States (CIS) and quick expansion of ties to Western European states was seen as provocative in Moscow; Georgian paramilitary attacks on ethnic minorities could have led to destabilizing refugee crises spilling across borders. Many Russians made no secret of their desire to see Shevardnadze removed. As a result, Shevardnadze kept his friends close and his enemies closer. He incorporated many Georgian warlords quickly, such that his Ministry of the Interior became a virtual state-within-a-state.

In Tajikistan, by contrast, Russia lent its armed forces and intelligence to support the Rakhmonov regime against domestic challengers. Alexander Shishlyannikov, a representative of the armed services of Uzbekistan, and

---

de facto independence throughout the 1990s. The Mingrelians in western Georgia were also slow to forgive the elites in Tbilisi for the overthrow of Gamsakhurdia and the brutal counterinsurgency campaign against the Zviadists.

7 This is my own distillation of events, but for associated insights see Gretsky (1995), Nassim Jawad and Tadjbakhsh (1995), Atkin (1997a), Centlivres-Demont (1998), Dudoignon (1998), Zviagelskaya (1998), and Akbarzadeh (2001).

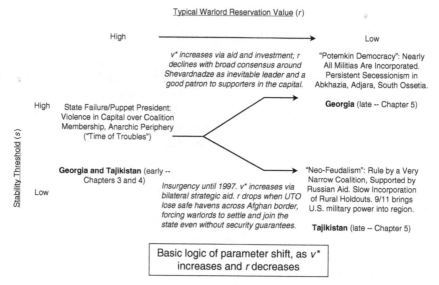

FIGURE 5.1. Divergent Consolidation Pathways: How do the parameters shift?

Saidamir Zukhurov, a representative of the KGB, were both members of Rakhmonov's first cabinet. There was a shared consensus among CIS states to keep the Afghan civil war in Afghanistan – and to keep American-funded Islamic fundamentalists or Iranian clerics from coming to power. As a result, I model the stability threshold as comparatively low, which is only to say that Russian support gave the president of this fragile new state more latitude to pick and choose among various local warlord allies than his counterpart in Georgia. Relatively low lottery odds also translated into high-stakes in Tajikistan, which manifested as fierce friction between various members of the insider coalition. The president was nearly removed from power by warlords who could see that as the peace process unfolded and additional warlords were incorporated, their bargaining position would be eroded.

But what did it mean for their position to be eroded? What were the warlords really after? Did they simply wish to skim cash off foreign charity money coming in (v^*)? Perhaps, but they also sought foreign recognition of their coalition to keep a stream of rents coming from both foreign aid (v^*), *on top of all of the rents that came from future domestic sources* (v).[8] In the medium, and

---

[8] This issue is somewhat confused in many political science treatments, with much piled into the term "spoils." See, for instance, Collier and Hoeffler (2004), particularly their interpretation of the "primary commodity exports" variable. Markowitz (2013), in an argument that resonates with the one in this book, shows that the ability of weak states in Central Asia to survive depends on local elites' ability to divide up "immobile capital" among themselves.

certainly in the long run, many commanders came to realize that domestic rents (v) would greatly outweigh any short-term incoming foreign cash (v^*). There are bribes, and then there are longer-term ways to avoid taxes and control regulation, permits, and other forms of rents.[9] The distributional politics that allow for v and v^* to be distributed are messy and unpredictable, which is why, to return briefly to the jargon of game theory, any equilibrium that "sticks" needs to be subgame perfect.

The president is a focal symbol of order and stability in a state recovering from failure. A confident and secure president sends a signal to investors and foreign donors that a country is open for business, and v^* follows. Warlords who are embedded in the state infrastructure – siphoning off wealth to pay their private armies, which they have not disarmed – have an interest in participating in the theater of civilian governance. The logic of the model is that gangsters realize that they can do better laundering money from naïve foreign donors and investors through a corrupt state apparatus than they can fighting among themselves to rule the state. Recall also that the *partial incorporation* and *full incorporation* equilibria both describe a peace that is self-enforcing without the need for an external guarantor. Order may be financed by outsiders, but it is monitored and enforced by locals.

But how does political power become centralized in the president's hands in this noninstitutionalized bargaining situation? The model in Chapter 2 answers this question. Warlords face a collective action problem once the president is installed. If all the security ministries act together, they can remove a president from power without bloodshed, but a warlord acting alone against a president is likely to fail. In the model, a warlord usually cannot carry out a coup alone – defection of multiple warlords from the president's coalition is almost always necessary to bring down the state. Tactical alliances between warlord factions do not easily congeal into a stable opposition coalition. In the absence of an institutionalized bargaining environment, and with no rules to structure coalition-building, no authority to enforce contracts between warlords, and the constant possibility that intrigue or accidental gunfire could eliminate a key coalition member, blocking coalitions can dissolve overnight.[10] The president is well positioned to take advantage of splits in warlord coalitions as they

---

9 Some of the criminals who gained power probably did not actually think very hard about the long run; some of these actors were actually driven by short-term payouts. It is likely the case that least two of the Tajik warlords analyzed in this dataset "exited the data" because they became addicted to heroin, stopped showing up for their jobs, and simply disappeared into the gray maze of street stories.

10 In the absence of formal institutions capable of structuring relationships between armed actors, warlords needed to use informal institutions with high transaction costs. For an excellent overview of the various sorts of efficiency losses associated with the use of informal institutions, see Dixit (2004), especially chapters 3 and 4. A partial exception to the "no counter-coalitions" rule was the United Tajik Opposition, but as the case study that follows demonstrates, it was, in the end, highly vulnerable to divide-and-rule strategies from the center.

emerge, using divide-and-rule strategies to become an indispensable member of the winning coalition. And though it is extra-model, the president's role as the primary spokesperson for the country's foreign policy means that he has a central role in negotiations with international companies, banks, and donor organizations. The fact that his signature is required on privatization documents, and that he is granted the symbolic power to appoint ministers, deputy ministers, and fill other state positions at a timing of his choosing, puts him in a position to distribute favor selectively and shape the overall bargaining space.

The model shows that, once in power, the president should *always* be able to buy off a coup. Warlords should understand that once a president is installed, they will lose leverage over him, even if they keep their guns. This is a central problem of civil war settlement in this framework. All players realize that different order-providing coalitions are sustainable equilibria. Donor-funded institution-building projects are important sources of liquidity, but v^* is divisible and fungible. The pie can be cut to accommodate myriad possible distributions.[11] The decision to install a president in the first place is a risky gamble.

Warlords weigh their odds of success in this unpredictable coalition formation lottery against their reservation value r for staying outside the state. As warlords' reservation values drop, presidents in consolidating states will be able to offer deals to incorporate warlords selectively into the state apparatus. The warlords who install a president at the beginning may be trusted allies, but the model assumes that they are functionally interchangeable with late-joiners. Though the strategy profile in Appendix B emphasizes that the president should pay exactly s warlords exactly what they would get in a coup, in the real world a very good strategy for staying in power is for the president to assemble *multiple* warlord coalitions, with overlapping memberships, that could each pass the stability threshold, and to distribute the spoils of statehood widely. As outside options fall, he can assemble a cheaper coalition and gradually keep more of the distribution for himself.[12]

As the warlords slowly capitulated to presidential authority, the president began to create a coalition of armed men with a shared interest in keeping him in power. Most of these men were still not loyal to the president in any meaningful way, and many of them would probably have liked to see him replaced. But there was sufficient uncertainty about who exactly would replace the president, and what the warlords' position would be in the new government, that most of these men were willing to opt for the relative safety of the current regime. Everyone understood that, unless it succeeded dramatically, any challenge to the president's coalition meant becoming a target for dismemberment by other militia leaders whose loyalty had been proven. Bit

---

[11] See Proposition 4 and the associated proof in Appendix B.
[12] Ferejohn (1986) presents a lucid and elegant exposition of the rationale for this assertion.

by bit, the old militia structures were replaced by sprawling and bloated power ministries, staffed with a mix of untested newcomers and co-opted militia members, opaque patronage networks, overlapping spheres of authority, and an earned reputation for corruption and unaccountability.

With wartime militia networks diluted in the new ministry structures, friendships and obligation chains that led upwards to the president were critical for long-term survival. Rather than a coup threat, new police forces became a constituency for the status quo. And with foreign military support, economic aid, and diplomatic recognition, this new warlord-backed regime became impossible to dislodge. Some warlords outside the coalition initially found they could thrive by operating independently at the periphery of state control, but eventually rural holdouts were squeezed into submission. Presidents sometimes used these newly incorporated warlords against the old, taking advantage of splits in the warlord coalition. Ultimately, both men insulated themselves from warlord challenges and emerged dominant.

SUMMARY OF STRATEGIES

Eduard Shevardnadze ascended to power in Georgia at the behest of a paramilitary junta, but quickly realized that gaining leverage over the leaders at the top of the power pyramids would be insufficient. There were actually dozens of self-financing militia factions within the Mekhedrioni and the National Guards, each backing a different leader (or, as the side-switching analysis in the previous chapter discussed, dividing their loyalty among a number of potential leaders). Shevardnadze was also keenly aware that as he deployed his unique asset – his celebrity status in Western capitals, with the promise of delivering huge bilateral and multilateral aid flows – whatever successes he achieved would provoke Russian hard-liners in Moscow. Georgian militias invited Shevardnadze to lead because of his unique potential to enrich the state (high v^*). Owing to external pressures, he needed the support of virtually all n of the militias to rule (implying a high stability threshold s).

Shevardnadze's strategy was to incorporate as many warlords as quickly as possible. He used the hierarchical structure of the ministries to break down "umbrella militia groups," which claimed huge memberships, into smaller constituent parts by promoting sub-lieutenants and lieutenants independently of each other. They were lured into these positions by the possibility of amassing personal wealth. Most were given their own semi-independent fiefdoms, housed within the labyrinthine Ministry of the Interior. By explicitly committing to policies such as rapid privatization, a restricted state role in economic policy, an uncompromising position toward the secessionist territories of Abkhazia and South Ossetia, and, most of all, non-interference into the affairs of his own Ministry of Interior, he lowered the political stakes between potential coup-plotters. The situation was made even more attractive once it became clear that, so long as he was at the head of the state, stable order and "Potemkin democracy" would allow his state to extract huge rents as a regional pivot player between Russia and the West.[13] The equilibrium that emerged gave the president the upper hand in bargaining with individual warlords, but little room to maneuver or steer domestic policy. This situation endured until the Rose Revolution.

A different kind of strategy, pursued effectively and ruthlessly by Emomalii Rakhmonov, was to *raise* the stakes of politics, heaping favors upon a pivotal warlord constituency to the exclusion of others. This strategy emerged naturally in Tajikistan once it became obvious that Russia would support any coalition capable of guaranteeing the security of the southern border with Afghanistan, and able to check the hegemonic aspirations of Uzbekistan and Iran. In the language of the model, Russia's support allowed the game to be played with an artificially low stability threshold s. Other parameters differed from the Georgian situation as well: the relatively low gains to stability ($v^* > v$, but only just) and the high reservation wage r for noncooperative warlords (stemming from the Afghan drug trade, the mountains, and the support from across the Uzbek and Afghan borders) slowed the speed of state consolidation.

Full incorporation emerged because, by 1997 (and even more so by 2003), two global parameters had shifted in ways that eventually changed warlords' strategic calculations. The first was a gradual rapprochement between Russia and Uzbekistan over the composition of the Tajik government, which lowered the reservation value r for warlords previously able to hide across international borders, or hold out hope of foreign support to keep the fight alive. As r dropped, and more warlords opted into the state, the inclusion of new warlords into the ruling coalition gave the president the ability to choose his allies, setting off violent opposition by marginal members of Rakhmonov's original coalition. A condominium between Uzbeks and Russians emerged only after the warlords who constituted the Tajik government demonstrated that they could fulfill certain basic functions, especially guaranteeing traffic through the overland routes necessary for the Afghan heroin trade and marginalizing, or silencing, radical Islamic voices. But it was the U.S. invasion of Afghanistan in 2001 that really cemented Rakhmonov's hold on power. Security assistance increased v^* available to the Tajik government. The reservation value r for most warlords was high when they were operating in the impenetrable Pamiri mountain range against ground forces, but modern air power changed the calculations. A shy man, whose only political experience before ascending to the position of head of state was working as the head of a collective farm in the agricultural region of Kulob, "Rakhmon" proved himself an adept political survivor. Today he heads of the only relevant political dynasty in Tajikistan.

---

[13] I borrow this clever phrasing from King (2001*b*).

EDUARD SHEVARDNADZE: THE INDISPENSABLE GEORGIAN

It is no secret why Eduard Shevardnadze was selected as the figurehead to pull the Georgian state back from the abyss: in the West, the recently retired Soviet Foreign Minister was probably the second most popular Soviet politician (after Mikhail Gorbachev) and the second most famous Georgian in history (after Josef Stalin). Shevardnadze was simply far ahead of the typical post-independence learning curve when it came to matters of international diplomacy, geopolitics, and the practical necessities of using international norms and rules to a new state's advantage. His personal friendships with foreign leaders and dignitaries – especially Bill Clinton and James Baker – were critical for getting international recognition of Georgia with territorial boundaries defined to include the territories of Abkhazia and South Ossetia. He was the first president from the Caucasus or Central Asia invited to visit the White House, and on his visit, Clinton promised $70 million in bilateral aid and signed policy directives for the CIA to train and equip a special unit of bodyguards to protect the new Georgian president.[14] More broadly, Shevardnadze's unique set of diplomatic contacts gave him the ability to seek multilateral and bilateral aid from both Russia and the West simultaneously. He proved successful in this task beyond anyone's expectations. On a per capita basis, Georgia received more democracy promotion assistance from the United States than the rest of the former Soviet Union combined. From Western European states, Georgia received approximately $172 million per year during the Shevardnadze era.[15]

Shevardnadze understood that the West wanted a geopolitical foothold in the Caucasus and that he was considered a "known quantity" in a confusing and chaotic region. He successfully branded Georgia as a potential energy corridor, securing contracts with multinational oil companies to build pipelines connecting Caspian oil to Western markets by way of a route that bypasses both Russia and Iran. In the imaginations of certain Western defense intellectuals this transformed Georgia from a forgettable ethnic oddity on the far side of the Black Sea to the geopolitical pivot of the Caucasus. Shevardnadze's status as a celebrity diplomat, and his personal involvement in all of these negotiations, made him seem larger than life. If he was not literally irreplaceable, he certainly was a unique national asset for a state confronted with a bewildering

---

14 See O'Ballance (1997), 138–139 and Areshidze (2007), 36.
15 Between 1995 and 2000, more than $700 million of bilateral aid arrived from the United States. In 2000 USAID's budget amounted to $200 per Georgian citizen, as compared to merely $1.25 per Russian. In addition to being the fourth-largest per capita recipient of USAID the 2002–2003, Georgia also received some 400 million Euro in the decade before the Rose Revolution from the coffers of the European Union, with additional contributions from many individual member states. Tudoroiu (2007), 323. See also Stephen Jones (2006), 41–42.

set of challenges.[16] In the words of Georgian political scientist Ghia Nodia, Shevardnadze's unique skills and autonomy in matters of foreign policy were the starting point for his domestic power grab: "It was on the image of this indispensability that he started building his internal legitimacy – and was later able to translate this into real power."[17]

At the same time he was cultivating relationships with the United States and Europe, Shevardnadze had a great deal of experience and many relationships in Moscow. He made the most of his ties to the Russian foreign policy apparatus to extract critical concessions and aid from Russia. This meant devoting a great deal of personal energy and political capital to trying to convince Russians that a Georgian government funded by the West would not be a threat to Russia's traditional sphere of influence. He was substantially successful in this task – certainly more successful than any credible alternative would have been. He used his contacts in the Russian military to make sure that the terms of the Tashkent Agreement (which divided the spoils of the Soviet military machine) were actually implemented, thus transferring tanks and heavy weapons to the Georgian state despite its "less than legitimate credentials."[18] Later he apparently convinced Yeltsin to authorize the use of the Black Sea Fleet to help rout the Zviadist insurgency.[19] At Moscow's insistence, he also appointed a Russian protege (Vardiko Nadibaidze) as the Minister of Defense and a Russian general (Igor Giorgadze) as the Head of the Internal Security Services. Placing Russian agents at the head of the army and internal police meant that Moscow could closely monitor Shevardnadze's actions, exert an independent role in military and foreign policy, and have an obvious route to a military coup if it so desired.

Shevardnadze gambled that if he allowed a system to evolve with multiple spheres of influence, he would be the most capable of navigating the resulting maze of coalition politics. He became famous in Georgia in the early 1990s for developing overlapping spheres of authority, a tactic that undermined

---

[16]   One of the often overlooked aspects of the Shevardnadze legacy was his quiet promotion of the idea among influential Georgians that this kind of aid and investment – the sort that does not come with Russian strings attached – should always be preferred to Russian bilateral aid or investment from Russian banks. Interviews with Vladimer Papava, Conducted in Tbilisi, February 7, 2006 and November 4, 2006. See also Papava and Chocheli (2003), generally.

[17]   See Nodia (2002), 428.

[18]   See Trenin (1995), 137. On the same page the author editorializes further: "[T]he Russians gave the Georgians more than enough weapons in 1992 to impose a military solution in all internal disputes. It is certainly not the fault of the Russian army that Tbilisi made such poor use of them."

[19]   It remains unclear whether these sailors were acting under orders from Moscow. A credible alternative tale of how the Black Sea Fleet was drawn into the conflict was that Shevardnadze took advantage of the fact that Moscow and Kiev both claimed the fleet as their own. As the tale is often told, Shevardnadze traveled in person to bribe the Ukrainian Admiral Baltin, the naval commander at the time, to move his artillery into position, reportedly with a briefcase filled with cash and two cases of Armenian cognac.

his credentials as a reformer, but also made his friendship and cooperation completely indispensable for anyone who wanted to actually get anything done. He was a relentless, tireless worker, and most of his work was done in meetings where he would sit down to build relationships, face to face, with individuals from every possible walk of society. He was notorious for postponing difficult decisions and shrewdly "maneuvering between different political forces... to broaden his power base and to neutralize major warlords."[20]

Although he eventually centralized political authority in a hegemonic party structure, the Citizens' Union of Georgia (CUG), for his first two years in office he exercised power in a personalist and deinstitutionalized fashion, preferring to "balance between opposing political factions."[21] This allowed the militia rank and file to convince themselves that they could accept favors from Shevardnadze without betraying their militia brethren or blood oaths. So long as there was a common external enemy in the form of Russia, it provided an impetus for warlords to work together. From the perspective of individual psychology, there was nothing particularly difficult about being anti-Russian in a political environment that was so virulently nationalist and anti-communist.[22]

In mid-September 1993, at the height of the Abkhaz crisis but before the final loss of Sukhumi, Shevardnadze appointed himself the Minister of the Interior, and asked the Georgian State Council to dissolve itself and approve a state of emergency. He was essentially proposing that the coup-plotters abrogate their roles, granting him what amounted to sweeping dictatorial powers. When this proposal was met with resistance from Ioseliani and other Mkhedrioni loyalists, Shevardnadze – in what was apparently a brilliantly improvised piece of political theater – publicly resigned and stormed out of the chamber. He resumed his position only after massive street demonstrations and a revolt of the professional state bureaucracy made it clear that no one wanted to see him go. He could, in fact, bring the whole state down with him if opponents rejected his ultimatums. But as the model suggests, for an equilibrium to be possible, most of the wealth must ultimately fall into the pockets of the warlords who control the raw tools of violence and those most symbolic institutions of statehood, the security ministries. Shevardnadze was the leader of a state with no army, other than the National Guard and the Mkhedrioni. The ongoing

---

20 See Jones (1997), 527 and Nodia (2002), 419.
21 Wheatley (2005), 85.
22 A few interview respondents went further, stating that once Shevardnadze came onto the scene, they realized that they had the possibility of provoking a serious war with Russia then waiting for the United States and Europe to come to their aid as a state-building strategy. It was a familiar kind of argument: state-building requires reducing a lot of the complex issues – including the transition from communism to capitalism, emotional decolonization for a multiethnic and multisecretarian society, and more – down to "all of us vs. them." The problem (though I did not interrupt the interviews to point this out) was that the Russian language was – and continues to be – the way that many *non-Russian non-Georgians* communicate with each other. For the 30 percent of Georgia's citizens who did not speak Georgian at home, persistent war between Georgians and Russians leaves them trapped between worlds.

battles with Zviadist insurgents and Russian-backed secessionists demonstrated that the Georgian state required both. Having secured foreign help to keep the state afloat, yoking the military strength of these private armies without bowing to the demands of the warlords was the core governance problem for Shevardnadze.

One of the first effects of Shevardnadze's celebrity status and foreign policy prowess was that events in the South Caucasus played out in a way that was a bit more "public" than they would have been otherwise, in terms of international news reporting. When Shevardnadze declined Russia's offer to have Georgia join the CIS – claiming to be executing the will of the consensus governing body – the challenge was understood violently. Clandestine arrangements introduced paramilitary armies from the North Caucasus to fight an undeclared war against the Georgian state, infiltrating through the secessionist regions.[23] Russian troops enforced a cease-fire in South Ossetia, provided support for the Abkhaz against the Georgian militias, and threatened to do the same in Adjara and the Armenian enclaves. Russia's threat to keep the small mountainous country fragmented indefinitely was very credible.

As diplomatic efforts to mend fences with Moscow occurred against the backdrop of Russian military and diplomatic support to Abkhaz and South Ossetian secessionists, this two-level gamesmanship required all the skill of a master politician. Shevardnadze needed to convince the Russians that he was extracting costly concessions from Georgian nationalists, while simultaneously convincing those same skeptical Georgians that he had not "gone native" during his years inside the Kremlin. Against the hopes of many in the United States and the demands of Georgian nationalist warlords, Shevardnadze finally opted to join the CIS. Though none of these positions were ratified by Parliament, Shevardnadze acceded to the presence of Russian peacekeepers along the unrecognized border with Abkhazia, the deployment of Russian border guards along the Turkish border (encircling Georgia), and negotiating – but, in the end, not signing – the Treaty on Russian Military Bases on the Territory of the Republic of Georgia, which would have granted Russia's military basing rights in Georgia for 25 years.[24]

---

[23] See Derluguian (2005), 260–273.

[24] At the end of many days of negotiating the minutiae of the treaty session, Shevardnadze apparently agreed, shook everyone's hand, and left the room without actually affixing his signature to the treaty. The Russian delegation left with a verbal agreement and publicized the treaty as a foreign policy success. The matter was thought settled, and the news cycles marched on. But it turns out that with no signature the treaty was technically nonbinding under international law. Apparently no one from Moscow's delegation felt they had the gravitas to "make him" sign. This technicality allowed Shevardnadze to renegotiate the content of the treaty at an OSCE meeting in 1999 – now with no war in the background and support from the West. He negotiated the withdrawal of troops by July 2001 rather than 2020. If he had signed,

In the mid-1990s, there was a general sense that the "frozen conflicts," which had left unrecognized states in Abkhazia, South Ossetia, and Adjara, would be reincorporated into the Georgian territory after patient diplomatic negotiations.[25] This would not be the case. The Russian leadership was not shy about using facts that emerged haphazardly in these conflicts to press foreign policy interests. As it became progressively clearer that Shevardnadze was not a disposable figure in the Georgian political scene, and that he had aspirations – indeed tangible plans – to move Georgia out of Russia's sphere, the Kremlin's position hardened. Military and political assistance to ethnic minority regions was provided. In the language of the model, this lowered the cost of war and raised the reservation value r for Abkhaz, South Ossetian, and Adjaran warlords. This might have begun as a strategy for punishing Shevardnadze for not joining the CIS and weakening his coalition formation project, but, over time, Georgian coalition politics evolved in the face of these new constraints.

The citizens of Abkhazia, South Ossetia, and Adjara became bargaining chips in a geopolitical game played between Russia and Georgia, which was trying mightily to reframe the issue as a conversation between Russia and the West. Protected from Georgian interference by the presence of a Russian military garrison, Aslan Abashidze and his family accrued fantastic personal wealth as the lords of Adjara during the 1990s (and, in a lesser known part of the transaction, would regularly lend his party's parliamentary votes to Shevardnadze's party in exchange for non-interference).[26] Abkhaz and South Ossetian "shadow states" persist to this day, now with established customs houses, foreign ministries, flags, national histories, and many other trappings of statehood.[27] These frozen conflicts provided Russia with a substantial source of leverage over the successively more Western-leaning Georgian governments. Though these regional hold-outs had no ability (or ambition) to seize the capital of Tbilisi, they remained territorial outposts for Russians. More importantly, they were lightning rods for Georgian nationalists, who fed off the anger of the displaced refugees who had been ethnically cleansed from the conflict zones. In May 1998, a six-day war broke out in the Gali district, the buffer region that straddles the unrecognized Georgia–Abkhazia border. The frozen conflict went hot in hours, yielding around 250 casualties and temporarily displacing between 30,000 and 40,000 Georgians from their homes. Shevardnadze was blamed by one faction for having coddled the guerrillas and blamed by the other faction for not doing enough to protect ethnic Georgians in Gali, who had been driven from their homes twice in five years. These events led almost immediately

---

the South Caucasus would be different today. Interview with Archil Gegeshidze, October 17, 2006. See also Larsson (2004), 406–409.

[25] For two examples of prominent area experts who committed to this position in print, see Suny (1995) and Laitin (2001).

[26] See Derluguian (2005), 230–233.

[27] See King (2000).

to a military uprising in Senaki (Mingrelia), reportedly led by former Zviadists – now incorporated into the Georgian army and Interior Ministry. The mutiny was put down the same day, but the entire set of events served as a reminder of the fragility of the arrangements that kept order in Georgia.

Meanwhile, back in the capital city of Tbilisi, processes of gradual alignment with the West were yielding huge social dislocations. The high-stakes politics of privatization that accompanied the end of socialism were usually decided behind closed doors. I asked a key informant within the Georgian Ministry of the Interior ("Levan") how former militia members got their share of foreign aid, which seemed (to me) to be accruing in the bank accounts of Europeans and the new class of nongovernmental organization employees ("NGO-nicks"). His response is worth reproducing here at length:

"So, you have the big men at the top in the Ministries. They are the bosses, and they make sure that things get divided fairly, so that nobody causes trouble. If there's trouble, there's sometimes a scandal, and then someone from Parliament or from the Chancellery [Executive Branch] will have to get involved, and then maybe everyone loses their jobs. Those of us at the bottom pay up, and if we have problems [with another Ministry employee] we take the problem to our bosses and let them sort it out … But most of the time, everyone knows who is connected, and they pay up to make sure that they keep a roof, you see? We are like tax collectors. Say you're a rich man, you speak English, you run an NGO – you still have to rent your building, yes? You have someone to drive your car? You still eat at restaurants? You have cousins and brothers and family, and you want them to all get jobs and stay out of trouble? Then you need to know people, to do favors. … Everyone needs soap and clothes and [music] tapes, and even the pensioners have kids sending money home from abroad, so the police who get [to work] the bazaars are always fine … but everyone does better when the Tiblesei [Georgian elite that have lived in the capital for more than 3 generations] are getting rich. Then, it's just a matter of dividing up the plate."[28]

As a former Minister of Public Order and Minister of the Interior for Georgia, Shevardnadze immediately understood what most Western journalists covering the region did not: although the large militia factions (the Mkhedrioni, the National Guard, the White Eagles, etc.) pretended to be organized based on strong ideology and dense social capital, their unity and hierarchy were based more on rhetoric than reality.[29] As described at length in the previous chapter, these umbrella organizations were composed of much smaller networks, recruited using family and criminal ties. The Mkhedrioni in particular claimed

---

[28] Interview conducted in Tbilisi, November 1, 2006.
[29] Shevardnadze was tremendously sophisticated as a student of contemporary street politics and local hierarchies of deference – he had a reputation for going out of his way to pay respect to the pecking order that militias established, address individuals by their self-appointed rank, and ask permission from superiors before speaking with subordinates. This was primarily a way of signaling to the militia members that he took their honorifics very seriously – and it set him apart from most of his peers, who could not convincingly hide their class biases.

an enormous membership but, by this point, most of the members were tied to a particular protection relationship with a captain, a local political boss, or a politically connected "businessman" organizing imports and exports. Shevardnadze understood that if he were to pull at loose threads and quietly deal with militia captains individually, he could centralize authority without rocking the boat or directly confronting the celebrity leaders of the umbrella factions, Tengiz Kitovani and Dzhaba Ioseliani. He slowly tightened this web and let warlords turn on each other, while simultaneously assuring "insider" warlords that he would look the other way while they looted the state. His eyes could not be everywhere, but a lot of different kinds of people were beginning to think of Shevardnadze as their "roof."

One of the central problems that Shevardnadze faced – a problem that motivated the model in Chapter 2 – is that militia captains who were *already* controlling lucrative bottlenecks in the informal sector were skeptical of the idea that they could do better by giving their loyalty to Shevardnadze. Recalling a conversation with Georgi Karakashvili (the commander of the White Falcons, a group that was a relatively early convert to Shevardnadze's consolidation project) about promotion into the Border Guards, a former Mkhedrioni lieutenant told me:

"[The offer] was a better and safer life, yes, with a salary and good opportunity to get noticed ... but it would take me away from my home and friends. And once I was all alone, how could I be sure that they would not later say 'him – he's a criminal, and I do not need to keep my word to him.' Who would blame them? ... But I took the promotion, in the end. It was a risk, but what was my choice?"[30]

This captures two facets of the general dilemma warlords faced: a leader cannot credibly pre-commit to a particular distribution of wealth, so warlords have no real reason to take him at his word. But if the warlords foresee a time in the future when their reservation values will slip toward zero, they might be convinced to throw in their lot with the president anyway, being forced to take a risk just to keep what they have. This process of gradually lowering profitable options for warlords outside of the state was the core of the state-building and incorporation project in Georgia. The offers came in the form of promises of autonomy within the ministries, which was valuable, even if it was understood that the autonomy could, in theory, be revoked at any time.

All the while, Shevardnadze and his economic team used the transition to a market economy to make the office of the president indispensable to the functioning of the domestic economy. New aid projects and foreign investment meant new opportunities for entrepreneurship, especially for Georgians who could speak English. The influx of wealth also brought new opportunities for graft, corruption and personal enrichment. The creeping formalization of

---

30 Interview conducted in Kvimo-Kartli on November 13, 2006.

the economy brought a proliferation of permits and regulations, as well as the inevitable back room payments and bribes that could circumvent the new regulatory regime. As the organization on the front lines of enforcement, the Ministry of the Interior was well positioned to tax the informal bottlenecks in this new era of entrepreneurialism. But it was the office of the presidency that was the true beneficiary of this new culture of corruption, as the president was a focal point for the emerging class of criminally connected businessmen who made huge profits from skewed privatization processes. In a transitional society, where the national currency was worthless and property rights could not really be enforced outside of personalist connections, the president's continuing friendship and patronage was invaluable. Once all the major players came to realize they had a shared stake in their friendship with the same man – and that no one else could offer the same degree of wealth creation that Shevardnadze could – contemplating a coup became much more difficult. Former Minister for Economy Vladamir Papava described the situation well: "While the laws were sometimes ambiguous, Shevardnadze was quite careful to not renege on promises regarding a person's [privatized] property. Investors and wealthy Georgians needed to trust the rules, trust the system. And, of course, because sometimes his promises overlapped, he *was* the system."[31] (*L'état, c'est moi.*)

Shevardnadze's ability to promote militia members within the shells of the formal security institutions inherited from Soviet times was also a powerful commitment mechanism. Portfolios with independent hiring and firing authority were particularly coveted, as they allowed warlords to formalize their patron relationships with their subordinate clients and screen recruits for personal loyalty. When loyalty to a gang leader was the paramount consideration for promotion and advancement, it led many career bureaucrats and competent, honest armed agents to retire. This led to a strange situation where superficially similar security institutions – with the same buildings, names, and even uniforms as in Soviet times – emerged with completely different personnel and a different sort of corporate culture. The institutionalization of unaccountable pockets of authority at the top levels of the bureaucracy had a corrosive effect on overall morale, with terrifying long-term consequences for Georgian civilians.[32]

While the Constitution of 1995 gave Shevardnadze power to selectively dismiss individuals anywhere in any ministry, this sweeping power was less threatening to warlords than it might have appeared for a few reasons. First,

---

[31] Emphasis in original interview February 6, 2006.

[32] Charles King has observed that in some respect this culture was not new: underpaid traffic police using their positions of authority to extract bribes from drivers' security was a fixture of late Soviet life in the Caucasus, and those technologies of extortion were replicated in the new security ministries (2006). See Zverev (1996), Nodia (1998*a,b*), and Areshidze (2007) for descriptive accounts of this phenomenon.

it was assumed that if a particular individual was dismissed after a few years, it would only be after the ousted person had used his time in the ministry to install loyal subordinates who could continue to make payments to him or his family. Second, it was fairly well understood that micro-managing the complex personal relationships that greased bureaucratic wheels inside the Ministry of the Interior would have been an impossible task for anyone, especially a president whose attention was mostly focused on foreign relations. This gave lieutenants a great deal of practical autonomy. Third, constant reshuffling of portfolios would have created perceptions of instability and uncertainty, which would be as bad for Shervardnadze's rule as it was for the warlords themselves. This third point is discussed in more depth in the text that follows.

Over time, the ability to set up miniature fiefdoms within the Ministry of the Interior freed members from the "umbrella" militia hierarchies that had emerged in the 1988–1991 period. Shevardnadze understood, perhaps better than anyone in Georgia, how to pit the career incentives of different short-sighted men against each other. Alex Rondeli recalled: "He was a man who saw the whole board... always calculating, always thinking about promoting with one hand and installing your worst political enemy one step below you in the hierarchy at the same time. He could manage relationships with the best of them. He was the finest product of the [Soviet] system."[33] He met with a great number of police captains, militia lieutenants, and other subordinates in the Mkhedrioni and National Guard hierarchies, always formally, being careful to respectfully ask the permission of the State Council first. But very slowly, using his powers of appointment over the security ministries, Shevardnadze began to promote lieutenants and sub-lieutenants, re-shuffling security personnel at almost monthly intervals during the 1993–1995 period. He created entirely new security sub-bureaucracies within the Ministry of the Interior with overlapping mandates, including the Border Guards, the Special Emergency Response Corps, Tbilisi Rescue Corps, Government Guard, Internal Troops of the Ministry of Internal Affairs, the American-trained Special Unit Alpha and a CIA-Trained Presidential Guard, and several even smaller forces. A zone of autonomy within the security services, even if its mandate overlapped with someone else's authority, could be transformed into lucrative business opportunities. Most leapt at the opportunity to guarantee themselves a piece of the pie.

What this meant was that real power increasingly lay outside the official institutional framework. Stephen Jones described politics during this period as "feudalized," in the sense that it was "fracured politically and geographically into unofficial power centers [which were] dominated by holders of important political office but who run their spheres of influence on the basis of informal networks, mutual favors and obligations."[34] Formal institutions were evolving

---

33 Interview in Tbilisi on November 19, 2006.
34 Jones (1997), 525.

during this period in a way that made Georgia appear like it was following an Eastern European script of legal and economic reform, parliamentary accountability, and engagement by civil society groups. However, as in Soviet times, these formal structures worked only intermittently without the aid of personal networks. Because these personal networks and informal institutions are difficult to monitor or map, particularly for outsiders, it is hard to make inferences about anyone's actual influence during this period by following official posts, or any metric other than their network distance from Shevardnadze. Dzhaba Ioseliani, for instance, spent virtually all of 1993 as a mere Parliamentary Deputy. In the aftermath of the 1992 elections, Kitovani was forced out of his position as Minister of Defense, but, in practice, retained influence by naming his own replacement and by that point was managing a controlling stake in Georgia's partially privatized energy sector.

What of the non-Georgian ethnic minorities? On the whole, their warlords fared well under this system. Georgia is often presented by political scientists as a laboratory to observe how ethnic boundaries can be constructed as static and militarized.[35] Ethnic secessionist regions – Abkhazia, South Ossetia, and Adjara – all fit neatly into spaces on old Soviet maps and can provide extensive historiographic evidence of their cultural distinctiveness from Georgians. Recall, however, that a large number of lesser known Armenian and Azeri enclaves (Akhalkalaki, Dmanisi, Ninochminda, Kvemo-Kartli, Marneuli, and Bolnisi) and the Mingrelians in Western Georgia, were all accommodated by the Georgian state. All were potential sources of leverage for Russia, but, in the end, most of these enclaves organized arrangements functionally similar to that of Adjara's "warlord" Aslan Abashidze, brokering their votes in parliament to Shevardnadze's party in exchange for food, fuel, and non-interference.[36] Shevardnadze's guaranteed voting constituencies were ethnic minority areas, which would deliver their votes for the CUG en masse. In the early stages of power consolidation, he appointed Otar Pacacia and Avatandil Margiani, symbolic representatives of Mingrelian and Svan ethnic lobbies, respectively, to the State Council and then to high positions in his government, assuring them that the informal governance structures those communities were using to distribute favors would be protected in the new state. By the 1999 parliamentary elections, even Aslan Abashidze's "Union for Democratic Revival" was boxed into defining itself as a national party and part of the opposition coalition.[37]

What evolved over time was an "off-the-books" economy where between 60 percent and 70 percent of economic activity in the country – certainly

35 See for instance, Toft (2005), 1–33, 87–126.
36 See, Marten (2012), 68–86.
37 Jonathan Wheatley suggests that the police "cleared away the local warlords" (88) in some districts, but in my reading of the period it was far more common for these men to remain in place (with their authority legitimized) and then find themselves enmeshed in the president's favor economy.

much of the trade in manufactured goods, alcohol, tobacco, and food – was unreported and untaxed.[38] Former Prime Minster Zurab Zhvania estimated that smuggling had cost the state 60 million lari ($29 million) from uncollected tobacco revenue alone in 2003 and almost $200 million from nondeclared oil products.[39] Thomas de Waal of International War and Peace Reporting quotes a corruption specialist who put the issue in even starker terms, saying that "The [Georgian] government could eliminate its fiscal deficit if it would just fully collect the taxes on two products, imported gasoline and cigarettes."[40] Despite the fact that the government retained the bloated state apparatus of Soviet times and continued to promise a huge range of social services (health care, pensions, etc.), tax collection was about 9 percent of reported gross domestic product (GDP). It was a system where no state employees were paid enough to live on, and so they had to marketize their place in the bureaucracy. It was structural corruption on a societal scale, which made it impossible to invest money without high-level personal connections. Given that the Ministry of the Interior was incorporating criminal militias, it is not surprising that this sort of corruption was particularly pervasive in the security services. Svante Cornell claimed that the Georgian police forces in the late Shevardnadze era were the most corrupt in the region, thoroughly penetrated by criminal interests.[41]

An overlooked part of this strategy was turning the lower tiers of the militias against their factional commanders. Once the warlords were substantially co-opted, it was possible for Shevardnadze to order the arrest of prominent warlords (such as Kitovani in September 1994 or Ioseliani in 1995). The deeper proof of Shevardnadze's political prowess was not when Ioseliani's Mkhedrioni forces were deployed to dismantle Kitovani's National Guard, but when co-opted Mkhedrioni members later turned on Dzhaba himself. Jailing the spiritual head of the Mkhedrioni would have been extremely threatening to the remaining militias, had the president not already demonstrated – repeatedly – that certain new rules of the game were fixed. The regime had demonstrated that, even given the opportunity, it would not liquidate the assets of new businessmen, who would be permitted to keep the wealth and property that they acquired during the scramble for Soviet spoils. The commitment by the president to keep the state extremely weak in certain areas, especially public administration and taxation, was made credible by handing entire bureaucracies over to incorporated militia members as explicit side payments for their loyalty. In this regard, the incremental moves to "crack down" on

---

38   King (2004*b*), 16 and Slade (2007).
39   Ratiani (2004).
40   Quoted in de Waal (2005), citing MacPhee (2004).
41   Cornell (2003), 33. Though drugs are neither produced nor consumed in Georgia in commercially interesting quantities, according to Shelley (2004), Interpol estimates that 10 percent of Afghan heroin moving to Europe moves through the South Caucasus. Georgia was hyperbolically identified as "the most" corrupt Soviet state by Ekedahl and Goodman (1997), 280.

prominent Mkhedrioni leaders who had kept aloof from Shevardnadze in early 1995 were more important than local scholars have tended to recognize, as most of the police lieutenants who enacted the arrest warrants had themselves sworn blood oaths to the Mekhedrioni a few short years before. It was a public warning by Shevardnadze that Dzhaba Ioseliani was no longer above politics. Shevardnadze could order one group of Ioseliani's men to attack the other group, and they would listen. Whatever arrangements were enforced, they would be enforced primarily through the Ministry of the Interior.

The failed assassination attempt against Eduard Shevardnadze was an important turning point for Georgia. According to rumor this assassination attempt was a direct response to Shevardnadze's affront on Ioseliani's leadership. Shevardnadze used the event to dismiss the Russian head of his military, Igor Giorgadze (who had fled the country in a Russian aircraft), order the arrest of Ioseliani and his lieutenants, and pass a new constitution – finally formalizing his presidency and established the current legal framework for the Georgian state. The legitimacy conferred through his mass-based political party was used to channel latent anti-Russian resentments into an energetic, Western-oriented foreign policy on the European model. But what Shevardnadze did not do proved just as important. He did not use the assassination attempt to purge the lower ranks of the security agencies, despite the fact that he would have had public support in doing so. Again, my interpretation of this inaction is that the non-prosecution of former regime opponents who had joined the ranks of the state sent a clear signal that certain rules of the game would be sacrosanct. As a high-placed former cabinet official wryly commented, "He was magnanimous in his victory after the car bomb. That was why he survived [instead of Gamsakhurdia]. He understood that there was plenty to share."[42]

As the model suggests, the promise of increased wealth opportunities for warlords who colluded with the state rather than challenging it was what brought unruly militias to heel. Importantly, Shevardnadze was removed from the day-to-day functioning of the shadow economy that managed to enrich the Georgian militia captains. This is consistent with the model, given the extremely high stability threshold (s). Shevardnadze gave his armed agents a relatively free hand domestically, so long as they did not take actions (generating violence or scandal) that would disrupt the flow of aid and threaten the entire system. Only when an individual stepped out of line would a punishment materialize, and even then, only with the firm backing of various other power centers in society poised to take advantage of the deviant's fall. The mechanism that was used to punish failure was *kompramat* (compromising information), a strategy from the Soviet era of maintaining a secret file of illegal dealings for the purposes of blackmail. For all of the disadvantages of the rampant corruption in the favor economy described previously, it had the virtue of creating a paper trail. Almost

---

[42] Interview conducted in Tbilisi, November 29, 2006.

anyone who had grown rich and powerful in Georgia during the 1990s had done so by running roughshod over some obscure legal barrier. With everyone implicated in the same ponzi scheme, there was a constant threat that the government would expose an individual criminal's misdeeds and expropriate all of his family's wealth. Zurab Zhvania, then chairman of the Parliament and manager of Shevardnadze's 1999 electoral campaign, reported to Keith Darden that all of the so-called "anticorruption" campaigns carried out in Georgia were actually thinly veiled purges.[43] To understand how this worked in practice, consider one militia member's account of Shevardnadze's "magic desk":

"American democracy is old … you do not know court politics. Here [in Georgia] we have to make our democracy work in the shadow of an older history, in the shadow of the Tsars. … Ioseliani was at first like a court magician – like Rasputin! – using his eyes and his voice to make Soviet bureaucrats lose their balls … but I think he [Ioseliani] didn't know what he was up against … Shevardnadze had those gifts too, you see: He had a magic desk, with a permanent memory. If you worked for him, he would have a file on you. All your history, every mistake. And when it came time for you to go, he would call you in, open the drawer, show you that he had you. But if they quit, and went quietly, his way, it would stay safe and forgotten in the desk. … The magic trick was that you *believed* that he would actually forget and forgive, and leave the file in the desk, if you did what he said. He had *that* power. The power priests have. The power to bless and forgive."[44]

This equilibrium was propped up by huge sums of Western development aid. But life grew more difficult for most Georgians. In spite of the proliferation of NGOs and the rhetorical promises that Western European–style welfare socialism was around the corner, it was evident that the individuals most capable of paying bribes were also the individuals with the connections to place money in offshore accounts or purchase property. By the end of 2003, in spite of huge infusions of Western aid, internal debt in unpaid salaries and monthly pensions for state employees (which had by this point dropped to less than $7) had reached $120 million. Half of the population was living below the international poverty line.[45] Although there was great care taken with the facade of safety and normalcy in downtown Tbilisi, economic transactions took place against a social backdrop where violence was just below the surface, precisely as one would expect, given the fact that many of the police officers were rehabilitated militia members.[46] The relationship between citizens and the police during this period harkened back to the late Soviet period:

43 See Darden (2008), 52.
44 Interview conducted in Tbilisi, May 8, 2007.
45 To give a sense of the size of this untaxed and illegible "shadow economy": the reported per capita GDP of the state divided by the best population estimates gave a per capita GDP figure roughly on par with that of Swaziland. See King (2004*b*) and Papava (2006).
46 Wheatley (2005) reports that "on at least six occasions between 1997 and 1999, suspects are said to have 'committed suicide' by jumping out of the top windows of MIA detention centers during police interrogation."

representatives of the Ministry of the Interior were dangerous, and you did not want them to think you owed them a favor. According to a survey conducted in the waning months of the Shevardnadze administration, only 32 percent of Tbilisi residents said they would turn to the police after being victims of a violent crime.[47]

EMOMALII RAKHMONOV: THE SLOW TALKER

When the militias seized the capital city of Dushanbe in December of 1992 in the name of the Popular Front of Tajikistan (PFT), Emomalii Rakhmonov had been the Head of State for just a few weeks. Rakhmonov was named head of state in a special session of the Supreme Soviet convened in territory held by the Popular Front. This former *kolkhoz* collective farm head from Kulob was a compromise candidate, in that both the armed groups from his home region of Kulob and Khojandi financiers with political ties to Tashkent and Moscow believed that they could control him.[48] For years afterwards, Rakhmonov was commonly referred to as *Rais Rudaki Prospect* ("President of Rudaki Avenue") because his administration was unable to enforce its edicts even a mile from the presidential palace.[49] Rakhmonov faced a situation even more harrowing than that of Shevardnadze in Georgia. He was literally a hostage to Kulobi war criminals in his own inner circle, while the Khojandi elite schemed to replace him and recapture high state offices. A rebel army launched guerrilla raids from the mountains in the country's east, where the elites were toying with secession. The economy was nonexistent.

Shevardnadze's tactics of exploiting factional and interpersonal divisions within paramilitary umbrella groups to seize control "from below" were foreclosed to Rakhmonov because of dense *avlod* ties within militias. In a conversation with a high-ranking member of United Nations Mission of Observers in Tajikistan (UNMOT) with firsthand knowledge of the consolidation process, I described Shevardnadze's strategy of dismembering large umbrella factions by

---

[47] Wheatley (2005), 132–133 reports that this survey also reported that only 20 percent of citizens (across the country) would involve the state in a land or property dispute.

[48] Various Lakai Uzbek and Hissori militias – both minorities – were wary of returning a Khojandi to the regime's top office, and rationalized the rise of a Kulobi. Most hoped Kulobi rule would be temporary, and some – Kenjayev in particular – even held out hopes that they would eventually be able to emerge as pivotal in the new power structure, if the country aligned closer to Uzbekistan.

[49] Even after the 1997 Peace Process, many warlords continued to control territory in which neither the government nor UN observers could enter without the permission and escort of these warlords. The most prominent of these locations were Darband (controlled by Mullo Abdullo), Tavildara (home of the Minister of Emergency Situations Mirzo Zioyev), and even the Leninsky District, twenty kilometers from downtown Dushanbe (controlled by Rakhmon "Hitler" Sanginov).

exploiting frictions between sub-commanders for comparison. His response to this is worth quoting here at length:

"He [Rakhmonov] did the same thing here – you peel away the label of the Popular Front and you find Kulobis, Hissoris, Lakai, Leninobodi financiers, Uzbeks – a real mixed bag. And he exploited those divisions, certainly … but I can't think of a time when he successfully turned a lieutenant against a commander if they were from the same region … that just couldn't happen, you see. I know that it sounds strange, but these guys are all related to each other. … That's part of why the competition got so fierce and bloody, and why it was so difficult to reach compromises at first: Everyone knew that everyone else just wanted to hand things over to their brothers-in-law. … Even today, everything worth owning is owned by someone who has sealed the deal not just with a joint business venture, but by arranging a marriage between someone in their family to someone with ties back to Dangara [the President's home region]. That's how it is here."[50]

Despite these obstacles, Emomalii Rakhmonov developed a strategy for political survival. He realigned domestic institutions and economic policy to make it difficult for elites from different regions to cooperate. Rakhmonov's coalition came to power as a client of Uzbek and Russian interests: essentially to hold the line against the civil war in Afghanistan from moving north. When frictions between Uzbekistan and Russia began to emerge, Rakhmonov allied his small nation strongly with Russia and proceeded to purge Uzbek-backed factions from the Communist old guard. The eventual settlement of the Tajik civil war came at the prerogative of Moscow and at the expense of Tashkent. Being a peacemaker strengthened Rakhmonov's legitimacy with the population and introduced new players into the governance shell-game. A combination of symbolic autonomy and large shares of the Afghan narcotics trade smoothed this transition. Eventually, he freed himself of dependence on the Kulobi warlords who put him into power. Cumulatively, the first decade of Rakhmonov's rule saw the fragmentation of the Popular Front coalition and the political disenfranchisement of every region other than the president's own. Unlike Shevardnadze, there is little temptation to call him a genius. But if power politics in for Tajikistan were a scored game, Rakhmonov – now "Rakhmon" – won it.

Emomalii Rakhmonov lacked Eduard Shevardnadze's gravitas, celebrity, external confidence, and foreign policy experience. He came to power supported by politically untested rural criminal-clan networks, with no friends in Moscow or Tashkent, let alone Europe or the United States. But he proved a remarkably quick student of geopolitics. Tajikistan was unique among the Central Asian republics in that it was spared the cadre purges of early 1980s because the Soviet Union was fighting its war in Afghanistan.[51] What

---

50 Interview conducted in Dushanbe August 15, 2005.
51 Going after cotton corruption was a luxury that Moscow could afford in republics like Uzbekistan, but in Tajikistan, Moscow was more or less willing to leave Khojandi elites in

Rakhmonov took from this historical period is that Moscow could be counted on to come to the aid of his government so long as Islamic radicalism was kept on the other side of the border. The civil war demonstrated that Rakhmonov and the Kulobi mafia networks that backed him were capable of controlling the demographically dense lowlands of their country, making these Kulob-based militias indispensable coalition partners for the time being. The key to the centralization of power in the hands of a shrinking clique was international public relations with Moscow – "He was a fast learner and a great salesman."[52]

In broad brushstrokes, the story of Tajik politics in the 1990s is the story of Emomalii Rakhmonov slowly learning the political skills that Eduard Shevardnadze had spent a lifetime perfecting. He became adept at mapping the frictions between different coalitions, exploiting divisions to split his enemies, and acquiring a sense of timing and political theater. Russian military power gradually eroded the UTO's will to fight. Rakhmonov's foreign policy gradualism facilitated a slow rapprochement between Russia and Uzbekistan over the composition of the Tajik government, which finally strangled the ambitions of certain Uzbek-backed militia captains who dreamed they could capture the state apparatus with Tashkent's blessing. The Tajik government's control of the major north–south roads gave the Ministry of the Interior a virtual monopoly on the rents from the Afghan heroin trade. The eventual arrival of American strategic bilateral aid after the invasion of Afghanistan gave the regime new resources to buy off warlords. As the logic of the model anticipates, while warlords were losing outside options this pulse of external funding led to a broader ruling coalition – not a democratic outcome, but a stable outcome that expanded the president's opportunities for divide-and-rule.

For the first few years in office, Rakhmonov acquired a reputation as a patient, methodical, nonthreatening force in Tajik politics – not at all ruthless, not at all relentless, very interested in listening, and not quick to give voice to his opinions. Like Shevardnadze, he found that delaying difficult tradeoffs and acquiring a reputation for indecision was a decent strategy for building trust between warlords. Also like Shevardnadze, he developed a remarkably consistent foreign policy orientation that allowed him to make the most of a

power so long as they served as a loyal "buffer state" against the chaos in their southern neighbor. Kathleen Collins argues that the social solidarity *against* these purges was what created interclan elite pacts in other regional states. She hints that in 1991, these pacts allowed Uzbekistan and Kyrgyzstan to avoid Tajikistan's violent fate with clandestine clan pacts. See Collins (2006), Chapters 4 and 5.

[52] Quote from former Ministry of Foreign Affairs official. A member of the United Nations Tajikistan Observation Mission (UNTOP) observed the following: "Rakhmonov always gave a warning before he went after you. He'd warn once, twice … he'd wait for months or years, giving people a chance to remove themselves from politics once they were becoming too threatening. He always gave everyone opportunities to get away.… He was not a genius, no … more of a 'slow talker,' if you know what I mean." Interview conducted in Tajikistan, July 22, 2007.

bad geopolitical hand. He succeeded in convincing Russia, Uzbekistan, and the United States that it was better to prop up his corrupt and fragile state than to risk state collapse that might infect the region. Rakhmonov needed no urging to commit his country to the CIS Collective Security Treaty. The 1993 Russian–Tajik Agreement on Friendship, Cooperation and Mutual Assistance made Tajikistan a Russian military outpost. Rakhmonov also proved to be extremely skilled at controlling the flow of information to the Russian security services, gradually convincing Moscow that power sharing with Hissori, Lakai, or Khojandi groups would only produce an Uzbek puppet state, which would be adverse to Russian geopolitical interests.

Russian support – manifesting in the language of the model as a low stability threshold *s* – facilitated a hard line against challengers to Rakhmonov's regime. Despite a number of high-profile meetings and international mediation efforts, the internationally recognized government in Dushanbe refused to make concessions to the United Tajik Opposition (UTO). Some elites in Gorno-Badakhshon (GBAO) declared independence in 1993, but failed to achieve any hint of international recognition.[53] As they grew more and more desperate, the Islamist rhetoric of the UTO increased in tone and frequency in an attempt to attract financing from Iran, the Gulf States, and Afghanistan. This backfired, making the worst-case threat of the Kulobi hard liners more credible to distant elites in Moscow. Any doubts that the elites in Dushanbe were the last line of defense against militant mujahideen, potentially poised to export revolution to the soft Muslim underbelly of the former Soviet Union, were belied by intelligence reports that included quotes from certain radical clerics affiliated with the UTO.[54]

Similar tactics were used to trim the membership of the Popular Front coalition of anyone whose influence network stretched to Uzbekistan. Prominent Khojandi, Hissori, and Lakai warlords would cry foul to distant cousins and one-time patrons in Uzbekistan, hoping that Uzbekistan's president Islam Karimov would be able to intercede on their behalf to Moscow. But appeals through Tashkent backfired in the same way: they were reframed as evidence that Uzbekistan was trying to direct Tajikistan's political development and limit Russia's role.

Because the president inherited an impoverished state apparatus and faced militias recruited with dense social capital, it was not easy to use patronage

53 Recall that GBAO has cast votes in the 1994 election with 96 percent for Abdullajanov and only 4 percent for Rakhmonov.
54 I honestly have no idea how one would, with the full benefit of hindsight, assess the voracity of these sort of claims. I suppose it is possible that there were pockets of angry Salafi jihadist radicals lurking in the mountains, poised to seize fragile states. What can be stated with certainty is that many journalists in the immediate aftermath of the September 11th attacks found it convenient to take this propaganda at face value. See, for example, Rashid (2002) – and take special note of the cover art.

opportunities to subdivide the militia captains.[55] The first priority was the restructuring of domestic institutions to formalize the bargaining advantage that the Kulobis had earned with their military victory. It took no time at all for the Kulobi ruling class to grasp that independence meant sovereign debt. Functionally, the war's winners were in a position to borrow money using the bodies of the war's losers – laborers residing in the rural, but economically productive, cotton-producing regions of the south – as collateral. The internal boundaries of the state were redrawn to give Kulobis semipermanent dominance over the cotton-producing agricultural southwest, essentially reappropriating the institutional advantage that the Khojandis had used to rule the country unchecked for decades.[56] Khojandis were passive participants in the disenfranchisement of the other non-Kulobi members of the Popular Front, apparently willing to gamble that the disenfranchisement of other groups with ties to Uzbekistan would give them an effective monopoly on ties to Tashkent.[57]

As Rakhmonov and his network of Kulobi apparatchiks began to monopolize power within the state apparatus, this centralization came first at the expense of groups with ties to Uzbekistan. Time and again, Uzbekistan would have the opportunity to play the part of the spoiler. The political maneuvering that followed took on many aspects of a proxy war between Uzbekistan and Russia, for reasons outlined at the beginning of this chapter. Briefly, over

[55] The fact that the warlords' families were clustered by geographic region and connected by political marriages meant that wealth transfers had some positive spillover effects. As such, warlords from Kulob could convince themselves that their fortunes were lifting together, at least for a time, even as individual Kulobi warlords were purged from the ruling coalition. Over time, however, this intra-Kulobi optimism proved misplaced. At the time of this writing, it has been nearly two decades since the official end of the civil war and more than two decades since the Kulobis unambiguously seized control of the state apparatus, yet is not clear that the so-called "Kulobization" of postwar power structures led to much public investment in the region of Kulob. In winter of 2007, the city center of the regional capital of Kulob still did not have a constant power supply.

[56] Successive waves of population displacement had transformed the demographics around Kurgan-Tubbe in a way that favored Uzbek-affiliated ethnic groups. As it was articulated to me, the fear was that Kurgan-Tubbe could ally with the Khojandis in the north, giving Uzbekistan potential influence over two of Tajikistan's five electoral districts. A military coup or popular revolution at the center by Uzbek-backed fifth columnists, it was feared, could be 3/5. The solution was simple: redraw regional boundaries to create only four regions. This crude gerrymandering was achieved by revising the constitutional framework to combine the administrative districts of Kurgan-Tubbe and Kulob into a single district of "Khatlon," an ancient name of Kulob. This effectively disenfranchised Uzbeks and Hissori populations in the south under the demographic weight of Kulob, reified in the 1994 election when 99.5 percent of Khatlon was reported as having voted for Rakhmonov (see Chapter 4). The capital and surrounding regions remained a district, but one under control of Kulobi militia formations. Khojandis could then be played against the Pamiris. The government cemented this advantage further by resettling many Kulobis in western Khatlon, installing them at the heads of collective farms after the murder or displacement of previous district heads. See Roy (2000), especially 97–98, and ICG (2005).

[57] Interview conducted in Dushanbe January 28, 2006.

generations at the top of the Tajik status hierarchy, many Khojandis had come to see themselves as closer, culturally and economically, to Tashkent than to Dushanbe. In recognition Khojand's special status in Moscow, the Russian foreign policy apparatus was convinced to keep a consulate open in Leninobod until 1996. The mass expulsions of the Gharmis during the civil war had left about half of the population of Kurgan-Tubbe as ethnic Uzbeks, who could have emerged a natural power base for Uzbek-backed factions. Kurgon-Tubbe, whose commander Mahmud Khudoiberdiyev maintained close contact with Tashkent, simply did not pay taxes to Dushanbe for years. The Uzbek government made no secret of the fact that they did not trust the Kulobis' "soft" approach to incorporating Islamists, and resented Russian efforts to cultivate a client in the region that was not linked through Tashkent.[58] An embassy representative described the problem in the following way:

"So, today, we know how the story ends, and we look back and think 'you'd have to have been crazy to think Rakhmon was an Islamic fundamentalist, or sympathetic with Iran, or anything like that! He's old-school! He's as conservative as they come! He's a Party man!' But we were getting fed those lines all the time [from the Uzbeks]. The truth is that, midway through the 1990s, nobody had any idea who was really running this country behind the scenes. Everything got mixed up in the war: Tajik nationalists who were talking about redrawing the map to get the old cities [Bukhara and Samarkand] back ... Iranian money ... nutty ideas floating in from Pakistan by way of Afghanistan along with the drugs. And all we knew, really, was that these rural guys from Kulob had the whole *golosovaniya* [voting] machine locked down. But what did they believe, really? It was hard to know."[59]

Military reforms to institutionalize Kulobi military control were another way to delay confronting the Khojandis. Control of the military was primarily a fight between Uzbeks, Hissoris, and Lakai, which was not directly threatening to the Khojandi industrialists. A former PFT fighter opined: "The Khojandis thought it would be like power sharing, where they ran the party and the Kulobis ran the army."[60] In early 1993, Rakhmonov announced plans to form armed forces exclusively out of Kulobi units under the command of "Baba" Sangak Safarov, the most influential of the Kulobi warlords. This was a terrible blunder. It alienated non-Kulobi members of the Popular Front and led many to publicly consider abandoning the regime, which would have effectively opened a third front in the ongoing civil war. But soon after, on March 30, Sangak

---

[58] For a brief overview on how Uzbek domestic policy considerations shaped their approach to the Tajik civil war, see Horsman (1999). Uzbekistan's President Karimov encouraged uncompromising, brutal punishment toward any faction linked to transnational Islamic networks. In part this was surely because many of these same leaders had, in the heady days of Tajik nationalism, voiced irredentist aspirations toward the Tajik cultural capitals of Bukhara and Samarkand.

[59] Interview conducted in Dushanbe, February 8, 2006.

[60] Interview conducted in Dushanbe, March 3, 2007.

Safarov was killed in a shootout with Fayzali Saidov. It was extrordinarily convenient for Rakhmonov to be able to plausibly claim that the whole ham-fisted centralization of the state had been Safarov's idea in the first place. Starting in 1993, representatives of Russian intelligence "essentially set up shop" in Dushanbe, sharing maps and military intelligence to aid Rakhmonov's counterinsurgency against the United Tajik Opposition. These security ties provided a critical conduit for the Kulobis to feed information to Moscow's military and political elites on Uzbek-backed coup plots, completely bypassing the Ministry of Foreign Affairs and other state organs where the Khojandis kept power. "Rakhmonov convinced the Russian military intelligence that they could work with his people ... they let the military make the case to Yeltsin. The Leninobodis [Khojandis] in the Foreign Ministry thought that their friends in Moscow's Academy of Sciences would save them ... [T]hey got completely outmaneuvered."[61]

Between 1993 and 1995, the Kulobis set about the more ambitious task of purging Khojandi influence from the state. The reversal of status hierarchies was sudden and total. The second round of Deputy Ministry appointments pushed out virtually every Khojandi with ties to the old guard from the security forces, tax administration, and the presidential inner circle. Faced with the prospect of being completely excluded from the seat of power in the republic, Khojandi militias and political parties took a number of steps to disrupt power consolidation. There were assassination attempts, terrorist bombings, and urban riots. In August 1993, Rakhmonov deployed several Kulobi "police units" to the northern regional capital of Leninobod, which led the Khojandi regional governor, Abdujalil Khamidov, to blow up the only bridge on the only road connecting Dushanbe and the northern regional capital.[62] In response, in the space of a single week, Rakhmonov fired Abdumalik Abdullojonov (the Khojandi Prime Minister since 1992) along with his brother Abdugani (the mayor of Khojand) and Governor Khamidov (also a Khojandi).

Russian military intelligence moved quickly to quash secessionist aspirations, urging the Khojandis to challenge Rakhmonov within the framework of the Soviet-inherited state borders. They acceded. Abdumalik Abdullojonov, who had been in the government alongside Rakhmonov since the beginning, ran against Rakhmonov for the office of president in 1994. The older generation of Khojandi *nomenklatura* gambled that with the regime in Dushanbe controlling only some 35 percent of the land mass of the country, former patrons in Moscow and Tashkent would engineer the reunification of the state under their

---

[61] Both of the preceding quotes from the same interview conducted in Dushanbe, February 24, 2007.

[62] Although reasonable people disagree, many believe that this was an effort to "test the waters" at the opportunity of secession in the Abkhaz or South Ossetian model with the military backing of Uzbekistan. See Neumann and Solodovnik (1996), 97 and Nourzhanov (2005).

leadership. Their confidence in foreign patrons proved misplaced. The day after a dubious election in which 99.5 percent of the inhabitants of Khatlon were reported to have voted for Rakhmonov, the Yeltsin government legitimized results with a statement declaring elections "free and fair."[63]

It did not take long for Abdullojonov to be charged with embezzling state assets and being barred from holding public office or standing in future elections. Just after the elections, Rakhmonov dismissed the heads of the KGB, Ministry of the Interior, and Prosecutor-General in Leninobod, as well as thirteen out of sixteen district chiefs who were seen as being sympathetic to Abdullojonov. The influx of Kulobis to fill these posts provoked large demonstrations in Khojand, and the ensuing wave of arrests and prosecutions finally crushed Abdullojonov's network. General Mamajanov, Khojand's provincial military commander, led an abortive armed uprising that was put down in January 1996, with aid from Russian secret police forces.[64] Residual Khojandi elites were forced to content themselves with symbolic and cosmetic posts, mostly in the Ministry of Foreign Affairs. Kathleen Collins goes so far as to state that they have been so cut off from political and economic assets that they are today "the poorest faction in the state."[65]

An obvious disadvantage to this transparently maximalist bargaining strategy was that it made it difficult for Rakhmonov to credibly offer anything to the UTO. Memories of brutality, atrocity, and broken promises were still fresh in the minds of many opposition elites. In 1995, opposition field commanders saw little reason to make concessions. But as we shall see, over the next two years, it became obvious that enough warlords had quietly committed themselves in the same kind of order-providing bargain. Previously uncommitted warlords began to recondition their strategies, aligning with Rakhmonov's regime in a cascade of collusion and collaboration.

In the freezing Tajik winter of 1996, a coordinated mutiny from within the PFT coalition nearly collapsed the state. The forces of two prominent field commanders surrounded Dushanbe. They seized the airport, cutting off supplies of electricity and food. The revolt was led by Ibodullo Boimatov, who had at one point controlled the lucrative aluminum factory at Talvidara, and Mahmud Khudoiberdiyev, who ruled the southern agricultural hub of Kurgan-Tubbe as an independent city-state. Both warlords claimed to speak for powerful constituencies. They had helped to install Rakhmonov, but feared that as Rakhmonov's "peace process" unfolded, they would lose influence in the ruling coalition. Acknowledging that their fears had merit, President Rakhmonov offered generous compensation to the blackmailers. Boimatov was appointed to the position of special trade envoy for cotton and aluminum, the

---

63 For a description of the circumstances surrounding this election, see Chapter 4.
64 Akbarzadeh (2001).
65 Collins (2006), 280.

country's two largest export items. Khudoiberdiyev became the First Deputy of the Presidential Guard.

Starting in the summer of 1996, there were special shuttle diplomacy meetings between representatives of the Rakhmonov government and individual UTO warlords, trying to convince them to switch sides and incorporate their soldiers into the Tajik army. These individual negotiation sessions were replaced with large working groups in the immediate run-up to the comprehensive peace process, with meetings conducted in Khojand and Kulob.[66]

Just over one year after his first attempt to collapse the state, Khudoiberdiyev raised the stakes with another uprising. Bolstered by foreign support from Uzbekistan and promises of support from shadowy financiers, he declared the establishment of the "Autonomous Defense Council of Central and Southern Tajikistan in Kurgan-Tubbe and Hissor." Few allies rallied to his cause this time. Boimatov, in particular, let Khudoiberdiyev flail in the wind. An improvised counter-coalition of rehabilitated rebel field commanders, many of whom had been branded as "criminal insurgents" and "Islamic terrorists" only weeks earlier, drove Khudoiberdiyev from the country in humiliation. Reports of what happened next are contradictory, but a common story is that he fled to Afghanistan and took refuge with the Uzbek warlord Abdul Rashid Dostum. When Dostum was defeated in 1998, Khudoiberdiyev tried another uprising in Tajikistan, this time in Khojand. It failed. He was finally forced to flee in disgrace.[67]

In 1996, Khudoiberdiyev was pivotal and could extort the president. By 1998, this was no longer the case. His final abortive coup was put down quickly and decisively by recently rehabilitated opposition warlords. This is wholly consistent with the interchangeability assumption in Chapter 2. That warlords in the initial ruling coalition feared that the integration of new armed groups into the state would come at their expense also fits the logic of the model.[68] But the main lesson that most observers drew from these abortive coups was that Rakhmonov was a permanent fixture. Even at the height of the 1996 uprising, it is telling that neither Khudoiberdiyev nor Boimatov, nor any official

---

[66] Interview conducted in Dushanbe, June 18, 2007.

[67] It should also be noted that the 1996 uprising was not first time Khudoiberdiyev and his army switched sides in the war. By my rough count, it was the third of six switchings. His uneven political fortunes provide a lens through which to view the kaleidoscopic complexity of Tajikistan's warlord politics in the 1990s. Khudoiberdiyev served in the Soviet military until its collapse, contracted his services to the elected postwar government (1991), joined the Popular Front and played a key role in installing Rakhmonov as president (1992), withdrew from Dushanbe politics and installed himself as a feudal lord in Kurgan-Tubbe (1993–1994), led an Uzbek-backed revolt against the state (1995–1996), became a first deputy in the presidential guard (1996), led a doomed revolt in 1997, reinvented himself as an Afghan "frontliner" in 1997–1998, and finally led his doomed insurgency in 1998. As of this writing, reasonable people disagree about whether he is alive and living in Uzbekistan or dead.

[68] Recall from the model: Because s is static, warlord payoffs are decreasing with k, meaning that as the coalition size increases, every warlord within it does strictly worse.

spokesperson for the regime in Tashkent, called for Rakhmonov's resignation. Instead, they demanded that certain hard line Kulobi warlords be dismissed and that the district of Khatlon be divided into its two original halves, returning to a framework for regional economic redistribution that was not weighted toward Kulob. Even with no meaningful formal institutions and distributional politics being decided at gunpoint – literally – by positioning himself as an intermediary between Mosow and the Tajik state organs, Emomalii Rakhmonov had become a permanent fixture in Tajik politics.

This power would only grow as Rakhmonov widened his governing coalition during the peace process. Promises to redraw district boundaries were forgotten. On June 27, 1997, Rakhmonov and the head of the UTO, Said Abdullo Nuri, officially concluded a "General Agreement on the Establishment of Peace and National Accord."[69] The executive branch of the government, which included all state ministries, regional and local government departments, and law enforcement bodies, pledged to incorporate UTO representatives on the basis of a 30 percent quota.

Parallel to the high-level diplomatic negotiations was a process of warlord incorporation negotiated between various Tajik warlords between 1995 and 1997. Opposition field commanders struck separate deals with government negotiators or Russian military forces, allowing them to become state representatives of their region, delivering votes and keeping order in exchange for a share of the emerging state spoils. These agreements were reached piecemeal at first, but once the state had reached a number of side-agreements and the UTO warlords began to feel that the writing was on the wall, they began to come forward to negotiate collectively in two separate, yet informal, roundtables (the "Gharm protocol," which recognized the central role of decentralized field commanders in the forthcoming Peace Process) in the summer of 1996. The rebels chose to agree to a settlement because the warlords who were fighting on their behalf had abandoned them, having struck side deals to keep their drug routes, rural fiefdoms, and positions in the lucrative state ministries.

In virtually all cases, these arrangements explicitly allowed warlords to keep their armies intact. Commanders handed over almost none of their weapons, or merely transferred them (with documentation) to "the government," where they were assigned to the weapons locker of the particular unit where they

---

69 See, for instance, Brenninkmeijer (1998) for a representative review of the International treatment of the conflict up until the time of the 1997 Peace Process or Akiner (2001) for what is certainly the most-cited general review of the politics surrounding the Peace Process. For a magisterial and critical insider's view of the implementation of the Tajik Peace Process, see Nakaya (2009) and Heathershaw (2009). The centerpiece of the agreement was the creation of a twenty-six-member Council on National Reconciliation, composed of thirteen opposition and thirteen government representatives. This body was tasked with the practical details of monitoring and upholding the ceasefire, dealing with refugees, amnesty, and key aspects of local government and representation. See "Key Points in the 1997 General Agreement," in Abduallev and Barnes (2001).

were assigned. Most military commanders, regardless of standing, were offered positions in the Ministry of the Interior MVD (Ministerstvo Vnuternnikh Del), the Army, the Ministry of Defense MOD (Ministerstvo Oborony), the Ministry of Emergency Situations MChS (Chrezvychainykh Situatsii), the Ministry of State Security MB (Ministerstvo Bezopasnosti) or the State Committee on the Protection of Borders KOGG (Komitet Oborony Gosudarstvennoi Granitsy). In the aftermath of integration, the same wartime hierarchies persisted, with the army in particular "operating much like a collection of militia groupings rather than as a vertically organized militia structure."[70] The Peace Process made certain field commanders' de facto control of rural populations de jure, coupled with informal understandings that opposition commanders would be allowed to rule the mountainous highlands (specifically the Rasht and Tavildara Valleys, and Gorno-Badakhshon), with no real interference from Dushanbe. Most of the security guarantees of the peace accord were simply never implemented, or implemented and then flagrantly reneged upon.[71]

The Peace Accords succeeded in their primary mission, which was to provide a face-saving framework by which opposition militia commanders could be incorporated into the state, and for warlords to legalize the holdings they had acquired over the course of the civil war. Many field commanders transitioned to the class of "businessmen," having reappropriated Soviet state property (apartments, land, factories, bazaars, cotton-fields and processing facilities, and even shopping centers) for themselves and their families. Sometimes these opportunities emerged out of ministry appointments, and sometimes they were simply legalizing what had been seized during the war. Torjensen and MacFarlane (2007) document a number of examples of these sorts of arrangements. Hoji Akbar Turajonzòda, a religious figure who moved between the military and political wings of the UTO, ascended to the post of Vice Prime Minister. A few years later, it was reported that he acquired "a cotton-processing plant in Vakhdat (Khatlon), the main shopping center in Vakhdat (the *Univermag*), and two flats in downtown Dushanbe," as well as years of rents from monopoly contracts importing wheat from Kazakhstan. Shurob Kasimov, a Popular Front Field Commander, owns a string of businesses and properties, including the rights to many of the properties in the Varzob district where embassy and NGO workers picnic in the spring. After Ghaffor Mirzoyev fell from Rakhmonov's favor in 2005, his assets were seized. It was revealed that he owned of over 30 apartments in Dushanbe, the bank *Olimp*, a

---

[70] Torjensen and MacFarlane (2007), 319.
[71] It could be argued that the UN provided political cover for domestic purges of incorporated militia members who officially joined the state in the framework of comprehensive peace. When the UN Observer Mission criticized corrupt practices and intransigence on the part of incorporated UTO militia members in 2001, Rakhmonov seized the initiative and fired anyone suspected of disloyalty from the ranks of the Ministry of Defense and Ministry of the Interior.

few factories, a major Dushanbe casino, and the Sultani Kabir car bazaar (the largest in the country at the time).[72]

And what of the Islamic fundamentalist ideology that was so threatening to conservatives in Tashkent and Moscow? For an overall summary response to this important question, it is hard to improve on Matveeva (2009):

On a provincial level the Islamic orientation of seemingly irreconcilable field commanders subsided substantially, even in Karategin Valley. Following the peace agreement the former *mujaheddin* became directors of state farms and heads of enterprises, or obtained appointments in the local authority. These new roles deprived them of the advantages of being in opposition, made them share the burden of everyday management with the secular authorities and forced them to act within the secular law. In this context their ideological positions and behavior changed radically. It appears that the Islamic movement was unable to sustain a mass following with the civil war was over. For example, Mirzo Zioyev, a UTO commander (his family originated from Talvidara, but Zioyev himself came from a resettlers' stock in Vakhsh) transformed himself into an Islamist warrior and cultivated a strict Wahhabi rule in the Tavildara district, enforcing Islamic order by force of arms if necessary. The terrified population obeyed. Alcohol, cigarettes, music, civic marriages and secular dress was prohibited. As soon as Zioyev was gone and became a minister in the new government, the local people returned to their normal practices. Across the former opposition areas, as the power of Islamist commanders withered away after the civil war, the population returned to the 'degree' of Islamism it had practiced before; i.e., socially conservative, but not extreme.[73]

The 1998 parliamentary election might have provided the opportunity for various factions who remained outside of Rakhmonov's direct control to form a coherent counterweight to Rakhmonov's party. These parliamentary elections were delayed, then cancelled, by presidential fiat. The 1999 presidential election proceeded as scheduled, reifying Rakhmonov's authority in a crude spectacle of consent. By this point, virtually all armed groups in the country were implicated in Rakhmonov's favor economy in one way or another; none of them had any interest in giving "the people" the opportunity to strangle their golden goose. Pro-regime terrorism cast a long shadow over the election – a barely contested exercise that included death threats, total media control by the president's party, and over a dozen publicized political assassinations of prominent candidates, journalists, and financiers. The only contender, Davlat Usmon of the Islamic Renaissance Party, was listed on the ballot only days before the vote. Usmon's son was kidnapped the day before ballots were cast. One of the most notable and symbolic deaths in the midst of this election was that of the original founder of the Popular Front, Safarali Kenjaev. Kenjaev was widely believed to have been planning to run for the November presidential race. He was shot and killed by unidentified gunmen on his front porch.

---

72 *The Financial Times*, August, 2005.
73 Matveeva (2009) 40.

By early in 2000, it was possible to observe that "a new coalition of warlords from Kulob, Gharm, and the Pamirs has presided over a massive redistribution of wealth ... [and] secured dominant positions in rent-seeking activities such as distributing foreign aid and drug trafficking."[74] As one would expect in a relationship fundamentally based on armed extortion, dynamics between Rakhmonov and the new warlord coalition were complex and contentious throughout this period. Just like Shevardnadze in Georgia, the president was constantly rotating the portfolios of important security ministers so that none of them could grow too powerful. As the peace process unfolded and more warlords joined the coalition, Rakhmonov gained flexibility to purge, promote, and reshuffle to his liking. Consider the career of Yaqubjon Salimov – the head of the Dushanbe mafia turned Minister of the Interior (1992–1994). Salimov was dismissed in 1995 and replaced by Saidamir Zukhrov (himself a former head of the Ministry of Security in Kulob) because Rakhmonov became concerned with the extent of Salimov's influence within the Dushanbe police force and the amount of wealth he had acquired. It was amicable: Salimov was appointed ambassador to Turkey, then reinstated in 1996 as Chair of the Customs Committee. Just over a year later, Salimov saved Rakhmonov's life in Khojand, pushing the president out of the way when a grenade was thrown at him. But Salimov's decision to throw his support behind Mahmud Khudoiberdiyev's August 1997 Rebellion was a terrible miscalculation. After the coup was put down by Kulobi warlords and incorporated UTO units, Salimov was forced to flee Tajikistan – first to Saudi Arabia, then to Moscow. He was arrested in February 2004, extradited to Tajikistan, and sentenced to 15 years in jail.

The fates of the three most prominent Kulobi warlords that spearheaded the government assault on Khudoiberdiyev in 1997 are also illustrative of how fragile coalition politics were during this period. Ghaffor Sedoi Mirzoyev, who guaranteed security at the largest bazaars in Dushanbe, had been the head of the Presidential Guard since 1995. Sukhrob Kasimov, a commander of the Special Forces of Dushanbe Police in 1992–1994, was promoted to the head of the Ministry of the Interior Rapid Deployment Brigade by Rakhmonov to "keep Mirzoyev under control."[75] Sulton Kuvvatov, the former head of the Ministry of the Interior's Unit of Combatting Economic Crimes, had been head of the Tax Committee since 1995. All were "Popular Front Men" who managed to rise from relative obscurity to prominence during the consolidation phase. And all three have since been purged. Kuvvatov was dismissed in 1998, stripped of his Parliament seat in 2002 and placed under arrest for the vague charges of "insulting Rakhmonov" and "inciting ethnic hatred" in 2005. Mirzoyev was arrested and sentenced to life imprisonment in 2004. Kasimov was dismissed in 2005 and quickly disappeared.

---

74 See Nourzhanov (2005), 124.
75 Nourzhanov (2005), 120.

Pamiri warlords, in general, were capable of making good on their bargains with the state where their Kulobi and Hissori counterparts were not. The impassable mountains make self-governing arrangements a practical necessity, which reduces a warlord's fear of the regime reneging down the road. On the regime side, it is unlikely that an uprising by a coalition of police chiefs in distant mountain villages poses the same existential threat as a coup by military generals in the capital city. Pamiris are also deeply resented by many ethnic Tajiks in Dushanbe, who are quick to fall back on old stereotypes of the insular religious group as wealthy elitists. The events of the early 1990s suggest that it would be very difficult for this group to seize national-level political power. The overland narcotics trade route from Afghanistan provides strong incentives for cooperation and opportunities for personal enrichment. The risk that the profitable drug transit corridor would be disrupted by violence outweighs any possible gain to Rakhmonov that could come from targeting a particular field commander's career. There is little in Badakhshon worth taxing or harvesting other than this drug trade or hydropower rents. In both cases, security is guaranteed by local agents with arrangements brokered in Dushanbe.

How did an oligopoly of violence emerge in Tajikistan? Warlords willing to pledge personal loyalty to Rakhmonov and commit their troops to supporting the Tajik government were integrated into the state. There could be no long term political guarantees, as the warlords themselves were the enforcing agents for contracts. Field commanders observed Rakhmonov as he carefully and methodically applied divide and rule logic to this coalition, occasionally inducing warlords to turn on each other in exchange for a larger share of state spoils. This risk was weighed against alternatives, which changed substantially over the fifteen year consolidation period. In general, warlords were offered the same kind of deal regardless of their characteristics: they were given amnesty, permitted to make large sums of money for a few years, and were then squeezed out of the governing coalition. The relative winners in the shell game were the Pamiris of Gorno-Badakhshon and actors with allies in the KGB. The relative losers were the Hissoris, who could not shed their association with Uzbekistan.

THE LOTTERY: EVIDENCE OF WARLORD INTERCHANGEABILITY

The differences that emerge between the consolidation projects of Shevard-nadze and Rakhmonov are consistent with what the model would predict if one country had a high stability threshold and the other had a much lower threshold (recall Figure 5.1). In Georgia, where Russia was interested in undermining the government and backing a coup, Shevardnadze needed to keep his friends close and his enemies closer (maneuvering while constrained by an extremely high s). Shevardnadze had enormous success at incorporating Georgian warlords quickly, but was then unable to steer the state apparatus once they were all inside his Ministry of the Interior. In Tajikistan, by contrast, Russia lent its armed forces and intelligence to *support* the Rakhmonov regime

TABLE 5.1. *Former Paramilitaries in the Georgian Ministry of the Interior*

Faction	Ministry Affiliation 1992–2003 (%)	Ministry Affiliation 2004–2007 (%)
Mkhedrioni ($n = 55$)	89	51
National Guard ($n = 18$)	67	44
Forest Brotherhood ($n = 6$)	67	50
White Eagle ($n = 8$)	88	75
Zviadists ($n = 13$)	77	69
Adjaran Police Force ($n = 5$)	0	100

against domestic challengers in a straightforward effort to keep Islamists or clients of Uzbekistan from coming to power. This allowed Rakhmonov to pick and choose among various local warlord allies (maneuvering with a much lower *s*). The high stakes in Tajikistan also led to fierce friction between the members of the insider coalition and the other warlords, as well as between these members and the president himself, over the peace process and efforts to incorporate additional warlords.

In Georgia, one can observe the rapid incorporation of most of the warlords into the state apparatus. Once Eduard Shevardnadze was the face of the franchise, near-universal buy in to the state-building project was the trend. Much of Shevardnadze's institution building was aimed at reassuring as many people as possible that he was a servant of the state and the nation, subordinate to the interests of the people. The Abkhaz, Adjar, and South Ossetian warlords were the exceptions, not the rule. Though the junta's State Council endured for months, in practice it did not last long as a consensus body. The statute that created the State Council allowed new members to be admitted by a two–thirds vote, and by May 1992 it had evolved into something like a "pseudo-parliament" of warlords, fragmented political party elites, and representatives of ethnic enclaves.[76] Shevardnadze assumed the pivotal role of coalition formation, acting both from behind the scenes and from the bully pulpit, taking responsibility for forging consensus and voting super-majorities from different interest groups, civil society figureheads, and warlords. He did all of this without a hint of subterfuge.

As a result, official membership in the Ministry of the Interior – headed symbolically by Shevardnadze himself for a time – swelled to nearly 30,000 by 1995, with at least as many unofficial affiliates. Much of the personnel for this new Ministry of the Interior – so often cited as the key to Shevardnadze's centralization of power – came from the ranks of various nationalist militias.

[76] Wheatley (2005), 70.

Table 5.1 reports the percentages of interviewed militia members who reported Ministry of Interior affiliation during this time.[77] The trend toward joining the Ministry of the Interior held for urban and rural members, for members whose time in the militia preceded the Gamsakhurdia coup (e.g., in the National Guard), for groups that fought against the state (e.g., the Zviadists), and for opportunistic joiners (e.g., in self-identified "Mkhedrioni" units in Tbilisi during the Time of Troubles). The exception is the Adjarans, who had seceded in the 1990s with the help of Russian aid and were part of their own parallel police force under the direct command of Aslan Abashidze. Table 5.1 also reveals that despite the Rose Revolution and recent anti-corruption campaigns in the Georgian state, the institutional footprint of the Shevardnadze compromises with nationalist militias persists in the composition of the modern police force.[78]

The civilianization of militia structures slowly eroded the power base of those militia commanders who could not learn new tricks. Sociopathic behaviors, radical political slogans, and anarchism were shed by many members, given the chance at a secure job and a pension in a patronage hierarchy. A labyrinth of corruption emerged in Shevardnadze's Ministry of the Interior. In the words of Mark Mullen, the former Georgian director of the National Democratic Institute and Transparency International:

"A state within a state is what it was ... They collect[ed] their own taxes, elect[ed] and promot[ed] their own officials through a process that nobody saw, and [weren't] accountable to anyone for anything ... it was the same Mkhedrioni, the same guys ... everybody knew who they were, what they were capable of. That was the point. That was their power."[79]

Co-opting challengers by bringing them into the Ministry of the Interior ultimately led to the creation of a bloated, factionalized, and inept police force – but one whose members saw the president at the head of a hierarchy. The empirical record suggests that, by 2003, many in the security services believed they would keep their jobs even if the president was forced to step down from power in the face of street protests. The Georgian polity had a centralized police apparatus a decade after Sheverdnadze ascended to power, with substantial authority vested in the head of state. This is where our narrative will pick up at the end of this chapter.

77　Responses add up to more than eight-four interviews – an artifact of side-switching between groups.

78　Fairbanks (2012) forcefully articulated this argument just days before the election that removed Saakashvili from power.

79　Interview conducted in Tbilisi on March 10, 2006. This runs in tandem with the descriptions of Jonathan Wheatley (2005, 78–83), Ghia Nodia, and many others who misleadingly describe Ministry of Interior "crackdowns" against criminals and isolated Mkhedrioni leaders as if the two groups were distinct.

In Tajikistan, consolidation was slow and grinding. An original dataset of warlord biographies allows a statistical assessment of how much time passed before an incorporated warlord was purged from the ruling coalition. I use statistical regression to compare warlords' political fortunes in the consolidating Tajik state. Using Russian- and Tajik-language newspaper archives and embassy reports, a team of Tajik researchers employed by the Small Arms Survey compiled a list of the most prominent "field commanders."[80] With the aid of two research teams based in Bishkek and Dushanbe, I revisited the Small Arms Survey's secondary source materials and identified an additional twenty-seven field commanders, for a total of ninety-seven observations.[81] Between 1992 and 1997, fifty-seven of these ninety-seven Tajik warlords accepted positions in the new bureaucracy, subordinating their armies to Emomalii Rakhmonov's political hierarchy.[82] About half of these warlords represented the core of the Popular Front coalition that seized the capital city in December 1992. Another major wave of warlord integration came with the 1997 Peace Accords, which guaranteed 30 percent of the positions in the "Power Ministries" (State Security, Defense, and Interior) to members of the UTO. Other field commanders integrated into the state apparatus piecemeal.

The column on the far right of Table 5.2 displays the number of years, rounded up, that a warlord served alongside his militia, after he had been incorporated into the state in an official capacity but allowed to retain his men. A few of the warlords departed voluntarily and retired as militia captains, removing themselves from politics and withdrawing from public life. Others were transferred to a non-security ministry or fired outright, which meant they effectively lost their private army. These purged warlords were often killed. When they were not, they were usually imprisoned, exiled, or simply disappeared once it was clear that they had lost their political protection.[83]

The final column in Table 5.2 reveals that warlords from some regions fared systematically better than others. A warlord's home region was a good predictor of which side they fought on in the civil war. Of the fifty-seven warlords who joined the state through the 1992–1997 period, by December 2006 only

---

[80] Torjensen (2005).

[81] For a discussion of coding rules and criteria, see Appendix C.

[82] When a warlord did not join the state it usually meant that he was killed in the course of civil war violence, though a small number of non-joiners fled to Afghanistan, disappeared into the criminal underworld, or simply refused to disarm or compromise. Even after 1997, many warlords continued to control territory in which neither the government nor United Nations observers could enter without the permission of these warlords and armed escort of their subordinates. The most prominent of these locations were Darband (controlled by Mullo Abdullo), Tavildara (home of the Minister of Emergency Situations Mirzo Zioyev), and even the Leninsky District, about twenty kilometers from downtown Dushanbe (controlled by Rakhmon "Hitler" Sanginov).

[83] I estimate that in roughly a quarter of the cases, the warlord's exit from state security services involved his death, but there are so many cases of "disappearances" that this generalization is mostly impressionistic.

TABLE 5.2. *Tajik Warlord Summary Statistics: Average Time Until Purge Varies by Region*

Region of Birth	Warlords (Total)	Warlords (UTO)	Warlords (PFT)	Joined 1992–1993	Joined 1996–1997	Average Years Until Purge
Kulob	24	5	18	13	3	6.7
Gharm	18	13	5	3	8	6.2
Hissor/Uzbek	10	1	9	8	0	2.5
Badakhshon	25	21	0	0	14	7.6
Other	20	3	8	7	1	7.3

sixteen remained. In the cabinet reshuffle of December 2006, the final remaining high-level UTO warlord in the dataset, the Minister of Emergency Situations Mirzo Ziyoev, was discharged. Anecdotally, it is well established that every prominent warlord in the Popular Front who installed Rakhmonov has either retired from politics, fled the country, landed in jail, or died under mysterious circumstances.

Appendix C provides an expanded statistical analysis of these data, but the main results can be easily summarized. Warlords from the president's home region of Kulob were purged at a rate that is statistically indistinguishable from the average. Subsections of the winning and losing sides of the civil war tended to be more likely to survive, but not in a manner that was predictable in advance. Indeed, whether one believes that the civil war was defined by competing ideologies ("Islam vs. Rump Communists") or regional politics ("Kulob, Hissor, and Khojand vs. Gharm and GBAO"), in the aftermath of the war, the coalition formation process yielded strange and unpredictable bedfellows, political alliances that transcended easily-codeable divisions. Strong warlords, defined as those who controlled large armies, were ultimately no more likely to emerge as members of the ruling coalition than weak warlords who controlled small armies. The inference that I draw from these patterns is that intracoalitional commitment problems were at least as serious as the "master" commitment problem between the winners and losers in the civil war. In retrospect, it is strange to remember that the Hissori/Uzbeks were the ones who looked like they had "won" the war back in 1992. As these statistical patterns show, they proved the most vulnerable warlords in the coalition formation process. By contrast, the most insulated warlords – Pamiris from GBAO – were clearly on the wrong side of the war in the early 1990s. I see this as evidence that the warlords could not predict themselves who would be a winner or a loser over the long run, once the president was installed.

What happened? The short answer is that all of these people were interchangeably awful, and recognized as such by civil society. Despite Russian ethnocentric stereotypes, Dushanbe and Tbilisi are cities that are full of thinking, educated, civilized people. Most of them understood that it was morally unnatural for rapists and murderers to hold positions with social power, respect, legal immunity, and institutionalized protection. Most people did not want criminal warlords managing property disputes. They understood exactly how outrageous a hand fortune had dealt them when they saw civil war commanders rising to positions in the state and handing out patronage. Temporary exceptions to this basic moral rule, which were justified by the temporary anarchy of the early 1990s, did not actually void the rule in the minds of most Georgians and Tajiks. So once the worst periods of violence had passed and normalcy returned, first the perceived Uzbek clients were pushed out, then the obvious sociopaths were trimmed, then the patrons who hired the sociopaths, and finally the leftovers. Rakhmonov simply rode successive waves of popular opinion and doled out what these men already "had coming" to them.

The long answer is that over the course of the fifteen-year observation period, membership of the ruling coalition changed substantially. In the early 1990s, friction between the new Tajik and Uzbek governments manifested as friction between Kulobis and Hissoris in coalition politics. The Hissoris were purged. In the late 1990s and early 2000s, the Pamiri Opposition commanders, who had reinvented themselves as police officers in rural Badakhshon, were kept in the state as subsequent rounds of purges removed former UTO combatants from Gharm and elsewhere.

The story of the "de-Uzbekification" of the Tajik ruling structure has already been previewed in this book. The district of Hissor, to the west of Dushanbe, produced a number of prominent warlords in the Tajik Civil War – most famously Safarali Kenjayev, the original founder of the Popular Front, and Ibod Boimatov, who led a 1996 mutiny against Rakhmonov's peace process and brought the state to a standstill.[84] The Soviets also relocated several seminomadic Uzbek tribes (Lakai, Kungrat, and Durman) to the agricultural lowlands of southern Tajikistan near Kurgon-Tubbe, creating local frictions over access to scarce land and water. The most prominent warlord to emerge from this region was Mahmud Khudoiberdiyev, the commander of the First Brigade at Kurgon-Tubbe. During the heady days of Tajik nationalism in the late Soviet period – when it became clear that Russian-enforced cosmopolitanism was breaking down and no one could predict what would replace it – these Uzbek groups were natural recruits for counterrevolutionary militias. Conservative elites in Tashkent, who feared that a new regime in Tajikistan might invite the conflict in northward or revisit territorial claims to Samarkahd and Bukhara, were interested in helping local co-ethnics gain influence and establish a protectorate. Yet once the Popular Front established itself in the capital city, the

---

[84] The district of Hissor is identified by Olivier Roy as a textbook example of the irrationality of the Soviet Border system – it is a district with approximately 60 percent Uzbek speakers facing directly across the border with the region of Sukhan Darya, a majority Tajik-speaking enclave in Uzbekistan (68–69).

dominant Kulobi faction saw these field commanders as a potential fifth column for Uzbek influence in the consolidating state, or as likely allies for a power grab by the northern Khojandi faction. Hissori warlords found themselves early targets for purges and persecution. To revisit the metaphor from Chapter 2, they had played the state-formation lottery and lost.

Ten warlords in my data are identified as being born in one of the Uzbek-dominated southern regions of the country, and nine of them were affiliated with – indeed were founding members of – the Popular Front. These Uzbek warlords formed nearly a quarter of the warlords in the initial ruling coalition. The Uzbek government made no secret of the fact that they saw their weak neighbor Tajikistan as a natural protectorate, and these warlords thought that their affiliation with a powerful foreign patron would act as a security guarantee. The strategy backfired. After 1995, these warlords were singled out for elimination.[85] The longest surviving warlord from this group, Safarali Kenjayev, was murdered outside his home (along with his bodyguard and driver) on March 30, 1999. With a seven-year tenure in the state, he was still purged faster than the average warlord in these data, despite the fact that he literally *founded* the political movement that captured the state apparatus. Kenjayev miscalculated, and Kenjayev was liquidated.

Contrast this narrative with the fates of the other significant ethnic minority group, the Pamiris. The GBAO makes up 45 percent of the land area of the Tajik state, but only contains 3 to 4 percent of the population. This inhospitable Mountain range is the home of the Pamiris, a distinct ethnic group distinguished by language (Shugni), religious sect (Ismaili), and physical appearance. After the Popular Front seized the capital city in December 1992, the militias that had supported the previous government fell back to the impenetrable Pamiri mountains, while in the capital hundreds of Pamiris were targeted for ethnic cleansing, with their homes and property expropriated by the victorious Kulobi militias. Shortly thereafter, the autonomy of Gorno-Badakhshon was rescinded in Dushanbe. Representatives in the regional capital of Khorog responded by declaring independence. In the spring of 1993, a compromise was reached. GBAO agreed to recognize the suzerianty of Dushanbe in exchange for a return to autonomous status, a promise to not disrupt the activities of the Aga Kahn (who was delivering aid to the starving populations), and a set of soft promises that the region would be allowed to manage its own security. This bargain generally held through the civil war, and its broad contours persist as of this writing – though it is not advised to pay too much attention to the particulars of the security arrangements. Formal autonomous status is one of the few formal protections of the civil war settlement that can said to have any teeth. Of the twenty-five Badakhshoni-born warlords identified in the data, none of them served in the Popular Front. Yet returning to Table 5.2, these warlords were

---

[85] The estimated median and mean survival times for Uzbek warlords are 2.4 and 2.5 years, contrasted with 8.3 and 8.4 for other warlords.

clearly capable political survivors.[86] In the consolidation lottery, they were relative winners.

But all of this is an ex post rationalization of trends that could not have been forecast by actors at the time they made their decision to back Rakhmonov or keep fighting. Many warlords could not predict coalition winners and losers. They were playing the odds in a high-stakes consolidation game.

A CODA FOR v^*: AID AND POLITICS AFTER COUP-PROOFING

The visualizations in Figure 5.2 demonstrate the degree to which the economies and state budgets of Georgia and Tajikistan have been "floated" by foreign aid (v^*). Although there were important differences between Shevardnadze's and Rakhmonov's governance styles, the countries have also been socialized by different geopolitical audiences. The content of targeted aid programs varied by country.[87] Tbilisi continues to pivot between Moscow and Washington, and Western aid to Georgia aimed at "strengthening civil society" and "democracy promotion" has geopolitical overtones. Dushanbe continues to be judged by both great powers on the same criteria: its ability to "hold the line" against radical Islam. Both states have grown into these roles.

Georgia is probably the best Eurasian example of a country where democracy promotion activities by the United States and Western Europe can be said to have "worked." With 55 percent of discretionary spending in the 2003 state budget filled by Western donors and a constant stream of rhetorical commitments to democratization, Shevardnadze could not easily interfere with the actions of foreign democracy-promotion NGOs in his own

---

[86] The estimated median and mean survival times for former field commanders from Gorno-Badakhshon are 8.8 and 10.1 years, contrasted with 5.1 and 6.4 for other warlords. Half (8/16) of the warlords who were still members of the state security apparatus in December 2006 were Pamiris – most of whom had, one point or another, taken up arms against Rakhmonov's regime.

[87] Whether and how foreign aid works to transform the institutions of target societies is the subject of a vast literature. For a useful review of this literature's findings, see Wright and Winters (2010). For a good review of how aid applies to fragile states, see Girod and Tobin (2015) and Girod (2012). For more on how political debates over the effectiveness of aid have coevolved with best practices as understood by the discipline of economics, see Easterly (2001) and Helpman (2004). The central difficulty for analysts is that institutions in societies adapt dynamically to expectations of foreign assistance: governments show donor states what the donor states expect to see in order to receive more aid. As Moscow's central planners came to appreciate: local actors become quickly aware of the incentives created, and in a general equilibrium framework they can act strategically. At some risk of cultural stereotyping, one of the legacies of the Soviet experience in Central Asia and the Caucasus is a mentality of "learned helplessness" from a century of colonial condescension. The myth of the Potemkin village captures an important cultural response to totalitarian rule: peripheral republics became extremely sophisticated about figuring out what metrics the social scientists in Moscow were using to judge "success" and producing those metrics. They are practiced at telling program evaluators what they need to hear and generating data to confirm theoretical priors.

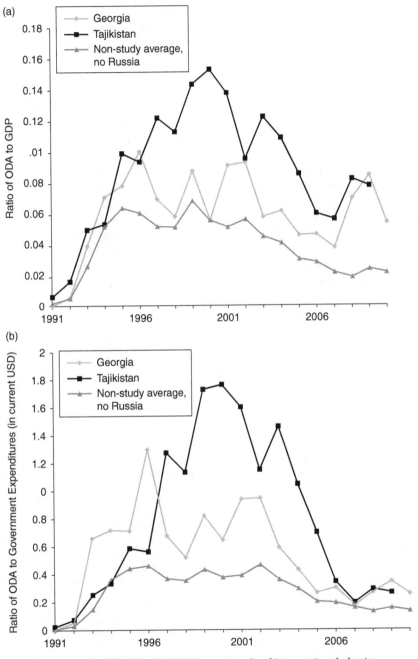

FIGURE 5.2. Georgia and Tajikistan: wards of international charity.

country. Georgian citizens themselves, taking their president at his word when he invoked the promises of democracy and legitimacy, were ultimately unwilling to tolerate the regime's perceived manipulation of elections in 2003. Civil society groups found themselves aided substantially by foreign-funded NGOs, including active participation by embassy employees and American and European expatriates. The gridlocked police apparatus did not respond to orders to dismiss crowds of demonstrators.[88] Peaceful protests swept Eduard Shevardnadze and his regime from power in November 2003 – a set of events that have come to be known as the Rose Revolution.[89]

In the years since the Rose Revolution observers have witnessed a reenergized presidency governing over what even cynics agree is a substantially more transparent version of the same superpresidential state structure. The new president, Mikheil Saakashvili, rode the nationalist euphoria to make a few institutional changes that earned him credentials as a reformer – notably firing the entire 60,000-person "traffic police," which made it possible for citizens to drive around the streets of Tbilisi without constantly stopping to pay bribes. He dramatically simplified the tax code. Saakashvili dominated the political landscape as completely as his predecessor through a similar mix of informal networks and formal institutions, particularly the judiciary and Parliament.[90] Shortly after the change in government, the breakaway republic of Adjara was

---

[88] The historical record on this point remains muddled, but the bulk of the evidence supports Fairbanks (2004) account, that Shevardnadze gave orders to disperse the demonstraters which were not carried out (117). I strongly suspect there was an uncomfortable psychological resonance with the 1989 attack on Tbilisi citizens which initiated the cycle of violence in late-Soviet Georgia.

[89] By far the most comprehensive and responsible review of the structural and political conditions that created the Rose Revolution, both in terms of strategy and tactics of all the major actors, is found in the work of Jonathan Wheatley (2005), chapters 6 and 7. For useful extension and descriptions of the event itself, see Fairbanks (2004), King (2004b), Miller (2004), Stephen Jones (2006), and Papava (2006). Mitchell (2004) reports that Shevardnadze appealed to Aslan Abashidze to send a goon-squad from Adjara to organize a counterdemonstration in front of the Parliament – to no effect (344). Protesters eventually stormed the (ungarded) doors of parliament. As he fled, Shevardnadze apparently attempted to declare martial law but he was informally abandoned by his security forces on November 22 and then formally repudiated by them on November 23. He was then forced to resign. One interpretation of these events, offered by Lincoln Mitchell, is that Shevardnadze "became aware that he no longer controlled the military and security forces. Bloodshed was avoided largely because the president was too politically weak to command it." 348. The facts are also consistent with an alternative theory of which I am fond: That after the death of his wife and a decade of thankless labor, the old man was tired. The determined opposition in the Rose Revolution forced his hand, leaving him the relatively easy choice to leave office as a temporarily disgraced hero for historians to rehabilitate, or as tinpot despot who fired into crowds of his own citizens.

[90] After the 2008 Parliamentary Election was resolved, Saakashvili's party, the United National Movement, controlled 119 seats in the 150-member Parliament, providing a comfortable cushion of safety above the 100 votes that would be necessary to change the constitution. The second largest faction – the United Opposition, consisting of eight small parties and a few individual politicians – has only seventeen seats.

reincorporated into Georgia proper. The Rose Revolution had the effect of rehabilitating the regime in the imaginations of many Western defense analysts, who rediscovered their optimism for the regime and doubled-down on their aid packages. Georgia's defense budget saw an unbelievable 50-fold increase between 2002 and 2007. To demonstrate support for Georgia's government in the opening phases of its disastrous war with Russia in 2008 over disputed secessionist territories, the United States pledged $1 billion in reconstruction and development aid.

Under Saakashvili, NATO membership became a political totem for Georgian citizens. While continuing to mouth the same promises of peaceful compromise and negotiation in English, in Georgian the tone of discourse changed. Talk of "internationalizing the conflict" – that is, introducing U.S. and European mediators into the conversation, backed by a muscular military presence – was thought to be the best route to a permanent settlement on Georgia's terms. Georgian troops were quick to volunteer for the coalition of the willing in Iraq, and the Georgian Train and Equip Program (GTEP) was extended to create pockets of professional leadership within their Ministry of Defense. But the events of 2008 brought to the fore just how easy it would be for an accidental war between NATO and Russia to break out over a forgettable flashpoint in the South Caucasus.

As we approach the two-decades mark from the end of the "Time of Troubles," the fundamental commitment problem that fueled the conflict in the first place is still present in Georgian society. In Georgia today, the events of the early 1990s tend to be recounted with a selective memory that borders on collective amnesia. In a nationally representative survey designed by the author and implemented through the Caucasus Research Resource Centers in Georgia in fall 2008, just after the war, an overwhelming majority of Georgian citizens prioritized reclaiming control of the "lost" territory of Abkhazia and South Ossetia over all other political issues, including good relations with the West (prioritized by only 7.1 percent of respondents) or relations with Russia. More than three-quarters of the respondents would reject any peace settlement that did not include a "right of return" for displaced Georgians.[91] Two generations

---

91 It is the official position of the Saakashvili government that reintegrating Abkhazia would come only with provisions of autonomy. Yet, given the broad, deep trends in Georgian public opinion on minority issues, the Abkhaz in particular can be perhaps forgiven for being skeptical of claims that they would be treated magnanimously by Georgians if the frozen conflict were resolved in Georgia's favor. When Georgian citizens were asked a variety of questions related to the practical meaning of "autonomy" for the Abkhaz, 71 percent of respondents believed that "Georgians should be able to purchase whatever property they wanted regardless of the wishes of the provisional Abkhaz government," 61 percent of respondents believed "Abkhaz and South Ossetians should be denied the right to serve in the Georgian military, police, or border guards," and 78 percent of respondents believed "schools and universities in Abkhazia should not be allowed to teach classes in only Russian or Abkhaz." These data are evidence of what most Georgia watchers have identified through anecdotes for years: a deeply immature

of Georgian politicians have promised that ties with the West would help the Georgians reclaim territory, with the unspoken implication that this territory was stolen by traitors at the behest of Russia.

What Russia's policies have incentivized is an equilibrium in which national-ist Georgian parties – which no longer have paramilitary wings, but one senses that they could be recruited at any time – hold pivotal coalition roles, and the West provides liquidity (v^*) in exchange for basing rights, a non-Russian oil pipeline transit route to get Caspian oil to Europe, and the satisfaction of helping to create a pro-Western political environment in a traditionally Russian-speaking region. From the perspective of many in Moscow, the failure to reach a lasting diplomatic settlement to these longstanding territorial disputes in Georgia has had the unanticipated – but tangible – benefit of halting NATO expansion to the South Caucasus. Every time the frozen conflicts thaw, European and North American observers are reminded that it is probably not in the national interest of any NATO member state to be obligated by treaty to consider defending distant Georgia against Russian "invaders." As the 2008 war between Georgia and Russia clarified, Georgia has no hope of reclaiming these statelets by force. Furthermore, its desire to join NATO, participate as a full member in European development and security dialogues, and present itself as a fully functioning member of the community of "normal" states will continue to be held hostage.

The presidency of Saakashvili was criticized as failing to live up to the promises of the Rose Revolution. The incumbent president and his party enjoyed a number of structural benefits, including favorable media coverage and free time on state television networks. Critics charged that Saakashvili's party, the United National Movement, used dirty tricks to monopolize political power. The incumbent party benefitted from an inherited Soviet culture of bureaucratic compliance, and a broader cultural expectation that private behaviors can and will be monitored and reported to authorities.[92] Local bureaucrats – particularly in poor and rural areas – know that they are expected to deliver their district to the ruling party in order to prove their loyalty and keep their jobs. In a pre-election survey conducted in the lead-up to the 2008 Parliamentary Election, 32 percent of voters reported that people had to "vote a certain way to keep their jobs." An additional 34 percent of voters admitted that this happens "sometimes."[93]

---

and self-referential rhetoric has been allowed to fester in the Georgian political discourse. The survey was nationally representative, stratified by region, with $N = 2,700$ respondents. For additional information and open-use documentation contact the Caucasus Research Resource Centers.

[92] See Harris (2004) and Paxson (2005).

[93] About a quarter (23 percent) of survey respondents in the average study precinct reported that these beliefs were widespread, with a standard deviation of 22 (e.g., in some precincts no one reported this fear and in others it was reported by a plurality).

For all the disappointments of the post–Rose Revolution era, however, Saakashvili's decision to concede electoral defeat to Bidzina Ivanishvili's *Georgian Dream* party in 2012 bucks a powerful regional trend. His is one of the only examples of a post-Soviet leader in Central Asia or the Caucasus losing an election and voluntarily stepping down from power. The experiences of Georgia in the last decade have me wondering whether the Soviet experience may have created favorable conditions for the transition to an "open access" political order.[94] Time will tell. For all the conspiracy theories of rampant corruption and offshore accounts that motivated angry protesters during the Rose Revolution, Eduard Shevardnadze passed away in July of 2014 in a small house on the outskirts of Tbilisi. As historians debate his legacy, it should be remembered that many contingent outcomes – a peaceful regime transition, progress toward democratization, and a Western-oriented foreign policy – are all, at least in some small part, a result of his decisions.

A peaceful regime transition is much more remote in Tajikistan. The totality of power consolidation by Rakhmonov became transparent in 2003 when the government proposed fifty-six amendments to the Constitution. Hidden among the list was a clause to extend the current presidential term to the maximum of two seven-year periods, making it possible for Rakhmonov to stay in power until 2020.[95] In 2006, the final high-profile UTO representative, Mirzo Ziyoev, was discharged. In 2007 the president dropped his surname's Russified suffix and demanded to be named in all official documents by his purer Persian name "Rakhmon." Virtually every prominent warlord in the Popular Front who installed him has either retired from politics, fled the country, landed in jail, or died under mysterious circumstances. The warlords who survive in the Tajik state are mostly co-opted Pamiris, managing neighborhood politics in GBAO. Russia underwrites the security of the whole arrangement while keeping plausible deniability over any of the particulars.

Tajikistan's geographical position and high mountain ranges made it a natural corridor for the Afghan narcotics trade. The rents of the drug trade came from guaranteeing low-risk transit from its southern border to the northern border on the way to the lucrative Western European market. This meant control of key roads and border checkpoints, and the formal institutions of the state – the military, police, and border guards – had every incentive to make sure that particular trucks were not harassed at road blocks or stopped for not having the right papers. Though in principle this suggests myriad

---

94 North, Wallis, and Weingast (2009), 148–154. The authors identify three "doorstep conditions" for a transition to an "open access" society, while being very clear that they do not have a predictive model explaining when exactly a country will transition from a closed to an open access society: "DC#1: Rule of law for elites. DC#2: Perpetually lived organizations in the public and private spheres. DC#3: Consolidated control of the military." 151.

95 The government claimed 96 percent voter turnout and 93 percent approval of the amendment.

opportunities for entrepreneurial youth to try to smuggle heroin independently, in practice any sophisticated international syndicate capable of buying heroin by the truckload probably wants to deal with a local partner in the Ministry of the Interior.[96]

Then, practically overnight, NATO military forces were in Afghanistan. For a time, a great deal more Western attention was devoted to the region. Was this increase in security assistance responsible for keeping Afghanistan's contagion of improvised explosive devices (IEDs) from spreading north to infect Tajikistan? Or was Tajikistan inoculated against this sort of violent extremism even before the influx of United States Agency of International Development (USAID) and European security aid? One cannot prove a negative, and many different theories can be laid atop an observational dataset of zeroes. What can be said, with confidence, is that the new security assistance strengthened Rakhmon's hand.

Tajikistan occupies the same place in the imagination of most American and Russian diplomats: a hardship post at the edge of the map. If not for the small border with China on the far side of the Pamiri mountains, it would be landlocked by other landlocked countries. Development aid continues to be frustrated by a "culture of corruption."[97] What is important to the great powers, in this context, is that a Salafi Jihadist subculture is not permitted to thrive. Certain Tajiks in the security infrastructure are digging in for a long war.[98] Most Tajiks have difficult but predictable lives. Pockets of extreme poverty and structural violence are in plain sight for anyone who cares to observe. But there is no war today, and probably there will be no war tomorrow. For that, most Tajiks are grateful. These observations are unlikely to become obsolete any time soon. Change comes very slowly in Tajikistan.

---

[96] At the time of this writing, the website of the U.S. embassy proudly declares that it helped provide the Tajik government with a $28 million state-of-the-art border checkpoint facility for the Tajik Customs Service.

[97] Mirzoev (2002) reproduces survey data revealing nearly universal acknowledgment by Tajik citizens that the state is highly corrupt (358, 360), and indeed that basic life is impossible for a household – regardless of income – without paying bribes for virtually everything (365, 375).

[98] The strategies and technologies that will be used to cauterize future threats are well understood. The cultural response for many powerless people, in my limited experience as an ethnographer, is to retreat from reality into imagination and conspiracy. Conspiracy theories allow people to find meaning, even in silences. Some of my Tajik informants never talked on the phone. Nothing I could say would convince these men – who suspected my motives, and who had been raised on a vision of the CIA gleaned from some mix of *Alias*, *The Dark Knight*, and their own experiences living in an Orwellian police state – that there were not "ghosts in the phones." But this paranoia does not capture the daily troubles of most Tajik citizens, or find resonance with their lived social reality.

6

Implications

The processes described in this book are hard to square with the picture of peace building that is typically put forward by optimistic liberal interventionists. The "root causes" of the wars were in no way resolved. Conflict identities between factions were not transformed in any fundamental way. The winners in the consolidation process did not demobilize so much as they *became* the state. Soldiers watched the daily drama of the consolidation process anxiously, hoping that they were backing the right horse. Many switched factions based on perceptions of whose star was on the ascent. Aid and investment increased the value of the "prize" being fought over in the streets, creating perverse incentives for militia expansion. A ruling coalition formed out of the violent sorting through processes of attrition on the streets. Losers in this process demobilized when they could no longer improve their life chances through violence, but not because there was any sort of security guarantee making them feel safe. Presidents gained power not by legitimizing or strengthening the state, but by subtly influencing the distributional politics associated with its cannibalization. All of this went on under the noses of foreign observers and Russian military peacemakers.

The post-socialist presidents of Georgia and Tajikistan inherited situations of intense institutional weakness. Paramilitary warlords and private armies emerged as power brokers in the chaotic aftermath of state collapse, and the new presidents were forced to incorporate armed factions and known criminals into ruling coalitions. These warlords and their men proceeded to pillage state institutions from the inside, rendering the state increasingly weak and useless. This entailed a great deal of violence and side-switching as coalitions formed and re-formed according to kaleidoscopically complex local logics. Yet over time both Shevardnadze and Rakhmonov were able to use a fairly weak set of institutionalized powers – their ability to bestow selective favors, create redundant ministries with overlapping mandates, bypass the written rules governing transactions between state bodies, and play a focal role in international affairs – to insulate themselves from the threat of a coup. Substance followed form in the post-socialist states. The symbolic functions of the head of state transmogrified into real power.

The theoretical contribution of this book is a model of state-building as a problem of *coalition formation* by amoral and interchangeable violence entrepreneurs. The process of dividing the rents of sovereignty has been modeled formally. Thinking of civil war settlement through the lens of coalition formation, rather than two-player problems of bargaining or commitment, emphasizes the ability of some warlords to extort rents from inside the coalition by threatening to remove the president and return the country to a state of war. Foreign patrons and multinational corporations desire order, not war, but this requires that they recognize *someone* to take responsibility for what occurs inside the territory of an internationally recognized state. To shape local incentives, they dangle aid. Warlords swap their fatigues for business suits to gain access to these income streams. They do not disarm. Wealth is distributed in the form of ministry positions, tacit nonenforcement of the tax code, closed-bid contracts, and rigged privatization schemes. When the guns go silent, order is self-enforcing without third-party policy enforcement. Peace is the result of jointly determined warlord strategies.

The empirical contribution of this book is a description of a process that unfolded in Georgia and Tajikistan, straightforward in its logic and banal in the brutality of its implementation. A small number of militia captains realized that they could do better by working together to install a president and reinventing their careers as security officers and politicians in the new regime ministries. They estimated that, once installed, they would be able to continue self-financing through racketeering, smuggling, and contract enforcement, while also extorting the president through the constant threat of removing him from power in a coup. The struggle over ruling coalition membership was violent, shifting from rural to urban areas once the "conventional" phase of the war was resolved. Collusion and coalition formation among various militia captains, based on the incentive to eliminate imitators and purge opportunists, was critical, as it revealed the bargaining power of the warring factions. Destructive urban warfare eventually ended, and a semblance of order reemerged in the capital cities. Shevardnadze used his celebrity to petition the West for multilateral aid, but doing so provoked Russia and required that he buy off most of his opponents simultaneously. In Tajikistan, by contrast, the president's strategy for political survival rested on playing both sides of the Western-Russian divide, *narrowing* the social bases of state power and *raising* the stakes of politics.

But if all of that is correct, then certain realists will feel entitled to ask difficult questions: Why persist with the idealist fictions of the liberal state-building canon? Why not be uncompromisingly honest about the processes that are likely to unfold? A cynical answer is that democratic legislatures in wealthy

[handwritten top margin: I.E., STEALING + SQUANDERING THE HARD EARNED WAGES OF THE VOTERS WHOSE INTERESTS THEY WERE ELECTED TO REPRESENT.*]*

states could not justify voting for humanitarian assistance if they believed that they were financing the kinds of militia politics described in this book.[1] Even if aid rents are just a form of divisible postwar spoils (v^*) that the warlords divide up, more is better than less if consolidation is the desired outcome. An ideological script for how civil war settlement ought to unfold – with an optimistic role for loans, grants, and training – may be a political necessity to securing humanitarian aid from donor states.

[handwritten left margin: what a laugh*]*

A better, more optimistic answer is that the university-educated class of multilingual elites who manage the modern humanitarian aid complex see themselves in solidarity with innocent people whose rights are trampled by very bad post-war states. These privileged, well-meaning bearers of v^* have social protections that are often not afforded to the citizens of the countries in which they temporarily reside, and they believe they can write a script to a better future. And perhaps they can. Because this book focuses on the warlords, their armies, and the gritty and corrupt distributional politics between them, the tone of the narrative implies a tradeoff between stability in the short term and strong and accountable institutions in the long run. But perhaps there is no such tradeoff. Perhaps we should acknowledge that our social scientific models of nonviolent social transformation have low predictive power. As recent Georgian political history has demonstrated, large numbers of NGO-funded idealists can, occasionally, completely overhaul the constraints of a warlord-saturated political system and induce lasting social change. It is sufficient to acknowledge that the liberal state-building canon, with its normative emphasis on democratic institutions in the Weberian mode, is at odds with processes described in this study. But that is not a sufficient warrant for torching the canon.[2]

[handwritten right margin: UNLESS TRUTH AND (BAD THINGS APPARENTLY...)*]*

Some liberals, anxious for an endorsement of their missionary spirit and disappointed with this stubbornly amoral and materialist account, are sure to ask a different set of equally-difficult follow-up questions. Is there truly no relevant role for democratic accountability in peace-building? No role at all for public goods? For holding government agents accountable to some kind of social contract? What are aid professionals supposed to imagine they are engaged in, if not trying to move societies toward a Weberian state?[3] And for

[handwritten: UHH, RIDING THE GRAVY TRAIN, FEATHERING THEIR OWN NESTS, VIRTUE-SIGNALING + ADVANCING LEFTEE-ISM??*]*

[1] A humanitarian functionalist might be able to look the other way, justifying large aid flows by arguing that short wars save lives, even if the money ends up lining the pockets of unsavory characters. But it is unlikely these arguments could survive sustained debates in a democratically accountable legislature. Olivier Roy, the OSCE head of mission to Tajikistan, who arrived on the scene fully fluent in Persian, left a digital treasure trove of English- and French-language emails for some future historian of the Tajik civil war. The fact that these emails are archived, not part of the official OSCE reports, is evidence that he believed plain speech could undermine the process that the OSCE mission was involved in: helping to oversee a transition to peace.

[2] Even Halford Mackinder (1942), a hardened geopolitical realist, recognized a role for idealism and values. 6.

[3] Weber (1953), following Trotsky, defined the state as "a human community that (successfully) claims the monopoly of the legitimate use of physical force within a given territory." 78. At

[handwritten right margin: I.E., HONESTY + TRUTH*]*

that matter, what of civil society? What of the *content* of all the different aid programs, troop trainings, education exchanges? Is v^* from the U.S. actually interchangeable with v^* from the Russia – or, for that matter, from Iran?

Of course not. The model in this book is merely meant to provide an account of how foreign involvement in the closing phases of a violent civil war might facilitate settlement *even if* there are no security guarantees and no value added by the foreign aid programming specifics. The model does not differentiate between different sources of v^* in the interests of simplicity, readability, and parsimony. Chapter 3 makes clear that the fear of what social institutions would look like in state where the v^* came from Iran motivated many Tajik militants to take up weapons. The fear of what social institutions would look like if they were forcibly integrated into a state where the v^* comes from the West motivates many Abkhaz and South Ossetians to remain outside of Georgia's state-building project to this day. In both states expectations of future foreign aid unleashed tremendous violent social energy precisely because the motives of foreign audiences were so easily anticipated.

IMPLICATIONS FOR POLICY

At the broadest level, the prognosis implied by this analysis is optimistic. If the leader of a postwar state can quickly tap into international aid (in the form of loans, charity, and security assistance) and then credibly commit to distributing it to warlords (who are prepared to carry out a coup against him if he does not make good on promises), a president may be able to quickly "buy" peace. Though this account is primarily meant to apply to small and centralized states, the model in this book provides an integrated lens through which to interpret the decline of civil conflict since the end of the Cold War. It is more difficult for warlords to survive outside of a state without superpower funding (e.g., the end of the Cold War lowered reservation values r).[4] There is also a greater

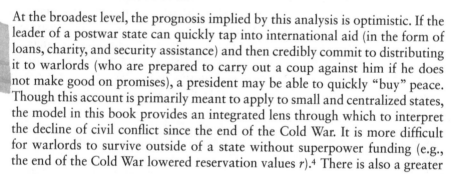

least since William Reno (1998), it has been difficult to square the Weberian benchmark of "monopolizing violence within recognized borders" with what everyone understands about political institutions in weak states. What we really mean when we talk about strengthening the state, in this account, is often associated with that elusive variable of "development." To quote Robert Bates (2001): "Development involves the formation of capital and the organization of economic activity. Politically, it involves the taming of violence and the delegation of authority to those who will use power productively." 25. But a "monopoly of violence" sets the bar too high. Many states have ungovernable rural or sub-proletarian pockets. Many leaders remain in power by exploiting their pivotal roles as the mediator between the international system and key providers of violence. In the tail of the distribution, some state leaders clearly thrive while ignoring – or even terrorizing – the majority of their citizens, and selling partial (or probabalistic) protection from the state's own agents. The empirical work of Karen Barkey (1994) and Ferguson (2005), and the theoretical work of Jackson (1990) and Wagner (2007) develop these intuitions further.

4 See Kalyvas and Balcells (2011). Face and voice recognition software, the proliferation of camera phones, mobile money – all of these make it more difficult for war criminals simply to

availability of credit and multilateral aid (e.g., higher levels of v^*) for states that make cosmetic efforts to democratize.

The threat of mass-casualty terrorism has raised the stakes of getting good intelligence. This in turn requires assistance from local partners and cooperation between the permanent veto players in the United Nations Security Council. It has also raised the stakes of inaction. The idea that pockets of toxic beliefs are going to simply be permitted to metastacize strikes many military professionals, and this author, as quaint. I cannot imagine a constellation of political circumstances that would allow the great powers to outgrow the temptation to tinker in the top-left "Postmodern Imperialism" corner of Figure 1.1, in the first chapter of this volume. Technology is rapidly expanding the scope of governments' ability to monitor individuals. Neither social scientists nor intelligence analysts in the employ of the great powers can credibly commit to ignoring what goes on in distant war zones. What the great powers *can* credibly commit to ignoring, as an empirical matter, is the indefinite persistence of very bad governance practices, so long as those governance practices serve the function of keeping threats contained. But common diagnosis of a shared problem for the great powers is in some sense good news for interstate cooperation at a global level.

Regionally, the picture is murkier. With China and Russia as permanent veto-players in the United Nations Security Council, UN Peacekeeping Operations (UNPKOs) in Eurasia are relatively rare.[5] As a new generation of post-Soviet elites come of age, it remains an open question whether these states will remain economically and culturally dependent on Russia. Human capital could easily begin to flow East or South. Geopolitically speaking, Eurasia is impossible to ignore: the rise of China and India, the persistent risk of Pakistani state failure, and the long-term viability of the nonproliferation regime are all challenges that will pull the attention of Western analysts. Over the next century, as Russian gradually contracts into a regional power centered on the ancient Christian city-states of the Rus, it will become more tempting for regional and great powers to assertively press their advantage in Russia's backyard.[6] I have argued that part of the key to quick and decisive civil war settlement in the post-Soviet wars was an absence of proxy-war dynamics in the early 1990s, out of deference to creaky politics in Moscow. In the future, proxy wars – of the sort that may be emergent in Ukraine – are more likely. As such, the prognosis for quick settlements to future Eurasian civil wars is not clear. If there were another episode of state failure or insurgency in Tajikistan, or a new conflict in Uzbekistan, Kyrgyzstan, or the South Caucasus, it is not

---

fade away into state security structures via the processes described in this book. I am not certain whether this ought to be modeled as increasing or decreasing the reservation wage of staying outside of the state. I suspect that all of these technologies will vastly increase the capacity of relatively weak states to manage unruly populations.

5 See Stedman (2003).
6 Cooley (2012), especially 16–29 and 162–178.

obvious that Russia would be capable of dictating the terms of the settlement in quite the same way. Bullying and bribing the warlords in Afghanistan and the government in Uzbekistan to stop supporting would-be clients from across their borders worked reasonably well as a strategy for Russia to end the Tajik civil war on its own terms in the mid-1990s. Many doubt whether these strategies could, or would, be replicated today. It is even more unlikely that the United States could play a unilateral stabilizing role from across an ocean. Russia's gradual disengagement from the region may have discouraging implications for human security in Central Asia.

In Tajikistan, a *partial incorporation* equilibrium gave way to *a full incorporation* equilibrium with time. I have argued in this book that this is largely due to the complimentarity of great power interests, with Russia acting as the lead state, to shield Central Asia from the chaos in Afghanistan or ideological infiltration from Iran. Reservation values for unincorporated warlords dropped gradually through the 1990s, and precipitously when NATO forces entered Afghanistan. Interest convergence between the great powers saved many lives, and kept the borders intact.

But the Georgian case is also worth considering, given that the weak states of Central Asia are boxed in from every direction by nuclear states that have demonstrated a willingness to support proxy wars in their neighbors. In the case of Georgia, reasonable people disagree about whether the contemporary situation represents a *partial incorporation* equilibrium (in which certain warlords in Abkhazia and South Ossetia remain stubbornly outside state control) or a *full incorporation* equilibrium (with revised boundaries that the Georgian government refuses to recognize).[7] But what almost no one disagrees upon is that in Georgia today Russian and American strategic assistance represent substitutes, not compliments.

This ambiguity in how one ought to even describe the Georgian case suggests that a "partial incorporation" can endure as an equilibrium indefinitely, or at least for a very long time. Nonconsolidated states – not only Georgia, but also contemporary Somalia and Afghanistan – may represent stable, self-enforcing equilibria. What we observe is persistent low-intensity conflict between one coalition of criminal gangsters in the capital city and various potential counter-coalitions of rural actors that have built their own shadow state institutions with assistance from foreign actors (e.g., Russia, Ethiopia, Pakistan, respectively). Insurgent warlords may desire political reconciliation, but calculate that there is more to be gained at the fringes of state control.

I am often asked for my opinion on whether and how soon Georgia should be admitted to the NATO alliance. Alexander Rondeli, the gregarious head of

---

[7] For a useful description of the overlapping zones of political control that define Georgia's internal hinterlands, see Marten (2012), 86–101.

the Georgian Foundation for Strategic and International Studies, once put the matter to me in the following way:

"The problem is easy to diagnose. The problem is that there are certain people in charge in Moscow who act like they don't know where Russia's borders are. ... America says it wants Georgia to develop independent of Russia. We agree! We don't *want* to be like Armenia, like Uzbekistan, like your Tajikistan ... we want to be free, to be like the Baltic states in Europe. And you [Americans] say you want the same thing for us. We have democracy. We train with your army. We sent troops to Iraq. What is left for us to do?"[8]

I will violate a Georgian taboo by answering Rondeli's well-asked question in plain language: If Georgian leaders wanted to get serious about getting NATO membership, a good first step would be to abandon territorial claims to the break-away territories. If Saakashvili had been the visionary he imagines himself to be, he would have used the afterglow of the Rose Revolution to do this in 2004. He instead took a number of provocative steps that led to war. Now the territories are almost certainly gone for good anyway, though it will fall on some future statesman to pay the domestic costs of admitting it. The blunt truth is that many in the Georgian political class continue to plan for a war with Russia. Their enthusiasm for this outcome is frankly disturbing. Most Americans do not want to fight a war with Russia at all, and certainly not over who owns what hotel in Sukhumi. As I am not myself a Georgian, it is not appropriate for me to pass judgment on Georgians' collective unwillingness to consider giving up their historical claims to the land of Abkhazia and South Ossetia. But I hope that my Georgian friends will extend me the reciprocal courtesy of acknowledging that, from the point of view of American national interests, the events of the August War of 2008 are exemplary of why Georgia is a potential security liability.[9] Russia has demonstrated a willingness to keep reservation values for Abkhaz and South Ossetian warlords higher than any offer from the Georgian center – even when foreign aid was flowing into Tbilisi at an unsustainable rate. Georgia has been a stalwart ally to America, especially since 2003, but if Georgians want to be part of a Western security community and the NATO defensive alliance, it a problem to be floating in quantum uncertainty between a *full incorporation* equilibrium and a *partial incorporation* equilibrium, depending on whose version of the map prevails. Georgia does not need Russian help or permission to withdraw from disputed territory. It could unilaterally transform itself into a better ally, if only Georgians wanted to. But I fear that a plurality of Georgians do not want to. Many believe they can wait Russia out. Many believe that they can spend another few decades continuing to enjoy massive flows of foreign aid, slowly shame the West into providing security guarantees, and eventually reclaim their

8 Interview with Alexander Rondeli Febuary 27, 2006 in Tbilisi.
9 See King (2008*a*, 2008*b*).

lost territory by some combination of military coercion and Western mediation. In my view, this kind of thinking is the heart of the problem – the worst kind of violent utopianism, celebrating escalation scenarios that culminate in war between Tbilisi and Moscow. And the problem is increasingly understood in exactly the same way in Brussels and in Washington.

One of the main policy-relevant lessons that should emerge from this book is that locals have strong incentives to misrepresent regional history. Given this, it important for policy audiences to be skeptical when either regional experts or armchair grand strategists claim to know what armed groups in a distant part of the globe are "really fighting for." Interview data do not cut this knot if the soldiers themselves either do not know why they are fighting or are strategically misrepresenting their own interests for the camera. And answers to the question can be tailored to the desired policy prescription in very predictable ways. If armed groups reflect deeply held political beliefs or social divisions, perhaps no international gendarmerie will be able to resolve long-term grievances or even stop the killing.[10] But if, on the other hand, armed groups rest on thin kinds of social capital that are just cover for criminal opportunism, perhaps it is morally incumbent on military professionals from the developed world to either buy them off with aid – as the model in Chapter 2 suggests is possible – or destroy these groups and spare civilians the horror of war.[11] Between these two extremes lie a universe of gradations.[12] But a healthy dose of humility is justified when it comes to predicting outcomes internal to civil wars, or the high-stakes coalition politics that accompany the settlement.

When it comes to predicting outcomes, Russia's failure to shape Georgian and Tajik domestic politics in the wake of their "order first" policies in the early 1990s can also serve as a cautionary tale. Russia and CIS forces had access to regional intelligence networks – acquired over decades of patient penetration and cultivation – that the United States can never really hope to acquire in Eurasia. Yet in both cases, Russia's foreign policy goals were thoroughly subverted by locals. Recall that Moscow's overarching goal was to build a strong buffer state and stable power-sharing in Tajikistan and to undermine Georgian efforts to orient their foreign policy toward the West and NATO. Russians superficially succeeded on both accounts in the short

---

[10] See Laitin (1999*b*) and Luttwak (1999).

[11] John Mueller has diagnosed the central problem of the twenty-first century military interventions as one of "policing the remnants of war." He posits that many of the armed groups responsible for civilian deaths in the developing world are disorganized criminal affairs run by gangs with very fragile ties to the society for which they claim to speak. Given the huge moral costs associated with standing on the sidelines while local criminals terrorize their populations, and given that any minimally competent military force should be able to rout and dismiss disorganized bands of "thugs," he argues that a liberal attitude toward intervention could save countless lives. See Mueller (2003) and Mueller (2004), 8–23 and 117–160.

[12] See Kalyvas and Kocher (2007) and Fearon (2007) for an example from recent history of how subtly different interpretations of these questions translate into radically divergent policy recommendations, holding geography and time constant.

term, but in a longer view, their policies have backfired in certain respects. Efforts to weaken Georgia led Shevardnadze to respond by building a broad coalition of social actors oriented toward the West, leading to an increasingly confident and independent foreign policy. In its efforts to make Tajikistan an outpost of Russian interests in the near abroad, Russian foreign policy has been complicit in the creation of an extremely brittle state with a narrow governing coalition. This is not to say that Russian policies were doomed to fail, or that the United States ought to give up on local partnerships and good intelligence. It is simply to note that in the scramble to establish friendly regimes in Georgia and Tajikistan, the Russian government was incapable of monitoring distributive politics or having influence over who got what. Georgian and Tajik agents got their way more often than they did not.

In Georgia and Tajikistan, warlords were not just taking advantage of state weakness to advance criminal agendas – they were trying to *become* the state. Any model that does not account for the possibilities of tactical cooperation and long-term collusion between the state and militia actors is incomplete. Although most authors writing on this period imply that warlords were disarmed by "the state" once it became strong enough to confront the militias, this simplification actually obscures the defining political problem of the time: that violent militias had moved from the streets to become *explicitly* part of the state, well positioned to contest their share of the rents of statehood. This is a disturbing insight for policymakers and scholars. When distant observers see brutal killing of civilians during the closing phases of civil wars, there is a tendency to want to send aid to shore up state weakness. The argument in this book should be interpreted as a caution against the impulse to simply increase bilateral aid to provide more resources to the consolidating regime. Models that focus on state capacity – with rebel militias locked in zero-sum competition with state institutions to provide public goods – are certainly relevant to counterinsurgency and asymmetric warfare, but they can be misleading when the state itself is up for grabs. Though often the political instinct is to "prop up" our ally (the recognized government) with an increased flow of bilateral and multilateral aid (to signal our commitment and to strengthen the police and military), if violence is occurring because various armed actors within the state are attempting to secure a larger share of state rents, targeted aid transfers may just increase the value of the prize being contested. Chapter 4 demonstrated that in the closing phases of both the Georgian and Tajik civil wars, militia members were engaged in months of grueling and destructive attrition warfare in the hopes of *being admitted to* the state apparatus with a sufficiently large side payment. Expectations of aid increased the stakes in the war of attrition.

To summarize: The extortion dynamic described in this volume are necessary considerations for elites hoping to "buy peace." This has relevance for contemporary policy toward Ukraine, where a war by warlord proxies is underway.

IMPLICATIONS FOR UKRAINE

At the time of this writing there is an ongoing civil war in Ukraine.[13] Various militias and state forces are clashing. The Russian government's position is that the proximate cause of this violence is Ukrainian state weakness, and the permissive cause of the violence is Western meddling in Russia's traditional sphere of influence. The Ukrainian government's position is that this war amounts to an undeclared invasion of Ukraine by Russia. Prominent Western opinion leaders have invoked comparisons to the Anschluss.[14] Although the root causes of the war are disputed, the costs are not. Thousands have died, many thousands have been wounded, tens of thousands have been displaced, and tens of billions of dollars of lost productivity and damage to critical infrastructure are estimated. Formal ceasefires have come and gone. What happened? And does the theory in this book shed light on what might be expected in the future?

Though Russian- and English-language narratives diverge quickly, the basic sequence of events leading to the current conflict is not disputed. In the fall of 2013, President Viktor Yanukovych of Ukraine declined to sign an association agreement with the European Union in favor of exploring membership in Russia's Eurasian Economic Union (EEU). Many Ukrainians believed the window was closing on the possibility of labor mobility to, and economic and cultural integration with, the West. Broad-based opposition emerged, galvanized in opposition to the prospect of a geopolitical pivot to the East. A wide coalition of civil society groups organized protests. Weeks of escalation finally culminated in prolonged and violent clashes with state security forces in Maidan Square at the heart of Kyiv – a bloody, high-stakes, ideologically charged reenactment of the 2004 Orange Revolution.[15] On February 22, 2014, Yanukovych shocked domestic and foreign audiences by fleeing the country. He left behind a paralyzed, headless government. Russia's state media outlets decried the situation as a Western-backed coup d'etat against the legitimately elected government in Ukraine. Ukrainian state security services stood down. Ad hoc voices from civil society promised new elections.

Political power passed to the parliament, which quickly passed a resolution that would have made Ukrainian the sole state language at all levels. If enacted, parents of Russian speakers would have had to enroll their children in Ukrainian-language schools for them to have any chance at any job as a government clerk. The bill was vetoed a little more than a week later

---

[13] I employ the analytic category "civil war" not to imply that the causes of the war are indigenous to Ukrainian politics, or that third-party engagement is irrelevant to the conflict – simply to note that according to the coding rules employed elsewhere in this manuscript the events of 2014 qualify as a civil war. The death toll is disputed, but at least 1,000 people have died, and more that 100 of the deaths are on the government side.

[14] Rucker (2014).

[15] For an analytic postmortem on the Orange Revolution see Beissinger (2013). His analysis emphasizes the nonideological nature of the 2004 mobilization. See especially 16–17.

by the interim president. But the threat to force linguistic assimilation, and strip life opportunities from Russian-speaking citizens who refused to give up their native tongue, increased the stakes of the political conflict.[16] Self-defense militias began to form.

For narrative coherence, at this point it is necessary to posit an "internal explanation" for the actions of Vladimir Putin – to speculate about one particular human being's emotions, psychology, and state of mind.[17] My best guess into Putin's psychology is that his actions with respect to Ukraine were driven primarily by domestic considerations – namely a desire to maintain his position as the most popular person in the Russian-speaking world, and to thereby write himself into Russian history – and secondarily by a desire for symbolic confrontation with the West. I suspect he understands himself to be engaging in a battle of wills against hypocritical geostrategic competitors, and is practically daring them into a proxy war.

Though Putin's reasoning will remain the subject of speculation, what is known is that he seized on the anarchic situation in Ukraine as a proximate justification for intervention: more or less to remind everyone that he could, he broke one of the most basic rules of international sovereignty. On February 27,

---

[16]   The acting president of Ukraine, Oleksandr Turchynov, vetoed the bill on March 1, effectively stopping its enactment. In my opinion, the decision to remove Russian as an official language can best be understood as an emotional decision, driven by spite and aimed at punishing the eastern half of the country for electing Poroshenko in the first place. The best that can be said of this rash move by parliament is that the vote was quickly overridden – but it validated the worst-casing of Russia's propagandists. For a useful discussion of spite, see Petersen (2011) 49–50. Petersen (2002) and Petersen (2011) describe various mechanisms by which anticipated reversal of status hierarchies produce violent actions by individuals.

[17]   Recall from Chapter 1: Internal explanations, according to Ferejohn (2004), come from within an individual, such as psychological biases, emotional responses, and culturally contingent belief structures. For expert testimony on Putin's psychology, see McFaul (2014), especially 8:00–12:10 and 20:20–21:15. A different kind of expert testimony, drawing on different sources and articulated with different motives, can be found in Remnick (2014). Maybe Putin feared that Ukraine's normal political institutions – regular elections that facilitated slow rotations of power between Western- and Eastern-oriented governments – were in the process of being bypassed by street politics, to the disadvantage of Russia and the advantage of opportunists in the West. While a vast strata of the Ukrainian population was interested in orienting their futures toward the West, many other Ukrainians, especially in the East, felt their votes had been invalidated and the promises of democracy betrayed by the nonconstitutional transfer of power. Many feared being reduced to second-class citizens in an emergent status hierarchy that rewarded English-language skills, and worst-case scenarios were validated by the rash actions of Parliament, maybe Putin felt a genuine obligation to come to the defense of "his people." Maybe Putin was angry that clandestine Western agents – whom he imagined to have been orchestrators of Maidan – were getting away with regime change in his backyard. Maybe he feared that the United States was planning to use the same kinds of tactics in Moscow on him. Maybe he was interested in probing the limits of favorable media coverage, testing if he could "wag the dog" to push his own popularity so high that conversations about election falsification would be absurd. It is likely a combination of these, but no one can produce evidence to validate or falsify alternative hypotheses.

Russian forces seized the Crimean Peninsula. Many Crimean citizens greeted them as liberators. Others, particularly those of Ukrainian or Tatar ethnicity, were far more apprehensive. A referendum to join Russia was organized quickly and, on March 16, a substantial majority of Crimea's citizens voted in favor of unification – although interpreting these results was complicated not only by Russia's military occupation, but also by the fact that the ballot did not include an option to remain within Ukraine.[18] These actions were declared illegal by Western governments, and, as such, the map remains contested. In a number of public speeches, Putin made it clear that he considered these moves a correction of historical mistakes made by Soviet map makers under Khrushchev, and did not consider the internationally recognized borders of Ukraine to be the business of anyone except Russians and Ukrainians. He repeatedly reaffirmed his duty to come to the aid of Russian speakers, and painted Crimea's citizens as helpless hostages trapped in the anarchic and proto-fascist Ukrainian state. Shortly after, he began to invoke "Novorossia," which were – are? – imperial Russian territorial claims on southeastern Ukraine, which may extend to the entire north Black Sea coast.[19]

In response to Russia's military adventurism, and recognizing the impotence of the Ukrainian state to do anything at all about it, many more pro-Russian militias self-organized.[20] Pro-Ukraine self-defense militias organized in response.[21] Charismatic warlords used the same kinds of persuasion sketched in Chapter 3 of this book: the certainty of masculine glory and the chance to play soldier in the short term, vague promises of a good job in the security sector in the medium term, and romantic hopes of social recognition and a respectful place in an emergent nationalist narrative in the long term. The backbone of the labor for many pro-Russian militias seems to have been Afghan civil war veterans, though there was apparently no shortage of disaffected youth ready to join.[22] As weeks turned into months, dozens of militias declared autonomous "People's Republics" around their city or oblast in the hopes of being recognized and annexed by Moscow. Though diplomatic recognition did not materialize immediately, what did materialize was barely covert Russian assistance aplenty.[23] Over the next few months, pro-Russian separatists inflicted humiliating losses on the Ukrainian military, sometimes in full sight of Organization for Security and Cooperation in Europe

---

[18] The official vote tally was 96 percent in favor with 86 percent reported turnout.

[19] *New York Times*: August 29, 2014.

[20] *New York Times*: April 30, 2014, *New York Times*:June 4, 2014.

[21] *New York Times*: May 23, 2014.

[22] "One rebel group, Oplot, comes from the Ukrainian city of Kharkiv. Another, the Russian Orthodox Army, is composed of Russians and Ukrainians. A third, named for a river, Kalmius, is made up mainly of coal miners. This motley mix forms just part of the fighting force of Ukraine's eastern uprising. It is more patchwork than united front: Some groups get along with others. Some do not. And their leaders seem to change with the weather. 'I can't keep them straight anymore,' said a fighter ..." *New York Times*: July 09 2014.

[23] *New York Times*: May 27, 2014.

(OSCE) observers.[24] Clumsy attempts at counterinsurgency by the Ukrainian military destroyed entire cities. A quarter of the country's industrial and mining output was disrupted. The Ukrainian currency devalued 60 percent.[25] Tens of thousands of Ukrainian civilians on both sides have been brutalized by war and will carry bitter memories for the rest of their lives.

As of the fall of 2014, Ukraine was clearly at war. An intergenerational struggle for national reunification, and a deep sense of bitterness at being abandoned by the West, was the product being peddled to the next generation of Ukrainian light infantry recruits. In a September trip to Kyiv, I observed dozens of young, athletic, masked men recruiting for the "Azov" militia in front the ancient St. Sophia Cathedral. I observed a similar initiation ritual just hours later, as stoic young men prayed over machine guns near the Monument to the Martyrs of the Artificial Famine of the 1930s. My life history interviews provide a basis for informed speculation as to the motivations of these young idealists. They were angry. They were anxious to prove their manhood – to themselves, to each other, to their families, and to their girlfriends. They wanted to claim their place in a nationalist narrative, fighting the war of independence that was denied to their fathers and uncles when the Soviet Union broke apart peacefully. They wanted to grease the skids toward a respectable career as soldiers or police officers, and doubted that volunteering would hurt their chances.

The theoretical model from Chapter 2 can be laid atop the Ukrainian empirical record to generate a short sketch of an analytic narrative in the service of providing policy recommendations. State failure in Ukraine was imminent in early January 2014. Russia could have responded by sending military assistance to prop up Yanukovych's embattled regime, but it did not. As a Ukrainian academic who was part of the Maidan Coordinating Council put it,

> "If he [Yanukovych] has gotten on the phone to Putin and said 'I need help, I need tanks, I need police battalions, maybe military divisions, I am the elected head of state … come arrest these criminal protesters,' there is absolutely nothing anyone could have done. … but he [Yanukovych] fled, so we'll never know. … I think he was worried about being strung up, like Ceaușescu in Romania."[26]

Returning to the language of the model: Russia responded to the collapse of the government by pro-Western demonstrators by raising the stability threshold (s). In practice, this meant demonstrating its economic and energy leverage, flaunting its superiority in military hardware, and engaging in a disciplined propaganda war. Russian media portrayed the new regime as dominated by fascists. The voices of *Pravii Sektor* brownshirts were broadcast as if they were representative of the modal member of the Maidan protests. Consonant agreement and numbing repetition linked "NATO" with "Nazis"

24 *New York Times*: September 24, 2014.
25 *Al Jazeera*: September 28, 2014.
26 Interview conducted with Oleksiy Haran in Kyiv, June 23, 2014.

as a rote cognitive script in the minds of Russian-language media consumers. As for establishing facts on the ground, Russia demonstrated the efficacy of a variety of very low-cost military technologies – logistical support to locally recruited militias and bike gangs, unregulated border crossings for irregular infantry units from the North Caucasus, and plausibly deniable support from the Russian regular military – to impose costs on the interim government in Kyiv.

Consistent with the logic of the model, the warlords with the highest reservation values (r), the Russian-speaking warlords in the East, were the first to torch the Ukrainian social contract. Subsequent Russian support raised the reservation value for pro-Russian militias.[27] To keep order, the Ukrainian government would have had to commit to higher transfers of v^* than before, striking new deals with newly mobilized various warlord constituencies. The problem was that *there existed no functioning government* capable of striking politically difficult bargains. A new president, Petro Poroshenko, was elected in late May 2014, so finally there was someone to negotiate with Putin and appeal to Western states for assistance. Ukrainian army forces were hastily deployed, the word "invasion" was constantly repeated, mandatory conscription into the army was discussed, and the fledgling coalition did what it could to demonstrate to warlords in the East that a war of independence would entail horrible violence (high costs of war c). Early results were not promising. And at the time of this writing, Ukraine appears to be sliding toward either a *partial incorporation* equilibrium, with functionally independent statelets in the East analogous to Abkhazia or South Ossetia. A full-fledged *state-failure* equilibrium is not out of the question. In anticipation of the latter, capital flight set in and the economy contracted substantially ($v < v^*$).

What would be necessary to peacefully resolve this conflict, restore order, and reestablish domestic sovereignty in Ukraine? In the language of the model: What would it take to get back to a *full incorporation* equilibrium?

Georgian history suggests that pragmatism does not emerge in the absence of leadership and sustained political will. Applying this lesson to Ukraine, my opinion is that Ukrainian domestic actors will have to work together to "get over Crimea" as quickly as possible. It is imperative that Ukrainian historical claims to the Crimean peninsula not be allowed to become a litmus test for participation in Ukrainian politics. There is a pragmatic, nationalist rationale for a gag rule on the Crimea issue: The question of "whose history is more right" has no objective answer. The 2014 Parliamentary elections provided some cause for hope in this regard, and I hope Ukrainian politicians will be able

---

[27] Many armed spokesmen in Donetsk and Lukhansk gave statements making clear that they saw in Russia's actions a once-in-a-lifetime opportunity to shape an independent future for themselves. They believed that even if they failed, conditional on taking up arms and organizing militias, they would gain access to a future where they could credibly demand far more functional autonomy from Kyiv than would be possible otherwise.

to run for office successfully without having to go on the record establishing their nationalist credentials on Donbas and Crimea. If positions harden, and hostile position-taking on Crimea becomes a prerequisite for electoral viability in Ukrainian politicians, Georgia's past will likely be Ukraine's future.

Although the West has every reason to encourage the emergence of a pragmatic conservative coalition willing to compromise and strike politically difficult bargains, there are two huge problems that do not, at the time of this writing, have obvious solutions. The first is that many Ukrainian voters feel, with reason, that if they acquiesce on Crimea, then they will practically be inviting Russians into Odessa. The second is that the main tools that the West has at its disposal to shape domestic politics are financial incentives (v^*).

The general hope in Kyiv, after the Maidan events and the annexation of Crimea by Russia, was that Western states would come to the rescue with low-interest loans, generous International Monetary Fund (IMF) packages, as well as manipulation of the global price of oil and sanctions on Putin's inner circle in Russia. On the diplomatic front, negotiators in the winter of 2015 were hard at work trying to hammer out arrangements that would make credible federal guarantees acceptable to both domestic constituencies in Ukraine and Russian-speaking audiences.

Optimists hoped that Russia would stop waging its undeclared proxy war via warlords in breakaway provinces or contribute to the rebuilding effort by lending the assistance of its security forces to quickly settle the matter. If Russia were to close its border and begin forcibly disarming warlords, the kinds of collateral civilian damage on display in the summer of 2014 would not need to be repeated. But as a Ukrainian military veteran observed:

"So long as the conversation is about NATO and the EU ... I doubt the West is really going to be able to build things here in Ukraine's faster than Russia can tear them down ... it would be nice if we could get money like Georgia for a few years, but Russia ... they are so close, and we are so close [taps his heart] to them, here, and you [Americans] are so far away. ... Even Germany, France – they have no interest here. Only sentiment."[28] *SORRY TO HAVE TO TELL YOU, BUT ITS JUST NONE OF OUR DAMN BUSINESS, ANY MORE THAN RUSSIA HAS BUSINESS IN OUR FRONT YARD.*

For its part, the current Russian government has demonstrated to future generations of Ukrainians the kinds of costs they could expect if they continued to drift toward the cultural and economic embrace of the West: Russia can simply flood the region with irregular soldiers and biker gangs, with occasional clandestine support from special forces, to fight an undeclared war. And at any time, Putin could decide to march his forces further, link up with Transdeniestria, and claim all of the north shore of the Black Sea for Russia. It is next to impossible for Russia to credibly commit to *not* do such a thing, given Putin's recent actions. This possibility is widely recognized, and is itself a strong argument for *withholding* security guarantees to Ukraine. As in the South Caucasus, the benefit that Russia accrues from keeping its neighbor

---

[28] Interview conducted in Kyiv September 14, 2014.

destabilized – keeping the NATO alliance out of its immediate neighborhood – may outweigh the costs of absorbing refugees and enduring scolding from international diplomats and op-ed writers. Ukraine could face many years in an ambiguous *partial incorporation* equilibrium.

But what if the West did take a principled stand against Russia, pouring postwar reconstruction aid (v^*) into Ukraine in the kind of localized Marshall Plan that some have advocated? It is not impossible to imagine a consensus emerging to stand up to Putin's "aggression." The thought leaders would presumably be residents of the Baltic states, supported by offshore Anglophone idealists. The costs of persistent conflict would be borne by German, French, Dutch, Turkish, Spanish, Polish, Italian, and many East–Central European constituencies (measured in gas prices at the pump) and by many Ukrainian families (measured in acute human suffering). It is even possible to imagine scenarios in which Ukraine is invited into NATO without first settling the Crimea border issue. This would set the stage for a new Cold War–style standoff, with Crimea playing the role of East Germany. The argument in this book should remind policymakers that if the West decides to approach the problem in this way, two things should be expected.

First, once the aid arrives, the model emphasizes that Western donors will immediately lose control of how it will be distributed. The aid will become a source of rents, distributed in the service of keeping the government in power. Whatever our intentions, much of the v^* will almost certainly end up lining the pockets of the most loathsome kinds of intermediaries: not only warlords, but also cynical vote brokers, war profiteers with multiple passports, and real estate speculators. Georgian and Tajik history suggests that trying to purchase peace with foreign aid is an ugly business.[29]

Second, even if it were possible to target the aid toward reconstruction in the shattered cities, some of the main beneficiaries will be local warlords in the East – individuals who can, by force of arms, veto the particulars of distributional politics. Increased transparency and contemporary forensic accounting techniques may make it possible for tomorrow's social scientists to trace the side payments as they accrue to local mayors, regional governors, and police chiefs. These are the social actors best positioned to drag their feet, demonstrate their power to be disruptive, get their bribes from Kyiv, and then

---

[29] In the case of lethal aid, the risks are substantially higher. In my estimation there is a substantial risk of that Western military aid to Ukraine, advocated by many hawks in the West, could backfire. If Putin can credibly claim that the dead Russian soldiers who come back in body bags are dead because they are being killed by Americans, or by American guns, he may be able to ride his recent wave of wartime popularity indefinitely. It would actually be an ex-post validation of the Kremlin's most virulent propaganda claims. It is frustrating that many self-styled "realists" either do not understand this, or pretend as if they do not. It is very hard to falsify the conspiracy theory that the Maidan events were engineered by Western security agencies. Sending military technology one year after unconstitutional regime change is not exactly "disconfirming evidence" for Putin's theory. *i.e., maybe Putin is on to something.*

decide whether or not to play their part to keep their districts from joining the Ruble zone.[30] And it is already obvious to anyone paying attention that the security forces of the Ukrainian state plan to fight this war by working in tandem with patriotic militias representing a broad coalition of anti-Putin Russian-speakers of every ideological stripe. If this is to be a new Cold War over the future of Ukraine, it will be a war largely fought to the benefit of warlord proxies, using violence to build autonomous quasi-states in the zones of contestation.

It may be valuable, as an analytic exercise, to try to view this crisis from the East and not the West, and employ the value-neutral metaphor of bargaining, or a game of nerves. It might be the case that Putin is doing all of this to signal that, when it comes to the defense of core interests the Russian Federation in 2014, he is willing and able to fight dirty. Russia may no longer be a superpower, but even as a regional power it has many potential sources of leverage over Ukraine, and deep historical interests in the area – interests that precede the existence of the United Nations Charter by centuries.[31] These core interests were never at stake in Central Asia or in the South Caucasus.[32] If this interpretation of Putin's psychology is correct, the chorus of scolding voices claiming that the Crimea precedent will unravel the post–World War II international order may be somewhat off the mark. By redrawing the map conservatively, and provoking a containable war in a part of the world that is in Russia's sphere of influence, perhaps Putin was communicating where post–Soviet Russia's revised security red lines actually are.[33]

A *Levada* Center poll in late 2014 estimated Putin's popularity at 87 percent.[34] At that time, Western governments were imposing economic sanctions as the instrument of punishment – a completely different kind of Western response than that seen to Russian moves in Georgia or Tajikistan. These sanctions inflicted substantial costs on the Russian economy, felt across a wide stratum of Russian society.[35] It is too early to tell whether these sanctions will change Russian policy. I would be surprised if they did. It is easy to imagine scenarios in which Russians "rally 'round the flag" in response to the sanctions,

---

30 See Donetsk People's Republic Plans to Switch to Ruble (2014).

31 Putin's tactics also had the effect of drawing attention to asymmetry of interests between the United States and Russia in this particular part of the globe. Overall, there are simply too many issues related to global governance in which there is a natural complementarity of interests between the United States and Russia: maintenance of the nuclear nonproliferation regime, a grand bargain with Iran, future relations with China, the functioning of the UN Security Council, and more. Putin factored these geopolitical realities into his bargaining position.

32 Whether or not they exist in the Arctic or Siberia is a matter for another day.

33 I am heartened by Foreign Minister Sergei Lavrov's calls for a "Reset 2.0." "Now there's a need for what the Americans might call a 'reset' ... The current US administration is today wrecking much of the cooperation structures that it created itself along with us. Most likely, something more will come up – a reset No. 2 or a reset 2.0." BBC (2014).

34 See "Putin's Approval Rating Soars to 87%, Poll Says": August 6, 2014.

35 See Birnbaum (2014).

tightening their belts and blaming the West for their hunger. It is easy to imagine scenarios in which countersanctions on food and agricultural imports from the West ultimately deepen Russia's economic and security relations with post-Soviet republics.[36] It is difficult, by contrast, to imagine scenarios for either regime change in Russia, or for a policy reversal on Crimea without regime change. I am afraid that the standoff has no end in sight. Putin has demonstrated that he can engineer a situation in Eastern Ukraine analogous to the *partial incorporation* equilibrium in Georgia: an ambiguous posture that keeps Ukrainian politics permanently destabilized.

The Georgia analogy is not lost on Ukrainians. I asked a prominent Ukrainian intellectual how he thought his country would be different in thirty years. He did not hesitate to respond that he did not think his country would exist in thirty years. Surprised by his candor, I asked him what he meant. He explained that in the future "[T]here will be three Ukraines, just like how today there are three Georgias." I asked him if he would share his theory of what the borders of the three Ukraines would be; he gamely sketched the map that appears as Figure 6.1.[37] He went on: "We've already lost the East, with the destruction of Donetsk and Lukhansk … our politicians just don't know it yet. But those people will never think of themselves as part of Ukraine again. We'll never bring them back, just like Georgians will never get back Sukhumi or South Ossetia." He envisioned a rump state, or a collection of ambiguously federated city-states, emerging east of the Dnieper River to provide Russia with the strategic depth it demands.[38]

A final provocative observation: Much in this book contradicts the standard account of war termination that is often championed by advocates of the International Court of Justice. It is worth recalling that one of the first things that Shevardnadze did was publicly pardon and forgive Ioseliani and Kitovani. Political rehabilitation of war criminals is at the core of the consolidation game as presented here. An uncomfortable social fact is that the decent people and the bad apples work in close proximity in postwar state security ministries. In both the Georgian and the Tajik cases, processes of local justice worked themselves out, albeit slowly and imperfectly. But criminals were not actually locked in zero-sum competition with legitimate state institutions so much as the criminals were shielded from prosecution by these institutions. That was the whole point. In reference to Ukraine: I would be surprised if either the relevant heads of state (Vladimir Putin, Petro Poroshenko) or any of the prominent warlords (such as

---

[36] See Schenkann (2014).

[37] Interview conducted in Kyiv, September 8, 2014. Author name withheld by request. He was quick to caveat his prediction: "If Putin dies, then everything in Russia unravels, and it could easily be very bad … and then there will be more than three Ukraines."

[38] Another memorable excerpt from the interview: "I do not pretend to know what will happen up here … I hope we [in the West] keep Kyiv … and I think we will. And probably the whole territory out there, and maybe parts of the suburbs of Kyiv, would be contested for a while – this is to be expected."

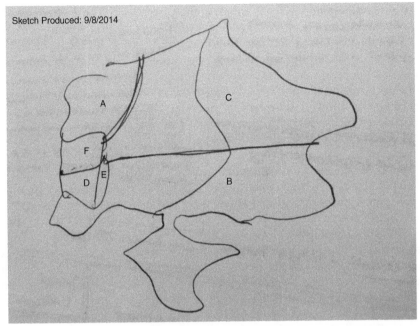

Sketch Produced: 9/8/2014

A = "Polish Ukraine" — Cities North of Romania, up to/including Kyiv (?)   D = Moldova
B = Novorossia — Essentially a straight latitude line from Transdniestria   E = Transdniestria
C = East Dniepr — Borders ambiguous; likely site of persistent civil conflict   F = Romania

FIGURE 6.1. Ukraine 2045: a predictive map.

Alexander Zakharchenko, the premier of the self-proclaimed Donetsk People's Republic) are ever indicted under the mechanisms of the Rome Statute. There is a gap between the universal rhetorical promises of international human rights law and the cynical reality of selective enforcement that is unlikely to be bridged in this part of the world any time soon.

IMPLICATIONS FOR THEORY

Civil wars are often treated by political scientists as contests between an "incumbent" and an "insurgent" player. This approach can shed light on attrition, asymmetric bargaining, and commitment dynamics, all of which are understood with a great deal more clarity today than they were two decades ago. Two-player models are attractive for their parsimony and tractability. These models generate policy-relevant insights that can be applied to many different settings. Because assisting incumbent regimes as they fight grinding wars against insurgents is a persistent problem, there is a permanent demand for analysts trained to deploy insights from these models.

For certain policy-relevant debates, there may be no real alternative to beginning the conversation by positing, by assumption, the existence of A and B: a legitimate state A, and an illegitimate rebel group B that is attempting to seize that state. But as scholars, we should notice that beginning the conversation in this way effectively forecloses the possibility of even asking a different question *that may be even more policy-relevant* in the closing phases of civil war: How is the practical boundary between "state" and "rebel" constructed by local actors trying to make peace?

My book is a direct attempt to answer this important question. All of the politics I describe revolve around strategic actors trying to manipulate the boundary of the coalition that would ultimately constitute "the state." Rather than just assuming Georgian and Tajik incumbents into existence, my approach draws attention to violent and cooperative processes that allowed corporate state actors to emerge.

The central problem with two-player "incumbent vs. insurgent" approaches is that they rely on assumptions that are inappropriate to the analysis of politics in failed states. Treating "insurgent" and "incumbent" players as fixed entities reifies the master cleavage of the civil war. It is not only postmodernists and radical constructivists who have noticed that treating ethnic groups as the unit of analysis – especially when combined with the language of "zero-sum conflict" – plays primarily to the advantage of military hard-line factions in the incumbent state.[39] As an empirical matter, civil wars since 1945 have rarely featured professional armies with coherent and unified lines of command-and-control. Analogies to two-player firm or interstate bargaining problems are therefore strained. This is especially the case in situations of acute state failure, when the incumbent regime faces off against multiple challengers. Side-switching in civil wars – especially highly fractious civil wars – is far more common than local politicians, foreign pundits, or political scientists have generally acknowledged. One of the main insights that emerges from the model in Chapter 2 of this book is that even if the figurehead president remains the same, the constellation of social forces that support a regime at the end of the civil war may not be the same constellation of social forces that supported the regime at the beginning of the war.

But once one abandons the analytic simplification of the two-player approach – the state vs. the insurgent terrorists, the red team vs. the blue team, our guys vs. their guys – where does one go next? It is one thing for aspirational policymakers to note in passing that "security problems for the great powers now emanate from weak states," but quite another for social

---

[39] Treating the ethnic group as the unit of analysis blurs distinctions between ruthless elites – who often generate fear and hatred cynically, with the expectation that they will be able to benefit in the aftermath of violence – and the ethnic masses who pay the costs of fighting. This critique has been well-treated by Gagnon (1995), Brown (1997), and De Figueiredo and Weingast (1999).

scientists to grapple with what this pithy observation actually implies for the future of security studies. This book, with its theoretical and empirical emphasis on the strategies of individual people (warlords), contributes to a literature that emphasizes agency over structure in civil war zones. But the research design endorsed by this book does, I fear, contribute to a dark trend: The size of the social unit that can be credibly described as a security threat is relentlessly shrinking, and the state's focus on these smaller units is relentlessly growing. Chapter 3 describes how and why certain individuals succeeded in politicizing grievance by quickly assembling private armies. To anticipate and cauterize this kind of threat in an era of mass casualty terrorism, some state agents already take it upon themselves to worry about individual people, map their social networks and institutional endowments, read their private correspondence, and ultimately judge whether or not they hold the "wrong beliefs." It is not clear where this line of inquiry should end. As a scientist, I am afraid that there is no end in sight. Sometimes it is possible to infer intent by the content of speech; sometimes language is intended to be "cheap talk." It is trivial to justify defensive war and preventative strikes if one takes certain angry people at their word. The world is full of angry voices and crazy ideas. Though I am not optimistic that there is a viable research program in studying grievance narratives in a comparative fashion, I am positive that the content of speech by people in the "belief creation" business – elected officials, clerics, teachers, and activists – is going to be the subject of sustained scrutiny by state-funded, computer-literate social scientists. I predict that epidemiological techniques will be brought to bear to track the prevalence and virulence of "dangerous ideas." All of this will occur in the name of national security.

These observations and predictions are not meant to be an apologetic for authoritarian practices. But I do not think liberal idealists or civil libertarians do themselves any favors by pretending that the problem is going to disappear. Scholars interested in understanding how to cauterize violence quickly and efficiently have no real alternative than to study autocratic practices, even if only in comparative context, even if only as a component of long-term peace-making processes in the liberal mode. I predict that in the coming decades, our field will devote considerably more attention to the direct and indirect technologies autocratic governments use to manage their populations. In so doing, scholars will surely notice analogous practices in well-governed "open access" societies.

The problem with making responsible inferences, testing theories rigorously, and generally advancing a research program on these kinds of questions is that those sort of data tend to be tremendously sensitive and difficult to gather. Even open, liberal, and strong societies enforce gag rules on topics that can inflame popular imaginations. The machinations of the secret police and domestic intelligence agencies are state secrets everywhere. All states have good reasons to keep researchers at arms' length from the inner workings of their police and military. It is not surprising that competent, strong states are much better at doing it.[40] But if we acknowledge this to be the case, we must also acknowledge that this creates a real inference problem for the research community. If the kind of research that generates theory and powerful narratives can be gathered only in the subset of countries where security services have broken down and allow researchers in, or where many of the basic tasks of governance is carried out by international NGOs under the watchful eye of the United Nations, we may be building theory based on a subset of civil wars that are not representative of what civil war settlements are likely to look like in the future. It may be telling, in this regard, that most civil wars occur in Asia, but most of the best social science on rebel groups and civil war dynamics since the end of the Cold War has emerged from countries in Africa.

Many Russians remember what it was like to live in a police state whose ideology was validated by confident social scientists. Today, all ethnic Russians live in close proximity to angry nihilists from different moral communities – potentially violent people who nurse real historical grievances. Their experiences may have something to teach the West about the limits of power in relation to populations that do not particularly want to be policed by a foreign-funded gendarmerie (or, one might add, be studied by well-meaning foreign social scientists). A Russian officer, when I asked what he meant when he said "all Chechens are crazy," met my eyes, and with great seriousness traced his finger in a line across the table:

"We don't try to understand them. That's what *you* do … To try to understand what is in their heads – that is an arrogant thing, you know. We have our culture. They have theirs. Maybe they are like us, and they don't always understand themselves. In war … we decide where the line is, and then we kill who crosses it. Let them believe what they want about us. If they don't cross the line, it's good for me. Who cares the 'why."[41]

If I were certain that I agreed with these sentiments, I would never have gone so far away from my home or stayed gone for so long. But if I were certain that these sentiments were irrelevant to the Russian cauterization of its peripheral wars, I would not reproduce them here. At the risk of cultural stereotyping: Russian foreign policy professionals were more willing than Americans to assume the worst about Georgian and Tajik social actors. Russian military professionals took for granted that their presence would be exploited in cynical and unpredictable ways by criminals and savages. Russia's ability to credibly commit to *ignoring* local nuance may have been an asset at times, if the logic of

---

[40] It may be that there is no practical solution to this problem, at least when dealing with ongoing civil wars. Collaboration with historians who can manage state security archives is where I anticipate new frontiers of empirical research. Alternatively, it is not difficult to imagine parallel sorts of coding and data aggregation projects, using crime statistics and field data on police and military characteristics across a variety of states facing low-intensity insurgencies.

[41] Interview conducted in Chicago, May 18, 2010.

this book is correct.[42] What interested Moscow, and what their policies actually incentivized, was the creation of a minimum threshold of stability and order. A government receptive to their interests could not be guaranteed. The civil wars provided an opportunity for Russia to sort the military strength of potential local partners and crudely leverage emerging coalitions in both states. They did not really try to do much more. Behaviors were judged, not motivations. This conservative approach, and a demonstrated willingness to allow a very ugly and cynical drama to play out under their noses in Georgia and Tajikistan, had the effect of limiting Russian liability for outcomes on the mountainous periphery. When things went wrong, the fault did not necessarily lie with Russia. That was important.

But over the long term, given the high stakes associated with mass-casualty terrorism, I fear that deterrence and in-group policing will only be able to take security studies up to the line traced by the Russian officer. Crossing that line requires very detailed kinds of individualized data. Many eager scholars and graduate students will surely talk themselves into helping the security forces of weak states collect and analyze these data. This will happen in the name of providing global public goods, in the name of combatting terrorists, in the name of helping the trains run on time. The Russian officer may have been ahead of the counterinsurgency curve. Somewhere on the far side of his line is what George Orwell called "thoughtcrime."

This has implications for how our research community thinks and talks about the people we study – and particularly how we discuss the phenomenon of "weak states." The experiences of fully collapsed states in West Africa and Yugoslavia in the mid-1990s are not representative of what goes on in most of the world's civil war zones. Yet they generated a powerful body of discourse – appeals to "anarchy" and "state failure" – which elites in the developing world, and agents of foreign security organs who are necessary intelligence partners, now cynically reappropriate. They too often use this language to absolve themselves of responsibility for their own actions. State weakness is real, of course, but "the absence of the state" can be the result of strategic design. State weakness can even occasionally be fully theatrical. What is publicly justified as an absence of capacity is often a lack of political will. Selling guns to local elites, sowing fear, and then saying "anarchy" to international observers is a common governance strategy in some parts of the world. It is important for researchers working in conflict zones to consider a variety of analogies and rival explanations for violence, rather than taking strategic elites at their word.

Social scientists are beginning to develop understandings of how violence markets work in weak states. This volume contributes to that literature,

---

42 Roy (2000) argued persuasively that Russian commitment to neither monitor nor meddle in post-independence affairs was made credible by generations of institutionalized pro-Slavic racism – but the multicultural hegemony of the United States does not leave its agents with that easy option.

emphasizing that relationships between militia captains and recruits involved a set of calculated risks, renewed as conflict parameters changed. I emphasize that outsiders' ability to model or second-guess how these processes would actually play out was very limited. The narratives that will endure in post war social memory are probably stories where local heroes had agency in resolving their own wars. The task will fall to future multilingual historians with a real stake in cultivating local social memory – whose first languages are Russian, Georgian, Abkhaz, Azeri, Armenian, Tajik, Shugni, and Uzbek – to decide what empirical details are worth remembering and passing along to their students. Meanwhile, if American social scientists cannot credibly commit to ignoring distant war zones, or to wondering what goes through the heads of very angry subalterns, we can at least tell other peoples' stories in a way that emphasizes their agency.[43] I have tried to remain carefully cautious about claiming to know what other people believed, or to passing judgement on the appropriateness of those beliefs. This book's approach is anchored in a "thin rationality" that does not depend on ideological or religious metaphors. This middle ground is aesthetically pleasing to me, and facilitates the cross-cultural conversations that I understand to be the essence of the comparative project in political science.

[43] I am increasingly of the opinion that if there are normative reasons to "get the story right," then there are also normative reasons to rewrite that story in the universal language of mathematics. Fearon (1997) argues that a great deal of diplomacy, translation, and communication might be reduced to an assurance game, where uncertain actors are trying to determine whether they understand the essence of the strategic situation in the same way. Haas (1992) and Satz and Ferejohn (1994) suggest that as a scholarly shorthand develops, ideas transverse disciplinary and linguistic barriers at progressively more rapid speed. Given that rational choice approaches show no sign of collapsing under the weight of accumulated contradictions on their own accord, the forced perspective of different roles, games, and constraints has independent value.

Appendix A

Case Selection and External Validity

This short appendix is meant to supplement empirical claims made in the first and last chapters of this book. It has two purposes. The first is to demonstrate that the countries in this study are outliers in terms of civil war duration. Even with numerous statistical controls, the wars resulting from the breakup of the USSR were unusually short. The second is to demonstrate that the broad

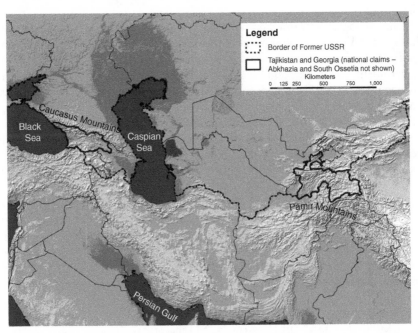

FIGURE APPENDIX A.1. Georgia and Tajikistan: unusually mountainous terrain.

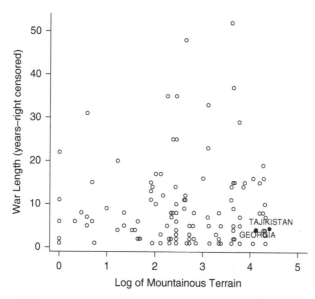

FIGURE A.2. Civil wars since 1945: mountainous insurgencies last longer on average.

contours of the settlement of the wars in these two countries can be squared with patterns observed after other civil wars in other parts of the globe since the end of the Cold War.

The coding conventions employed in this study follow Fearon and Laitin (2003), defining a civil war as a conflict taking place within a recognized state that results in 1,000 or more deaths, with more than 100 occurring on the government side (thus excluding one-sided massacres). These coding rules may overaggregate the phenomenon of "civil war," pooling very distinct processes together to gain statistical power. In an important article, "Why Do Some Civil Wars Last So Much Longer Than Others?" James Fearon (2004) notes that when one inductively examines the cases in standard datasets, one finds remarkable heterogeneity of the kinds of political violence that are counted as civil wars. When similar kinds of events are clustered, the "type" of war emerges as the best predictor of war duration.

As Figure A.1 shows, both Georgia and Tajikistan contain formidable mountains. To consider the effect of mountains on civil war length, Figure A.2 displays a simple scatterplot of mountainous terrain plotted against civil war length, using the Fearon (2004) dataset. Mountains are very good places for insurgents to hide from the state, so guerrilla wars tend to go on longer in very mountainous countries.[1] Tajikistan and Georgia – the cases that

---

[1]   For this reason, mountainous terrain is a critical component of the identification strategy for the latent "weak state" variable in Fearon and Laitin (2003). The authors demonstrate that mountainous terrain is a statistically robust predictor of civil war outbreak.

TABLE A.1. *Why Do Some Civil Wars Last So Much Longer Than Others?*

Variables	(1) Fearon (2004)	(2) Control Variables	(3) Controls, without Post-Soviet Dummy
Coup or Revolution	0.382***	0.398***	0.402***
	(0.083)	(0.090)	(0.093)
Sons of the Soil	2.135***	2.060***	1.992***
	(0.510)	(0.490)	(0.485)
Drugs	1.935***	1.892***	1.948***
	(0.459)	(0.454)	(0.475)
Mountainous Terrain	1.162**	1.145*	1.130*
	(0.082)	(0.081)	(0.081)
Post-Soviet Wars	0.302***	0.364***	
	(0.120)	(0.153)	
Anti-colonial Wars		0.806	0.826
		(0.242)	(0.253)
Ethnic Fractionalization		1.255	1.374
		(0.427)	(0.468)
Population		1	1
		$(5.20e^{-10})$	$(5.24e^{-10})$
Cold War (pre-1991)		1.223	1.359*
		(0.243)	(0.258)
p	1.073	1.088	−0.665
SE(p)	0.071	0.074	−0.665
Observations	149	149	149
Observations (ended)	135	135	135

Weibull regression results with *civil war length* (measured in years) as the dependent variable. Coefficients in the table report estimated multiplicative effects of a one-unit change in the independent variable on the average length of civil war. ***$p < 0.01$; **$p < 0.05$; *$p < 0.1$.

constitute the bulk of this book – do not conform to this trend. Contrary to the predictions of area specialists at the time – who confidently predicted long-running, hard-to-end conflicts based on hardened clan and ethnic hatred – the wars were resolved with unusual speed. When relevant control variables are taken into account, the puzzle of this speedy resolution emerges even more clearly. Model 1 of Table A.1 replicates the empirical findings in Fearon (2004) using an updated dataset of civil wars between 1945 and 2008.[2] The statistical

---

[2] This model adds a continuous *mountainous terrain* variable that emerges as statistically significant in the Fearon duration replication data, but does not feature in the write-up because of its low predictive power. In addition to expanding the temporal range of analysis to 2008, this dataset makes a number of small modifications to the original dataset based on evolving coding decisions since the original dataset construction. Most of variables presented in this model are coded according to variable descriptions in Fearon (2004). For *Coup or Revolution*, a country

and substantive significance of the coefficients is unambigious: postcommunist wars lasted about a third as long as civil wars in other parts of the world. The modal civil war since 1945 has been a rural insurgency in a relatively poor state, pitting ill-equipped regime militias against rebel armies. Mountainous terrain and narcotics production are associated with longer civil wars because they lower the costs of initiating or sustaining rebellions. The so-called "Sons of the Soil" rebellions – land disputes between an indigenous minority group that fears cultural extinction and state-supported immigrants hungry for land – are difficult to end. Coups and urban revolutions, by contrast, tend to be centered in the capital city and feature "tipping" dynamics. The rebellion either succeeds in toppling the government or it fails – but whatever happens, it happens quickly.[3]

Model 2 in Table A.1 demonstrates that many structural features of the state have little or no predictive value once the general type of civil war is taken into account.[4] Model 3 in the same table, which does not include a dummy variable

is assigned a "1" if the civil war is initiated with either a split in the military ("coup") or popular social movement in the capital in the style of the French or Iranian revolution ("revolution"), and "0" otherwise. For *Sons of the Soil*, a country is assigned a "1" according to Fearon coding rules, which relate to the internal immigration dynamics that define the identities of incumbents and insurgent groups, and "0" otherwise. *Drugs* is a binary variable that has been recoded in a number of cases, coded "1" in cases where a rebel group in the country funds itself substantially through the use of narcotics or other contraband and "0" otherwise. The *Post-Soviet Wars* include only the conflicts that emerged from the disintegration of the Soviet Union proper, excluding wars in Eastern Europe. In these data, this variable does not include Bosnia and the wars of Yugoslav secession (including Kosovo), the Romanian revolution, or the second Chechen war. This leaves the first war in Chechnya, Tajikistan, Georgia's various wars, the Karabakh conflict in Azerbaijan, and Moldova. To avoid arbitrary coding decisions, I included control variables that do not vary over the course of the civil war itself, and did not include variables that are clearly endogenous to the course of the war itself (and hence the dependent variable), such as fragmentation of rebel groups, battle deaths, GDP loss due to the civil war, and the like. Other variables are reappropriated from Fearon and Laitin (2003), Fearon (2004), or hand-coded. Following convention, I use 1997 as the end-point for the Tajik civil war.

3 Fearon admits that his model does not persuasively account for the post-Soviet wars quick end: "In the model, increasing one side's probability of decisive victory shortens expected war duration. However, the thrust of the analytical results on relative military capabilities is that matters are complicated, since imbalanced capabilities tend to reduce prospects for a negotiated settlement while balanced capabilities increase them.... In addition, the model highlights the problem of untangling relative capabilities from the propensity of different capabilities to produce decisive victory or stalemate." Fearon (2004), 298. Political scientists tend to reason that foreign military aid to rebels against a weak government should *prolong* civil wars. Nicholas Sambanis (2002), in a review of the large-*n* statistical literature on war settlement, makes this point forcefully: foreign interventions into civil war zones are often thought to strengthen rebellions that would otherwise "quickly be crushed by the government." 222. A stable settlement pattern allowing for prolonged "frozen" conflicts is not discussed in Sambanis and is rarely considered by civil war specialists in political science.

4 *Anti-Colonial Wars* are wars fought against a European metropole, primarily during the period of decolonization. Earlier statistical probes suggested that these wars were systematically shorter than their counterparts. Various working papers discussed in Sambanis (2002) support the finding that ethnic fractionalization increases civil war length, so an *Ethnic Fractionalization*

for the post-Soviet wars, is included to show that although post-1991 civil wars tend to be resolved faster than wars fought against a backdrop of superpower competition, this trend is statistically attributable to the rapid resolution of wars along Russia's new frontier.[5] It would be reassuring to believe that benign aspects of the post–Cold War world system – such as the replacement of superpower "proxy wars" with the emergence of regular multilateral peacekeeping missions under UN auspices – are responsible for this statistical trend. Though these data are not inconsistent with that interpretation, the mechanisms suggested by this volume may be an understudied components of the system-level pattern.

In the formal model that anchors this book, coups in postwar states should usually not occur. Presidents should be able to anticipate them and buy them off. In the real world coups do occur. Approximately one in five of the "Peace Processes" in the Doyle and Sambanis (2006) dataset are interrupted by coups. That means that 80 percent of postwar governments manage to insulate themselves from coups, by either good fortune or good strategy. Are the subset of postwar governments that are capable of coup-proofing their regimes less likely to return to war?

Yes, they are. Empirical data from the Doyle and Sambanis (2006) dataset, which uses the "Peace Process" since 1945 as its unit of analysis, is well suited to address this question.[6] The primary explanatory variable of interest in this analysis is whether the peace process was interrupted due to coalition infighting and instability, punctuated by a coup. I developed an original *coups* variable. Using the Goemans, Gleditsch, and Chiozza (2009) leadership dataset as a baseline, I hand-coded *coups* when leaders left power in an irregular manner, internal power struggle, or an uprising by armed agents of the state.[7] The

---

control was added. The *Cold War* variable is coded "1" if a conflict was initiated before 1991, and "0" otherwise. Owing to space constraints, additional model specifications were omitted. Including regional or decade dummy variables, GDP-per capita measures (for the beginning and end of the war) and other control variables had no statistically significant impact beyond cluttering the model.

5 Various mechanisms by which superpower competition in the Cold War affected civil conflict are reviewed in Kalyvas and Balcells (2011).

6 Their data codes a variety of relevant characteristics, including data on the host state, the war itself, and the interveners. I reproduce several of their measures as control variables here. The *Politicide* variable is a binary variable for whether the civil war included instances of mass killing directed against an ethnic, religious, or political group. *Civil War Duration* is measured in months. *Rebel Victory* is a binary variable for whether the peace process was initiated at the end of a decisive military victory by a nonstate actor. *GDP* is a measure of per capita GDP from the start of the war, taken from Fearon and Laitin (2003). *Ethnic Heterogeniety* is a 0–1 scale for ethnic fractionalization developed by James Fearon (2003). *Strong UN* indicates the presence of a transformation United Nations mission – a cumulative category for Multinational Peacekeeping Operations, Peace Enforcement Operations, Transnational Administration, etc.

7 The variable correlates with the dependent variable (*Peace Process Failure*) at 0.18, with a variety of cases (Argentina, Guinea Bissau, Laos, Pakistan, Paraguay) having coups but no civil war resumption and many more having civil war resumptions without coups.

TABLE A.2. *Which Civil Wars are Most Likely to Restart?*

Variables	(1) Basic	(2) "Decisive Victory"	(3) Best Fit
Coup (Goemans, & Gleditsch, and Chiozza, 2009)	0.989** (0.477)	1.249** (0.618)	1.065* (0.626)
Politicide		1.224** (0.505)	1.741*** (0.602)
Civil War Duration		−0.006** (0.003)	−0.007** (0.003)
Rebel Victory		−0.954* (0.559)	−1.208* (0.701)
Per Capita GDP			−0.276** (0.107)
Ethnic Heterogeniety			2.679*** (0.824)
Strong UN Mission			−3.378*** (0.876)
Constant	−0.073 (0.208)	0.109 (0.336)	−0.665 (0.517)
Observations	138	133	133
Pseudo r^2	0.026	0.111	0.270

Logit regression results with *Failed Peace Process* as dependent variable Clustered Standard Errors by Country. ***$p < 0.01$; **$p < 0.05$; *$p < 0.1$.

outcome variable for the models displayed in Table A.2 is a binary indicator *Peace Process Failure*, which measures whether the civil war restarted within five years of the beginning of the peace process. The statistical model used to analyze these data was a simple logit regression with clustered standard errors by country.

During the fragile transition after a peace process, a coup within the incumbent government makes civil wars more likely to restart. Table A.3 displays the substantive impact of varying a few "usual suspects" from the civil war literature.[8] These results validate general intuitions: the small fraction of civil wars lucky enough to receive strong international peace enforcement

[8] Because the substantive interpretation of logit coefficients in Table A.2 is not straightforward, I use CLARIFY to run Monte Carlo simulations of the model to produce the parameter values, using Model 3 in Table A.2. The change in outcome values for binary variables is displayed for switching the independent variable to 1; for continuous variables the change comes from switching the independent variable from the 25th percentile to the 75th percentile. For simplicity of presentation, these results are interpreted in terms of their individual impact on the probability that a country will "return to war," while holding all variables at either their mean or median value.

TABLE A.3. *Model 3: Internal Politics and Civil War Resumption (Simulations)*

Variable	Mean Value	Proposed Variation	All at Mean (%)	All at Median (%)
Return to War (DV)	0.57	0–1	49 (Baseline)	44 (Baseline)
Coup (G&G)	0.20	0–1	+19	+22
Politicide	0.33	0–1	+24	+31
Duration (months)	0.73	14–111	−19	−17
Rebel Victory	0.22	0–1	−21	−27
Per Capita GDP	1.79	0.59–2.34	−12	−13
Ethnic Heterogeneity	0.56	0.33–0.77	+29	+26
Strong UN Mission	0.09	0–1	−43	−49

missions – generally cases from the 1990s – are good candidates for peace to endure. International interventions matter, third-party peace enforcement works, civil wars settled by rebel victory at the end of a long civil war are likely to stay settled, mass killing during the civil war raises the probability of the war restarting, and countries that are poor or ethnically heterogeneous are at a somewhat higher risk of renewed war. But Table A.3 shows that, *even taking all of this into account*, countries that experience coups are about 20 percent more likely to return to war than identical postwar regimes that successfully manage intra-coalition politics.

The theory and the empirics of the cases suggest that armed actors had incentives to build new institutions quickly to attract foreign wealth and manage distributional politics among each other. But what kind of institutions? Are there any patterns to the kinds of institutions that emerge and endure after civil war? And do global patterns match with the story of patronage politics buttressed by strong, personality-based party networks to monitor defections, described in Chapter 5?

Yes, they do, though with the caveat that the answer depends critically on what time period is being studied. Military regimes can certainly manage distributional politics. These regimes, however, had their heyday in the 1970s, against the backdrop of Cold War competition, and are relatively rare today. For the purposes of exposition, postwar regime types were coded based on what form of government was sustained for the five-year period after the peace process commenced. Mechanically, I added a number of columns to the Doyle and Sambanis (2006) replication dataset of all civil war settlements since 1945, based on a coding scheme developed by Magaloni (2008), who classifies different kinds of dictatorships based on their "launching organization" and the number of viable political parties. For simplicity in interpretation, binary variables were identified for *Military Dictatorships* (23 percent of the sample), *Hegemonic Party Regimes* (23 percent of the sample), *Single Party Regimes*

(11 percent of the sample), and "true" *Democracies* (11 percent of the sample). For the purposes of this statistical analysis, these categories are exclusive.[9] Control variables were included for characteristics that might affect postwar institutions (e.g., wealth, oil, the degree of fragmentation caused by the war, and a few other common control variables).[10]

During the Cold War, coup leaders could seize power and then extort the two great powers for recognition simultaneously – threatening, implicitly or explicitly, to offer their territory and assets to the geopolitical competitor. Marxist ideology provided a moral and scientific justification for single-party dictatorship. With the end of the Cold War, *Hegemonic Party* systems – similar to the caricature of Chicago politics, where one party wins predictably, but voters are permitted to waste their vote on opposition parties if they choose – come into prominence. UN peacekeepers were deployed more often, increasing the prominence of the residual *Transition* category (a government assisted by a transnational presence).

Some authoritarian regimes seem to be systematically better "coup-proofed" than others, as the next set of regressions show. Each of the seven models is a simple logit estimator with clustered standard errors by region, with *Coup*, a binary indicator of a leader's irregular exit in the first five years after the initiation of the peace process, as the dependent variable. Fully institutionalized democracies are the most coup-proof, as we see in Models 4, 5, and 7. The 11 percent of regimes that manage to emerge from civil war with consolidated democratic institutions and the 9 percent of countries that received large peace-enforcement missions were relatively successful at avoiding coups.[11] In the aftermath of civil conflict, regime investments in party infrastructure – with elections used to legitimate the regime and then distribute patronage – inoculate regimes against coups. *Hegemonic Party* regimes appear unusually resilient, as do single party regimes. Military dictatorships are vulnerable. Table A.5 displays the substantive interpretation of the coefficients via simulation for

---

[9] A *Hegemonic Party* regime is a regime that allows multiparty competition, but where the incumbent dominates the state apparatus. A *Single Party* regime is one in which there is only one legal party (overwhelmingly communist regimes). A *Military* regime is one in which authority ultimately rests within the armed forces. *Democracies* are defined as countries that achieve a Polity score of 6 or higher any time in the five years after the peace process.

[10] Rather than fully replicate the full Magaoloni structure here, I also included a scaled polity variable that runs from 0 to 20, which provides a rough measure of the distinction between "soft" and "hard" authoritarian nondemocracies.

[11] There is substantial crossover between these two categories, and a glance at the these twenty-three cases suggests that they were not analogous to the highly fragmented political reconstruction projects in Georgia and Tajikistan. Rather, they tend to be peripheral secessionist insurgencies in states where democratic institutions were strong in the country's "core" (e.g., India, the Philippines) or countries where combatants came to the table peace was underwritten UN peacekeeping and international peace guarantees (e.g., Cyprus, Mozambique, South Africa, El Salvador).

TABLE A.4. *Which Post-War Institutions Are Most Coup-Prone?*

	(1)	(2)	(3)	(4)	(5)	(6)	(7)
Hegemonic Party	−2.158** (0.251)	−2.248** (0.092)	−2.468** (0.248)	−2.294** (0.214)	−2.437** (0.251)	−2.407** (0.337)	−3.339** (0.375)
Military Regime	0.889* (0.458)	0.854++ (0.521)	0.734 (0.615)	0.179 (0.604)	0.674 (0.558)	0.819 (0.601)	−0.784 (0.966)
Single Party Regime		−0.217 (1.028)	−0.630 (1.134)	−1.195 (1.002)	−0.756 (1.124)	−0.639 (1.136)	−2.224++ (1.189)
Number of Warring Factions		0.165** (0.054)	0.207** (0.049)	0.188** (0.027)	0.248** (0.038)	0.195** (0.045)	0.188** (0.033)
GDP per Capita (Start of War)			−0.370* (0.192)	−0.376* (0.156)	−0.371++ (0.199)	−0.335 (0.230)	−0.364 (0.279)
Postwar Democratization (Polity Score 6+)				=1 (if=0) [18 dropped]			=1 (if=0) [18 dropped]
Strong UN Mission					=1 (if=0) [12 dropped]		=1 (if=0) [15 dropped]
Oil Exporter						−0.374 (1.020)	−0.372 (1.098)
Polity Score Scaled (0–20)							−0.049 (0.071)
Constant	−1.368* (0.459)	−1.827** (0.421)	−1.275* (0.584)	−0.655 (0.450)	−1.260++ (0.615)	−1.258* (0.582)	0.507 (0.651)
Pseudo r^2	(0.109)	(0.122)	(0.162)	(0.184)	(0.163)	(0.164)	(0.226)
N	138	134	134	116	122	134	93

Logit regressions with clustered standard errors by region, with "Coup within five years of the start of the Peace Process" as the dependent variable. Robust standard errors are in parentheses. ++$p < 0.1$; *$p < 0.05$; **$p < 0.01$.

TABLE A.5. *Institutions after Civil War: Practical Coup-Proofing (Simulations)*

Variable	Mean Value	Proposed Variation	All at Mean (%)	All at Median (%)
Coup (G&G) (DV)	0.20	0–1	15 (Baseline)	27 (Baseline)
Hegemonic Party	0.23	0–1	−11	−23
Military Regime	0.23	0–1	+8	+6
Single Party Regime	0.11	0–1	−4	−8
Warring Factions	3.23	2–4	+4	+7
GDP Per Capita	1.79	0.59–2.34	−9	−12

Model 2, the most straightforward to interpret.[12] Results are interpreted in terms of their individual impact on the probability that a government will suffer a coup, holding all other variables at either their mean or median value. Postwar authoritarian institutions matter, and building parties after civil wars is a common strategy for keeping mass violence from breaking out again.

The inference I draw from these trends is that Georgian and Tajik actors engineered the same kinds of outcomes that can be observed in other states since the end of the Cold War, only faster. Though the experiences of these two states exposes processes of civil war termination that have resonance in other settings, I leave rigorous cross-national tests to future work. Following King, Keohane, and Verba (1994), most of my inferences come from "increasing my *n*" within countries rather than across countries – comparing the life experiences of many soldiers, and the consolidation strategies of many warlords, while holding the real estate constant. It would be a simple matter to assemble anecdotes from around the globe that echo the logic of the model. I prefer to let data sourced from the Georgian and Tajik streets tell their own story.

---

[12] Obviously, this model pools the twenty-three cases with either consolidated democracies or strong UN Enforcement Missions (which both predict the outcome perfectly and are thus unsuitable for simulations in CLARIFY). The substantive effects of this pooling are that the "baseline" probability of a country suffering a coup is lower than it would be if these cases were excluded. As previously, the change in outcome values for binary variables is displayed for switching the independent variable to 1; for continuous variables the change comes from switching the independent variable from the 25th percentile to the 75th percentile.

Appendix B

Mathematical Proofs

This appendix presents formal propositions to supplement the presentation in Chapter 2. To recap:

- Each of n warlords chooses simultaneously whether to battle for total dominance of a state ("Fight"), or to support the candidacy of a civilian president ("Install"). Call the full set of warlords W. Call the total lootable resources in the country v. If the total number of warlords supporting a president is less than a commonly known stability threshold s, the outcome is war. In war, each warlord who played "Fight" gets $\frac{v}{n} - c$ and each warlord who played "Install" gets $\frac{v}{n} - c - w$.
- Define the number of warlords who play "Install" as k. Call this subset of k warlords W^P. If $k \geq s$, a president is installed. Warlords who played "Fight" in the first stage get a reservation value r. The game ends for these warlords.
- The lootable resources of the state v increase to v^*. A figurehead president P is installed. He selects l warlords, such that $k \geq l \geq s$. Call this subset of l members W^L. P proposes a distribution of v^* among these l warlords and himself, $x = (x_i, x_j, \ldots x_q, x_P)$. Warlords in W^P but not in W^L get a payoff of zero. The game ends for these warlords.
- Each warlord in W^L observes his distribution and either "Accepts" or "Coups" the president. Playing "coup" imposes costs c on a warlord, but this warlord will succeed in installing himself as president (claiming v^*) with some probability p. The "Coup" payoff, then, is $pv^* - c$. If s or more warlords play "Accept," the president's distribution x is implemented. If fewer than s warlords play "Accept," the president receives zero and each warlord receives his coup payoff. The game ends.

The appropriate solution concept for this game is a subgame perfect Nash equilibrium (SPNE), in which no player can promise or threaten actions that he would not take if presented with the option. To simplify matters and highlight essentials, my analysis focuses on simple strategies in which a warlord conditions second-stage actions only on whether or not a government formed, without reference to particular composition of the coalition.[1] Even with this constraint, the game contains many such equilibria. Once we eliminate strategies that are weakly dominated – in other words, once we restrict analysis to equilibria sustained by strategies by which players could do no worse, but possibly improve their welfare, regardless of strategies chosen by other players – it turns out that only a few of these equilibria are important for analysis.

Proposition 1. This game has a subgame perfect Nash equilibrium in which no player plays a weakly dominated strategy in which all warlords choose "Fight" in the first period. Call this a *State Failure* equilibrium.

Proof. One has only to consider a defection by a single warlord in the first stage. Consider the simple case where $n = 3$ and $s = 2$. If i knows that both of the others will choose "Fight," second-stage payoffs will not be realized. A comparison between $\frac{v}{n} - c$ and $\frac{v}{n} - c - w$ makes "Fight" the best reply. Any strategies off the equilibrium path can be chosen, but "All Fight" will still remain an equilibrium.

This essentially captures the situation described in Chapter 3: many warlords fight, each hoping to control the capital. This is an inefficient equilibrium for two reasons. First, war is costly. Fighting destroys productive assets, leaving v smaller for whatever warlord succeeds in the military contest. Second, fighting in the first stage foregoes the wealth associated with international recognition $(v < v^*)$. Nevertheless, if other warlords are planning to try to violently seize the statehouse, any warlord i can only make himself worse off by not taking part in the scramble. As in Rousseau's stag hunt and Jervis's security dilemma, gains from cooperation do not easily overcome incentives for defection when trust is low and stakes are high.

We now move to analysis of the final subgame, with the assumption that warlords will backward-induct strategies in the first "installation" stage of the game based on expectations of what will unfold in the second "consolidation" stage. Because warlords have the last move in the game, it is intuitive that they

---

[1] It is reasonable to object that this is not how the game would play out. In a two-stage game, warlords should be able to condition their strategies in the second stage on what becomes known about the outcome of the first stage. In actual play, there are good reasons to expect that the content of the coalition membership should matter. Warlord i should be able to identity of the warlords who joined the government. His strategy should allow him to "Coup" if warlord j is part of W^P and "Agree" if j is not part of W^P. In this more complex and realistic setting the set of outcomes for the first round is an n-tuple containing 2^n possibilities in the (pure) strategy space and kaleidoscopic complexity as various actors attempt to "out think" each other. This is certainly what happens when I play this game in class with my students.

will be well positioned to extort the president. Yet, as has been shown in many contexts, an early mover with proposal power in a bargaining game can extract substantial advantages from the ability to limit her strategic opponents' choice sets.[2]

Proposition 2. In the final subgame (starting with P's proposal), there is always a subgame perfect Nash equilibrium where P distributes x such that $x_i = pv^* - c$ to each of s warlords in W^L.

Proof. First consider defection by a single warlord i who has been offered $x_i = pv^* - c$. By changing strategies to "Coup," i will only receive $pv^* - c$, which he is already getting as x_i. Next, consider whether P, who can keep for himself what he does not transfer, can improve his welfare by changing his distribution. P knows he will receive o in the event of a successful coup by any warlord i, or if fewer than s warlords play "Accept." Looking down the game tree, he knows he must devise transfer schemes that induce exactly s warlords to play "Accept." Because P gets to keep for himself whatever part of v^* he does not distribute in the form of x_P, he loses utility if he transfers any more than the minimum necessary. Consider the most constraining case for collusion, where $s = n$. In this example, each warlord must be included in W^L, and if a single warlord plays "Coup" P will receive zero. P can pay each of n warlords $x_i = pv^* - c$ and keep a positive transfer $x_P = nc$ for himself (the rents from sparing all warlords the cost of fighting). Because neither the president nor any of the warlords can change strategies and improve their welfare, this is a SPNE.

Every warlord $i \in W^P \ni W^L$ will receive zero. At the time that a warlord chooses to play "Install" or "Fight" he understands that P, if installed, only needs the loyalty of s warlords to pass the stability threshold,. Though there is nothing in the structure of the game that requires that the president select exactly s warlords to be in W^L, as P gets to keep what he does not distribute, P will have the ability and incentive to offer exactly s warlords exactly what they would receive in a coup, and no more. P cannot credibly commit to paying all k warlords who install him if $k > s$.

Proposition 3. In the final subgame, any outcome in which P is removed in a coup, or any outcome in which the sum of P's proposed transfer to warlords $x_1 + x_2 \ldots x_n$ exceeds $s(pv^* - c)$, requires the play of weakly dominated strategies on the equilibrium path, off the equilibrium path, or both.

Proof. Because the president P gets to keep $v^* - l(pv^* - c)$ for himself, his payoff is strictly decreasing in l. P should want to include exactly s warlords in l, which is the minimum necessary to keep himself in power. If $c \geq pv^*$,

---

[2] See Schelling (1960) and Osborne (2004) generally, but especially Ferejohn (1986).

then the president is no longer incentivized to keep the coalition small, but can no longer credibly commit to any transfer of wealth to any warlord. As shown in *Proposition 2*, P should always be able to stay in power through some correctly-calculated allocation x. For a warlord i to be induced to play "Accept," he must be transferred $x_i \geq pv^* - c$.

If warlords understand the broad contours of the game, in other words, if they understand that the president will pay exactly s warlords their coup value, understand that they are interchangeable, and they choose strategies accordingly, then in the installation stage, they are essentially gambling when they install a figurehead president. This gamble can be justified. It is possible to support a subgame perfect Nash equilibrium in which every warlord opts to join the state. I will refer to this as a *full incorporation* equilibrium.

Proposition 4. Subgame perfect Nash equilibria can exist in which (a) no warlord plays a weakly dominated strategy and (b) all warlords play "Install" in the first period. Call these *Full Incorporation* equilibria.

Proof. For "Install" to be a best reply, it must be true that $r \leq (\frac{s}{k})(pv^* - c)$. This is true for every warlord i if $r \leq (\frac{s}{n})(pv^* - c)$. Many distributions of x by P are supportable equilibria, but in each distribution the president will select s warlords and transfer each of them $pv^* - c$. There are $\frac{n!}{s!}$ SPNEs of this sort. For example, if W={A, B, C, D, E, F}, and $s = 5$, there are six different distributions of x that are six different SPNEs – one where each of A, B, C, D, E, and F is transferred $x_i = 0$, while the other five are transferred $x_i = pv^* - c$ and P keeps $x_p = v^* - 5(pv^* - c)$ for himself. If $n = 6$ and $s = 4$, there are thirty different SPNEs. In each of these, four warlords receive $x_i = pv^* - c$, 2 warlords receive zero, and the president retains $x_p = v^* - 4(pv^* - c)$. When "Install" is chosen, this distribution x is unknown.

As a general principle, each warlord i should compare his life opportunities in W^P to his reservation value r. Because s is static and warlords are symmetric, i's utility is strictly decreasing in k. Every warlord who plays "Install" worsens the W^L lottery odds for every warlord in W^P. Still, if r is low, v^* is high, and s is high, that is, the lottery odds are good, it is possible to support situations where every warlord strictly prefers joining the state to staying outside of it.

Proposition 5. Subgame perfect Nash equilibria can exist in which no warlord plays a weakly dominated strategy where some $k \geq s$ warlords play "Install" and join W^P, but at least one warlord plays "Fight" in the first period and remains outside of the consolidating state. Call these *Partial Incorporation* equilibria.

Proof. There can exist a k' such that $r \leq (\frac{s}{k'})(pv^* - c)$ but $r > (\frac{s}{k'+1})(pv^* - c)$. If one more warlord were to enter, it would no longer pay (in expectation) for any of them to enter.[3] In this setting, k' is approximately equal to $(\frac{s}{r})(pv^* - c)$.

As a simple extension: Consider a more realistic model that introduces initial heterogeneity in the warlords' value for the outside option if the state consolidates, but they opt to stay out of the state. Instead of having all warlords symmetric in r, assume r_i is not the same for all $i \in W$, and that they cannot (at low cost) mimic the characteristics of the "high reservation wage" types to get the best deal. In that case, $F(.)$ represents the cumulative distribution of r_i, meaning that $F(z)$ is the share of warlords with $r_i \leq z$ and $nF(z)$ is the number of warlords with $r_i \leq z$. The equilibrium is determined by a cutpoint value r^*

$$r^* = \left(\frac{s}{nF(r^*)} \right)(pv^* - c)$$

Note that the left-hand side of the equation is increasing in r while the right-hand side is decreasing. This means that the equilibrium will be unique. All warlords with $r_i > r^*$ will stay out, and those with $r_i \leq r^*$ will enter. All the comparative statics on s, v^*, and the average r value from above still hold in this richer setting. But now the game produces a natural result in which warlords who stay out have an idiosyncratic feature – such as safe refuge across an interstate border or sustained military support from a great power – that gives them better payoffs outside the consolidating state.

---

3 Reaching this arrangement, where some stay in and others stay out, still requires that the warlords solve a coordination problem among themselves. To understand why this is so, imagine a symmetric mixed strategy equilibrium, where all the warlords are identical, and each warlord plays "Install" with an identical equilibrium probability. In this case, where the question of whether the stability threshold s is passed is resolved probabilistically, the players may or may not reach consolidation (enough to select P) in equilibrium.

Appendix C

Ninety-Seven Anonymous Warlords

The purpose of this appendix is to provide details about the data on Tajik warlords who joined the state and to expand on the brief presentation in Chapter 5.

With the aid of research teams based in Bishkek and Dushanbe, I revisited the Small Arms Survey's secondary source materials. My aim was to identify additional characteristics of each field commander's private army and resolve a number of inconsistencies in the application of coding categories. The data collection effort, conceived in the spring of 2006, began as an attempt to systematically collect information on recruitment techniques, control of resources, political connections to groups in the capital, financial support, and characteristics of command and control for each warlord who fought in the Tajik civil war. Additional interviews with area specialists, military and embassy professionals, and journalists filled in the gaps left by interviews with former combatants. All final coding decisions were my own. None of my research assistants retain project materials.

What is a warlord, exactly? The coding rules used admitted an additional field commander to the dataset if (1) it was possible to find at least three secondary or two primary sources that confirmed that an individual actually existed (e.g., that the newly discovered commander was not simply a pseudonym or *nom de guerre*), and (2) at least one source suggested that the warlord could call on the services of at least twenty-five men through channels other than the official state hierarchy (e.g., being a general or police colonel did not automatically lead to inclusion in the dataset).[1] The dataset likely includes at least one individual who may have had a bigger public presence than he

---

[1] The twenty-five threshold is admittedly arbitrary. Though most of the selective violence during the consolidation phase was perpetrated (or threatened) by a small core of trusted killers kept on close retainer, to put on a public face and "lobby," it was important to be able to organize rallies and occasionally stage large-scale violent demonstrations (see Chapter 4).

actually commanded in terms of street recruits, but because their names exist in the historical record it was decided at the time that excluding them would have been arbitrary. Individuals who remained completely outside of the political consolidation scramble – apolitical criminals and drug dealers who kept their heads down and never entered militia politics – are also excluded from these data. These ninety-seven warlords represent what I believe to be the universe of independent Tajik militia leaders as best as they could be identified.[2] The unit of analysis in the regression analysis that follows is the individual field commander. The period of observation is 1992–2006.

The post-incorporation longevity of warlords in my dataset diverged dramatically. A few were still affiliated with the regime at the end of the study period. Many more were purged, jailed, or killed. The model, which treats field commanders as symmetric and indistinguishable, makes no attempt to explain this variation in side payoffs or tenure in the ruling coalition.[3] Indeed, if it were possible to compare post-incorporation political fortunes, the model's prediction would be that, conditional on joining the state, all warlords should be on equal footing when it comes to keeping their position and avoiding a purge. This seems a poor fit with the narrative data presented in the book. Ethnic minority warlords were easily marginalized, and strong

---

[2] There are two caveats. First, There were thirteen warlords for whom it was not possible to determine a precise place of birth. In these cases, two additional criteria were employed. For eight of the observations, interviews with former combatants made it possible to determine the area where the field commander's men were primarily recruited. For the remaining five we coded based on the region of the country where the warlord was known to carry out operations, on the assumption that his men were probably relying on nearby family for shelter and aid. This criteria may would have the effect of slightly inflating the percentage of Gharmis in the dataset. There were five warlords where birthplace data existed but was contradictory, and we had no trusted source to settle the issue. Five warlords were coded as having multiple birthplace regions. These ambiguities mostly relate to the misuse of the term "Gharmi" to refer either to someone from the region of Gharm *or* or a collective slur against the tens of thousands of families that were forcibly relocated moved from the mountains ("Gharm") to the cotton-producing lowlands as part of Soviet population transfer policy in the 1940s, 50s, and 60s. In the summary statistics in Table 4.3 each warlord is counted only once for each area; in the statistical analysis duplicate birthplaces are "double-counted," meaning the effects of the additional dummy variables are incorporated into the Weibull simulation results. Family membership also posed a problem. In more than two cases, brothers were identified as warlords operating in tandem. This created a problem. Should these men should be treated as independent observations, or a single one? It seems unlikely that they would turn on each other, and in practice the research team never found an example of a particular pair of brothers shooting at each other. Yet if we choose to treat them as a pooled observation, should we do the same for warlords who are cousins? Or warlords from the same clan-regional faction? To avoid a difficult mapping project, a decision was made to treat all warlords as independent observations *unless* they were immediate familial relations. Individuals who were literally brothers were treated as single observation.

[3] If the warlords themselves could have predicted ex ante which characteristics would maximize their odds of successful coalition survival, I assume they would have adopted those characteristics. Though clan/regional affiliation and place of birth are fixed for an individual, strategic marriages allow flexibility even for these "immutable" characteristics.

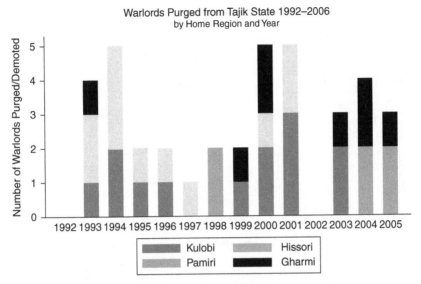

FIGURE C.1. The dependent variable: purges over time.

warlords seem to have done better than weak warlords. Statistical rigor is the antidote to anecdote, however. A dataset of Tajik warlord biographies allows for a transparent evaluation of the model's most controversial starting assumption.

The dependent variable used in this analysis is the number of *years* that a warlord was permitted to take part in the bonanza of postwar state corruption before he was dismissed or disappeared. Figure C.1 provides a basic visualization of these purges, grayscale-coded by warlord home region. Warlords were removed from the state apparatus at a rate of approximately three per year. Every purge could be interpreted as a failure by a warlord to correctly anticipate the value of acting to install a president – either strategic misplay, or (as this book argues) a bet that simply did not pay out. Figure C.2 shows the Kaplan–Meier survival estimate, with "failure" defined as leaving the state. For most field commanders, the arrangement that initially convinced them to join the state was void within seven or eight years.

Survival analysis can be used to assess if regional patterns reported in Chapter Five (Table 5.2) are spurious. Multivariate Weibull analysis displays transparently which individuals were more or less likely to politically survive successive rounds of coalition formation (with implications for physical survival). The reported coefficients are expressed as the multiple by which a field commander's expected time in the state will change when the factor is present. The independent variables in the dataset are either individual characteristics of warlords or characteristics of their army. A binary *UTO*

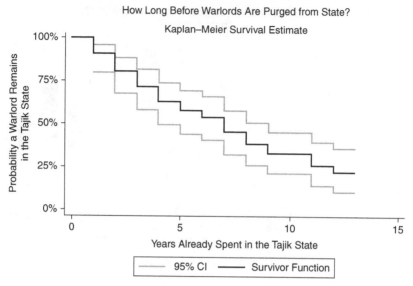

FIGURE C.2. Time trends: almost all warlords get purged sooner or later.

variable was created to capture the master cleavage of the civil war, coded "1" if a warlord joined the state as part of the 1997 United Tajik Opposition (UTO) amnesty agreement. As militias fought with similar weapons technology and deployed light infantry tactics, an estimate of *Troop Strength* (the total number of soldiers under a warlord's command at the time of integration) was triangulated through a variety of sources. As an additional indicator of relative warlord power, a binary variable was constructed to identify commanders that had careers in the Soviet army, the MVD (Ministerstvo Vnutrennikh Del) (police), or KGB (security service). The *Soviet Security* variable was intended to serve as a proxy for leadership and tactical training beyond the standard single tour of conscripted service.[4] A few trends emerge clearly from these data.

---

4   Although the secondary literature notes that these commanders had little training, it is still striking how few of the field commanders had any real military expertise before the fighting broke out. Despite the fact that one would think military and police professionals would be perfectly positioned to take advantage of the breakdown of order, only thirteen of the ninety-seven warlords identified by the coding project had previous experience in the Red Army or the KGB, and eleven of the fifty-eight analyzed in the subsample of "joiners" came out of the security structures. The armies that these men led were no larger on average than the armies of their counterparts who lacked their institutional advantages. One explanation for this might be that the Russian army stayed carefully neutral in the Tajik Civil War until a clear military victor emerged and it could play kingmaker, and career military officers within the army unlikely to be identified as "warlords" precisely because they had the resources to remain aloof from consolidation politics and keep their names out of the newspapers. Another potential explanation for the unusual trend in the data is that training in the security services

TABLE C.1. *Which Warlords Are Purged Quickly? Which Warlords Survive?*

	Model 1	Model 2	Model 3	Model 4	Model 5	Model 6	Model 7
Hissori/Uzbek	0.361**	0.422**	0.412**	0.416**	0.387**	0.375**	0.315**
	(0.097)	(0.107)	(0.108)	(0.109)	(0.112)	(0.95)	(0.106)
Gorno-Badakshon (Pamiri)	1.349	1.583++	1.641++	1.569++	1.468	1.681*	1.530
	(0.364)	(0.408)	(0.450)	(0.408)	(0.416)	(0.427)	(0.467)
Soviet Military/KGB		2.122**	2.125**	2.103**	2.159**	2.246**	2.286**
		(0.621)	(0.619)	(0.620)	(0.640)	(0.644)	(0.670)
Political Opposition (UTO)			0.914				0.872
			(0.221)				(0.224)
Gharmi (from Gharm region)				0.939			0.879
				(0.245)			(0.267)
Kulobi					0.835		0.736
					(0.216)		(0.223)
Strength/Troop Estimate						1.000	1.000
						(0.000)	(0.000)
p	1.469	1.567	1.575	1.569	1.556	1.626	1.627
SE (p)	(0192)	(0.201)	(0.203)	(0.201)	(0.199)	(0.214)	(0.213)
N	58	58	58	58	58	58	58
N(ended)	42	42	42	42	42	42	42

Weibull regression with length of time serving in the state, or in cooperative arrangement with state officials (measured in years) as the dependent variable. Coefficients in the table report the estimated multiplicative effect of a one-unit change in the independent variable on the average duration that a warlord will remain in the state; e.g., 0.294 means that a one-unit change is associated with a reduction in the mean length of time in the state by a factor of 3. Standard errors in parentheses. $^{++}p < 0.1$; $^{*}p < 0.05$; $^{**}p < 0.01$.

The central trend of note is that most warlords were, statistically speaking, equally likely to be purged in a given year. This is consistent with the theoretical assumption that they were functionally indistinguishable coalition members. Winners of the civil war were no more likely to survive successive rounds of coalition reshuffling than losers. Whether one considers the civil war as being fundamentally a matter of ideology ("UTO Islamists vs. PFT Rump Communists") or regional politics ("Kulob, Hissor, and Khojand vs. Gharm and Badakhshon"), the master cleavage of the war provided no predictive power in terms of which warlords were most likely to endure as coalition members.

Warlord military power – measured by the number of troops at the time of incorporation – had no statistically significant impact on warlord tenure in the state. This suggests two things. First, the same "multiple equilibria" problem that makes coalition formation games difficult for political scientists to productively analyze from a distance made the consolidation process difficult to navigate for strategic actors on the ground. Given the opportunity, a large number of weak warlords could (and did) substitute for a single strong warlord in securing domestic order.

Ethnicity matters. Minority warlords faced different opportunities and constraints compared to warlords from the national group when navigating the contours of coalition politics. Pamiri warlords – who held out against Rakhmonov's consolidation project in the impenetrable mountains of Badakhshon – tend to last a long time in the state once they joined it, about 50 percent longer than average. Hissori warlords, and other groups who had historically traced their patronage to Tashkent, were by contrast easy targets for purges once geopolitical frictions emerged between Russia and Uzbekistan. They exit the ruling coalition about three times as fast as the average warlord. Though it is unlikely that these trends could have been predicted ex ante with either existing models of civil war settlement or expert area knowledge, these trends contradict the model's assumption of simple warlord interchangeability.

Commanders who had prior careers in the Soviet security services emerged as unusually successful survivors, lasting about twice as long as average. As of 2006, five of these eleven warlords still held official state positions, putting their survival rate far above average. My interpretation of this trend is that access to clandestine networks of former Soviet security officials provided these men advantages in identifying lucrative niches in the Tajik shadow state as it consolidated. The president turned on warlords from his home region at a rate that is virtually indistinguishable from the average. In this light, the "Kulobization" of the state apparatus under Rakhmonov represents a general

allowed unusual social mobility – languages, contacts, and access to foreign currency – which allowed these men to flee the state with their families between 1988 and 1992.

victory for Kulobi apparatchiks at the expense of the men who fought to put the civilian apparatus into power. But it is also interesting to note that the subrepublic, local informal networks that mattered so much in mobilization – clan, family, *avlod*, and *kolkhoz* ties – were less robust predictors of political survival over time than the informal networks of security personnel.

The primary inference that I draw from these regression results is that the ruling coalition changed over time. Warlords simply could not predict how the coalition would change fifteen years into the future. Though there are certainly omitted variables in this analysis, I am confident that there is nothing that distant scholars could code ex post that would have been known to the actors ex ante.[5]

Certain area specialists, who have no interest in external validity or generalization beyond the Tajik case, might find it useful to lower the microscope and add more granular data to the analysis. Modern social science methods could shrink the error term on predictions of longevity in the Tajik state even further. Software for mapping social networks or forensic accounting technologies could be brought to bear. Drug routes and ministry positions could be coded. When I began this data collection process, I had vague ambitions to do all of these things. After all, I had chosen my research question, in part, out of a desire to revisit an understudied period of history and bring new facts to light. But as I describe in Chapter 1, at some point along the way I became uneasy with the task to which I had set myself. Social memory is a complicated and contingent thing. I did not trust all of the data I was collecting. I also began to fear that my research team was taking risks by asking too many sensitive questions. I remember the exact moment that it dawned on me that the process of collecting systematic information on individual people, in the way that I was doing it, was difficult to distinguish from putting together a targeting list. As I slowly internalized the implications of this, I decided that continuing to add either columns or rows to the dataset exposed all of my research assistants to charges of treason or espionage. Drawing a map of these social networks could easily have unanticipated effects, potentially exposing my host family in Tajikistan or my research team to violence. To limit my own liability, and set an example for future scholarship in this vein, replication data are stripped of names and identifiers.

---

5   For additional visualizations of the trends described earlier, see Driscoll (2012).

References

Abduallev, Kamoludin, and Catherine Barnes. 2001. "The Politics of Compromise – The Tajikistan Peace Process." Conciliation Resources, London. Available on http://www.c-r.org/accord/tajikistan

Akbarzadeh, Shahram. 1996. "Why Did Nationalism Fail in Tajikistan?" *Europe-Asia Studies* 48(7):1105–1129.

Akbarzadeh, Shahram. 2001. *Abdullajanov and the "Third Force."* Conciliation Resources, chapter 7, Retrieved from http://www.c-r.org/our-work/accord/tajikistan/third-force.php.

Akhmedov, Said. 1998. Tajikistan II: The Regional Conflict in Confessional and International Context. In *Conflicting Loyalties and the State in Post-Soviet Russia*, ed. Michael Waller, Bruno Coppiters, and Alexei Malashenko. Frank Cass, pp. 171–186.

Akiner, Shirin. 2001. *Tajikistan: Disintegration or Reconciliation.* The Royal Institute of International Affairs, London.

Akiner, Shirin. 2005. "Violence in Andijan, 13 May 2005: An Independent Assessment." Silk Road Paper, Central Asia-Caucasus Institute Silk Road Studies Program.

Albini, Joseph, R. E. Rogers, and Victor Shabalin. 1997. "Russian Organized Crime: Its History, Structure, and Function." *Trends in Organized Crime* 3(1):39–40.

Allison, Graham, and Robert Blackwill. 1991. "America's Stake in the Soviet Future." *Foreign Affairs* 70(3): 77–97.

Anchabadze, Jurij. 1999. History: The Modern Period. In *The Abkhazians*, ed. George Hewitt. Curzon Press, pp. 132–146.

Anderson, Benedict. 1991. *Imagined Communities: Reflections on the Origin and Spread of Nationalism.* Verso.

Anderson, Jon Lee. 2007. "Inside the Surge: The American Military Finds New Allies, but at What Cost?" *The New Yorker*. Available on http://www.newyorker.com/magazine/2007/11/19/inside-the-surge, last accessed November 19, 2014.

Areshidze, Irakly. 2007. *Democracy and Autocracy in Eurasia: Georgia in Transition.* Michigan State University Press.

Atkin, Muriel. 1997a. Tajikistan: Reform, Reaction, and Civil War. In *New States, New Politics: Building Post-Soviet Nations*, ed. Ian Bremmer and Ray Taras. Cambridge University Press, pp. 604–634.

Atkin, Muriel. 1997b. Thwarted Democratization in Tajikistan. In *Conflict, Cleavage, and Change in Central Asia and the Caucasus*, ed. B. Parrott and K. Dawisham. Cambridge University Press, pp. 277–311.

Atkin, Muriel. 2002. Tajikistan: A President and His Rivals. In *Power and Change in Central Asia*, ed. Sally N. Cummings. Routledge, pp. 97–130.

Aunger, Robert. 1995. "On Ethnography: Storytelling or Science?" *Current Anthropology* 36(1):97–130.

Auten, Brian. 1996. "Tajikistan Today." *Studies in Conflict and Terrorism* 19:199–212.

Aves, Jonathan. 1993. Underdevelopment and the New Georgian Nationalist Movement. In *In a Collapsing Empire: Underdevelopment, Ethnic Conflicts, and Nationalisms in the Soviet Union*, ed. Mark Buttino. Feltrinelli Editore Milano, pp. 225–236.

Aves, Jonathan. 1996. *Georgia: From Chaos to Stability?* The Royal Institute of International Affairs, London.

Ayres, Sabra. 2014. "Amid Staggering Destruction, Eastern Ukraine Looks to Rebuild." *Al Jazeera America*. Available on http://america.aljazeera.com/articles/2014/9/28/east-ukraine-reconstruction.html, last accessed September 28, 2014.

Babak, Vladimir, Demian Vaisman, and Aryeh Wasserman. 2004. Republic of Tajikistan. In *Political Organization in Central Asia and Azerbaijan: Sources and Documents*, ed. Vladimir Babak, Demian Vaisman, and Aryeh Wasserman. Cummings Center for Russian and Eastern European Studies. Frank Cass Publishers.

Balta, E. 2007. *Military Success, State Capacity, and Internal War-Making in Russian and Turkey*. PhD thesis, City University of New York.

Barkey, Karen. 1994. *Bandits and Bureaucrats*. Cornell University Press.

Bates, Robert. 2001. *Prosperity and Violence: The Political Economy of Development*. W. W. Norton and Company.

Bates, Robert H. 1984. *Market and States in Tropical Africa*. University of California Press.

Bates, Robert H., Avner Greif, Margaret Levi, J. L. Rosenthal, and Barry Weingast. 1998. *Analytic Narratives*. Princeton University Press.

Bates, Robert H., Avner Greif, Margaret Levi, J. L. Rosenthal, and Barry Weingast. 2000. "The Analytic Narrative Project." *The American Political Science Review* 94(3):696–702.

BBC. 2014. "Russia's Lavrov Says Time for a 'Reset 2.0' in US ties." *BBC News*. Available on http://www.bbc.com/news/world-europe-29401840, last accessed September 28, 2014.

Beissinger, Mark. 2013. "The Semblance of Democratic Revolution: Coalitions in Ukraine's Orange Revolution." *American Political Science Review* 107(3):1–19.

Beissinger, Mark R. 2002. *Nationalist Mobilization and the Collapse of the Soviet State: A Tidal Approach to the Study of Nationalism*. Cambridge University Press.

Berman, Eli. 2009. *Radical, Religious and Violent: The New Economics of Terrorism*. The MIT Press.

Birnbaum, Michael. 2014. "Western Sanctions for Ukraine Conflict Hurt Russian Economy, Open up Rifts." *Washington Post*. Available on http://www.bbc.com/news/world-europe-30436200

Blasi, J., M. Kroumova, and D. Kruse, eds. 1997. *Kremlin Capitalism: Privatizing the Russian Economy*. Cornell University Press.

Blattman, Christopher and Eduard Miguel. 2009. "Civil War." NBER Working Paper No. w14801. March. National Bureau of Economic Research.

Blauvelt, Timothy. 2013. "Endurance of the Soviet Imperial Tongue: The Russian Language in Contemporary Georgia." *Central Asian Survey* 32(2):189–209.

Bornet, Jean-Marc. 1998. The International Committee of the Red Cross and the Conflict in Tajikistan. In *Tajikistan: The Trials of Independence*, ed. Shirin Akiner Mohammad-Reza Djalili, and Frederic Grare. Curzon Press, pp. 219–228.

Bowen, John, and Roger Petersen. 1999. Critical Comparisons. In *Critical Comparisons in Politics and Culture*, ed. John Bowen and Roger Petersen. Cambridge University Press, pp. 1–20.

Brass, Paul R. 1997. *Theft of an Idol: Text and Context in the Representation of Collective Violence*. Princeton University Press.

Brenninkmeijer, Olivier A. J. 1998. International Concern for Tajikistan: UN and OSCE Efforts to Promote Peace-Building and Democratisation. In *Tajikistan: The Trials of Independence*, ed. Shirin Akiner Mohammad-Reza Djalili and Frederic Grare. Curzon Press, pp. 180–216.

Brown, Archie. 2007. *Seven Years that Changed the World*. Oxford University Press.

Brown, Bess A. 1998. The Civil War in Tajikistan, 1992–1993. In *Tajikistan: The Trials of Independence*, ed. Shirin Akiner Mohammad-Reza Djalili and Frederic Grare. Curzon Press, pp. 86–96.

Brown, Michael E. 1997. *The Causes of Internal Conflicts*. MIT Press, pp. 1–31.

Buford, B. 1993. *Among the Thugs*. Vintage Press.

Bukharbaeva, Galima. 2005. "Testimony: Statement of Galima Bukharbaeva, Correspondent—Institute for War and Peace Reporting." Helsinki Commission Hearing.

Bunce, Valerie. 1999. *Subversive Institutions: The Design and Destruction of Socialism and the State*. Cambridge University Press.

Bushkov V., and Mikulskii, D. 1995. *Anatomiya grazhdanskoi voiny v Tadzhikistane (ethno-sotsial'nye protessy I politeskaya bor'ba, 1992–1995*. Moscow.

Capote, Truman. 1965. *In Cold Blood*. First ed. Vintage International.

Carothers, Thomas, ed. 2006. *Promoting Rule of Law Abroad: In Search of Knowledge*. Carnegie Endowment for International Peace, Washington, DC.

Centlivres Pierre, and Micheline Centlivres-Demont. 1998. Tajikistan and Afghanistan: the Ethnic Groups on Either Side of the Border. In *Tajikistan: The Trials of Independence*, ed. Shirin Akiner Mohammad-Reza Djalili, and Frederic Grare. Curzon Press, pp. 3–13.

Chwe, Michael Suk-Young. 1998. "Culture, Circles, and Commercials: Publicity, Common Knowledge, and Social Coordination." *Rationality and Society* 10(1): 47–75.

Collier, P. H., and A. Hoeffler. 2004. "Greed and Grievance in Civil War." *Oxford Economic Papers* 56:563–595.

Collins, K. 2006. *Clan Politics and Regime Transition in Central Asia*. Cambridge University Press.

Cooley, Alexander. 2012. *Great Games, Local Rules: The New Great Power Contest in Central Asia*. Oxford University Press.

Cornell, Svante E. 2001. *Small Nations and Great Powers: A Study of Ethnopolitical Conflict in the Caucasus*. Curzon Press.

Cornell, Svante E. 2002. "Autonomy as a Source of Conflict: Caucasian Conflicts in Theoretical Perspective." *World Politics* 54(2):245–276.

Cornell, Svante E. 2003. The Growing Threat of Transnational Crime. In *The South Caucasus: A Challenge for the E.U.*, ed. Dov Lynch. Chaillot Papers, No. 65.

Cunningham, David E. 2006. "Veto Players and Civil War Duration." *American Journal of Political Science* 50(4):875–892.

Daly, John C. K. 2005. "The Andijan Disturbances and Their Implications." *Central Asia-Caucasus Analyst* 29. Available on http://www.cacianalyst.org/publications/analytical-articles/item/10049-analytical-articles-caci-analyst-2005-6-29-art-10049.html, last accessed 29 June, 2005.

Daniel, E. Valentine. 1996. *Charred Lullabies*. Princeton University Press.

Darchiashvili, D. 1997a. *Georgia: The Search for Security*. Caucasus Working Papers, CISAC, Stanford.

Darchiashvili, David. 1997b. "Georgia: A Hostage to Arms." Saferworld Arms and Security Programme, London.

Darchiashvili, David. 2005. Georgian Defense Policy and Military Reform. In *Statehood and Security: Georgia after the Rose Revolution*, ed. Bruno Coppieters and Robert Legvold. MIT Press, pp. 117–154.

Darchiashvili, David, and Ghia Nodia. 2003. The Weak State Syndrome and Corruption. In *Building Democracy in Georgia: Power Structures, the Weak State Syndrome, and Corruption in Georgia*. International Institute for Democracy and Electoral Assistance.

Darden, Keith. 2008. "Graft and Governance: Corruption as an Informal Mechanism of State Control." *Politics and Society* 36(1):35–60.

Davenport, Christian. 2007. *State Repression and the Domestic Democratic Peace*. Cambridge Studies in Comparative Politics. Cambridge University Press.

De Figueiredo, R., and B. Weingast. 1999. The Rationality of Fear. In *Civil Wars, Insecurity, and Intervention*, ed. B. Walter and J. Snyder. Columbia University Press.

de Waal, Thomas. 2003. *Black Garden: Armenia and Azerbaijan through Peace and War*. New York University Press.

de Waal, Thomas. 2005. Georgia and Its Distant Neighbors. In *Statehood and Security: Georgia after the Rose Revolution*, ed. Bruno Coppieters and Robert Legvold. MIT Press, pp. 307–338.

Demetriou, S. 2002. "Politics from the Barrel of a Gun: Small Arms Proliferation and Conflict in the Republic of Georgia." Small Arms Survey, Geneva.

Denber, Rachel, Barnett Rubin, and Jeri Laber. 1993. "Human Rights in Tajikistan in the Wake of Civil War." Human Rights Watch (Organization), Helsinki Watch, New York.

Derluguian, G. M. 2005. *Bourdieu's Secret Admirer in the Caucasus: A World-System Biography*. University of Chicago Press.

Devdariani, Jaba. 2005. Georgia and Russia: The Troubled Road to Accommodation. In *Statehood and Security: Georgia After the Rose Revolution*, ed. Bruno Coppieters and Robert Legvold. MIT Press, pp. 153–204.

Dixit, Avinash K. 2004. *Lawlessness and Economics: Alternative Modes of Governance*. The Gorman Lectures in Economics. Princeton University Press.

Donetsk People's Republic Plans to Switch to Ruble. 2014. Retrived from http://www. kyivpost.com/content/ukraine/donetsk-peoples-republic-plans-to-switch-to-ruble-not-ready-for-own-currency-366278.html

Doyle, M., and Sambanis, N., 2006. *Making War and Building Peace*. Princeton University Press.

Driscoll, Jesse. 2012. "Commitment Problems or Bidding Wars? Rebel Fragmentation as Peace Building." *Journal of Conflict Resolution* 56(1):118–149.

Driscoll, Jesse, and Timothy Blauvelt. 2012. Translation Bottlenecks and Truth Hierarchies: A Language Experiment in Post-War Georgia. In *Association for the Study of Nationalities Annual Meeting*. Association for the Study of Nationalities, Columbia University, New York.

Dudoignon, Stephane A. 1998. Political Parties and Forces in Tajiksistan, 1989–1993. In *Tajikistan: The Trials of Independence*, ed. Shirin Akiner Mohammad-Reza Djalili and Frederic Grare. Curzon Press, pp. 52–85.

Easterly, William. 2001. *The Elusive Quest for Growth: Economists' Adventures and Misadventures in the Tropics*. MIT Press.

Ekedahl, Carolyn McGiffert, and Melvin A. Goodman. 1997. *The Wars of Eduard Shevardnadze*. Pennsylvania State University Press.

Ellis, S. 1999. *The Mask of Anarchy: The Destruction of Liberia and the Religious Dimension of an African Civil War*. C. Hurst.

Elster, Jon. 1989. *Nuts and Bolts for the Social Sciences*. Cambridge University Press.

Elster, Jon. 2000. "Rational Choice History: A Case of Excessive Ambition." *American Political Science Review* 94(3):685–695.

Emerson, Robert M., Rachel I. Fretz, and Linda L. Shaw. 1995. *Writing Ethnographic Field Notes*. University of Chicago Press.

Enloe, Cynthia H. 1980. *Ethnic Soldiers*. University of Georgia Press.

Espiritu, Yen Le. 1996. Racial Killing or Barroom Brawl? Multiple Explanations for the Killing of Vincent Chin. In *Riots and Pogroms*, ed. Paul Brass. New York University Press, pp. 221–234.

Fairbanks, C. H., Jr. 1995. "The Postcommunist Wars." *Journal of Democracy* 6:18–34.

Fairbanks, C. H. 2002. Weak States and Private Armies. In *Beyond State Crisis?: Post-Colonial Africa and Post-Soviet Eurasia in Comparative Perspective*, ed. M. Beissinger and C. Young. Woodrow Wilson Press, pp. 129–159.

Fairbanks, Charles. 1996. Party and Ideology in the Former U.S.S.R. In *Left, Right and Center: Party and Ideology after the Cold War*, ed. Richard Zinman and Jerry Weinberger. Cornell University Press.

Fairbanks, Charles. 2004. "Georgia's Rose Revolution." *Journal of Democracy*, 110–124.

Fairbanks, Charles. 2012. "Georgia's Prison Rape Scandal – And What It Says About the Rose Revolution." *The Atlantic*, Available on http://www.theatlantic.com/international/archive/2012/09/georgias-prison-rape-scandal-and-what-it-says-about-the-rose-revolution/262720/, last accessed September 24, 2012.

Fanon, Franz. 1968. *The Wretched of the Earth*. Grove Press.

Fearon, J. 2004. "Why Do Some Civil Wars Last So Much Longer Than Others?" *Journal of Peace Research* 41(3):275–301.

Fearon, J. D. 2007. "Iraq's Civil War." *Foreign Affairs* 82(2):2–16.

Fearon, James. 1997. Deliberation as Discussion. In *Deliberative Democracy*, ed. Jon Elster. Cambridge University Press, pp. 44–68.

Fearon, James. 2003. "Ethnic and Cultural Diversity by Country." *Journal of Economic Growth* 8(2):195–222.

Fearon, James, and David Laitin. 1996. "Explaining Interethnic Cooperation." *American Political Science Review* 90(4):715–735.

Fearon, James, and David Laitin. 2000. "Violence and the Social Construction of Ethnic Identity." *International Organization* 54(4):845–877.

Fearon, James, and David Laitin. 2003. "Ethnicity, Insurgency, and Civil War." *American Political Science Review* 97(1):75–90.

Fearon, James, and David Laitin. 2004. "Neotrusteeship and the Problem of Weak States." *International Security* 28(4):5–43.

Fearon, James, and David Laitin. 2007. "Civil War Termination." Prepared for the 2007 Annual Meetings of the American Political Science Association.

Felter, Joseph. 2005. *Taking Guns to a Knife Fight: Counterinsurgency in the Philippines.* Unpublished doctoral dissertation, Stanford University.

Ferejohn, J. 1991. Rationality and Interpretation: Parliamentary Elections in Early Stuart England. In *The Economic Approach to Politics: A Critical Reassessment of the Theory of Rational Action*, ed. Kristen Renwick Monroe. HarperCollins.

Ferejohn, John. 1986. "Incumbent Performance and Electoral Control." *Public Choice* 30(Fall):5–25.

Ferejohn, John. 2004. Internal and External Explanation. In *Problems and Methods in the Study of Politics*, ed. Ian Shapiro. Yale University Press, pp. 144–166.

Ferguson, James. 2005. "Seeing Like an Oil Company: Space, Security, and Global Capital in Neoliberal Africa." *American Anthropologist* 107(3):377–382.

Filkins, Dexter, and Carlotta Gall. 2010. "Taliban Leader in Secret Talks Was an Impostor." *New York Times.* November 22, 2010, page A1. Available on http://www.nytimes.com/2010/11/23/world/asia/23kabul.html?pagewanted=all

Fortna, Page. 2008. *Does Peacekeeping Work?* Princeton University Press.

Gagnon, V. P. 1995. "Ethnic Nationalism and International Conflict: The Case of Serbia." *International Security* 19(3):130–166.

Gambetta, D. 1996. *The Sicilian Mafia: The Business of Private Protection.* Harvard University Press.

Gambetta, Diego. 2002. Corruption: An Analytical Map. In *Political Corruption in Transition*, ed. Andras Sajo and Stephen Kotkin. Central European University Press, pp. 33–56.

Geertz, Clifford. 1977. *The Interpretation of Cultures.* Basic Books.

Girod, Desha. 2012. "Effective Foreign Aid Following Civil War: The Nonstrategic-Desperation Hypothesis." *The American Journal of Political Science* 56(1):188–201.

Girod, Desha and Jennifer Tobin, "Take the Money and Run: The Determinants of Compliance with Aid Agreements," International Organization (forthcoming).

Giustozzi, Antonio. 2009. Bureaucratic Facade and Political Realities of Disarmament and Demobilization in Afghanistan. In *Reintegrating Armed Groups after Conflict*, ed. Mats Berdal and David Ucko. Routledge Studies in Intervention and Statebuilding, pp. 67–88.

Gleason, Gregory. 1997. *Central Asian States: Discovering Independence.* Westview Press.

Goemans, H. E., K. S. Gleditsch, and G. Chiozza. 2009. "Introducing Archigos: A Dataset of Political Leaders." *Journal of Peace Research* 46: 269–283.

Goldenberg, Suzanne. 1994. *Pride of Small Nations: The Caucasus and Post-Soviet Disorder.* Zed Books.

Goldgeier, James, and Michael McFaul. 2003. *Power and Purpose.* Oxford University Press.

Goldsmith, Aurthur A. 2008. "Making the World Safe for Partial Democracy? Questioning the Premises of Democracy Promotion." *International Security* 33(2): 120–147.

Goldstone, Jack A. 1994. "Is Revolution Individually Rational? Groups and Individuals in Revolutionary Collective Action." *Rationality and Society* 6(1): 139–166.

Gorvin, Ian. 1998. The Human Rights Situation in Tajikistan (1992–1993). In *Tajikistan: The Trials of Independence*, ed. Shirin Akiner Mohammad-Reza Djalili and Frederic Grare. Curzon Press, pp. 229–236.

Gourevitch, Peter. 1978. "The Second Image Reversed: The International Sources of Domestic Politics." *International Organization* 32(4):881–912.

Gretsky, S. 1995. Civil War in Tajikistan: Causes, Development, and Prospects for Peace. In *Central Asia: Conflict, Resolution, and Change*, ed. Roald Sagdeev and Susan Eisenhower. Center for Post-Soviet Studies, The Eisenhower Institute, MD. http://www.amazon.com/Central-Asia-Conflict-Resolution-Change/dp/0967023319

Gretsky, Sergei. 1997. *Russia's Foreign Policy Toward Central Asia.* Carnegie Endowment for International Peace. Moscow.

Grossman, Dave. 1996. *On Killing.* Back Bay Books.

Grossman, H. I. 1999. "Kleptocracy and Revolutions." *Oxford Economic Papers* 51:267–283.

Grotz, Florian. 2001. Tajikistan. In *Elections in Asia and the Pacific: A Data Handbook*, Vol. 1; *Middle East, Central Asia and South Asia*, ed. Florian Grotz, Dieter Nohlen, and Christof Hartmann. Oxford University Press.

Haas, Peter M. 1992. "Introduction: Epistemic Communities and International Policy Coordination." *International Organization* 46(1):1–35.

Handelman, S. 1995. *Comrade Criminal: Russia's New Mafiya.* Yale University Press.

Harris, Colette. 2004. *Control and Subversion.* Pluto Press.

Heathershaw, John. 2007. "Peacebuilding as Practice: Discources from Post-Conflict Tajikistan." *International Peacekeeping* 14(2):219–236.

Heathershaw, John. 2008. "Seeing Like the International Community: How Peacebuilding Failed (and Survived) in Tajikistan." *Journal of Intervention and Statebuilding* 2(3):329–351.

Heathershaw, John. 2009. *Post-Conflict Tajikistan: The Politics of Peacebuilding and the Emergence of Legitimate Order.* Routledge.

Helpman, Elhanan. 2004. *The Mystery of Economic Growth.* Belknap Press of Harvard University Press.

Herman, Edward S., and Noam Chomsky. 1987. *Manufacturing Consent.* Pantheon.

Herr, Michael. 1968. *Dispatches.* ed. Vintage International.

Hobbes, Thomas. 1651. *Leviathan.* 1991 reprint ed. Cambridge University Press.

Horsman, S. 1999. "Uzbekistan's Involvement in the Tajik Civil War 1992–1997: Demostic Considerations." *Central Asian Survey* 18(1):37–48.

ICG. 2004. Tajikistan's Politics: Confrontation or Consolidation? Technical Report. International Crisis Group. Bishkek/Brussels.

ICG. 2005. "The Curse of Cotton: Central Asia's Destructive Monoculture." *Asia Report* (93). Bishkek/Brussels, pages 1-50 http://www.crisisgroup.org/en/regions/asia/central-asia/093-the-curse-of-cotton-central-asias-destructive-monoculture aspx.

IDEA. 2011. "IDEA: International Institute for Democracy and Electoral Assitance. Voter Turnout for Tajikistan." Retrieved from http://www.idea.int/vt/countryview.cfm?CountryCode=TJ

Ilkhamov, Alisher. 2006. "The Phenomenology of 'Akromiya': Separating Fact from Fiction." *China and Eurasia Forum Quarterly* 4(39):39-48.

Jackall, Robert. 2005. *Street Stories: The World of Police Detectives*. Harvard University Press.

Jackson, Robert H. 1990. *Quasi-States: Sovereignty, International Relations, and the Third World*. Cambridge University Press.

Jalali, Ali A. 2006. "The Future of Afghanistan." *Parameters* Spring 36(1):4-19.

Jankowski, Martin S. 1992. *Islands in the Street: Gangs and American Urban Society*. University of California Press.

Jones, Stephen. 1997. Georgia: The Trauma of Statehood. In *New States, New Politics: Building Post-Soviet Nations*, ed. Ian Bremmer and Ian Taras. Cambridge University Press, pp. 505-546.

Jones, Stephen. 2006. "The Rose Revolution: A Revolution Without Revolutionaries?" *Cambridge Review of International Affairs* 19(1):33-48.

Jones, Stephen F. 1996. Adventurers or Commanders? Civil-Military Relations in Georgia Since Independence. In *Civil-Military Relations in the Soviet and Yugoslav Successor States*, ed. Daniel Zirker and Constantine P. Danopoulos. Westview Press.

Jones-Luong, Pauline. 2002. *Institutional Change and Political Continuity in Post-Soviet Central Asia: Power, Perceptions, and Pacts*. Cambridge University Press.

Jonson, Lena, and Shirin Akiner. 1998. *Tajik War: A Challenge to Russian Policy*. Royal Institute of International Affairs, London.

Kaldor, M. A. 1999. *New Wars: Organized Violence in a Global Era*. Polity Press.

Kalyvas, S. 2003. "The Ontology of "Political Violence": Action and Identity in Civil Wars." *Perspectives on Politics* 1(3):475.

Kalyvas, S. 2004. "The Urban Bias in Research on Civil Wars." *Security Studies* 13(3):160.

Kalyvas, S. 2006. *The Logic of Violence in Civil War*. Cambridge Series in Comparative Politics. Cambridge University Press.

Kalyvas, S., and M. Kocher. 2007. "How "Free" Is Free Riding in Civil Wars? Violence, Insurgency, and the Collective Action Problem." *World Politics* 59:177-216.

Kalyvas, Stathis. 2007. Civil Wars. In *Oxford Handbook of Political Science*, ed. Carles Boix and Susan Stokes. Oxford University Press, pp. 416-434.

Kalyvas, Stathis, and Laia Balcells. 2011. "International System and Technologies of Rebellion: How the End of the Cold War Shaped Internal Conflict." *American Political Science Review* 104(3):415-429.

Katz, Jack. 1988. *Seductions of Crime: Moral and Sensual Attractions in Doing Evil*. Basic Books.

Kaufmann, Chaim. 1996. "Possible and Impossible Solutions to Ethnic Civil Wars." *International Security* 20(4):136–175.

Keegan, J. 1994. *The History of Warfare*. Vintage International.

Keen, David. 1998. "The Economic Functions of Violence in Civil Wars." Vol. 320: Adelphi Paper. (Oxford University Press for International Institute for Strategic Studies).

Kendzior, Sarah. 2006. "Inventing Akromiya: The Role of Uzbek Propagandists in the Andijon Massacare." *Demokratizatsiya: The Journal of Post-Soviet Democratization* 14(4):545–562.

Kennan, George F. 1997. "A Fateful Error." *New York Times*, February 5.

King, Charles. 1997. "Ending Civil Wars." Adelphi Paper (Oxford University Press for International Institute for Strategic Studies).

King, Charles. 2000. "The Benefits of Ethnic War: Understanding Eurasia's Unrecognized States." *World Politics* 53:524–552.

King, Charles. 2001*a*. "The Myth of Ethnic Warfare." *Foreign Affairs* November/December:n/a.

King, Charles. 2001*b*. "Potemkin Democracy." *The National Interest* Summer.

King, Charles. 2004*a*. "The Micropolitics of Social Violence." *World Politics* 56(3):431–455.

King, Charles. 2004*b*. "A Rose among Thorns: Georgia Makes Good." *Foreign Affairs* 83(2):13–18.

King, Charles. 2008*a*. "The Five-Day War." *Foreign Affairs*. November/December 2008 Issue; available on http://www.foreignaffairs.com/articles/64602/charles-king/the-five-day-war

King, Charles. 2008*b*. "Salon Radio: Professor Charles King on Russia/Georgia." Salon Radio. Retrieved from http://www.salon.com/2008/08/11/king_7/

King, Gary, Robert Keohane, and Sidney Verba. 1994. *Designing Social Inquiry*. Princeton University Press.

Kotkin, Stephen. 2002. "Trashcanistan: A Tour through Wreckage of the Soviet Empire." *The New Republic Magazine*, 226(14):26–38.

Kotkin, Stephen. 2008. *Armageddon Averted*. Oxford University Press.

Kramer, Andrew. 2014. "Ukraine Picks Motley Group to Exchange for Prisoners." *New York Times*, September 24, A4

Krasner, Stephen. 2001. *Sovereignty: Organized Hypocrisy*. Princeton University Press.

Kubicek, Paul. 1999–2000. "Russia's Foreign Policy and the West." *Political Science Quarterly* 114(4):547–568.

Kuran, Timur. 1991. "Now Out of Never: The Element of Surprise in the Eastern European Revolution of 1989." *World Politics* 44:7–48.

Kuzmin, A. I. 1997. *Grazhdanskaya Voina v Tadzhikisstane: Istoki I Perspektivy*. TsMI, MGIMO, Moscow.

Lacina, Bethany. 2006. "Explaining the Severity of Civil Wars." *Journal of Conflict Resolution* 50(2):276–289.

Lacina, Bethany. 2014. "India's Stabilizing Segment States." *Ethnopolitics* 13(1):13–27.

Laitin, David. 1977. *Politics, Language, and Thought: The Somali Experience*. University of Chicago Press.

Laitin, David D. 1994. "The Tower of Babel as a Coordination Game: Political Linguistics in Ghana." *American Political Science Review* 88(3):622–634.

Laitin, David D. 1998. *Identity in Formation*. Cornell University Press.

Laitin, David D. 1999a. National Revivals and Violence. In *Critical Comparisons in Politics and Culture*, ed. Roget Petersen and John Bowen. Cambridge University Press.

Laitin, David D. 1999b. Somalia: Civil War and International Intervention. In *Civil Wars, Insecurity, and Intervention*, ed. Jack Snyder Barbara F. Walter. Columbia University Press, pp. 146–180.

Laitin, David D. 2001. "Secessionist Rebellion in the Former Soviet Union." *Comparative Political Studies* 34(8):839–861.

Laitin, David D. 2006. "Caucasuan Crucibles." *New Left Review* 38.

Laitin, David D., and Rogers Brubaker. 1998. "Ethnic and Nationalist Violence." *Annual Review of Sociology* 24:423–452.

Larsson, Robert L. 2004. "The Enemy Within: Russia's Military Withdrawal from Georgia." *Journal of Slavic Military Studies* 17(3):405–424.

LeBon, Gustave. 1895. *The Crowd: A Study of the Popular Mind*. Second – 1982 reprint ed. Cherokee Publishing Company.

Leeuw, Charles Van Der. 1999. *Storm Over the Caucsus in the Wake of Independence*. Curzon Press.

Levitsky, Steven and Lucan Way. 2005. "International Linkage and Democratization." *Journal of Democracy* 16:20–34.

Lezhnev, Sasha. 2006. *Crafting Peace: Strategies to Deal with Warlords in Collapsing States*. Lexington Books.

Lichbach, Mark I. 1995. *The Rebel's Dilemma*. University of Michigan Press.

Licklider, R. 1995. "The Consequences of Negotiated Settlements in Civil Wars, 1945–1993." *The American Political Science Review* 89(3):681–690.

Luttwak, Edward. 1999. "Give War a Chance." *Foreign Affairs* 78(4):36–44.

Lyall, Jason. 2010. "Are Coethnics More Effective Counterinsurgents? Evidence from the Second Chechen War." *American Political Science Review* 104(1):1–20.

MacFarlane, Neil. 1999. Realism and Russian Strategy after the Collapse of the USSR. In *Unipolar Politics*, ed. Ethan B. Kapstein and Michael Mastanduno. Columbia University Press, pp. 218–260.

MacFarquhar, Neil and Andrew Kramer. 2014. "Praising Rebels, Putin Toughens Tone on Ukraine." *New York Times*, August 29, 2014, page A1.

Mackinder, Halford. 1942. *Democratic Ideals and Reality: A Study in the Politics of Reconstruction*. Classic ed. National Defense University Press.

MacPhee, Craig. 2004. "Expert on Georgia Explores 'Can Saakashvili Outdo Shevardnadze?'." Newswise. January 5, 2004. Available on http://www.newswise.com/articles/expert-on-georgia-explores-can-saakashvili-outdo-shevardnadze

Magaloni, Beatriz. 2008. "Credible Power-Sharing and the Longevity of Authoritarian Rule." *Comparative Political Studies* 41:715–741.

Mardin, Serif. 1978. "Youth and Violence in Turkey." *Archives of European Sociology* XIX:229–254.

Markowitz, Lawrence. 2011. "Unlootable Resources and State Security Institutions in Tajikistan and Uzbekistan." *Comparative Political Studies* 44(2):156–183.

Markowitz, Lawrence. 2013. *State Erosion: Unlootable Resources and Unruly Elites in Central Asia*. Cornell University Press.

Mars, Gerald, and Yochanan Altman. 1983. "The Cultural Bases of Soviet Georgia's Second Economy." *Soviet Studies* XXXV(4):546–560.

Marten, Kimberly. 2012. *Warlords: Strong-Arm Brokers in Weak States*. Cornell Studies in Security Affairs. Cornell University Press.

Martin, Terry. 2001. *The Affirmative Action Empire: Nations and Nationalism in the Soviet Union, 1923–1939*. Cornell University Press.

Mason, T. David, and Dale A. Krane. 1989. "The Political Economy of Death Squads: Toward a Theory of the Impact of State-Sanctioned Terror." *International Studies Quarterly* 33(2):175–198.

Matveeva, Anna. 2009. "The Perils of Emerging Statehood: Civil War and State Reconstruction in Tajikistan." CSRC Working Papers, 2(46):1–57.

McCormick, Gordon, Stephen Horton, and Lauren A. Harrison. 2007. "Things Fall Apart: The Endgame Dynamic of Internal Wars." *Third World Quarterly* 28(2):321–367.

McFaul, Michael. 2001. *Russia's Unfinished Revolution*. Cornell University Press.

McFaul, Michael. 2002. "The Fourth Wave of Democracy and Dictatorship: Noncooperative Transitions in the Postcommunist World." *World Politics* 54(2):212–244.

McFaul, Michael. 2014. "Michael McFaul on Vladimir Putin and Russia." Retrieved from https://www.youtube.com/watch?v=iHgp9fLUzpE

Miller, Eric. 2004. "Smelling the Roses: Eduard Shevardnadze's End and Georgia's Future." *Problems of Post-Communism*, 51(2):12–21.

Mirzoev, Tokhir. 2002. Post-Soviet Corruption Outburst in Post-Conflict Tajikistan. In *Political Corruption in Transition*, ed. Andras Sajo and Stephen Kotkin. Central European University Press, pp. 353–382.

Mitchell, Lincoln. 2004. "Georgia's Rose Revolution." *Current History* 103(675): 342–348.

Mueller, John. 2000. "The Banality of 'Ethnic War'." *International Security* 25(1): 42–70.

Mueller, John. 2003. "Policing the Remnants of War." *Journal of Peace Research* 40(5): 507–518.

Mueller, John. 2004. *The Remnants of War*. Cornell University Press.

Naimark, Norman. 2002. *Fires of Hatred: Ethnic Cleansing in Twentieth-Century Europe*. Harvard University Press.

Nakaya, Sumie. 2009. *State Reconstruction in Tajikistan*. PhD thesis, City University of New York.

Nassim Jawad, and Shahrbanou Tadjbakhsh. 1995. *Tajikistan: A Forgotten Civil War*. Minority Rights Group. London.

Neumann, Iver, and Sergei Solodovnik. 1996. The Case of Tajikistan. In *Peacekeeping and the Role of Russia in Eurasia*. Westview Press, pp. 83–102.

Nodia, G. 2002. Putting the State Back Together in Post-Soviet Georgia. In *Beyond State Crisis?: Post-Colonial Africa and Post-Soviet Eurasia in Comparative Perspective*, ed. M. Beissinger and C. Young. Woodrow Wilson Press.

Nodia, Ghia. 1996. "How Different Are Postcommunist Transitions?" *Journal of Democracy* 7(4):15–29.

Nodia, Ghia. 1998a. The Conflict in Abkhazia: National Projects and Political Circumstances. In *Georgians and Abkhazians: The Search for a Peace Settlement*, ed. Bruno Coppieters, Ghia Nodia, and Yury Anchabadze. BIOst.

Nodia, Ghia. 1998b. "Causes and Visions of Conflict in Abkhazia." Working Paper: Berkeley Program in Soviet and Post-Soviet Studies.

North, Douglass C. 2006. *Understanding the Process of Economic Change.* Princeton Economic History of the Western World. Princeton University Press.

North, Douglass C., John J. Wallis, and Barry R. Weingast. 2009. *Violence and Social Orders: A Conceptual Framework for Interpreting Recorded Human History.* Cambridge University Press.

Nourzhanov, K. 2005. "Saviors of the Nation or Robber Barons? Warlord Politics in Tajikistan." *Central Asian Survey* 24(2):109–130.

Nourzhanov, Kirill, and Christian Bleur. 2013. *Tajikistan: A Political and Social History.* Australia: Australian National University E-Press.

Nunn, Samuel. 1991. "Soviet Defense Conversion and Demilitarization." Congressional Hearings.

O'Ballance, Edgar. 1997. *Wars in the Caucasus, 1990–1995.* New York University Press.

Olcott, Martha Brill. 1994. Emerging Political Elites. In *The New Geopolitics of Central Asia and Its Borderlands*, ed. Ali Banuazizi and Myron Weiner. Indiana University Press. Warsaw.

Olcott, Martha Brill. 1997. *Central Asia's New States.* United States Institute of Peace Press.

Olson, Mancur. 1965. *The Logic of Collective Action: Public Goods and the Theory of Groups.* Harvard University Press.

O'Prey, Kevin. 1996. Keeping the Peace in the Borderlands of Russia. In *UN Peacekeeping, American Politics, and the Uncivil Wars of the 1990s*, ed. William J. Durch. Stimpson Center Press. Warsaw.

Orwell, George. 1952. *Homage to Catalonia.* Harcourt Brace and Company.

Osborne, Martin J. 2004. *An Introduction to Game Theory.* Oxford University Press.

OSCE. 2005. "Preliminary Findings on the Events in Andijan, Uzbekistan, 13 May 2005." OSCE Office for Democratic Institutions and Human Rights, pp. 44–67.

Panfilov, Oleg. 2003. *Tajikistan: Journalists in Civil War (1992–1997).* Russian ed. Goryaie Tochki.

Papava, Vladimer. 2006. "The Political Economy of Georgia's Rose Revolution." *Orbis,* 50(4): 657–667. Available on http://www.sciencedirect.com/science/article/pii/Soo 3043870600779

Papava, Vladimer, and Vepkhia Chocheli. 2003. *Financial Globalization and Post-Communist Georgia: Global Exchange Rate Instability and Its Implications for Georgia.* iUniverse.

Paxson, Margaret. 2005. *Solovyovo: The Story of Memory in a Russian Village.* Woodrow Wilson Press.

Petersen, Roger. 2001. *Resistence and Rebellion: Lessons from Eastern Europe.* Cambridge University Press.

Petersen, Roger. 2002. *Understanding Ethnic Violence: Fear, Hatred, and Resentment in Twentieth-Century Eastern Europe.* Cambridge University Press.

Petersen, Roger. 2011. *Western Intervention in the Balkans: The Strategic Use of Emotion.* Cambridge Series in Comparative Politics. Cambridge University Press.

Pevehouse, Jon C. 2005. *Democracy from Above? Regional Organizations and Democratization.* Cambridge University Press.

Pileggi, Nicholas. 1985. *Wise Guy.* Pocket Books.

Pirseyedi, Bobi. 2000. "The Small Arms Problem in Central Asia: Features and Implications." United Nations Institute for Disarmament Research (UNIDIR).

Popkin, S. 1979. *The Rational Peasant: The Political Economy of Rural Society in Vietnam*. University of California Press.

Popkov, Viktor. 1998. Soviet Abkhazia 1989: A Personal Account. In *The Abkhazians*, ed. George Hewitt. Curzon Press, pp. 102–131.

Posen, Barry. 1993. "The Security Dilemma and Ethnic Conflict." *Survival* 35(1):27–47.

"Putin's Approval Rating Soars to 87%, Poll Say". 2014. Retrieved from http://www.themoscowtimes.com/article/504691.html

Putnam, Robert. 1988. "Diplomacy and Domestic Politics: The Logic of Two-Level Games." *International Organization* 42(3):427–460.

Rakowska-Harmstone, Teresa. 1970. *Russia and Nationalism in Central Asia: The Case of Tadzhikistan*. Johns Hopkins University Press.

Rashid, Ahmed. 2002. *Jihad: The Rise of Militant Islam in Central Asia*. Yale University Press.

Rashid, Ahmed. 2008. *Descent into Chaos*. Viking Press.

Rashidov, Akbar. 1993. Family and Tribal Structures and Social Conflicts in Soviet Central Asia. In *In a Collapsing Empire: Underdevelopment, Ethnic Conflicts, and Nationalisms in the Soviet Union*, ed. Mark Buttino. Feltrinelli Editore Milano, pp. 291–299.

Ratiani, Shorena. 2004. "Georgia: Corruption Crackdown Makes Waves." IWPR Caucasus Reporting Service, no. 231.

Remnick, David. 1994. *Lenin's Tomb: The Last Days of the Soviet Empire*. Vintage International.

Remnick, David. 2014. "Watching the Eclipse." New Yorker, August 11, 2014. Available on http://www.newyorker.com/magazine/2014/08/11/watching-eclipse

Reno, William. 1998. *Warlord Politics in African States*. Rienner.

Reno, William. 2002. Mafiya Troubles, Warlord Crises. In *Beyond State Crisis?: Post-Colonial Africa and Post-Soviet Eurasia in Comparative Perspective*, ed. Mark R. Beissinger and Crawford Young. Woodrow Wilson Press, pp. 105–127.

Roeder, Philip G. 1993. *Red Sunset: The Failure of Soviet Politics*. Princeton University Press.

Roeder, Philip G. 2007. *Where Nation-States Come From: Institutional Change in the Age of Nationalism*. Princeton University Press.

Roth, Andrew. 2014a. "A Separatist Militia in Ukraine with Russian Fighters Holds a Key." *New York Times*. June 5, 2014, page A12.

Roth, Andrew. 2014b. "Ukraine Faces Struggle to Gain Control of Militias, Including Those on Its Side." *New York Times*. June 5, 2014, page A12.

Roth, Andrew, and Sabrina Tavernise. 2014. "Russians Revealed Among Ukraine Fighters." *New York Times*. June 5, 2014, page A12.

Roy, Olivier. 2000. *The New Central Asia: Geopolitics and the Birth of Nations*. New York University Press.

Rubin, Barnett R. 1993. "The Fragmentation of Tajikistan." *Survival* 35(4):71–79.

Rubin, Barnett R. 1998. Russian Hegemony and State Breakdown in the Periphery: Causes and Consequences of the Civil War in Tajikistan. In *Post-Soviet Political Order: Conflict and State Building*, ed. Jack Snyder Barnett and R. Rubin. Routledge, pp. 128–161.

Rucker, Philip. 2014. "Hillary Clinton Says Putin's Actions are Like 'what Hitler did Back in the '30s'". Retrieved from http://www.washingtonpost.com/blogs/po st-politics/wp/2014/03/05/hillary-clinton-says-putins-action-are-like-what-hitler-did -back-in-the-30s/

Rumer, Boris. 1989. *Soviet Central Asia: A Tragic Experiment.* Unwin Hyman.

Sacco, Joe. 2003. *The Fixer.* First ed. Drawn and Quarterly.

Sambanis, Nicholas. 2002. "A Review of Recent Advances and Future Directions in the Quantitative Literature of Civil War." *Defense and Peace Economics* 13(3):215–243.

Satz, Debra, and John Ferejohn. 1994. "Rational Choice and Social Theory." *Journal of Philosophy* 92:71–87.

Schelling, Thomas. 1960. *A Strategy of Conflict.* Harvard University Press.

Schenkann, Nate. 2014. "Band of Outsiders: How Sanctions Will Strengthen Putin's Regional Clout." *Foreign Affairs*, August 27, 2014. Available on http://www.foreignaffairs.com/articles/141941/nate-schenkkan/band-of-outsiders

Scheper-Hughes, Nancy, and Philippe Bourgois, eds. 2004. *Violence in War and Peace: An Anthology.* Blackwell Readers in Anthropology.

Scott, James. 1976. *The Moral Economy of the Peasant.* Yale University Press.

Shabad G., and Llera F. 1994. Political Violence in a Democratic State: Basque Terrorism in Spain. In *Terrorism in Context*, ed. Martha Crenshaw. Pennsylvania State University Press.

Shapiro, Jacob. 2013. *The Terrorist's Dilemma: Managing Violent Covert Organizations.* Princeton University Press.

Shelley, Louise I. 2004. "Organized Crime in the Former Soviet Union: The Distinctiveness of Georgia." TRACCC (Transnational Crime and Corruption Center), Tbilisi, Georgia.

Shleifer, Andrei. 2005. *A Normal Country: Russia after Communism.* Harvard University Press.

Simis, Konstantin. 1982. *USSR: The Corrupt Society: The Secret World of Soviet Capitalism.* Simon and Schuster.

Slade, Gavin. 2007. "The Threat of the Thief: Who Has Normative Influence in Georgian Society?" *Global Crime* 8(2):172–179.

Slider, Darrell. 1997. Democratization in Georgia. In *Conflict, Cleavage, and Change in Central Asia and the Caucasus*, ed. Karen Kawisha and Bruce Parrot. Cambridge University Press.

Smale, Alison, and Andrew Roth. 2014. "Ukraine Says That Militants Won the East." *New York Times.* April 30, 2014, page A1.

Solnick, Steven L. 1998. *Stealing the State: Control and Collapse in Soviet Institutions.* Harvard University Press.

Stedman, Stephen. 1997. "Spoiler Problems in Peace Processes." *International Security* 22(2):5–53.

Stedman, Stephen. 2003. "Where Do Peacekeepers Go?" *International Studies Review* 5(4):37–54.

Stinchcombe, Arthur. 1968. *Constructing Social Theories.* Harcourt, Brace and World.

Suny, Ronald Grigor. 1995. Elite Tranformation in Late-Soviet and Post-Soviet Transcaucasia, or What Happens When the Rulling Class Can't Rule? In *Patterns in Post-Soviet Leadership*, ed. Robert C. Tucker and Timothy J. Colton. Harvard University Russian Research Center, pp. 141–165.

Tadjbakhsh, S. 1993. "The Tajik Spring of 1992." *Central Asia Monitor* 2:21-29.

Tajima, Yuhki. 2014. *The Institutional Origins of Communal Violence: Indonesia's Transition from Authoritarian Rule.* Cambridge University Press.

Tarzi, Amin. 2005. "Disarmament in Afghanistan – Which Militias and What Weapons?" Radio Free Europe/Radio Liberty (RFE/RL).

Tavernise, Sabrina, and David Herszenhorn. 2014. "Patchwork Makeup of Rebels Fighting Ukraine Makes Peace Talks Elusive." *New York Times.* July 9, A4

Thelen, Kathleen. 1999. "Historical Institutionalism in Comparative Politics." *Annual Review of Political Science* 2:23-49.

Tilly, Charles. 1985. War Marking and State Making as Organized Crime. In *Bringing the State Back In*, ed. Theda Skocpol, Peter B. Evans, and Dietrich Rueschemeyer. Cambridge University Press, pp. 169-191.

Tishkov, Valery. 1995. ""Don't Kill Me, I'm a Kyrgyz!" Anthropological Analysis of Violence in the Osh Ethnic Conflict." *Journal of Peace Research* 32(2):133-149.

Tishkov, Valery. 1997. *Ethnicity, Nationalism, and Conflict in and after the Soviet Union: The Mind Aflame.* SAGE.

Toft, Monica. 2010. *Securing the Peace: the Durable Settlement of Civil Wars.* Princeton University Press.

Toft, Monica Duffy. 2005. *The Geography of Ethnic Violence: Identity, Interests, and the Indivisibility of Territory.* Princeton University Press.

Torjensen, S. 2005. "Tajikistan's Road to Stability: Reduction in Small Arms Proliferation and Remaining Challenges." Small Arms Survey, Geneva.

Torjensen, Stina, and S. Neil MacFarlane. 2007. "R Before D: The Case of Post Conflict Reintegration in Tajikistan." *Conflict, Security, and Development* 7(2):311-332.

Treisman, Daniel. 1999. *After the Deluge: Regional Crises and Political Consolidation in Russia.* University of Michigan Press.

Trenin, Dmitri. 1995. Russian Peacemaking in Georgia. In *Crisis Management in the CIS: Whither Russia?*, ed. Hans-Georg Ehrhart, Anna Kreikenmeyer, and Andrei Zagorski. Nomos Verlagsgesellschaft.

Tudoroiu, Theodor. 2007. "Rose, Orange, and Tulip: The Failed Post-Soviet Revolutions." *Communist and Post-Communist Studies* 40:315-342.

Tullock, G. 1971. "The Paradox of Revolution." *Public Choice* 11(1): 89-99.

Ucko, David. 2009. Militias, Tribes, and Insurgents: The Challenge of Political Reintegration in Iraq. In *Reintegrating Armed Groups after Conflict*, ed. Mats Berdal and David Ucko. Routledge Studies in Intervention and Statebuilding, pp. 89-118.

Van Atta, Don. 2008. "The Failure of Land Reform in Tajikistan." Paper prepared for the 13th Annual World Convention of the Association for the Study of Nationalities.

Van Evera, Stephen. 1994. "Hypotheses on Nationalism and War." *International Security* 18(4):5-39.

Varese, Federico. 2001. *The Russian Mafia: Private Protection in a New Market Economy.* Oxford University Press.

Venkatesh, Sudhir. 2007. *Off the Books: The Underground Economy of the Urban Poor.* Harvard University Press.

Venkatesh, Sudhir. 2008. *Gang Leader for a Day.* Penguin Press.

Vigil, James Diego. 1988. *Barrio Gangs: Street Life and Identity in Southern California.* University of Texas Press.

Volkov, V. 2001. Who Is Strong When the State Is Weak. In *Beyond State Crisis?: Post-Colonial Africa and Post-Soviet Eurasia in Comparative Perspective*, ed. M. Beissinger and C. Young. Woodrow Wilson Press, pp. 81–103.

Volkov, Vadim. 1999. "Violent Entrepreneurship in Post-Communist Russia." *Europe-Asia Studies* 51(5):741–754.

Wagner, R. Harrison. 2007. *War and the State: The Theory of International Politics.* University of Michigan Press.

Walter, Barbara. 1997. "The Critical Barrier to Civil War Settlement." *International Organization* 51:335–364.

Walter, Barbara F. 2002. *Committing to Peace: The Successful Settlement of Civil Wars.* Princeton University Press.

Walter, Barbara F. 2009. "Bargaining Failures and Civil War." *Annual Review of Political Science* Spring. 12:243–261.

Wantchekon, Leonard. 2004. "The Paradox of "Warlord" Democracy: A Theoretical Investigation." *The American Political Science Review* 98(1):17–33.

Warren, Camber, "Not by the Sword Alone: Soft Power, Mass Media, and the Production of State Sovereignty," International Organization (forthcoming).

Weber, Max. 1953. *From Max Weber: Essays in Sociology.* Oxford University Press.

Weinstein, Jeremy. 2006. *Inside Rebellion: The Political Economy of Rebel Organizations.* Cambridge University Press.

Wheatley, Jonathan. 2005. *Georgia: From National Awakening to the Rose Revolution – Delayed Transition in the Former Soviet Union.* Ashgate.

Whitlock, Monica. 2005. *The Land Beyond the River.* St. Martin's Press.

Whyte, William Foot. 1982. Interviewing in Field Research. In *Field Research: A Sourcebook and Field Manual*, ed. Robert G. Burgess. George Allen and Unwin.

Wood, Elisabeth. 2003. *Insurgent Collective Action and Civil War in El Salvador.* Cambridge University Press.

Wood, Elisabeth. 2007. Field Methods. In *The Oxford Handbook of Comparative Politics*, ed. Carles Boix and Susan Stokes. Oxford University Press.

Wright, Joseph, and Matthew Winters. 2010. "The Politics of Effective Foreign Aid." *Annual Review of Political Science* 13:61–80.

Zuercher, Christoph. 2005. *The Post-Soviet Wars: Rebellion, Ethnic Conflict, and Nationhood in the Caucasus.* New York University Press.

Zverev, Alexei. 1996. Ethnic Conflicts in the Caucasus. In *Contested Borders in the Caucasus*, ed. Bruno Coppieters. VUB University Press, pp. 13–71.

Zviagelskaya, Irina. 1998. The Tajik Conflict: Problems of Regulation. In *Tajikistan: The Trials of Independence*, ed. Shirin Akiner Mohammad-Reza Djalili and Frederic Grare. Curzon Press, pp. 161–179.

Index

CPSIA information can be obtained
at www.ICGtesting.com
Printed in the USA
LVHW091724271121
704625LV00003B/101